THE OWL AND THE NIGHTINGALE

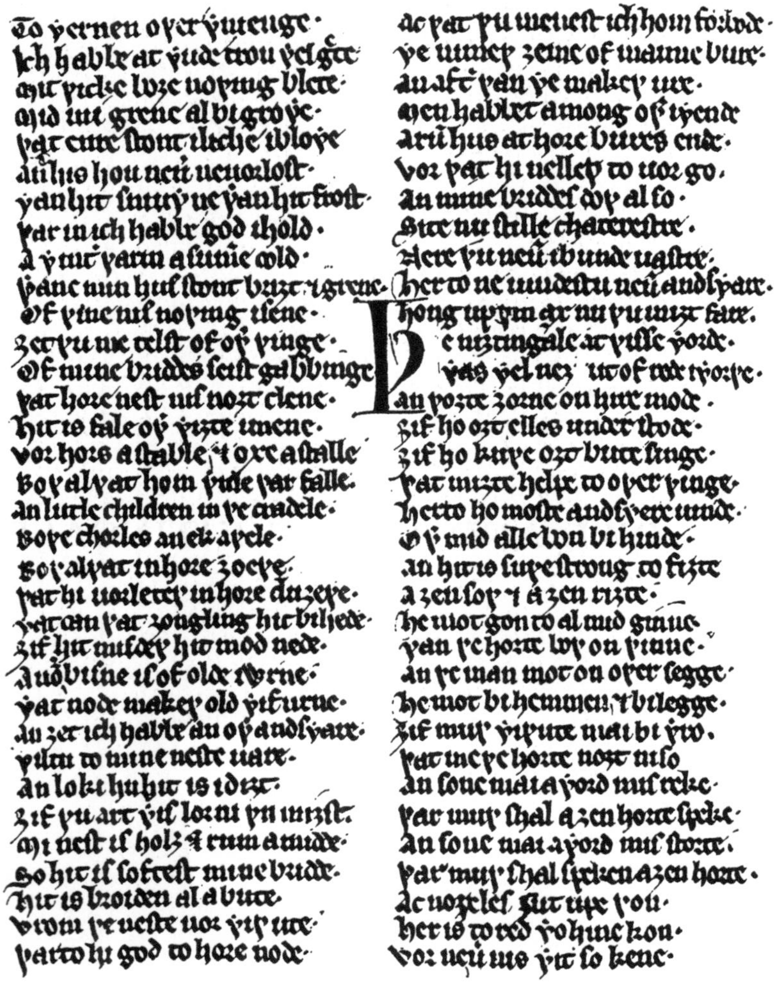

MS. Cotton *Caligula* A IX. (reduced), fol. 237, cols. c and d.
ll. 614–681.

⁊ so heo doþ voꝛ heo beoþ wode.
þat hure nette goþ to brode.
Wymmon is of neyſſe fleyſſe.
⁊ fleyſſes luſtes iſ ſtrong to queyſſe.
His wunder non þah he abide;
voꝛ fleyſſes luſtes hi makeþ ſlide;
he loþ heo nouht alle foꝛ loꝛe;
þ' ſtumpeþ at þe fleyſſes moꝛe;
voꝛ mony wymmone haueþ myſ do.
þat aryſt vp of þe slo.
He loþ nouht oneſ alle ſunne.
voꝛ þan hi loþ ofterre ikunne;
sum ariſt of fleyſſes luſte.
⁊ ſum of þe goſtes cufte.
þat fleyſ draþþ uſ iuo to druꝛenetto
⁊ to wlonk heꝛe.⁊ to golueſſe;
þe goſt myſ doþ þurh uþþ aud onde
⁊ leþþe myþd muelþye of moneſ hoꝛe;
⁊ wuuueþ after moꝛe aud moꝛe;
⁊ lutel reꝛþ of ꝗlte aud oꝛe.
⁊ ſtyþþ on heyþ þur modþneſſe.
⁊ ouer.howeþ. þane laſſe;
sey me ſoþ.if þu hit woſt.
h weþer doþ wurſe. fleyſ þe goſt.
þu myht ſegge if þu wile.
þat laſſe is þel fleyſeſ gult.
ayonymd iſ of his fleyſſe clene;
þat iſ myþd moꝛe deouel iuene;
he ſchal no mo wymmau bi grede.
⁊ fleyſſes luſtes hure vp broyde.
sucſ heo maꝛte beo of golneſſe.
þ' ſuneꝛeþ wurſe i moduieſſe;
h wer if it ſchulde a luue bringe.
wif oþer maýd h waune ic ſinge;
I e wolde wiþ þe maýde holde;
I f þu couſt aꝛyþt at holde;
L uſt uſ ic ſegge þe hwar voꝛe;

y þ to þe coppe from þe moꝛe;
I f maýde liueþ derneliche;
h co ſtumpeþ ⁊ falþ iauueliche;
v oꝛ paſþ heo ſu hwile pleýe;
h wo uſſ nohc teꝛ ve of þe weye;
h eo maý hure guld atweude;
A riþce weýe þurþ churche beuꝛ;
⁊ maý efc habbe to make;
h ire leof uuon wiþ vre ſake;
⁊ gon to hiu bi daýel lyhce.
þat er bi ſtal ou þeoſter uphce;
þ'youghlug not hwat ſuch þing iſ.
haſ youge blod hit draþþ auuýs
⁊ ſuu ſot mau.hit tyhþ þaꝛ to
ayid alle þan þat he maý do.
h e cuueþ ⁊ faiſþ. aud beod abiꝛ,
⁊ he biſtaꝛce au oþer ſiꝛ.
⁊ bi ſelþ.iloue aud louge;
h war maý þat child þaþ hit uſs for
h it uuſte nou hwat his weſ.
voꝛ þi hit þouꝛce fouꝛi þas,
⁊ wyſce iþis hwich beo þegouue;
þ' of þe wilde malieþ toine;
h e maý ic voꝛ reuþe lete;
h waune ic iſeo þe tohte ilete;
þ e luue bring ou me wunglinge;
þ at ic of uuurehþe hi ue ſinge;
I e theche heo bi myþue ſonge;
þ at ſuycſ luue. ne laſt nohc loug;
f oꝛ myþ ſong luꝛ wile uette.
⁊ luue ne doþ nohc buꝛe uette.
o u ſucſ childre ⁊ ſoue a geþ
⁊ falþ a dun þe heoꝛte bruꝛ;
I ſinge uýþ heo. one þuowe;
Bi gunne au heyþ ⁊ eudi lowe.
⁊ lete miue ſouger falle;
A luꝛe wiſe. a.dun uýþ alle.

MS. Jesus College, Oxford 29 (reduced), fol. 239, cols. a and b.
ll. 1385–1458.

THE OWL

AND

THE NIGHTINGALE

EDITED WITH INTRODUCTION, TEXTS, NOTES, TRANSLATION AND GLOSSARY

BY

J. W. H. ATKINS, M.A.,

RENDEL PROFESSOR OF ENGLISH LANGUAGE AND LITERATURE, UNIVERSITY COLLEGE
OF WALES, ABERYSTWYTH. SOMETIME FELLOW OF ST JOHN'S COLLEGE, CAMBRIDGE

Mes. n'il a fable de folie
u il nen ait philosophie
Marie de France, *Ysopet*, Prol. 23–4.

CAMBRIDGE
AT THE UNIVERSITY PRESS
1922

TO MY WIFE

CAMBRIDGE
UNIVERSITY PRESS

University Printing House, Cambridge CB2 8BS, United Kingdom

Cambridge University Press is part of the University of Cambridge.

It furthers the University's mission by disseminating knowledge in the pursuit of education, learning and research at the highest international levels of excellence.

www.cambridge.org
Information on this title: www.cambridge.org/9781107432123

© Cambridge University Press 1922

First published 1922
First paperback edition 2014

A catalogue record for this publication is available from the British Library

ISBN 978-1-107-43212-3 Paperback

PREFACE

THIS edition of *The Owl and the Nightingale* is mainly based upon the work submitted as a Fellowship dissertation at St John's College, Cambridge, some years ago, and since laid aside for various reasons. In the meantime the poem has received considerable attention, more especially at the hands of American and German scholars. Useful editions have appeared by Wells and Gadow: further light has from time to time been thrown upon dark places in the text: and altogether it may safely be said that the poem to-day is better understood than ever. But it is equally true to say that much remains to be done. There are many "desperate" places in the texts awaiting solution, besides difficulties connected with almost every aspect of the work: and it is in the hope of clearing up some of these difficulties that the present edition has at length been undertaken.

As to the methods employed in this edition, it may at once be said that the main effort has been concentrated upon providing a reliable text: and here the accurate work of Wells has been of considerable assistance, though, it must also be added, both MSS. have been carefully and independently examined. Thus the two versions have been given as the simplest way of providing all the available data: the texts are represented substantially as they stand: all departures from the MS. readings have been carefully noted: while the emended forms have been indicated by being placed in square brackets. As for the emendations themselves, they are concerned for the most part with the C. text, as being the earlier and more conservative of the two copies: but while this C. text thus becomes the main subject of study, the J. version will be found useful for purposes of collation and comparison. In the second place, the emendations are made mainly in cases where scribal error may be suspected on palaeographical grounds; so that all changes aim at restoring either the wording or the grammatical construction of the original. No attempt is made at obtaining a normalised spelling. The two orthographies of C., and the later spellings of J., the French scribal forms, and the numerous variants found in one and the same text have all been allowed to stand: for all such forms have their historical value. They are "landmarks" (in spite of Dryden) "so sacred as never to be removed." In certain sections of C., it is true, there are reasons for suspecting the original spelling to have been preserved. But to normalise the spelling on those lines would have been too hazardous a venture: and it has formed no part of the present edition.

Then, again, the interpretation of the text has been attempted in a somewhat wide sense. Efforts have naturally been made to deal with difficulties of a verbal kind: and it is hoped that solutions have been found for most, if not all, of the existing obscurities, notably in the emendations proposed in ll. 651, 748, 991, 1319–20, 1322, 1400, 1586, and in the explanations given of ll. 427–8, 816, 1128, 1206, 1230, 1754. But the task of interpretation has been taken to mean something more than this; though no attempt has been made to deal systematically with the phonology of the poem—a task already performed by Wells and others. The aim has rather been to deal with the poem as a piece of literary art, illustrative of the culture of the age that produced it: and an attempt has therefore been made to view the poem in its historical setting, and to regard it as a human document of its own particular age. And in this way, it is believed, some fresh results have been obtained. Apart from the question of authorship, which must still remain a debatable point, fresh light has been thrown upon the general significance of the poem by a detailed investigation of its sources, its form and its theme: and these results are not without their bearing on the intellectual activities of the age. If, as may truly be said, some knowledge of contemporary conditions is needed for an intelligent reading of the poem, it is equally true to say that the poem, intelligently read, is capable in its turn of adding to our knowledge of those conditions, by its reflection from new angles of the social and intellectual life of the times. And that a more adequate appreciation of the intellectual activities of that period is one of the *desiderata* of English studies at the present time, is, I venture to think, a statement that will scarcely be denied.

It now remains for me to record my obligations to various scholars, who from time to time and in different ways have assisted in the preparation of this work. To my old Cambridge teachers—the late Professor W. W. Skeat, Sir Israel Gollancz and Professor H. M. Chadwick—I wish in the first place to acknowledge my deep indebtedness. To them I owe not only an earlier training, but the guidance and the stimulus which only generous teachers can give: and their influence is such as no lapse of years can lessen. To Professor W. P. Ker, I owe, further, much encouragement and inspiration. More than any other living representative of English scholarship, he has helped to bring light into dark corners of the literature of the Middle Ages: and his assistance to me has not been confined to his written work. My best thanks are also due to Professor W. A. Craigie of Oxford and Mr G. G. Coulton of St John's College, Cambridge, both of whom have been most generous in supplying information and criticism on points connected with the texts: also to my Aberystwyth colleagues—Professor André Barbier, Professor E. Bensly, Mr L. C. Jane, Professor S. Roberts, and Professor H. J. Rose— who have consistently placed at my disposal their wide scholarship and learning: and above all to Mr Bruce Dickins of the University of Edinburgh, who has been good enough to read through the book in proof, and whose criticism and suggestions have been of a most valuable kind. There yet remains to be mentioned my indebtedness to Mr J. Ballinger, Chief Librarian of the National Library of Wales, and to Mr R. Farquharson Sharp, Deputy-Keeper of Printed Books in the British Museum, from both of whom I have received substantial assistance in the matter of books as well as unfailing courtesy in response to many inquiries.

And, lastly, I have to thank the Syndics of the University Press for undertaking the publication of the poem ; and, in particular, Mr A. R. Waller, for his generous and judicious advice on various points connected with the work, and the staff of the Press for their skill and consideration shown in the actual task of printing.

J. W. H. A.

UNIVERSITY COLLEGE OF WALES,
ABERYSTWYTH.
December, 1921.

CONTENTS

INTRODUCTION

§ 1. THE HISTORICAL SETTING OF THE POEM

SOME pieces of literature are slower than others in coming to
their own, and *The Owl and the Nightingale* is assuredly one of
the slow-footed kind. Unearthed in the 18th century after a
long period of neglect, it was made accessible through the labours
of Mid-Victorian scholars[1]: by the end of the 19th century it
had come to be regarded as a work of considerable linguistic
interest: but it is only of late years that its real value has begun
to be appreciated and a fairer idea formed of its importance in
English literature. With regard to its intrinsic value, one of the
most recent estimates is probably the best. It has been described
as "the most miraculous piece of writing...among the medieval
English books[2]": and the statement will stand without any sort
of reservation. But as a human document as well the poem is
highly significant, especially when viewed in its proper perspective.
Belonging, as it does, to a barren period of our literature, it helps,
for one thing, to correct our notions as to the literary activities of
the time. It suggests, for instance, that the English genius, even
then, was capable of something more than the *Ormulum* or even
the *Brut*: that the fable and debate forms were not confined to
Anglo-Latin or Anglo-Norman writers: and if we may judge from
the artistic merits of the work, it is more than likely that it was
preceded by earlier experiments which have since been lost. But
the poem has yet a greater interest for modern readers, in that it
stands for a phase of medieval life and thought earlier than that
which has become familiar in the pages of Chaucer. Great things
were happening in the 12th and early 13th centuries. With the
passing of the Dark Ages a new era had come. It was the age
above all in which Romance was born: when a new music was
heard throughout Western Europe: when a new secular spirit was
challenging the old religious tradition, and the medieval genius
was finding expression in a new art and a new learning. And these
things are reflected to some extent in *The Owl and the Nightingale*.
"What above all makes the study of medieval French works so
attractive and profitable," so writes Gaston Paris, "is the fact

[1] See Bibliography I.   [2] Ker, *English Literature Medieval*, p. 181.

that they reveal to us, better than all historical documents, the nature of the manners, the thoughts, and sentiments of our ancestors[1]": and this is in the highest sense true of our present poem. It enables us to see, as it were, into 12th century minds, to learn something of their tastes, their mental outlook, and their problems. Nor can quite the same revelation be said to exist anywhere else in contemporary English literature. Among the first of the vernacular works to appear after the Norman Conquest, this poem alone carries us back to the beginnings of things. Then, again, it has always seemed strange that English alone of the literatures of the West, should have failed to respond to the epoch-making influences of 12th century France. Yet if *The Owl and the Nightingale* be read aright, that failure would seem to have been more apparent than real: for our poet has shown himself to be alive to the main activities of his age, and his work is the English contribution to the great European concert. There are, in fact, but few, if any, literary works produced in medieval England that are better worth reading than *The Owl and the Nightingale*. Whether we have in mind its merits as a piece of art, or the significance it possesses from the historical point of view, the poem will be found to compare favourably with the best things done by any of Chaucer's contemporaries, while it has features which render it unique in the annals of our literature.

In approaching a work of this kind, no apology is therefore needed for attempting to recall the main features of the age that produced it. The historical background, for one thing, will help to bring out the many-sided interest of the poem. But since the poem is written darkly, in allegorical fashion, the presence of such a background becomes absolutely essential: indeed it is doubtful whether, apart from historical considerations, an intelligent reading of the poem is possible at all. It is therefore proposed, by way of introduction, to make an attempt at placing the poem in its proper historical setting. And that setting will be obtained not with England only as a background, but with Western Europe as it was in the 12th and early 13th centuries; with its common intellectual life, its common religious thought, and those various activities in literature which were shared in by all peoples of the West alike. To view the work as an English product merely, is to miss much of its meaning and value. For the civilisation of the 12th century was international in kind: a common spirit reigned

---

[1] G. Paris, *La Littérature française au moyen âge*, p. 32.

everywhere. Western Europe was still dominated by the Roman tradition of unity : it was subject to the common influences of Latin culture and Latin Christianity. And since England after the Conquest had become part of the European confederation, and thus shared in that civilisation, for the full tide of the great movements in which England was involved, we must turn to the Continent and above all to France. In short, to understand 12th century England, we must begin by understanding 12th century Europe.

Now the one outstanding fact, connected with Western Europe at this date, is that it witnessed a Renascence hardly less vital and far-reaching than the great awakening of the 15th and 16th centuries. The history of man, as is well known, has its periods of illumination, when the human spirit leaps forward to a higher plane of being. Such periods stand out as the great ages of the world : and among them must be reckoned the 12th and early 13th centuries in Europe: for it was then that vast changes came over the civilisation of the West, that new forces were liberated in every sphere of life, while a new spirit was generated, different from that of any other period of history. For the causes of this great awakening we must shortly recall the conditions precedent. The 11th century was a time of intellectual torpor and stagnation : of weakness and corruption within the pale of the Church. Under the feudal *régime*, moreover, order, liberty, and justice were everywhere wanting, while the state of the humbler classes was one of squalor and misery. Such conditions are wont to bring about a natural reaction: and the reaction came at the end of a prolonged period of migrations, when the various Teutonic peoples had become settled in different parts of Europe. Before the 11th century had closed, there was visible already a stirring of the waters. The Church, led by Hildebrand, had commenced its long struggle for the mastery of Christendom: and with the victory at Canossa (1077), and the subsequent triumph in the 12th century over the great Frederic Barbarossa, the Papacy became supreme in European affairs, a monarchy occupied with temporal and spiritual interests. And in other ways, too, the Church gave signs of fresh life and vigour. Under the inspiration of St Bernard, great reforms were effected in the life of the secular and regular clergy. What Cluny in the 11th century had begun was carried on by Clairvaux in the 12th. There was a wonderful development of the monastic spirit, a multiplication of religious orders: while attempts were also made to get rid of simony and lay investiture, and generally to root out the feudal characteristics of the Church.

But while the Church was thus flinging off the lethargy of the Dark Ages, a yet more momentous change was taking place in the awakening of the popular classes. This movement, which was general, was the outcome in part of the lawlessness of feudal conditions. Long subject to exactions of the most unscrupulous kind, the towns of Europe in the 12th century rose up against this reign of tyranny. From their feudal lords they claimed guarantees against arbitrary exploitation: and in the end they were successful in winning a certain measure of autonomy, as well as some recognition of their rights and liberties. But there were other causes at work in this first emancipation of the Commons: and most active and potent of all was the economic revolution of the period, which rivalled in its effects the economic developments of modern times. Wherever we look in 12th century Europe, we find signs, hitherto wanting, of commercial enterprise and life. The spirit of the time was one of adventure. It was an age of pilgrimages: the century of the Crusaders. And with the ever-increasing intercourse between the East and the West, new markets were opened, a new merchant class was formed; while fresh impetus was also given to the various local industries, which not only increased their output in response to the new demands, but also transformed their crafts by what they had learnt from the East. Thus Industry followed Commerce: and the economic revolution was complete. Nor were the effects slow to appear in social and political spheres. Increased prosperity changed the lot of all—the merchant, the artisan, and the serf, while a new *bourgeois* class was formed with an entirely new outlook on life. Strongly entrenched in their guilds and industrial corporations, the townsfolk presented a new problem to the feudal lords of the age: and it was a problem which could only be solved by the granting of liberties and rights. In this way a new factor entered medieval politics: and with it there went a new secular spirit, which was to challenge authority in all its forms, and to oppose the very principles and facts upon which the Middle Ages rested.

In the meantime, however, a similar awakening, no less important, was taking place in the intellectual life of the time: and indeed it is here that we find the finest fruits of the 12th century Renascence—in the awakening of the reason, the growing freedom of thought, and in the revival of learning which brought in its train a wider and a more humane culture. Nor are the causes of these changes far to seek. Men's minds expanded with the expansion of the world beyond the seas. They were encouraged to make a beginning of thinking for themselves, as a result of the newly-acquired liberties of a political kind. At the same time, too, Western thought was being fertilised by contact with the East. Arabic lore poured in through Constantinople, Sicily, and Spain : while further inspiration was derived from the works of Aristotle, many of which were expounded by Averroës, now for the first time. Nor must the activities of schools like Chartres and Paris be altogether forgotten: nor the work of the newly-founded Universities—Bologna, Paris and Oxford—in the century which followed. All alike were centres which fostered or disseminated the new learning, and gave birth in due course to 13th century Scholasticism. As for the results of this great movement, they may easily be traced in the intellectual activities of the time, which were mainly concerned with theological studies—the one form of knowledge which led to the salvation of man. Up to the 11th century, however, patristic theology, as expounded by Gregory, had been handed on unchanged. And it stood for a creed that was rooted in authority, a religion inspired by the terrors of Hell, from which there was no escape except by penance and tears. Then in the 12th and early 13th centuries great changes took place. There was a gradual recasting of Latin Christianity in an intellectual as well as an emotional sense. It was as if the medieval mind now for the first time had found itself, and was setting the impress of its genius on the patristic dogmas and doctrines. In the hands of Abelard, for instance, dialectic became the accepted means of attaining truth in both secular and religious matters. Scholasticism, again, aimed at giving a rational explanation of revealed truth by reconciling current doctrines with Aristotle's teaching. And in the heresies of the time similar activities were also displayed. They all gave evidence of the same intellectual unrest, of efforts to place Christianity on a more rational footing, while eliminating in some measure the superstition and the dead learning which had gathered round the creeds. Nor was this patristic teaching modified only in an intellectual sense. To the ancient doctrines was also given a fresh emotional value. They were shown to be capable of appealing to what was deepest in the hearts of men, through the love and pity, the beauty and the mystery enshrined in their thought. And in this imbuing of earlier doctrines with human elements lay perhaps the greatest achievement of the Middle Ages.

But while Latin Christianity was undergoing this humanising process, a similar change was at work in the secular studies of the time. To the 12th century, in short, belongs a great revival of letters, the result of a changed attitude towards the literature of antiquity. No longer regarded as merely a pedagogic instrument for the teaching of grammar and rhetoric, Latin literature was now approached from the humanistic point of view: it was commended and studied as a means of discipline and general culture. "Solace in grief, recreation in labour, cheerfulness in poverty, modesty amid riches and delights, faithfully are bestowed by letters[1]": so wrote John of Salisbury, the greatest of 12th century humanists: and he was not alone in feeling the spell of the classics. His humanism was shared by Bernard Silvestris, the interpreter of Virgil, by the versatile Giraldus Cambrensis, by Alanus de Insulis, Bernard of Chartres, Peter of Blois, Gilbert de la Porrée and countless others: though on the other hand, there were some who scorned these classical studies. It was to combat the position of such men—Cornificiani[2] as they were called—that John of Salisbury wrote his *Metalogicus* (1159), thus opening the first phase of the controversy between the Ancients and Moderns. And the humanistic position as a result was well defended, while one at least of the writer's arguments became a commonplace at a later date. "Bernard of Chartres used to say," so writes John of Salisbury, "that we were like dwarfs seated on the shoulders of giants[3]": and this dictum, which was doubtless well known to 12th century scholars[4], was resuscitated by Vives, and again at the end of the 17th century, when the dispute between the Ancients and the Moderns was fought out anew[5].

Such then were some of the main features of the 12th century Renascence—a movement which affected all spheres of contemporary life, which led to a general emancipation in social, political, and intellectual spheres, and which brought with it a new self-consciousness, a new attitude to life. It was not long, however, before this freeing of the human spirit gave rise to a desire for

---

[1] *Policraticus*, Prol. (Migne, *Pat. Lat.* 199, col. 385), quoted by Taylor, *Medieval Mind*, II. 115.

[2] See Appendix v.

[3] *Metalogicus*, III. 4 (Migne, *Pat. Lat.* 199, col. 900).

[4] Cf. Neckam, *De Nat. Rerum*, I. ch. 78. Haec relatio fabulosa illos tangit qui aliorum labores intrantes, gloriam aliis debitam in se praesumunt transferre. "Et" ut ait philosophus "nos sumus quasi nani stantes super humeros gigantum."

[5] Cf. "We must have more [knowledge] than the Ancients, because we have the Advantage both of theirs and our own, which is commonly illustrated by the Similitude of a Dwarfs standing upon a Gyants shoulders, and seeing more or farther than he" (Temple, *Essays*, ed. Spingarn (Oxford), p. 3).

self-expression: and here we have another aspect of the Renascence—its wonderful developments in literature and art. Early in the 12th century the medieval genius had already become articulate, voicing its hopes and its fears in forms of its own devising. And the first and most characteristic revelation had been in the architecture of the period, in the noble Romanesque churches, and the stately Gothic cathedrals, all alike symbols of the religious faith of the age. Here, indeed, carved in stone, lay the real poetry of the period; poetry written in characters that all could read, while suggesting by its gracious form, its wealth of detail, its wonderful effects of colour and light, something of the mystic yearnings of the Christianity of the age. Of less permanent value, perhaps, but still of considerable note, was the medieval Latin literature connected with this date: for in that work we see the freeing of the spirit, in the breaking-up of the balanced periods of classical prose, and in the creation of new kinds of prose composition, for which no models existed among classical forms. Instances of this occur in the *De Planctu Naturae* of Alanus de Insulis, in the *Metalogicus* of John of Salisbury, and in the contemporary works of other English scholars. In the Latin verse, however, the emancipatory movement is yet more clearly seen. There may be traced the abandonment of classical metres, and the adoption of accentual and rhyming forms more capable of expressing Christian emotion and thought. Works like the *Anticlaudianus*, it is true, preserve the old classical tradition: but, on the other hand, there are the splendid Latin hymns of Abelard and Adam de St Victor, as well as that mass of student songs, the *Carmina Burana* (1150–1225), which point clearly enough to new developments. Indeed these songs form one of the most striking phenomena of the time. Written by the wandering clerks found everywhere at this date, they parodied, in form and diction, the Latin hymns of the century: and consisting of drinking songs full of amorous and convivial *diablerie*, they introduced into medieval Latin literature a new secular and satirical note, which is found elsewhere only in the *nugae amatoriae* of the scholars, and in the Goliardic "debates" also due to the vagrant pens.

But, after all, it is not in these Latin works that the age finds its most complete and fitting expression. For that we must turn to the vernacular literatures then coming into being: and, more particularly, to the literature of France, where the spirit of the age is reflected in all its variety and colour. In the *Chansons de geste*, for instance, will be found depicted the lawless passions and manners of contemporary feudalism, just as in the *fabliaux* will be detected a new secular note, a realistic and cynical treatment of the *bourgeois* life of the time, with its customs, its humours, and its vices as well. Still more significant, however, was the love-poetry of the Troubadours, which flourished throughout the whole of the 12th century, and was associated with the names of William Count of Poitiers, together with Bertran de Born, Bernart de Ventadour, Arnaut Daniel, and hundreds of others besides. In this poetry may be seen new refining influences at work: ideas and sentiments which then were penetrating certain strata of society, and giving to life a more spiritual meaning. Foremost among these was the new cult of woman, the doctrine of courtly love, which was conceived in cultured circles as an ennobling passion, an inspiration to high deeds and generous thoughts. And this formed the common theme of these Provençal lyrics, which first gave expression to the chivalrous code of the Middle Ages, while founding the tradition of a finer art. Nor was it in this Troubadour poetry alone that the new chivalry found artistic expression. In "that world of fine fabling," the 12th century romances, the same influences are seen at work, fostered by the efforts of noble patrons alive in a new sense to things of the spirit. Thus love, under different forms, fills the romances of Benoît de Sainte-More and Chrétien de Troyes, by whom were narrated some of the great world-stories—the deathless tragedies of Cressida, of Guinevere, and Iseult. Love, again, is the theme of tales brought from the East, of which the most notable, perhaps, are the Floris and Blauncheflur story and the wonderful *Chante-fable* of Aucassin and Nicolette. But whatever be the origin of this variegated material, whether drawn from antiquity, from Celtic or Oriental stores, in every case it was refashioned in accordance with contemporary ideals, it was poured into the mould of 12th century "romance": and it enshrines, as a result, the living spirit of the age, its unrest, its aspirations, its quest for beauty and strange adventure, in fact, all that was of significance in the 12th century attitude to life. And the influence of this new literature was felt throughout Western Europe. "The love of honour and the honour of love" became the themes of the Minnesingers in Germany, of the Troubadours who sang in Italy, Portugal, and Spain, as well as of particular poets like Wolfram von Eschenbach and Walther von der Vogelweide, all of whom continued what Chrétien de Troyes had begun. In the meantime, too, fresh inspiration had been given to vernacular literature generally: for it was now that the *Nibelungen Lied* assumed its extant form, that Spain produced in the *Cid* its first great epic, while farther north, the *Mabinogion* and the *Edda* were the fruits of other national activities. Thus France, having roused herself by her own energy, roused Europe afterwards by her example. A new era had begun for literature in the vernaculars: a great literary Renascence had come with the wider Renascence in social and intellectual affairs. And, of this movement, France was the centre and also the inspiration. If to Europe of a later date her literature has constituted a second antiquity, to Europe of the 12th century she gave a new art, a new culture, a new philosophy.

Such, then, were the European conditions when *The Owl and the Nightingale* appeared: and it remains to inquire how far England can be said to have come under the same influences and to have shared in the intellectual activities of the time. Upon the social and political changes in England there is no need to dwell. There was abroad in the land the same spirit of progress: there was the same growth of towns, the same awakening in regard to both industry and commerce: and this was accompanied by a stirring of the political waters, by administrative reforms under Henry II, which were to lead on naturally to the emancipation of the Commons. Less obvious perhaps are the intellectual achievements of the age. They are indeed but faintly reflected in contemporary English literature: so that it has become almost the fashion to regard this period in England as intellectually obscure and barren: notable for many things, it may be, but not for its culture. Yet there are many reasons for adopting this view with the utmost caution, and for anticipating great developments in both literature and learning. It was surely not for nothing that a rapid growth of the patronage system was witnessed under Henry I and Adelaide, and, later on, under Henry II and Eleanor: or that, again, throughout the same century, England remained in close touch with France, the literary centre of Europe. The two countries, for some time, were practically united under one king: Troubadours and French scholars frequented the English court: Englishmen flocked to the schools of France: all of which must have affected English intellectual life[1]. Nor was it with France alone that Englishmen had relations. At the court of Henry II all nations of Europe had their representatives: Henry's envoys were to be found abroad in every quarter: and while intercourse

---

[1] Wells (*O. & N.* p. xxxi) quotes the statement of J. Jacobs (*The Fables of Aesop*, I. 180) to the effect that two-thirds of the French writers of the period (1154–1206) were Englishmen or men connected closely with the English court.

with the far East was being opened up by the Crusaders, travellers, like Adelard of Bath, Michael Scott, and Daniel Morley, were bringing back from Bagdad, from Sicily, or Spain, much of what was valuable in Arabic letters and learning. And if men's minds were expanding as a result of this international traffic, at home there was also dawning a new national self-consciousness. Race-antagonism between the Norman and English sections of the community was rapidly becoming a thing of the past; the foundations of our national institutions were being slowly but truly laid. In short, politically and socially it was an age of enlightenment and progress in England: and in intellectual matters, too, the same impulses were at work.

And this is seen in the literary output of the period, which in England was as considerable as it was varied in character. No-where else, save in Paris, were so many writers to be found, men filled with an ardour for learning, or devoting their whole energies to literary work. In certain directions, indeed, England may be said to have led the way. The Latin Chroniclers, for instance—Geoffrey of Monmouth, William of Malmesbury, Henry of Huntingdon, Benedict of Peterborough, and the rest—must certainly be regarded as outstanding during this period. There was nothing elsewhere to correspond to their achievement, or to dispute their supremacy in this sort of work. Then, too, England at the time was the home of the medieval fable. All the important versions of Aesop were due to writers who belonged to 12th century England: and it was the lost collection of Alfred of England, together with the *Anonymus Neveleti* of Gualterius Anglicus, and the *Ysopet* of Marie de France, that introduced the Aesopic fable to Western readers. But in the general activities of the time, England also played a conspicuous part. There was no branch of literature that was not cultivated by her men of letters: works of the ripest scholarship, fanciful collections of stories and legends, romances and *lais*, Latin hymns and lyrics, letters and commonplace-books, debates and fables, all were represented, either in Latin or Anglo-Norman form: and the result was a standing witness to the wide interests of the age, and to the versatile genius of contemporary writers. Of the details of this literature but little need here be said. It was associated with great names like John of Salisbury and Giraldus Cambrensis: it took its colouring from court, castle, and monastery: while it was representative of all the main movements of the age. Much of it, for instance, was concerned with satire, with shrewd reflections on men and things—the product, as a rule, of an alert and cultured society: and this is seen in such works as Map's *De Nugis Curialium*, and Nigel Wireker's *Speculum Stultorum*, counterparts of that Goliardic verse, which elsewhere voiced the feeling against ecclesiastical tyranny and corruption.　At the same time the love-story or the romance was making its appearance in the *lais* of Marie de France, and in the forms of the Grail and Tristram stories set forth by Robert de Boron and the Anglo-Norman Thomas.　Debates were common both in Latin and Anglo-Norman form: native stories like those of Bevis, Horn, and Havelok were being revived: while books of edification, including Lives of the Saints, were still being written in very great plenty. Even law fell under the literary spell, as is seen in the treatises ascribed to Glanvill and Fitz Neal: and over and above all this, it was now that popular literature emerged in the form of the ballad, the *carole* and the May-day songs.

This, then, suggests some sort of setting for *The Owl and the Nightingale*.　It was the product of a great Renascence period, inspired by influences, national and international, the effects of which are seen in the social, political, and intellectual spheres. Written in an age of great legal activities, when the debate was a characteristic literary form, when fables and proverbs were acceptable reading, and when the romance of love came as a revelation to men, there is much in the poem that belongs to its age, and reflects its surroundings: and it is only in the light of that environment that the poem can be properly read.

§ 2.　THE MANUSCRIPTS

The text of the poem has come down in two separate forms, one found in the MS. Cotton *Caligula* A ix in the British Museum, the other in the Jesus College Collection (MS. Jesus Coll. Oxon. 29) at present deposited in the Bodleian Library.

The Cotton MS. (C.) consists of a small parchment quarto of 261 ff. with double columns written in different hands, all of which belong to the 13th century.　On its first leaf is found the autograph of Sir Robert Cotton.

The MS. contains the following items:

(i)　A version of Laȝamon's *Brut* (ff. 3—194).

(ii)　Chardry, *La vie de Seint Josaphaz*. A.-Fr. verse (ff. 195–216).

(iii)　Chardry, *La vie de set Dormanz*. A.-Fr. verse (ff. 216–29).

(iv) An account of the Anglo-Saxon and Norman kings down to the accession of Hen. III. A.-Fr. prose (ff. 229–32).

(v) *The Owl and the Nightingale* (ff. 233–46).

(vi) Seven short poems (*Long Life, Orisun of Ure Lady, Will and Wit, Doomsday, Death, Ten Abuses, A Lutel Soth Sermun*) included by Wright in his Percy Soc. volume and by Morris in *Old English Miscellany* (E.E.T.S. 1872) (ff. 246–9).

(vii) Chardry's "debate." *Le Petit Plet.* A.-Fr. verse (ff. 249–61).

The C. text of *The Owl and the Nightingale* is in a single hand-writing of the first half of the 13th century, and it has the following scribal peculiarities and abbreviations. For *w* the O.E. runic symbol (*wen*) is employed with a dot above to distinguish it from the other runic letter (*thorn*) of similar form. When the dot is omitted, as is not infrequently the case (cf. l. 151), the symbols are apt to be confused. Occasionally the French *w* is employed: and while this *w* might also stand for *vu* (cf. *wl* l. 31) sometimes a single *u* (*v*) is used to denote O.E. *w* (cf. *svete* l. 358, *suich* l. 405). For O.E. þ (= *th*) both þ and ð are used, though the latter occurs only after l. 911. O.E. *r* is represented by two symbols: *u* and *v* occur indiscriminately (cf. *iui* l. 617, *vrom* l. 646): O.E. pal. *ġ* is represented by ȝ (very rarely *y* as in *ey* l. 104): while there are also two symbols for *s* (long and short). Of the abbreviations the following are among the most common: *þurh* (*þurȝ*) is denoted by þ with a horizontal stroke though the lower part of the letter: *þat* by þ with a short oblique stroke ending in a hook placed above. A nasal is represented by a wavy line (~) placed above the preceding letter: *-ri*, *-re* by an *i* or *e* written above the letter following: *-er* by an oblique stroke with a hook at the end: *and* by the usual symbol (ꝼ), though the form *an* is also fairly common. The poem is moreover divided into paragraphs of un-equal length, the initial capital of each paragraph being in red ink. The spacing is as a rule correct and regular (cf. however l. 1602). A rough attempt at punctuation has been made by means of stops placed at the ends of the lines: and the absence of such stops (cf. l. 667) rightly denotes run-on lines. Corrections are occasion-ally made by means of *puncta delentia* (cf. *stude* 966): and there are frequent marginal corrections due to a later hand.

The Jesus MS. (J.) consists of two quarto MSS. partly paper, partly parchment, bound together. The paper part belongs to the 15th century and contains one item only, i.e. the first. The parch-ment section contains numerous items, all written in one and the same hand, and is catalogued as belonging to the 14th century, though it would seem to be more correctly described by Morris as late 13th century. At all events, this portion of the MS., and therefore the J. text of *The Owl and the Nightingale*, is certainly later than the C. text mentioned above. The MS. itself, as is stated on a fly-leaf, was presented to Jesus College, Oxford, by "Tho. Wilkins, LL.B. rector B.M. super Monte in Agro Glamorganensi," c. 1660: and like the Cotton MS. it is clearly and regularly written. Both are in fact excellent specimens of 13th century book-hand, "less grand than that of the 12th century, less pliant than that of the 14th."

The contents of the Jesus MS. are as follows:

(i) A Chronicle of the Kings of England 900–1445 (ff. 1–216).

(ii) *The Passion of Our Lord* (ff. 217–28).

(iii) *The Owl and the Nightingale* (ff. 229–41).

(iv) A group consisting mainly of English poems, of which all except one are printed in Morris' *O.E. Miscellany*, pp. 58 ff. (ff. 242–73).

(v) *Le Doctrinal* (O.Fr.) (ff. 274–80).

(vi) Chardry, *La vie de set Dormanz*. A.-Fr. verse (ff. 280–95).

(vii) Chardry, *La vie Seint Josaphaz*. A.-Fr. verse (ff. 296–317).

(viii) Chardry, *Le petyt ple*. A.-Fr. verse (ff. 317–30).

This MS., it will be noticed, contains not only the three Chardry poems, but also six of the seven short poems that appear in C.

Among other features that call for notice is the statement made by Thos. Wilkins[1] (one-time owner of the MS.) on f. 228 r., the statement being as follows:

"On parte of a broaken leafe of this MS. I found these verses written, whereby the Author may bee gues't at (viz.):

Mayster Johan eu greteþ of Guldeuorde þo.
And sendeþ eu to seggen Þat synge nul he no.
Ac on þisse wise he wille endy his song.
God louerd of Heuene, beo vs alle among.

Amen."

This reference to "a broaken leafe" is rather puzzling, as nowhere does there appear any trace of a leaf cut out or torn. There does, however, exist some irregularity in the MS., as Wells

---

[1] Wells (*O. & N.* Intro. p. xxvii) describes the note as being "probably" due to Thos. Wilkins. Mr Richard Ellis, of Jesus College, Oxford, has since definitely identified the handwriting as being that of Wilkins.

pointed out[1], which seems to throw some light upon the difficulty. Thus it is curious to note that f. 253 v. contains a fragmentary poem (*O.E. Miscellany*, XXI) which breaks off abruptly at the bottom of that page, while the following page (f. 254 r.) begins with the last 7 ll. of a poem (*O.E. Misc.* XI), the first 11 ll. of which are found on the lower half of f. 261 v. The probability therefore is that certain folios of the MS. have been displaced in the process of binding, for it is evident that f. 261 v. must in any case come before f. 254 r. But if f. 261 is moved to this earlier position in the MS. then ff. 258–60 must also go with it, since the sequence of verses is unbroken throughout those pages: that is to say, one poem begins at the top of f. 258 r. and from there on to f. 261 v. the poems overlap from page to page, as do also the poems from f. 254 r. to f. 257 v.

The pages as restored would therefore run as follows:

(i) f. 253.

(ii) A possible gap to allow for the completion of the fragmentary poem on f. 253 v.

(iii) ff. 258 r.–61 v.

(iv) Another gap for the completion of the poem begun on f. 261 v. and ended on f. 254 r.

(v) ff. 254 r.–57 v.

After this would come f. 262 r. where the irregularities cease, except for the fact that f. 262 r. begins with the closing lines of a poem so that yet another gap seems likely here. Hence it would seem that, in the MS. as it stands, there are probably three gaps, all of which suggest missing leaves. It is noteworthy that similar *lacunae* are found in the French sections of the MS.[2] and it is probably to one of these (loose?) leaves in the English section of the MS. that Thos. Wilkins in his note refers.

With regard to the scribal peculiarities of this J. text of *The Owl and the Nightingale*, it will be found that the symbols and abbreviations employed are much the same as those of C. The French *w*, however, is more consistently used; and while the symbol *þ* (*th*) is as a rule preserved, to the exclusion of *ð*, sporadic forms of *th* do occur (cf. ll. 1206, 1449). The symbol *y* also appears

---

[1] See Wells, *O. & N.* Intro. p. xxviii.

[2] See Chardry, *Josaphaz, set Dormanz, und Petit Plet*, ed. J. Koch (Heilbronn, 1879), p. vii : " durch ausreissen von blättern sind drei grosse lücken entstanden, welche in die vv. *Jos.* 751–874, 1382–1510, und *Pet. Plet* 440–568, von L (i.e. MS. Cott.)...fallen." A note to the same effect is also inserted on the inside of the binding of the MS. by J. Koch, 1876. It is stated that a leaf is missing between ff. 228 and 229, 232 and 233, 247 and 248 respectively.

frequently for *i*, and regularly for O.E. pal. *ġ* (cf. *seyde* 1. 61, *yerd* 1. 777). There are the same paragraph divisions as in C.: each line begins with a capital, and the initial capitals of the paragraphs are coloured alternately blue and red.

§ 3. THE TWO TEXTS

In studying the texts of any literary work the first and foremost object is to discover as accurately as possible what the author actually wrote. In the present instance we have two versions, copied at different dates: and it will therefore be necessary in the first place to investigate the genesis of the two texts, i.e. the relation in which one text stands to the other and the relation of each to the original.

(*a*) THEIR RELATIONSHIP.

(i) From what has already been said with regard to the two MSS. it is clear that *J. represents a later version than C.* The respective handwritings make this clear, while the spellings will also be found to point in the same direction.

(ii) It is equally certain that *the texts are independent copies,* and that J. is not based on C. The evidence for this is as follows:

(*α*) J. supplies a few lines that are missing from C., viz. ll. 86, 770, 771, and the latter half of 1. 1254: and the fact that these lines formed part of the original poem and are no mere scribal insertions, is proved by the rhymes.

(*β*) Certain errors found in C. are absent from J., which again supplies what were clearly the original forms. For instance the scribe of C. occasionally writes *r* for *t*, and in two places *an* for *t*, where J. has the *t* correctly. Errors of this kind were not uncommon owing to the similarity of the scribal forms for *r*, *t*, and *and* (ꝥ): Ex.: C. *þar*, J. *þat* (1. 918): C. *iwarte*, J. *warre* (1. 1221): C. *sortes*, J. *sottes* (1. 1471): C. *an o*, J. *to* (ll. 1476, 1489). Moreover C. reads ꝥ *honge* (1. 1195), ꝥ *storue* (1. 1200), where J. more correctly has *anhonge*, *astorue*: and these details point to the independence of J.

(iii) But while J. is a later and independent version, it is clear that *both texts were copied from a common original,* for both C. and J. have certain faulty readings in common, apart from other details which suggest this common origin.

(*a*) Erroneous readings are common to C. and J. Thus both MSS. read *þe* for *þu* (1. 805): *for* for *fox* (1. 812): *an* for *am* (1. 364): *ne ne* for *ne* (1. 1358): C. reads *hoȝeþ*, J. *howeþ* for *ho gᵤþ* (1. 1602): C. *bo þe*, J. *beo þat* for *boþe* (1. 1681). Moreover C. and J. read *þule* for *hule* (1. 411), where the error is due to the rubricator, while in l. 1711 both scribes wrongly begin a new paragraph.

(β) Both MSS. are obscure in much the same places, viz.: C. *þes*, J. word omitted, with *bles* added in later hand (l. 748): C. *chil*, J. *chid* (l. 1315): C. *inune*, J. word omitted, *inome* added later (l. 541): C. *fueʒel*, J. *fuoel* (l. 1135): C. *dreache*, J. *theche* (l. 1449). In many other places the J. scribe had avoided difficulties by substituting different words for forms obscure in C., Ex.: C. *breche*, J. *beche* (l. 14): C. *foʒe*, J. *soþe* (l. 184).

(γ) Moreover the fact that the MSS. in which the two versions are found, contain several items in common (see Introduction, § 2) apart from *The Owl and the Nightingale*, seems to suggest that the scribes had before them one and the same MS.

(δ) And this is supported by the existence of orthographical peculiarities in certain identical sections of C. and J. (see (iv) below).

(iv) Lastly, *this common original of C. and J.* was not the author's text but *an intermediate copy* of that text. This is suggested by the two systems of orthography found in C., where one spelling extends over certain sections of the text while another system is found in the remaining sections (see (c) below). This double system of spelling seems to point pretty conclusively to the work of two different scribes. But such collaboration is impossible with regard to C. itself, for the handwriting of that text is the same throughout. The double system must therefore have existed in the text from which C. was copied; and since it is unlikely that the author himself would employ two spellings, the only possible inference is that C. was copied from a copy of the author's text, and that this intermediate text was copied by two different scribes, who undertook different sections of the work— one beginning with the first line, the other half-way through the poem—and transcribed their original in accordance with their respective scribal practices.

Nor does the absence of this double system of spelling from J. raise any difficulties as to the common origin of C. and J. The single system of J., which is consistently used throughout, is identical with neither of the C. orthographies: and the probability therefore is that the J. scribe, who modernised and corrected his text, also levelled all variations in spelling, as he went along. On the other hand, there are signs that the J. scribe, too, has worked from an original that contained some variety of scribal practices. Thus it is characteristic of those sections of C. in which the second system of orthography (i.e. β, see p. xxix) appears, that abbreviations are used for *þat* and *þer*, whereas elsewhere in C. those words are written in full. But in the J. text a similar practice may be traced[1];

[1] See Wells, *O. & N.* note l. 902.

the abbreviations are employed in the sections corresponding to those of C. in which the same abbreviations occur; and only in those sections. And the inference to be drawn from these facts is clear. It would seem certain that both scribes had before them a version of the original text written by two copyists: and that while the scribe of C. has faithfully reproduced the different spellings of the two copyists, the J. scribe has preserved but one of the peculiarities of one of the copyists. Hence the genesis of C. and J. might be briefly represented as follows:

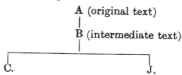

(*b*) THE TWO VERSIONS.

When we turn to consider more closely the two MSS. described above, we shall find that they contain two versions of the poem, differing in various details: and that while the C. text, on the whole, supplies the better version, the J. text is the result of a freer handling of the original, and thus contains modifications which detract very considerably from its value as a copy of the original text.

(i) In the first place, the J. scribe will be found to *omit frequently certain necessary words*. He omits, it is true, only one line (l. 1308) completely: but his total omissions are considerable, and are far more numerous than those of C. Sometimes he drops a word apparently for metrical reasons, in order to obtain what he regarded as a more regular line. He seems to have disliked the elision of unstressed vowels (whether inflexional or before *r*): and in order to give a stress to these light syllables he frequently omits unimportant monosyllabic words from the text; Ex.:

C.　nó, þu háuest wel schárpe cláwe.
J.　nó, þu háuest schárpe cláwe. (l. 153.)

There are over fifty cases of such omissions in J., the words *wel* and *eure* being most frequently dropped, though *no, ӡet, þat, forþ* and *ut* are all treated in similar fashion. Ex.: J. [*no*] l. 283: [*forþ*] l. 356: [*ut*] l. 444: [*sum*] l. 1040: cf. also ll. 615, 667, 714, 1022, 1207. Many of these omissions, it might be added, spoil the scansion, and therefore can scarcely have been characteristic of the original text[1]. Then, again, a word is occasionally omitted from J. because its meaning was apparently unfamiliar to the scribe: Ex.: [*hoӡe*] l. 701: [*þes*] *bles* (in later hand) l. 748; while in other

---

[1] It is of course possible that some of the omissions were due to the fact that, in the scribe's opinion, such words were redundant and unnecessary—a common cause of omission from Latin MSS.

cases no doubt the omission may have been due to carelessness. Ex. [*suþe*] l. 667.

(ii) But besides omitting words, the J. scribe is often found introducing into his text *changes in the order and choice of words*.

   (a) The following are instances of such changes in the word-order, and it is significant that in each case the rhythm of the line in J. suffers as a result of the change: Ex. :

      C.   To me heo hire mone send.
      J.   To me hire mone heo send. (l. 1520.)
      C.   Herof þe lauedies to me meneþ.
      J.   Herof to me þe leuedies heom meneþ. (l. 1563.)

   There are, however, other instances where the rhythm is preserved in spite of changes in the word-order. Cf. ll. 433, 471, 649, 955.

   (β) Instances of the change of words are still more numerous. Failing to understand a word in his original (a word generally preserved in C.), the J. scribe would sometimes substitute a word with a totally different meaning: Ex.: C. *bov ne strind*, J. *bouh of lynd* (l. 242): C. *banne*, J. *barme* (l. 390): C. *chokeringe*, J. *cokeringe* (l. 504): C. *may telen*, J. *mahte beo* (l. 1415).

   Or again the substitution might be due to the desire to replace a word that was possibly becoming archaic, by one of a more familiar kind: Ex.: C. *chauling*, J. *changling* (l. 284): C. *weȝe*, J. *bere* (l. 1022): C. *itid*, J. *iwurþ* (l. 1256): C. *unhwate*, J. *unhap* (l. 1267): C. *wurþschipe*, J. *trevschipe* (l. 1344): C. *misrempe*, J. *misnyme* (l. 1353): C. *an fale londe*, J. *of alle londe* (l. 1371).

In each of these cases it is highly probable that C., rather than J., presents the original form: and this is suggested by the breakdown of the rhyme in J. in similar cases where the variation occurs in the rhyming position. Ex.:

C. *manne*	:	*banne*	J. *manne*	:	*barme*	(ll. 389–90)
C. *leue*	:	*reue*	J. *leue*	:	*teone*	(ll. 457–8)
C. *neor*	:	*meoster*	J. *norþ*	:	*mester*	(ll. 923–4)

Cf. also ll. 131–2, 135–6, 157–8, 589–90, 1149–50, 1277–8, 1487–8.

(iii) And, further, the J. scribe has consistently *introduced into his text modernised forms*, which, when they occur at the end of a line, frequently injure the rhyme. The existence of normal rhymes in such cases in C. points to the retention of the original forms in that version. Ex.:

C. *haȝte*	:	*wraȝte*	J. *hayhte*	:	*wrauhte*	(ll. 105–6)
C. *-daȝe*	:	*-slaȝe*	J. *-daye*	:	*-slawe*	(ll. 1141–2)
C. *fulieð*	:	*sulieð*	J. *voleweþ*	:	*sulieþ*	(ll. 1239–40)

Then, too, it is worth noting that in J. the old verbal inflexions are sometimes confused, and irregular forms are thus presented: Ex.: C. *bihold* (pret.), J. *biholdeþ* (l. 30): C. *biliked* (p.p.), J. *bilikeþ* (in spite of rhyme with *isliked*) (l. 842): C. *tobeteþ*, J. *tobete* (in spite of rhyme with *þreteþ*) (l. 1610): C. *ȝe schule*, J. *ye schuleþ* (l. 1703): C. *ich an* (indic.), J. *ich vnne* (l. 1739).

(c) THE THREE ORTHOGRAPHIES.

Apart from these verbal differences, however, it will be found that the C. and J. texts differ very materially in the matter of spelling. It has been already stated (see (*a*) (iv) above) that three systems of orthography are represented in the two texts, and this is evidently a matter that calls for some consideration. In the C. text, for instance, may be traced with a fair amount of consistency, one system of orthography (*a*), extending over ll. 1–901, 961–1183, a second system (*β*), extending over ll. 902–60, 1184–end, while the spelling of the J. text is different from either, and is used consistently throughout the whole text. The main features of these orthographies may be illustrated as follows:

W.S.	C.		J.	Examples					
	a	*β*		C.				J.	
				a		*β*			
					ll.		ll.		ll.
æ	e	ea (e)	e	del	870	deale	954	dele	954
ĕo	o	eo	eo	horte	37	heorte	947	heorte	947
ēo	o	eo	eo	bo	137	beo	1349	beo	137
āh	aȝ	ah (aȝ)	auh	aȝte	385	aht	1479	auhte	385
ĕah ēh	eȝ	eh (eȝ)	eyh	iseȝ	29	neh	1252	iseyh	29
īh	iȝ	ih (iȝ)	yh	niȝtingale	4	nihtegale	1512	nyhtegale	4
ōh	oȝ	oh (oȝ)	ouh	þoȝtest	157	biþohte	939	þouhte	1442
hw	w	hw (w)	hw	wan	459	hwi	909	hwanne	459
ġ	ȝ	ȝ	y	ȝer	101	ȝer	1259	yer	101
g (after r or l)	ȝ	ȝ (h)	w	{ sorȝe { folȝeþ	431 307	seorhe	1599	{ sorewe { foleweþ	431 307
g (medial)	ȝ	h (ȝ)	w	fuȝele	64	{ fuheles { itoȝen	1660 1725	{ vowele { itowen	64 1725
ð, þ	þ	ð	þ	boþ	296	beoð	911	beoþ	911

In addition the (*β*) orthography has other noteworthy forms, e.g. occasional instances of the doubling of vowels to denote length (cf. *cuuþ* l. 922, *sooþ* l. 1407, *stoone* l. 1167), also of the doubling of consonants to denote a short preceding vowel (cf. *Goddspelle* l. 1209, *hwucche* l. 936, ȝ*arre* l. 1222, *Godd* l. 1543.

Of the three systems, the (β) orthography must in all probability be described as belonging to the earliest date. In fact that system will be found to coincide in almost all its essential details (cf. the treatment of O.E. *ǣ*, *eo*, *hw*, medial *g*) with the spellings characteristic of works written about 1200, e.g. *O.E. Homilies, S. Juliana, Sawles Ward,* and *Ancren Riwle* (Titus MS.). And if a further suggestion may be hazarded, it is not at all unlikely that in those sections of the C. text where this (β) orthography appears, we have the text faithfully reproduced in its original form as it left the author's pen.

On the other hand, the (α) orthography suggests that some amount of modernising has taken place in the sections in which it is found. The use of ȝ (for O.E. *h* and O.E. *g*, gutt. and pal.) belongs to a slightly later date than the (β) orthography: the appearance of *w* (for O.E. *hw*) points to further scribal alteration: while the unusual and rather puzzling use of *o* (for O.E. *ĕo*) also seems to point in the same direction. What the scribe of the intermediate copy has apparently done in the latter instances is to substitute *o* for the *eo* of his original, the symbols being equivalent in Anglo-French forms. In *La Vie de Seint Josaphaz,* for example (one of the A.-Fr. poems included in the C. and J. MSS.), forms in *o* and *eo* occur as variants of *oe* forms, the common sound-value of all three probably being [ö]. Ex.: C. *quoer*, J. *queor*: C. *soen*, J. *seon*: C. *avogle*, J. *avoegle*: C. *dol*, J. *doel*: C. *joevne, jeovne,* J. *jofne*. It is, moreover, not without its significance, that in the C. text of *The Owl and the Nightingale,* alternative forms in *oe* (for *eo*) occasionally occur: cf. *boe* (l. 1303): or again forms in *eo* (for *o*): cf. *seorhe* (l. 1599), *weolcne* (l. 1682), *heom* for *hom* (l. 1534): whilst *wode* (l. 320), *node* (l. 388) have in each case an *e* placed after the *o* (in a later hand)[1]. These forms, then, point to the confusion which prevailed in the scribal use of *eo*, *oe* and *o*: and therefore the *o*-forms in the (α) orthography must be regarded as so many French scribal spellings[2], which have

---

[1] Similar variants occur elsewhere. In *Dame Siriz* (Digby MS. 86) the scribe writes *oe* (for *ŏ*): *Goed* (O.E. *God*) l. 210: *roed* (O.E. *rōd*) l. 254: *noen* (O.E. *nōn*) l. 433; while *hoe* occurs regularly in place of *heo*. This *hoe* (alongside *heo*) is also found in Laȝamon's *Brut*; ȝ*oe* (= *heo*) occurs in Robert of Gloucester's *Chronicle*. And while in *O.E. Homilies* the forms *soven* (O.E. *seofon*), *son* (O.E. *sēon*), *node* (O.E. *nēod*) appear, in Laȝamon's *Brut*, again, the spelling *eo* is frequently found in place of *o*.

[2] For other French scribal forms, see Appendix I. (*a*) (ii).

been substituted for the normal *eo*-forms found in the (β) sections of C., and throughout the whole of J.

But while the (a) orthography thus bears evident traces of modernising, the same can be said of the J. text and with yet greater certainty. The development of the diphthongs *au, ou, ey* (*ei*), before gutt. and pal. *h*, the use of *y* in place of an earlier ȝ, and the change of O.E. *g* to *w* after *l* and *r*, and in the medial position—all these details belong to a later date than the forms of either the (a) or the (β) orthography.

From the above considerations it therefore becomes clear, that in the matter of spelling, C. supplies a more accurate copy of the original than J. C. reproduces the double system of spelling which probably figured in the intermediate copy, where one scribe had attempted to modernise, the other being content to copy the text as it stood. J. on the other hand gives us the intermediate text, after some amount of revision, and after its spelling, in particular, had been brought up to date. Hence the sections of C. in which the (β) orthography appears, may reasonably be regarded as reproductions of the author's text: the (a) sections give us that original in a slightly modified form: while J. supplies a version that has undergone a systematic change of spelling.

(*d*) Scribal Errors.

In the foregoing sections, the main features in which the C. and J. texts differ from what may be regarded as the original version, have been noted. We have seen verbal changes in J., orthographical modifications in both C. and J.: and it now remains to examine those departures from the original which came about in the process of copying, and were due to scribal error. Such error is inevitable in all transcription of MSS.: but in the present instance, the risk was increased, owing to the fact that both MSS. were based on an intermediate copy, which itself doubtless contained some amount of inaccuracy. Hence there are two sources of scribal error in C. and J. Some errors have been taken over from the common original (see § 3 (*a*) (iii) above, for examples), while others are clearly due to the scribes of C. and J. themselves: and of the latter it may be said that whereas the errors of J. are largely due to the scribe's attempts at improving his text, those of C. are mainly of a mechanical unconscious kind—the result of an attempt to copy, rather than to improve, the text.

In general the scribal errors will be found to be those common to all transcribers: but they are by no means without a special interest, for apart from the more obvious emendations they suggest, they are not without their value in clearing up difficulties connected with certain *loci desperati*.

Thus we find instances of:

(i) *Dittography.* Ex.: C. *one one* l. 446: C. and J. *ne ne* l. 1358: C. and J. *lustes is* (for *lust is*) l. 1388: C. *of of* l. 1469.

(ii) *Haplography.* Ex.: C. *opere[s] song* l. 11: J. *nu þe* [for *nu suþe*) l. 205: C. *cliures [s]charpe* l. 1676: C. *his [s]chelde* l. 1713. Cf. also l. 767 (see note) and l. 930 (see note).

(iii) *Transposition of letters.* Ex.: C. *þurste* (for *þustre*) l. 249: C. *blod* (for *bold*) l. 317: C. *worþ* (for *wroþ*) l. 1218: C. *hlad* (for *hald*) l. 1576: C. *ihc* (for *ich*) l. 1698: C. *þorte* (for *þrote*) l. 1721.

(iv) *Wrong division of words.* Ex.: C. *is hote* (for *ishote*) l. 23: C. *is tunge* (for *istunge*) l. 515: C. *mani eine*, J. *mony eine* (for *manteine*) l. 759, see note: C. and J. *monnes honde* (for *monne shonde*) l. 1402: C. and J. *hoȝeþ, howeþ* (for *ho geþ*) l. 1602: C. *mann enne* (for *mankenne*) l. 1725.

(v) *Confusion of similar letters*[1].

    (a) *þ* written for *h*. Ex.: C. *þes* (for *hes*) l. 748, see note: C. *þurþ* (for *þurh*) ll. 1256, 1405, 1428: C. *neþ* (for *neh*) l. 1267: C. *innoþ* (for *innoh*) l. 1319: C. *heþ* (for *heh*) l. 1405: C. *houdsiþe*, J. *houþsyþe* (for *houhsiþe*) l. 1586, see note: cf. also l. 651.

    (β) *h* written for *þ*. Ex.: J. *bihouhte* (for *biþouhte*) l. 199: C. *floh* (for *floþ*) l. 920: C. *þunch* (for *þuncþ*) ll. 1649, 1651: see also C. *hwitestu* l. 1356 (note): J. *smithes* l. 1206 (note).

    (γ) *w* and *þ* confused[2]. Ex.: C. *wriste* (for *þriste*) l. 171: C. *þinne* (for *winne*) l. 670: C. *þi* (for *wi*) l. 905.

    (δ) *t* and *r* confused. Ex.: C. *dart* (for *darr*) l. 1106: C. *warte*, *ȝarte* (for *warre*, *ȝarre*) ll. 1221, 1222: C. *hite* (for *hire*) l. 1341: C. *awet* (for *awer*) l. 1342: C. *weþet* (for *weþer*) l. 1360: C. *mistempe* (for *misrempe*) l. 1353: see also C. *þar* (for *þat*) l. 918: C. *reache* (for *teache*) l. 1449.

    (ε) *m*, *n* and *u* confused. Ex.: C. *fron* (for *from*) ll. 135, 1614: C. *hon* (for *hom*) l. 881: C. *hin* (for *him*) l. 890: C. *wisdon* (for *wisdom*) l. 1482: C. *sun* (for *sum*) l. 1598: C. *inmeaþe* (for *unneaþe*) l. 1618: C. *wronehede* (for *wrouehede*) l. 1400, see note.

    (ζ) *d* written for *ð*[3]. Ex.: C. *wened* (for *weneð*) l. 901: C.

---

[1] See Napier, *O.E. Glosses*, p. xxxi, for similar scribal errors.

[2] Since the only distinction between the two letters was the dot placed above *þ* (for *w*), the confusion is easily intelligible. Wells however frequently reads *w* instead of *þ* in places where the *þ* written was probably original; cf. *þane* l. 165. See note.

[3] The use of *ð* (for *þ*) is found almost exclusively in the (β) orthography of

oder (for *oðer*) ll. 903, 905: C. *fulied* (for *fulieð*) l. 1239:
C. *sulied* (for *sulieð*) l. 1240: see also C. *houdsiþe* l. 1586
(note).

(η) *it* written for *u*. Ex.: C. and J. *bihaitest* (for *bihauest*)
l. 1322: J. *smithes* (for *snuwes*) l. 1206, see note: see also
notes ll. 759, 763, 1189.

(θ) *st* and *ȝt* confused. Ex.: C. *mist* (for *miȝt*) l. 78: C.
nuȝte (for *nuste*) l. 1751: see also ll. 642, 1300.

Of the errors mentioned above, those included under (v) are
worthy of close attention. They are all presumably due to badly-
formed letters in the intermediate copy, and an inspection of
the handwriting characteristic of the period (see *facsimiles*) will
show how easily such errors might arise, with a carelessly copied
text to work from. Most of the errors, it will be noted, occur in
the (β) section of the text, that section in which the scribe aimed
at mere copying, and took no liberties with his text. But what is
particularly valuable, in connection with these scribal errors, is the
fact that an acquaintance with the main tendencies will help
greatly in the solution of textual difficulties. In more than one
passage emendations suggest themselves for readings which seemed
hopelessly corrupt (e.g. ll. C. 748, J. 1206: C. 1322, 1400, 1586):
and these emendations will be found to commend themselves
because they are palaeographically easy.

By way of summary, it can now be stated that in C. and J. we
have two independent copies of a certain text, C. dating from the
first half, J. from the second half, of the 13th century. The text
from which they were both copied was itself a copy of the original
poem: and it was probably written by two scribes, one of whom
aimed at introducing a modernised spelling, while the other was
content to copy the text as it stood. The C. scribe, in due course,
made a transcript of this composite text, so that in his version we
have a double system of orthography preserved. The J. scribe, on
the other hand, aimed at making a thorough revision: he re-wrote
the whole poem in a more modern spelling, and altered the readings
wherever he saw fit. He has therefore taken considerable liberties
with the text. He has frequently omitted words which he considered unnecessary, or which presented difficulty: he has changed
the word-order in places, frequently to the injury of the metre:
he has introduced new words for various reasons, and at times he
is found confusing the older inflexions. It is therefore C. which

---

MS. C. and was probably characteristic of the second scribe of the intermediate
text.

preserves the original version with the greater fidelity: and if we allow for scribal errors which have to be eliminated, C. may be said to present us with a fairly accurate text.

§ 4. THE DATE OF THE POEM

In the various attempts made from time to time to date the poem, wide differences of opinion have been revealed. The earliest editor, Stevenson, followed Warton in connecting it with the reign of Richard I (1189–99): Ten Brink, Morris and Skeat placed it about the middle of the 13th century, and (according to Skeat) "certainly not later than the time of Henry III" (1216–72): while Madden and Hazlitt, in their respective editions of Warton's *History*, assigned as its date "the beginning of the reign of Edward I," or "not later than Edward I" (1272–1307). Others again have inclined to the earlier date. Wright, Mätzner and Wülcker connected it with the reign of John (1199–1216): Börsch suggested 1218–25, Morsbach and Hall c. 1220, Wells 1216–25, while Gadow would place it in the second or third decade of the 13th century.

In investigating anew this question of date, a start may perhaps safely be made from the fact that the handwriting of the earlier MS. (i.e. C.) belongs to the first half of the 13th century. From this it follows that the original text must have belonged, either to the opening decades of the 13th century or to the end of the 12th: for since C. is a copy of a copy of that original, some time—more or less—would have to be allowed for the transmission to be made. And this is roughly borne out by the orthographies of the C. text. Such modernisings as appear in the (a) sections belong to the earlier half of the 13th century, while the (β) orthography—which may reasonably be regarded as something like the original—bears close resemblance to the spelling characteristic of works c. 1200. There is this, however, to be added: that the more probable date is *after*, rather than before, 1200: for in the (β) orthography we find occasional forms[1] in *ou* (= O.E. *ū*), a spelling not found in 12th century work[2], as well as certain forms[3] in *o* (= O.E. *u*) which are rare in the 12th century. On the other hand, the comparative absence of French words from the vocabulary of the poem, and the fidelity with which the Old English inflexional system has been

---

[1] Cf. *houle* (l. 1662), *proude* (l. 1685).
[2] See Morsbach, *M.E. Gram.* § 121 a.1.
[3] Cf. *comen* (l. 1199), *come þ* (l. 1236).

preserved, seem to lend support to the earlier date. In any case, neither of these arguments can be called decisive; and all that can safely be said is that the handwriting and the orthographies of C., taken together, seem to point to the period 1190–1210 (or later), as that in which the poem was most probably written.

With regard to evidence of an internal kind, the poem, in the first place, contains a reference to a certain King Henry, which has an important bearing on this question of date. The reference is as follows:

þat underyat þe King Henri,
Jesus his soule do merci!   (ll. 1091–2.)

and from its very nature, it can only allude to a departed monarch, the form of benediction being one that was used in connection with the dead. That it refers to Henry III (d. 1272) is, at any rate, impossible: for such an assumption would throw the poem into the last quarter of the 13th century—a date ruled out by the evidence above. The allusion must therefore be connected with Henry II (d. 1189); with that generous patron of letters[1], whose munificence is commemorated by more than one writer of the period[2], and whose legislative reforms constitute a landmark in our national history. But if the Henry-allusion be thus interpreted, the forward limit of the date becomes the year of Henry's death: that is, the poem cannot have been written before 1189. And with equal certainty, it might be added, it cannot have been written after 1217: for in that year Henry III came to the throne, and, with the later Henry reigning, the reference would not have been free from some amount of ambiguity. The period 1189–1217 would therefore seem to be a likely one for the composition of the poem—a date in close agreement with the evidence set out above.

There is, however, yet another contemporary allusion that calls for consideration. In two places in the text, reference is made to a Master Nicholas of Guildford. He is described as a cleric, then living at Portisham, who had not hitherto received the recognition he deserved: and the question therefore arises, whether it is possible to identify the Master Nicholas thus mentioned, so as to throw some light on the matter of date. It would have to be a

---

[1] J. Hall suggests (*Selections from Early Middle English*, II. 566) that some recent instance of Henry's protection of minstrels is referred to in ll. 1093 ff., where some "minstrel go-between [is] saved, by the intervention of King Henry the Second, from the vengeance of a wronged husband."

[2] Cf. Guiot de Provins, *La Bible* (1206), l. 318; also in Peter de Blois, *De prestigiis fortunae*.

cleric of the name of Nicholas, one associated with the diocese of
Salisbury, in the jurisdiction of which both Portisham and Guildford then lay: while his condition in the early part of the 13th
century (or earlier) would have to be such as to suggest neglect at
the hands of the authorities. The chances are clearly against such
an identification: yet it would seem to have been done with some
amount of plausibility[1] and with results not without their bearing
on the question of date. Thus in *The Charters and Documents
illustrating the History of the City and Diocese of Salisbury in the
12th and 13th Centuries*[2], mention is made of one *Nicholaus capel-
lanus archidiaconi* who appears as witness to a document c. 1209.
Later on, in an inventory[3] taken at Godalming (near Guildford) in
1220, reference is also made to one *Nicholaus submonitor capituli
Gudeford*, who is said to have been connected with the Chapel of All
Saints, Hertmer, for the two preceding years[4]. If, as seems at least
possible, the archdeacon's chaplain of 1209 is the submonitor of
the Chapter of Guildford in 1220, we then have cognisance of a
cleric, Nicholas by name, who up to the year 1220 had associations
with the diocese of Salisbury and with Guildford in particular, and
who had held during that time no very lucrative office. It is true
that no contemporary record of his connection with Portisham
has as yet come to light, though the Nicholas in question may have
resided there before proceeding to Hertmer in 1217; a change
which may have resulted from a change of bishops, Bishop Herbert
Poore being succeeded by his brother Richard in 1217. In that
event, some date before 1217 would be the time to which the neglect alluded to in the poem would naturally apply: and though the
evidence is imperfect, since the identification is not complete, yet
it is not without its value in adding to the probability of the
opening decades of the 13th century as the approximate date of
the composition of the poem.

And in keeping with that date are certain other considerations,
none of which is conclusive, but which, taken together, afford
evidence of a cumulative kind. Thus the poet might well be expected to betray incidentally some knowledge of events connected
with the period: and some such historical reminiscence seems to

---

[1] See W. Gadow, *Eule und Nachtigall*, pp. 12, 13, where the case is stated
for the first time.

[2] Ed. W. D. Macray, London, 1891, I. 73.

[3] See *Vetus registrum Sarisberiense*, ed. W. Jones, London, 1883, I. 297.

[4] "Item est ibi capella de Hertmer, de Omnibus Sanctis: lignea adhuc,
quam tenet Nicholaus, submonitor capituli de Gudeford, pro dimidia marca,
et tenuit eam iam transactis duobus annis."

underlie the passage in which the Nightingale states her reasons
for not wishing to visit the countries of the North. She explains

> þeȝ eni god man to hom come,
> so wile dude sum from Rome,
> for hom to lere gode þewes,
> an for to leten hore unþewes,
> he miȝte bet sitte stille,
> vor al his wile he sholde spille.   (ll. 1015 ff.)

Here reference is apparently made to a certain Papal embassy,
sent some time before (cf. *wile* l. 1016) the date at which the poet
was writing, to visit the northern kingdoms. And although it might
be argued that the use of the word "Rome" is due to exigencies
of rhyme, yet it is difficult to avoid thinking that the allusion
here is to some definite Papal mission. It is significant, for one
thing, that the countries implied in the context are Ireland,
Scotland, Norway and Galloway. The Nightingale is replying to
the taunt of the Owl,

> þu neauer ne singst in Irlonde,
> ne þu ne cumest noȝt in Scotlonde.
> Hwi nultu fare to Noreweie
> an singin men of Galeweie?   (ll. 907–10.)

and the allusion is, without doubt, to the journey of Vivian, who,
in 1176, travelled to Scotland at the request of William and his
clergy for information in ecclesiastical matters, and who undertook
at the same time a Papal mission to Ireland, Norway and the
adjacent islands. The embassy is referred to in Benedict of Peterborough's *Chronicle* under the year 1176[1]: and the allusion to
that event, made by our poet, suggests that he was writing certainly after 1176, but sufficiently near to that date to make the
reference clear to his contemporaries. So important an event as a
Papal mission to the distant North would certainly not be forgotten by the early decades of the 13th century: and in the light
of this allusion, the poem may well be placed, either towards the
close of the 12th century, or in the opening decades of the 13th[2].

Or again we might point to the use made by the poet of Neckam's
De Naturis Rerum (see Introduction, § 8, pp. lxii, lxvii), a work

---

[1] I.e. "Missus est itaque ad eos Vivianus presbyter cardinalis, qui etiam
legatiam Hiberniae, Scotiae, et Norwegiae et aliarum circumjacentium insu-
larum suscepit."

[2] It is unnecessary to infer with H. B. Hinckley (see *Modern Philology*,
xvii. 5, pp. 63 ff.), mainly on the strength of this historical allusion, that
the poem was written as early as "1177 or 1178 or at least not later than
1189." Further evidence is available which demands a date somewhat later.

of considerable maturity and learning, which can scarcely have been written before 1186, when Neckam, aged 29, returned to England after a period spent abroad at the schools of Paris[1]. The use made of this source suggests, once again, a poet writing towards the end of the 12th century or early in the following century. It is true that the debt to Marie de France (see Introduction, § 8, p. lxii), with regard to the nightingale-episode, and the use of Alfred's name in connection with the proverbs of the poem are both compatible with an earlier date; for *Laustic* appeared c. 1175, and a version of the *Proverbs of Alfred* has come down from the 12th century. Yet the adoption of the debate form—a form which flourished on the Continent towards the close of the 12th century—and, more particularly, the elaborate form assumed by the debate in our present poem, these again are arguments for the later date: as is also the refusal on the part of the Nightingale to accept "the ordeal by battle" as a way of settling the dispute (see ll. 150 ff. note)[2]. That the C. MS. itself was written soon after 1216 is suggested by the fact that the short Anglo-Norman Chronicle of English Kings, which precedes our poem in that MS., breaks off abruptly at the year 1216, leaving some space for the continuation of the Chronicle at a later date: and, here again, it would seem that the poem, in all probability, had been composed some few years earlier.

So that, reviewing the evidence as a whole, however inconclusive each detail may in itself appear, a case would seem to be established for placing the poem in the early part of the 13th century, and for pointing to the reign of King John (1199–1217) as the period in which the poem was most probably written.

§ 5. THE AUTHOR

Who the author of *The Owl and the Nightingale* actually was, cannot be stated with any certainty. In neither of the two MSS. is any definite assertion made: there is no contemporary reference to supply the information: nor has tradition anything to say on this particular point.

In any discussion of the question, however, there are two names which obviously call for consideration. One is that of John of Guildford, who is described in the Jesus MS. as the writer of

---

[1] See Neckam, *De Nat. Rerum*, ed. Wright (Rolls Series), Preface.

[2] See also Hall's suggestion (*Selections from Early Middle English*, II. 566) that, in l. 1732, reference is made "to the good peace kept by the Justiciar Hubert Walter, during Richard the First's absence from England in A.D. 1194–8."

certain verses contained in that MS.: the other is Nicholas of Guildford who is mentioned at some length in *The Owl and the Nightingale* itself. And, since Stevenson first edited the poem, these two names have been discussed in connection with the authorship, but without any decisive result. While the earlier scholars, on the whole, inclined to accept Nicholas as the author, recent editors have considered rather more seriously the claims of John, though all alike have agreed to leave the question an open one.

In the first place, the case for John of Guildford rests mainly on the following considerations:

(1) In the note contained in the Jesus MS. (see Introduction, § 2) we have definite evidence of the fact that John of Guildford was a 13th century writer of verse. It is true that the statement to this effect has come down in a 17th century hand: but there is no reason for doubting the explanation given by the writer (at that time owner of the MS.), namely, that he had copied his statement from "a broken leafe" of the MS. as it had come into his possession. The present condition of the MS., with its several *lacunae* and its derangement of folios (see Introduction, § 2), makes it at least possible that omissions and misplacements had occurred in the process of binding: and thus indirectly lends support to the existence of a "broken leafe." Then, too, the linguistic forms of the four lines quoted are contemporaneous with the Jesus MS.[1] The passage is wanting in C.: and in all probability the lines were originally copied or added by the scribe of J. Hence they supply clear 13th century evidence as to the activity of John of Guildford as a verse-writer of the time.

(2) He is the writer of at least one of the verse-pieces originally included in the Jesus MS.: this also is explicitly stated in the note referred to above.

(3) His name suggests some sort of connection with Nicholas of Guildford, on whose behalf *The Owl and the Nightingale* was obviously written. The immediate object of the poem was to win recognition for Nicholas: and it would naturally have been written by someone interested in his welfare, such as John of Guildford might reasonably be taken to be.

(4) It has, further, been suggested[2] that the dialect of the C.

---

[1] Cf. the forms characteristic of J.: *eu* (C. *ow*), *Mayster* (C. *Maister*), *Guldeuorde* (C. *Guldeforde*), and *endy, synge*, where the *y*-spellings (instead of C. *i*) occur.

[2] I.e. by Professor Craigie, see Appendix I. (*a*).

text has traces of Kentish peculiarities (see Appendix I. (*a*)), and that the poem may therefore have been originally written in that particular dialect. This would make it possible for the author to have been a Guildford man—John of Guildford, for instance— who may well have sent a copy to his friend Nicholas in Dorset, where it would be copied by scribes, who would naturally give it the south-western peculiarities it now presents.

On the other hand, there are certain grave difficulties which prevent us from regarding John of Guildford as the author of our poem:

(1) To begin with, there is nothing in the scribal note to connect him definitely with *The Owl and the Nightingale*. Wilkins' transcript of that note appears on f. 228 r.; and as it stands, it refers apparently to the preceding verses, that is, to *The Passion of Our Lord*, though this on the whole is unlikely[1]. But then, this is not its original position: it has been transferred by Wilkins from "a broaken leafe": and whichever of the original folios may have been represented by that "broaken leafe" it cannot have been among those prior to f. 253, where the first irregularity occurs. In other words, the note cannot have been originally inserted in the neighbourhood of *The Owl and the Nightingale*, for that poem comes to an end on f. 241 v., some 12 folios before the irregularities begin. Moreover, had a reference to our poem been intended, the scribal note would surely have been written at the end of the poem, in the blank space left at the foot of f. 241 v. col. 2. Hence we may safely infer that the reference was intended to apply, not to *The Owl and the Nightingale*, but to some other poem in the MS.

(2) And this is also suggested by the terms of reference. The poem alluded to in the note is described as "a song": a description more in keeping with some of the shorter poems (ff. 243–72) than with *The Owl and the Nightingale*.

---

[1] It may be that Wilkins had some special reason for inserting the note where he did, thus apparently ascribing the *Passion* to John of Guildford. For instance, as J. Koch (*Angl. Beibl.* XXI. 231) pointed out, the metre of the four lines is the same as that of the *Passion*, and this may have weighed with Wilkins. At the same time there are reasons for thinking this assumption to be highly improbable. The transcript was probably inserted where it stands for reasons of space, the greater part of f. 228 r. and the whole of f. 228 v. having been left blank. Moreover it is significant, as Wells pointed out, that "the conclusion of the *Passion* is such as to render it very improbable that any such matter as is quoted in the note was attached to that poem." (See Wells, *O. & N.* p. xxviii.) So that on the whole there would seem to be no case for connecting John of Guildford with *The Passion of Our Lord*.

(3) Nor would the establishment of John of Guildford's claim to one of the other poems warrant a claim being advanced for him in connection with *The Owl and the Nightingale*. There is nothing in the poems (ff. 243–72) to suggest that any one of them was due to the author of our poem. On the contrary, in subject-matter, treatment, and general outlook upon life, there is a world of difference between the respective works, making it highly improbable that the writer of "the song" was also the author of *The Owl and the Nightingale*.

(4) Nor does the presence of occasional Kentish forms in one of the extant copies prove much in connection with the authorship of the poem. Even if the Kentish original be granted, for the sake of argument, the claims of John of Guildford would hardly be stronger than those of Nicholas. For both presumably hailed from the S.E. district; both would therefore be familiar with Kentish forms: and it is as easy to imagine Nicholas, though removed to Dorset, reverting to his native dialect in attempting a vernacular poem, as it is to imagine John employing the Kentish dialect for a similar attempt at Guildford. On the other hand, it is significant that the poet, whoever he may have been, shows that he is well aware of the value of variant forms in helping out his rhymes (see Introduction, § 9, p.lxxxvii). And it may well have been that the Kentish forms discharged this function in the original version. This would imply an original written in a dialect other than Kentish—the south-western dialect for instance—and in that case, the weight of the evidence would rest with Nicholas, who would naturally be familiar with both dialects employed, a claim that could not definitely be made on behalf of John. In any event, these Kentish elements leave us very much as before: they cannot be said to strengthen the claims of John.

This, then, is the case for John of Guildford. There is nothing which definitely points to him as the author; though, as a contemporary poet, whose verses were included in the same MS. as a poem devoted to the interests of a clerk of the same surname, he may possibly have been the writer of the latter poem as well. But the theory lacks probability: it is a bare possibility, and nothing more.

The case for Nicholas of Guildford, on the other hand, is of a different kind, and rests entirely on internal evidence. Reference is made to him in two passages of the poem (ll. 191 ff., 1746 ff.). There he is described as a well-known cleric, then living at Portisham in Dorset; a man, so it is stated, of considerable parts, famous for his writings (ll. 1756-8) and his taste in literary

A.   *d*

matters (ll. 195–8), besides being highly esteemed for his ripe wisdom, his sound judgment and his virtuous way of life. In the poem he figures as the umpire agreed upon by both disputants: and it is not without significance that his character is described at considerable length, and his qualities are presented in a most favourable light. Still more significant is the hint that is given of his neglect at the hands of the authorities. Distinguished man though he was, he is said to have been sadly in want of patronage. "He has but one living—to the great shame of the bishops and of all who have heard of him and of what he has done" (ll. 1760–3). Whoever may have been the author of the poem, one thing at least is certain, and that is, that one object—the main object—of the writer was to commend the case of Nicholas to the proper quarters for preferment. Such a conclusion is inevitable from the nature and the persistency of the allusions. Nor need such an object be regarded as in any degree surprising. "The idea of choosing a person as an honor and as a means of praising him and furthering his welfare, seems to have been generally the motive for choosing the judge in the Provençal *partimen*. The same seems true, for the most part, of the Old French *jeu parti*[1]." So that the poet, whoever he was, in thus advocating the claims of Nicholas, was but employing a familiar literary device of the time for the particular purpose he had in view.

In the absence of any definite statement as to the authorship of the poem, it was perhaps inevitable that the question should be raised, as to whether Nicholas himself might not have been the writer of the poem. And indeed this possibility has been considered by most of those who have dealt with the work. The two earliest editors were inclined to favour the theory: but since then the verdict has somewhat changed, and some of the later scholars have preferred to reject the idea. It will therefore be necessary, in the first place, to examine the grounds advanced for the confident rejection of Nicholas as author: for Wülcker and Ten Brink both regarded the idea as "impossible," while Mätzner, though rather more cautious, also inclined strongly to the same opinion. The main argument brought forward for discrediting the Nicholas theory was that the self-praise, thus involved, would be incredible in connection with such a man as Nicholas was said to be. "His self-praise," wrote Mätzner, "would surprise us, if he were the

---

[1] See Wells, *O. & N.* p. xxvi, n. 1, where Knobloch, *Die Streitgedichte im Provenzalischen und Altfranzösischen*, p. 48, and Selbach, *Das Streitgedicht in der Altprovenzalischen Lyrik*, 177, are also quoted.

author[1]." According to Wülcker, again, it would prove him to have been "one of the most conceited of men[2]." Or, as Ten Brink put it, "the manner in which his virtues, his justice, prudence, and wisdom are dwelt upon, makes it impossible to regard [Nicholas] as the poet himself, because such laudation would ill agree with those qualities[3]." But, it may fairly be asked, are arguments such as these sufficiently conclusive to warrant the use of the word "impossible"? To begin with, a wrong inference seems to have been drawn from the self-praise of Nicholas, granted that it was he who wrote the poem. It is clear that his motive in so writing would be, not the indulgence of personal vanity, but the attainment of a definite material end. He might therefore justly be taxed with being ambitious, shrewd and practical: but it would not necessarily follow that he was excessively vain. But apart from superficial reasoning, is there anything in the nature of the case that rules out Nicholas as author of the poem? The charge of excessive vanity, even if it could be maintained, would hardly be decisive, for modesty has not proved to be an essential ingredient in the artistic temperament. Is it, then, that a sense of fitness, some scruple of conscience, would have prevented any writer from adopting this device in order to further his own interests? But that is surely to test the matter by the application of modern standards. It was a period in which imaginative writings were, to a large extent, anonymous: and it is surely not inconceivable, that in an age of anonymity, an able and ambitious writer, fretting under a sense of unmerited neglect, might resort to means of winning recognition, which, although they could not be squared with a modern code, would involve no great sacrifice of self-respect under 13th century conditions. It would therefore seem that there has been an overstatement of the case, in maintaining it to have been impossible for Nicholas to have been the author—at least for the reasons specified. And the same holds true of the other objections that have been raised, as when Wülcker[4], for example, maintained that Nicholas and the poet stood for two separate persons, since the poet is present throughout the debate, whereas Nicholas "is always spoken of as an absent person who dwelt at Portesham." But there is surely no real difficulty here: for the disputants throughout are represented as unconscious of the presence of the poet, who overhears the dispute from a place of concealment (l. 3). Had the poet revealed himself at any time, and had a reference

---

[1] *Altengl. Sprachproben*, I. 40.   [2] Paul u. Braune, *Beiträge*, I. 70.
[3] *Early English Literature* (Bohn), I. 217.   [4] *P.B.B.* I. 70.

then been made to an absent Nicholas, the case would have been different. The existence of two separate personalities would then have been established. Equally irrelevant, too, is Wülcker's further argument relating to the fact that at the close of the poem (l. 1789) the disputants are represented as setting out to the abode of Nicholas. "If he" [i.e. the author who was present], writes Wülcker, "were one with Nicholas, why should [he] let the birds go away instead of coming forth from his concealment, or why could he not tell us the verdict[1]?" But here again the answer seems plain. It was no part of the "debate" convention for the poet, who overheard the dispute, to reveal himself to the disputants, nor was it at all necessary for any verdict to be given. In accordance with the rules of the literary "debate," the poet aims merely at presenting a case, at giving the pros and cons of the question at issue. As Wells correctly states: "the poet had no intention of giving a definitely formulated statement of his solution of the question that he had raised[2]."

These, then, are the arguments which have been advanced to prove that Nicholas could not possibly have been the author: and the case clearly rests on no very substantial grounds. In fact, there seems to be no definite reason why the authorship may not be attributed to Nicholas: while, on the other hand, there are certain considerations which render that theory not at all unlikely.

(1) In the first place, while undue importance need not be attached to the mere statement of Thomas Wright, that "the name of Nicholas of Guildford appears in the poem......in a way which would lead any one acquainted with the manner in which writers of the Middle Ages name themselves, to believe him to be the author[3]," yet it represents the conviction of one with a wide knowledge of medieval texts, and is therefore not without its definite value.

(2) On the other hand, there is the undoubted fact, that towards the end of the 12th century, when the oral tradition was beginning to decline, and increased patronage was being extended to poets for political and personal services, we find authors beginning to insert their names into their works in some fashion or other[4]. Such references were not always as direct as the well-known statement in *Ormulum*[5]. In the prologue to *Doon de Nanteuil*,

---

[1] *P.B.B.* I. 70.   [2] Wells, *O. & N.* p. xxvi.
[3] T. Wright, *Biog. Brit. Lit.* (Anglo-Norm. Period), p. 438. London, 1846.
[4] G. Paris, *Esquisse historique de la litt. française*, § 13. Paris, 1914.
[5] "This book is called Ormulum because Orm composed it" (Pref. ll. 1-2).

for instance, Huon de Villeneuve is mentioned as the poet from whom the work had been stolen: and this was, not improbably, a trick on the part of the author—Huon himself—who was thus enabled to praise his *geste* in impersonal fashion[1]. In connection with *The Owl and the Nightingale,* there would be other and obvious reasons for the use of a similar device, since the appeal on behalf of Nicholas would be far more effective if it came ostensibly from an independent quarter. Thus there is really no antecedent improbability about either the insertion of the name, or the method of disguise adopted. If Nicholas were indeed the author, it is precisely the procedure we should expect him to adopt.

(3) We may, however, go further and state that there are plausible grounds for identifying the author with both Nicholas of Guildford and Nicholas the chaplain of the Archdeacon of Salisbury in 1209 (see Introduction, § 4, p. xxxvi). All three seem to possess certain points in common: and although the identity may not be completely established, the evidence goes to suggest that we are here dealing, in all probability, with one and the same person.

To begin with, the broad characteristics of the author may be gathered from the poem itself, from that self-revelation which every poem, in a greater or less degree, involves. That he was a man of considerable learning is shown by the sources from which he drew his varied material (see Introduction, § 8). It would therefore be strange if he were not a cleric: indeed his learning would be quite consistent with the dignity of "Maister." But the author, whoever he was, also betrays a special acquaintance with judicial procedure. The legal atmosphere of the poem in general was noted by Ten Brink. But certain details connected with the conduct of the debate (see Introduction, § 6, pp. liii ff.), the references to such matters as "the King's peace" (l. 1730), and the hue-and-cry (ll. 1215, 1683), for instance, point unmistakably to a writer well versed in judicial matters, whose hand was subdued to what it worked in. Then, too, the poet is evidently a man of broad human sympathies, with no cloistered view of life, no lack of experience in everyday affairs. He had walked abroad with a keen observant eye, fully alive to the comedy of life, concerning which he has however formed his own independent judgment, as is shown by the theme he has adopted for his poem. Shrewd as a man of the world, original both as artist and thinker, he is clearly a man of forceful personality, possessed of much humour and a sound grip on life.

---

[1] See E. Faral, *Les Jongleurs en France au moyen âge,* p. 182. Paris, 1910.

And in this shrewd and humorous personality we may perhaps detect the Nicholas of the poem, who according to description, has many of the characteristics that have been ascribed to the author. The portrait of Nicholas, it is true, is possibly of a flattering kind: but that part of the description relating to verifiable facts, must surely be accepted as true and authentic, since deception in these matters would defeat the object of the poem. Thus we may take it for granted that Nicholas of Guildford was a contemporary cleric of considerable learning, whose merits had been ignored by the ecclesiastical authorities. That he was concerned with legal business may be reasonably concluded from the passage, in which reference is made to the sound judgments he had written (ll. 1755 –8). That he was something of a poet, moreover, is implied in ll. 195–6: and if any value is to be attached to the objections raised by the Owl (ll. 202–4), then we are to understand that he had figured as "a man of the world" in his youth, had devoted himself to *nugae amatoriae*, and as such, had acquired an unclerical knowledge of life, which, later on, was extended in the course of his judicial labours. It therefore requires no great stretch of the imagination to see in Nicholas the author of the poem. The device therein adopted might well have appealed to his shrewdness and sense of humour. He would merely have been adapting to his own uses a growing practice of the time: and, like Hamlet, he might have excused himself, "sith [he] had cause and strength and will to do it."

Whether this Nicholas of Guildford may be identified with the archdeacon's chaplain of 1209 and the submonitor of 1220 is, of course, uncertain: but, it should be added, it is by no means unlikely. The theory derives support, at least, from the subordinate position held by this Nicholas between 1210–20: while as chaplain to the archdeacon, who in those days was the legal official of the diocese, he would naturally acquire a special knowledge of legal matters, and would probably be responsible for the drawing up of many judgments connected with ecclesiastical cases of the diocese. With a fair amount of plausibility, therefore, the poem may be ascribed to Nicholas of Guildford; and he in his turn may possibly be Nicholas, the archdeacon's chaplain mentioned in the year 1209. Absolute certainty as to authorship is out of the question: but Nicholas of Guildford must at least be said to hold the field.

§ 6. THE FORM OF THE POEM

The type of literature to which *The Owl and the Nightingale* belongs, namely, the debate, was one which was specially characteristic of the 12th and early 13th centuries. Together with the *Chansons de geste*, the *fabliaux* and the Provençal lyrics, the debate may be regarded as the natural expression of the medieval genius at that particular period: and of the works that have come down, *The Owl and the Nightingale* represents not only the earliest poem of the kind in English, but also one of the greatest, if not actually the greatest, of all the medieval debates. Its form is therefore of considerable interest: and the origin and development of that form are also matters of the greatest importance. From the Carolingian era onwards, poems of the kind had been constantly appearing, in Latin for the most part, though occasionally in the vernaculars as well: and while the 12th and early 13th centuries witnessed the greatest popularity of the form, it is represented intermittently right on to the end of the Middle Ages. The debate had thus an extensive vogue: and it was known under a variety of names—the *conflictus, certamen, contentio, disputatio, altercatio, estrif, plet, disputoison*. But in every case, the essential element was the same: there was always a spirited contest in verse between two or more disputants, each of whom claimed supremacy for the views he held.

For the origin of this medieval form we must therefore go back at least to the Carolingian era, to those scholarly activities associated with the name of Alcuin, which had for their object the study of Latin as the key to the vast library of patristic thought. And among the literary works which have come down from that distant period are two Latin poems of great historical value: one the *Conflictus veris et hiemis*, ascribed to Alcuin or to some member of his school (8th century), the other, *De rosae liliique certamine*, due to Sedulius Scotus, an Irish-Scot grammarian who flourished in Lorraine during the 9th century. With these two poems the vogue of the medieval debate may be said to have begun. But they themselves were representative of a yet earlier tradition which went back to the pastoral eclogues of Theocritus and Virgil, and more particularly to those Virgilian eclogues consisting of a contest between two singers and concluding with a judgment pronounced by a third party[1]. To this class of work belonged, for

[1] In support of this statement see A. Jeanroy, "La Tenson provençale" (*Annales du Midi*, II. 281 ff.), E. Faral, in *Romania*, XLI. pp. 472 ff., and J. H. Hanford, "Classical eclogue and mediaeval debate" (*Romanic Review*, II. pp. 1–229).

example, the third and the seventh Eclogues of Virgil: and similar contests are to be found in the works of early imitators—Calpurnius (1st century) and Nemesianus (3rd century) for instance: still later in Vespa's *Judicium Coci et pistoris, judice Vulcano* (4th century), as well as in that famous Eclogue of Theodulus which, in the 12th century, appeared in the text-books of the schools. This, then, was the Latin tradition which more immediately led up to the medieval debate[1]. And it is important to note that the earliest examples (i.e. the *Conflictus* of Alcuin and the *certamen* of Sedulius Scotus) were, as their subjects suggest, little more than literary exercises of the schools, pedagogic efforts similar in kind to the *declamationes*, the riddles, and the *nugae poeticae* cultivated by scholars of that age.

How then are we to account for the great popularity of the debate in the 12th and early 13th centuries, for the fact that it then becomes, throughout all Western Europe, one of the characteristic forms of literary expression? The explanation is to be sought in the intellectual life of the times: and the key seems to lie in the activities of Abelard, who, dominating the 12th century with his personality and force, gave to medieval thought a new direction and a new method. He it was who set out on a search for truth amidst the conflict of authoritative doctrines current at the time. And in his famous *Sic et Non* his method is explained and illustrated. He held, to begin with, that an attitude of doubt should precede all scientific search for truth, since doubt led to inquiry and inquiry to truth[2]; moreover that this healthy scepticism was best induced by collating discordant opinions drawn from recognised authorities, thus setting the question at issue in the clearest light. To provide a solution, however, was no part of his method. In fact, it was essential that no solution should be given. The main objects of the method were said to be, firstly, to encourage beginners to search for truth; secondly, to put them in a position to acquire truth for themselves, and thus to sharpen their wits as a result of their search. In short, the first key to wisdom, Abelard defined

---

[1] There can be little doubt that, apart from the instances found in the Virgilian eclogues, the *certamen* was a familiar literary form in Latin. This at least is suggested by the following reference (due to Professor H. J. Rose): "Asellio Sabino sestertia ducenta donavit pro dialogo in quo boleti et ficedulae et ostreae et turdi certamen induxerat" (Suetonius, *de Vita Tiberii*, § 42). On the diffusion of the *certamen* in a great number of literatures see Greif's account in *Zeitsch. für vergleichende Literaturgeschichte*, N.F. I. 289–95.

[2] "Dubitando enim ad inquisitionem venimus: inquirendo veritatem percipimus" (*Sic et Non*, ed. V. Cousin, p. 16).

as "untiring and persistent inquiry[1]": and on this basis was erected that study of dialectic which, introduced by Abelard to 12th century scholars, took the place of grammar as the mistress-study of the age. Of the subsequent developments of this method there is no need to speak. It was at once applied to the study of theology[2] and law[3]: it was the instrument employed in the *Summae Theologiae* of the 13th century—those encyclopaedic works in which Scholasticism reached its highest point. And in all these applications of the method there was present the collating of discordant opinions as recommended by Abelard[4]. But attempts were also made to reconcile the contradictions, to arrive in the end at some positive truth—a process which involved a departure from the original method. In Abelard's *Sic et Non* no such harmonising had been attempted: the author had aimed, not so much at the imparting of truth, as at the sharpening of the wits of beginners in philosophy. And this was the method that influenced for the most part the intellectual activities of 12th century scholars. It everywhere developed the taste for argument and formal discussion, and it established incidentally the vogue of the 12th century debate. Written at first as a mere exercise in the new study of dialectics, the debate soon became one of the most popular of literary forms. Before the end of the 12th century it had rapidly developed and had become one of the most characteristic types in the literature of the period.

The history of that development has yet to be written and to deal with it at all fully would be out of place here. Yet some knowledge of its main features is needed for an appreciation of our poem: and in general it may be said that the debate in the 12th and early 13th centuries became everywhere a favourite literary device, and that many of its themes circulated throughout Western Europe, both in Latin and in the vernaculars, as freely as the romances, the *chansons* and the *fabliaux*. Among the most familiar were the debates between the Soul and the Body, between Summer and Winter, Water and Wine, Phillis and Flora: all of which appeared

---

[1] "Haec quippe prima sapientiae clavis definitur: assidua scilicet seu frequens interrogatio" (*ibid.*).

[2] E.g. Peter Lombard, *Book of Sentences.*

[3] E.g. Gratian, *Decretum aut Concordia discordantium canonum.*

[4] It is perhaps worth noting that the method reappears in Bacon's *Essays*, where the "pros and cons" of the various subjects are developed in accordance with Bacon's remarks on "the antitheses of things," which appear at the end of the sixth book of the *Advancement of Learning* (see *Bacon's Works*, ed. Ellis and Spedding, vol. IV. pp. 472 ff.).

in several versions. Others again were possessed of special significance. The growing popularity of the form, for instance, was illustrated by the *Visio Philiberti*, in which the O.E. (and Latin) *Address of the Soul to the Body* was transformed from a dialogue into regular *contentio* form. Traces of a pastoral origin are found in the obscene *Altercatio Ganymedis et Helenae*: while the Carolingian use of the debate as a literary exercise is illustrated in the charming dispute between the *Violet and the Rose*. In the 11th century *Conflictus ovis et lini* a fresh variety of theme had become visible: whereas the Goliardic note is heard in the satirical *Goliae Dialogus inter aquam et vinum*. As for the themes themselves, they are as varied as they are numerous. Some, for instance, were of a personal kind: and, as an example, might be taken the dispute between Urban II and Clement II with regard to the possession of the triple crown (1091). Others, moreover, like the *Disputatio inter cor et oculum* or Chardry's *Petit Plet* were of a purely didactic kind: the former dealing with the question whether the heart or the eye were the greater cause of sin, the latter with the old contest between optimistic youth and a despairing old age. In the Goliardic *De Clarevallensibus et Cluniacensibus*, on the other hand, may be heard echoes of earlier monastic differences, while in *De Mauro et Zoilo* and *De Presbytero et Logico* are discussed further matters of interest to contemporary clerics. Nor was the theme of love without a place in these debates. In one case, the dispute was concerned with the rival claims of Love and Gold: elsewhere (in the *Altercatio Ganymedis et Helenae*) it is a question of the love of youth as opposed to the love of women: while in the famous *De Phillide et Flora* and in the later versions of that debate[1], it is the respective merits of the cleric and the knight as lovers that are under debate.

But if the themes were of this varied kind, so were also the form and the conduct of the debate, which, in general, consisted of (1) a short introduction descriptive of the scene and circumstances of the dispute, (2) a spirited discussion with some amount of dramatic incident, and (3) a brief judgment pronounced by an appointed judge, though the judgment was not by any means always given. Into this framework, however, might be woven a great variety of detail, the most elaborate and picturesque results being present in the later, i.e. the vernacular, forms. Between the

---

[1] E.g. *Concile de Remiremont* (Lat.), *Florence et Blancheflour* (Fr.), *Blancheflour et Florence* (A.-Nor.), *Melior et Ydoine* (A.-Nor.). See E. Faral, *Romania*, XLI. pp. 474 ff.

Latin and the vernacular types, indeed, many broad differences are visible. The latter, as a rule, are less stiff and conventional: they omit the classical allusions and references that abound in the Latin works, they elaborate the narrative and the dramatic elements, they introduce some amount of local colour, and aim altogether at a more colloquial style. It was but seldom that a Latin debate opened without a descriptive introduction of some sort or other, though this is the case in the *Disputatio inter cor et oculum.* More regularly the scenes are sketched in considerable detail. It is generally spring-time: the dispute takes place under a shady tree[1], with the earth clad in its many-coloured robe[2]; or the scene might be a meadow near a shady brook[3], or a garden full of fragrant flowers[4], or else a wood containing all the trees known to classical story[5]. Then, too, the poet might be represented as overhearing the debate from a place of concealment, or the disputants might appear before him in the course of a vision[6]: and in one such vision the poet is wafted up to the third Heaven, where he hears the case argued before the divine tribunal[7]. After these preliminaries, the dispute would be carried on with but a minimum of narrative or dramatic incident. It is but seldom in these Latin *altercationes* that any circumstantial detail accompanies the dialogue, though an exception must be made in the case of *De Phillide et Flora,* where elaborate descriptions of the young girls and their equipment are found, as well as of the Court of Love to which they turn for a decision of their quarrel. For the most part, however, the arguments of the disputants follow on without interruption, each argument being comprised in a fixed number of lines, and all being drawn from Biblical or classical sources. And, in this regular fashion, the debate would move to a conventional close with the verdict of the appointed judge, who might represent either some personality such as Palaemon, the poet, the Pope or the Deity, or else certain abstractions like Reason, or Usus et Natura.

It is to the vernacular group of these medieval debates that *The Owl and the Nightingale* obviously belongs: from the Latin type it is marked off by certain clear differences. Its framework, it is true, remains much the same: there is still the introductory description, the dispute, and the closing reference to a formal

---

[1] *Conflictus veris et hiemis.*   [2] *De rosae liliique certamine.*
[3] *De Phillide et Flora.*   [4] *Dispute between the Violet and the Rose.*
[5] *De Clarevallensibus et Cluniacensibus.*
[6] *Altercatio Ganymedis.*   [7] *Goliae Dialogus inter aquam et vinum.*

judgment. But the treatment is modified in various particulars, and the ultimate form is something quite different from that of the Latin *Conflictus*. Some of the more general points of distinction have already been hinted at. In *The Owl and the Nightingale* there is, for instance, an absence of classical phrase and allusion, of those numerous references to Virgil, Ovid, Tibullus, found in the Latin works. Then, too, from time to time, the dialogue is enlivened by the introduction of narrative and dramatic details[1]: it becomes less stiff and formal, by reason of the varied length and tone of the several arguments. Fresh colour, again, is added by the numerous references to contemporary life and scenes: and while the dispute gains in vivacity in consequence of its more familiar style, it is also worth noting that the arguments are now supported, not by Biblical or classical authority, but by reference to that medieval fount of wisdom known as *The Proverbs of Alfred*[2]. But these departures from the *Conflictus* type do not altogether account for the novelty in the form of *The Owl and the Nightingale*. There are still points of difference, some of which suggest the influence of the Old French lyric. Such at least is highly probable in connection with the opening description, the realistic details of which are common to the *aubes*, the *pastourelles* and the *chansons dramatiques*, which sprang from the popular dance-songs of the May-day festivities. Then, too, the fact that the protagonists are birds is also suggestive of the same influence: the nightingale in these May festivals, and also in contemporary French lyrics, was frequently endowed with a symbolical meaning, and stood, as in the present poem, for the advocate or messenger of love. Whether the form of *The Owl and the Nightingale* owed anything to the influence of the courtly *tençons* or *jeux-partis* is perhaps more difficult to say: it is not unusual in such disputes to find a contemporary personality nominated as judge, and also to find judgment withheld at the end of the debate. These features are present in *The Owl and the Nightingale* and they represent departures from the Latin tradition. On the other hand, it would require no great measure of originality on the part of the poet to have devised these details for himself.

There yet remains, however, one other characteristic feature in the form of the poem, a feature which is perhaps the most distinctive and interesting of all. And that feature has reference to

[1] See Introduction, § 9, p. lxxv.
[2] Cf. similar references in Chardry's *Petit Plet* to the medieval *Distichs of Cato*.

the formal procedure of the debate, which follows very closely the lines of a 13th century law-suit[1]. It was commonly characteristic of the vernacular debates[2], that in them the language of legal procedure should, in a general way, be adopted: and indeed the terms *altercatio* and *plet* (*pluit*), as applied to such poems, are significant in themselves. In *The Owl and the Nightingale*, however, the poet not only uses the word *plait, plaid* (= plea), ll. 5, 1737, to describe his particular debate, he not only creates a legal atmosphere by introducing reminiscences of a legal kind, but he consistently employs both the terminology[3] and the procedure of contemporary advocates, so that the dispute throughout its various stages is closely modelled on the form of a 13th century law-case.

Thus the Nightingale as plaintiff begins the proceedings by stating the charge[4] (= *tale*, see note, l. 140) she wishes to bring against the Owl. But since her mere statement will not suffice, for no litigant could claim an answer to a bare assertion (*nude parole*, see note, l. 547), it is therefore necessary that she should bring forward some witness (= oath-helper, compurgator) on her behalf, and this she does by quoting in support of her statements certain proverbs of Alfred[5]. In the meantime, the Owl as defendant has denied the charge, and according to the usual practice has declared her willingness to defend her case by force of arms[6]. The wager of battle, however, is not accepted, and the Owl therefore proceeds with the statement of her defence[7], also citing in her support the proverbs of Alfred[8]. Now, according to present-day practice, the case would be at an end, and the verdict would forthwith be given. In the 13th century, however, it was competent to the defendant at this stage of the proceedings to claim the right of *exceptio*[9], i.e. to show cause why the action should proceed no further: and the Owl consistently puts forward her claim[10], pointing out that the plaintiff has formally stated her case (*bicloped*,

---

[1] Gadow was the first to point this out with any detail: see his edition of *O. & N.* notes on ll. 5, 550.

[2] See also *Goliae Dialogus inter aquam et vinum*, l. 12, where the disputants are called *actor* and *reus* respectively.

[3] Cf. *tale* (l. 140), *fals dom* (l. 210), *speche* (l. 398), *bare worde* (l. 547), *bicloped* (l. 550), *hes* (l. 748), *rem* (l. 1215), *sake* (l. 1430), *uteste, utheste* (ll. 1683, 1698), (King's) *pes* (l. 1730), *griþbruche* (l. 1784). See also ll. 1093, 1096, 1098, 1492. [4] Cf. ll. 215–52; 411–66.

[5] ll. 236, 294, etc. See Intro. § 8, p. lxxi, note 2.

[6] ll. 150–3. See note. [7] ll. 255–390; 473–542. [8] ll. 291, 301, 351, etc.

[9] See Pollock and Maitland, *History of English Law*, II. 587, 611–20.

[10] ll. 545–55.

l. 550, see note), and that it is now her turn to cross-examine her opponent. In virtue of this right, the Owl takes up the attack, and in the *exceptio*[1] she charges the plaintiff with many misdemeanours. The Nightingale follows with her "replication[2]," in which she defends herself against the charges of the Owl: and then the case degenerates, as frequently happened, into a loose irregular dispute in which the pleaders accuse one another in strenuous terms, each one striving to confute the other, so as to win in the end a judgment in her favour. This is why in the latter half of the poem we find the argument less clear and coherent. The Nightingale, it is true, expresses certain views as to the love-themes then current, and the question of superiority is never allowed to recede quite into the background. But the proceedings are now conducted with a less punctilious regard for formalities, and towards the end there are passages of indiscriminate revilings.

And while, in its broad outline, the debate thus follows the lines of a contemporary law-suit, equally close is the resemblance when we consider the method and the spirit in which the dispute is conducted. Throughout the action both pleaders are animated with one and the same object: each strives to catch her opponent tripping, and endeavours to point to some technical error in her pleading. A mistake in pleading would be likely to have very serious results. "Every mistake in pleading, every *miskenning* or *stultiloquium* brought an amercement on the pleader, if the mistake was to be retrieved[3]": and both of the disputants are evidently aware of that fact. Hence their pleading is like a fencing-bout between two wary and seasoned swordsmen: there are lunges, ripostes and feints, and each one remains on guard against the familiar tricks of legal debate (*plaites wrenche*, l. 472). Among the recognised tricks of pleading was the attempt to show that the charge was not a *bona fide* appeal, but was, on the other hand, the outcome of malice and hatred (*odium et atia*)[4]. To establish this point would mean the break-down of the case, and the Owl resorts to these tactics in l. 1183 where she accuses her opponent of *alde niþe* (ancient malice). Yet more general was the trick of angering an opponent, and of causing him, as a result, to make "a mistake in pleading." This also was attempted by the Owl, and in some measure she succeeded (l. 933). But the Night-

---

[1] ll. 556–668; 837–932.
[2] See Pollock and Maitland, *History of English Law*, II. 615. Also ll. 707–836; 955–1042.
[3] Pollock and Maitland, *History of English Law*, II. 519.   [4] *Ibid.* II. 614.

ingale is said to have seen through the trick in time: she recalled the
saying that "the angry man is seldom a good pleader" (ll. 943–4),
and so she manages to steady herself before replying to her opponent.
The Nightingale, on the other hand, is more successful in her
tactics as a pleader, when she convicts the Owl of a *stultiloquium*
(l. 1640), and claims that the defendant has lost the case through
boasting of her own disgrace (l. 1650). This claim, advanced by
the Nightingale, is not without its importance: it is endorsed by
the neighbouring birds, who rejoice that a decision has at length
been reached: and with this, the legal dispute comes practically
to an end, with the Nightingale triumphant.

The form of *The Owl and the Nightingale* is therefore one of considerable interest. Originally a development of the pastoral in
late Latin literature, it became, from the time of Alcuin, one of
the recognised medieval *genres*, until, in the 12th and early 13th
centuries, it reached the height of its popularity when it appeared
in the vernaculars as well as in the original Latin. In its general
outline the poem thus recalls the earlier *Conflictus* and *certamina*:
but in its various details it points to a development of those
earlier types. Its treatment, for instance, is freer and more
original: it has been influenced in places by the lyrical poetry of
France: its procedure has been modelled on that of contemporary
law-suits, and altogether the form is full of historical interest,
while it is also excellently adapted for the special object in
view.

§ 7. THE THEME OF THE POEM

Not less interesting than the form is the theme of the poem,
which will be found to deal with one of the outstanding developments in the literature of the age. It was usual for such debates
to take up questions of contemporary interest: and *The Owl and
the Nightingale* is certainly no exception to the general rule. As
to the actual nature of the theme, there has been some difference
of opinion. Earlier interpretations, for the most part, have
assumed a general form. The dispute has been said to stand for
the old conflict between pleasure and asceticism[1], between crabbed
age and youth, between gravity and gaiety[2]: or again, it has been
described as Art against Philosophy[3], the aesthetic as opposed to
a more serious view of life[4], the strict monastic party on the one

[1] Ten Brink, *Early English Literature* (Bohn), i. 215.
[2] Saintsbury, *Short History of English Literature*, p. 60.
[3] Ker, *English Literature Medieval*, p. 183.
[4] Wells, *Owl & Nightingale*, p. xli.

side, the more latitudinarian among the clergy on the other[1]; and for each of these suggestions there is something to be said, though, it must also be added, no one of them seems to suit all the details of the case. Indeed, there are specific references in the poem which seem to point to a subject less general: and in spite of the elaborate form of the debate, in spite, too, of the side issues and the personalities in which the disputants indulge, the main theme reveals itself with tolerable clearness, as a question that stood in intimate relation to the age.

In the first place, it would seem clear, that the dispute is concerned primarily with the singing of the two birds. So much might reasonably be gathered from the choice of birds as disputants, were it not also definitely stated, by the poet himself, before the contest begins (ll. 11–12). But it is further suggested by the opening words of the plaintiff, in which, according to legal custom, it was usual for a case to be stated in the plainest of terms. Thus the Nightingale opens the proceedings with remarks on the Owl's song (ll. 35–40): later on, she begins her formal plea with a more detailed indictment of the same (ll. 217 ff., 411 ff.). And although other charges are also brought forward from time to time, they are merely incidental: it is with the singing of the Owl that the plaintiff is primarily concerned, while an arraignment of the Nightingale's song is the main line of the defence.

The key to the allegory will therefore be found in the contrast of the two songs: and a hint as to the nature of that contrast may further be gathered from the particular birds chosen—the Owl with her fabled wisdom, the Nightingale associated with the passion of love. But the solution need not be based on mere conjecture: the poem itself is sufficiently explicit on the point. From the thrust and parry of the debate, the drift of the allegory becomes clear, and the disputants can be unmasked by noting what is said, first, of their songs, and secondly, of their personalities.

To begin with, there can be no mistake about the claim of the Owl, when she states that her songs urge men to repent and find pardon for their sins, that they inspire good men with longing, and fill the wicked with terror of the evils to come (ll. 869–92, 927–8). Nor can the Nightingale be misunderstood when she protests that her songs bring delight (*skentinge*, l. 986) to men, and that "soþ hit is of luue ich singe" (l. 1339). The contrast is, of a surety, sufficiently plain: the broad issue would seem to lie between two types of poets and poetry, between the religious didactic poetry

[1] Courthope, *History of English Poetry*, i. 134.

characteristic of the Middle Ages, and the new poetry with its love-motive, which originated in the century 1150–1250.

And this interpretation may be consistently applied throughout the poem, to what is said of the songs and the disputants alike. When the Nightingale, for instance, attacks the Owl for her lugubrious singing, which terrorises and depresses all who hear (ll. 220 ff.), or when she complains that the Owl sings only in times of trouble, as if envious of the happiness of men (ll. 412 ff.), the reference is obviously to that medieval religious poetry, which, based on patristic teaching, sought by thunderings and threats to bring men to God. But the Owl, too, lays stress on the didactic qualities of her song (ll. 535 ff.), on the knowledge she possesses of the symbolical meaning of things (ll. 1213–14): while she is found betraying the medieval ascetic temper, when she charges the Nightingale with making use of wanton themes to the abuse of young minds (l. 899). It is the religious poet as opposed to the secular love-poet. And the contrast is further emphasised by the personalities in which the disputants indulge. Thus in the references to the tyrannical behaviour of the Owl (ll. 61 ff.), and her uncleanly ways (ll. 91 ff.), we have obvious allusions to clerical abuses of the time[1]. Then, too, there are the Owl's boasts of her preference for a life of retirement (ll. 227 ff.), of her well-ordered singing at regular hours (ll. 323 ff.), and her care for the fabric of the Church (ll. 609 ff.). Here, it cannot be doubted, one of the regular clergy is meant. And, with equal certainty, the Nightingale may be described as the secular love-poet. Her songs are said to be sung only in cultured circles (ll. 1031 ff.): her technique is claimed to be finer than that of her opponent (ll. 48, 759 ff.): her defence of love (ll. 1378 ff.) finds a counterpart in many utterances of contemporary love-poets: while, later on, she is indirectly accused of being "al unihoded" (l. 1178), that is, being not ordained she does not possess the priestly prerogative of uttering a curse[2]. There is but one passage in the poem which seems to be inconsistent with this

---

[1] For owl = "monk" see St Anselm in Migne, *Pat. Lat.* 159, col. 699 d.

[2] Courthope (*History of English Poetry*, I. 134 n.) has curiously misinterpreted this passage. He translates "For prestes wike ich wat þu dest" (l. 1179) as "I know thou doest so for the sake of a priest's dwelling." In reality the word *wike* = "offices" or "duties"; and the Owl, instead of regarding the Nightingale as a cleric who aimed at winning a priest's dwelling, is, on the contrary, condemning her opponent for performing the priestly function, being as she was, "al unihoded" (i.e. "unordained," not "unheeding," as Courthope translates). The taunts of the Owl, which immediately follow, supply evidence on this point. (See ll. 1180 ff.)

A.   *e*

general interpretation, and there the difficulty is more apparent
than real. It is where the Nightingale claims that she, too, sings
of "chirche-songe" (l. 1036), and thus seems to emphasise the
didactic quality of her singing. Yet this passage is by no means
out of keeping with the rest of the poem, if interpreted in the
spirit of certain lines which precede it (cf. ll. 716 ff.), where the
Nightingale states that since all earthly songs are a preparation
for the harmonies of Heaven, therefore her singing is not without
its religious value. Elsewhere the point is repeated when the
Nightingale claims to teach the virtue of fidelity (l. 1347), and
the transitoriness of earthly passion (l. 1450). And this she does
mainly for a tactical purpose, in order to meet her dour opponent,
as it were, on her own ground. But the point scored is something
more as well: it is an argument drawn from the teaching of Latin
Christianity, according to which the Nightingale was praised, not
as the messenger of love, but as the songstress of the glories of
the Creator[1]. It is as the songstress of love that the Nightingale
figures in the present poem: but the old didactic notion is also
utilised as a sort of passado in a bout of dialectics.

The discussion in the poem may therefore be said to deal with
the respective merits of two different types of poetry—the old
religious poetry on the one hand, the new love-poetry on the
other—and we have yet to consider the attitude taken up by
the poet on this particular question. In accordance with the
debate convention, no definite decision is given at the end of the
poem: the discussion is broken off abruptly before the umpire
has time to speak. Yet the sympathies of the poet can be read
between the lines, and the statement may be hazarded, that although
the balance is held fairly between the two disputants, it is the
Nightingale who in the end seems to get the better of the argument.
For one thing, it is not without its significance that the Nightingale figures as plaintiff in the law-suit: she is out to remedy an
abuse, to right a wrong, and to claim for love-poetry its release
from the heavy hand of tradition. Then, too, it is noteworthy that
the Nightingale is represented on the whole as the better-tempered
of the two combatants: she is the more attractive personality, she
shows more self-restraint than the Owl, and she indulges to a
lesser extent in vile personalities and abuse. And in the end it is
the Nightingale who is made to triumph[2]: she accuses the Owl of
a technical blunder and claims for herself the victory, which is
joyfully endorsed by the company of attendant birds[3]. Indirectly·

[1] See note, l. 736.   [2] See ll. 1649 ff.   [3] See ll. 1658 ff.

therefore, the poet may be said to have given his verdict: he has declared against the monopoly of religious themes in literature, and has called attention to the claims of the new love-poetry for recognition[1].

But while this is true, it should also be added that the Nightingale—and consequently the poet—has incidentally some criticism to make on the love-themes that were characteristic of the lyrics of the age. While commending love-poetry she does so with reservation: she has a protest to make against the artificial conventional themes which figured in so many of the French *chansons,* and which also gave a bias to Troubadour work. In the ancient *chansons de danse* which accompanied the May-day festivities, the common theme was that of *la mal mariée,* according to which, marriage was represented as a hateful form of slavery, and the husband as an odious tyrant (*le vilain, le gelos*) who was wont to ill-treat his wife, clothing her badly, oft-times beating her and putting her under lock and key. This subject-matter entered into the *chansons dramatiques*: and the tradition persisted in the courtly poetry of the Troubadours, as well as in the doctrines formulated in the Courts of Love. Thus, love was seldom celebrated save in opposition to marriage, the love which preceded or accompanied marriage being generally excluded. In courtly lyrics, married women alone were idealised and their exploits with lovers sung: whereas songs in honour of young girls were comparatively rare. And again, in the Courts of Love it was decreed that a man could love only a married lady, while love in marriage was deemed impossible. It was against this artificial code that the Nightingale seems to have uttered her protest. Her sympathies lie with the loves of maids (l. 1419): for the peccadilloes of wives she has naught but condemnation (l. 1468). A wife, she maintains, should ignore the allurement of fools, even though her marriage should chance to be unhappy (l. 1471): while a virtuous wife might also taste of love and yet remain faithful to her marriage vows (ll. 1340–1). It is, in short, a plea for a more rational treatment that the Nightingale is here making, for love-themes more in keeping with ordinary morality: and that the poet would seem to have had this object in mind is clearly suggested by reminiscences of the *mal mariée* motive found here and there in the poem[2].

The main theme of our poet is therefore one of considerable interest. He discusses the respective merits of two types of poetry: and while definitely commending the poetry that took love for its

---

[1] See note, l. 1794.   [2] See Introduction, § 8, p. lxx.

theme, as opposed to the older sort of a religious kind, he also
passes judgment on the contemporary limitations of that theme,
and argues for a broader and a healthier treatment. Nor need we
be greatly surprised at finding an English writer of the early 13th
century handling in his poem such subjects as these, and handling
them too in so original and striking a fashion. The challenge of the
earlier religious tradition had already gone forth in actual literary
developments: and no alert contemporary, such as our poet must
surely have been, could possibly have remained ignorant of the
changes that were taking place at the time. Of the nature of those
changes something has already been said[1]: of the work of the
Troubadours who sang of love—to them a cult, almost a religion—
with a beauty and a refinement that made their lyrics something
new in the achievements of man: of those wonderful romances,
too, in which love appeared, not merely as the artificial convention
of the lyrics, but as a tremendous mysterious force, potent for
good or evil in its influence on mankind. And such works could
not but come into violent contrast with the literature that had
sprung from the patristic tradition, with such works as the *Dies
Irae*, the *Moral Ode*, the Legends of the Saints, or with others which
dealt with Visions of Heaven and Hell, with Vices and Virtues,
and the Seven Deadly Sins[2]. Nor could those developments on
French soil have been unknown to cultured Englishmen of the
time: for England under Henry II had become a true colony of
France in matters of taste, and the relations between the two
countries were of a most intimate kind. There is therefore nothing
improbable in attributing to an English poet of this period a discussion as to the relative values of the old and new schools of
poetry. The only wonder really is that French literary activities,
which produced such results in Germany and Italy and elsewhere,
did not lead to some similar result on English soil[3]. If, however,
we have nothing in England to correspond to the Minnesingers of
Germany or the Troubadours of Italy and Spain, there is at least
The Owl and the Nightingale to show that the new movement in
France did not pass altogether unnoticed, and that England too
played a part in the new European concert.

Apart from its pronouncements on the theme selected, the poem

[1] See Introduction, § 1, pp. xvii ff.

[2] See also F. A. Patterson, *The Middle English Penitential Lyric*, New York,
1911.

[3] Possibly, as Mr G. G. Coulton suggests, because the vernacular was not
spoken at the English court.

undoubtedly has qualities that command attention. In its freshness and originality, for instance, and in the independence of judgment shown in criticising the new tradition, may be found a striking witness of 12th century Renascence influences. Or again, to contemporary readers, the form, even more than the subject-matter, may possibly have offered attractions. For our poet has set out clearly the pros and cons of the question at issue: his poem is notably an exercise in dialectics: and with Abelard he might have said in submitting his case, "I present these contradictions to inspire my readers to search after truth, and to make their minds more flexible as a result of that search." But to modern readers, interest will, of necessity, gather around the theme, the significance of which could only be revealed in historical perspective. To us the poem stands out as a landmark in English literature, as the work of a herald announcing a new order of things. And although its utterance may be but an echo from abroad, it is yet the English voice in that widespread chorus which anticipated the coming of Dante and of Petrarch, and of all who were to find their inspiration in the theme of love.

§ 8. THE SOURCES

In seeking for the sources of medieval literature we have constantly to bear in mind the common modes of medieval thought and feeling. In spite of the barriers set up by the different languages, a free interchange of ideas went on throughout all Christendom, rendering it easy for a piece of literature to be transferred from one language to another without much loss of effect. Many of the works, in fact, which were written in English during the Middle Ages, were little more than adaptations of French or Latin originals: and therefore *The Owl and the Nightingale* may well have been the result of some such process. Like those other debates which appeared in variant forms in Latin, French or Anglo-Norman, that poem may stand for a re-working of an earlier debate which had dealt with the same theme in one or other of those languages. But no original of the kind has come to hand as yet. There exists nothing which can be regarded as even a rough draft of the poem: and in the absence of such text all conjecture seems futile. There is, in short, no reason for regarding *The Owl and the Nightingale* as other than an original piece of work.

At the same time, it by no means follows that we are unable to form some idea of the rough material upon which the poet worked.

To the making of the debate there went a great variety of learning —reminiscences and borrowings drawn from many sources. And if we may not always be able to track the various details to their ultimate sources, owing to the vast amount of material common to medieval works, yet a knowledge of the borrowings themselves will not be without its value, while furnishing some idea as to the reading of a 13th century clerk.

(*a*) Perhaps the most familiar of such borrowings is that of the "nightingale episode" (ll. 1049–1104), consisting of a story very popular at the time, which has come down from the 12th century in two slightly different versions found in the *Laustic* of Marie de France and in the *De Naturis Rerum* of Alexander Neckam. From each of these versions the English poet has apparently taken certain distinctive details. From *Laustic*, in the first place, he has borrowed his account of the capture of the nightingale and of the means devised to entrap that hapless bird. In *The Owl and the Nightingale*, for instance, it is stated that the jealous husband

> Liim ⁊ grine ⁊ wel eiwat,
> sette ⁊ leide þe for to lacche.   (ll. 1056–7.)

And whereas in Neckam no details of the kind are given, in *Laustic* the method of capture is carefully elaborated:

> Il n'ot vaslet en sa maisun
> ne face engin, reiz u laçun,
> puis les metent par le vergier.
> N'i ot coldre ne chastaignier
> u il ne metent laz u glu[1].   (ll. 95–9.)

From Neckam, on the other hand, the English poet probably took his account of the nightingale's death (cf. *O. and N.* l. 1062 "mid wilde horse were todraʒe"). In *Laustic* the neck of the captured nightingale is broken by the knight in the presence of his lady: whereas in *De Naturis Rerum* (I. ch. 51), the account runs as follows: "miles enim quidam nimis zelotes philomenam quatuor equis distrahi praecepit[2]." The poet has therefore made use of both the current versions, taking from each what suited his purpose. And moreover, certain other details he himself has added. From Marie de France's *Yonec* he has possibly taken the ideas of the jealousy of the knight, and of the ill-treatment to which the lady was subjected[3]; and again, when the knight as a result of his cruelty is said to have been outlawed, condemned and fined[4] by

---

[1] *Die Lais der Marie de France*, ed. K. Warnke, p. 149.

[2] Cf. also: "Sed o dedecus! quid meruit nobilis volucrum praecentrix, instar Hippolyti Thesidae, equis diripi?" (*Ibid.* I. ch. 51.)

[3] See p. lxx and note. l. 1081.   [4] See notes, ll. 1093, 1096, 1098, 1101.

order of King Henry—the addition is probably made out of compliment to the legal reforms brought about by that monarch.

(b) Equally clear, though more puzzling in some of its details, is the poet's indebtedness to the animal-fables current at the time[1]. Two well-known fables have been skilfully worked into the poem— one, the fable of the Owl and the Falcon (ll. 99–138), the other, that of the Cat and the Fox (ll. 809–37)—and whereas the latter is embodied in the argument with but slight modification, the former shows considerable divergence from versions then current, and opens up problems of a somewhat complicated nature.

(i) To begin with, the Owl and the Falcon fable is one of the most familiar of its kind. Its main idea is found in one of the bird-fables of Bidpai[2], according to which a small falcon which had fallen out of its nest is brought up by a hawk: but in spite of much kindness it soon flies away, whereupon the hawk observes that a bird's nature could not be changed, and that from a raven's egg, though it were hatched by a peacock, only a raven could possibly come. In medieval times the fable reappeared in variant and expanded form. It dealt with the ingratitude shown by one bird to another by whom it had been generously reared: and while this ingratitude generally took the form of defiling the nest—as in our present poem—it might also result in the slaying of the foster-mother, a variation of the theme based on observation, and commonly connected with the cuckoo legend[3].

It is when we proceed to investigate the relation existing between our poet's version and the several versions belonging to the 12th and following centuries, that our difficulties begin: for with all the variant forms of the fable our poet has certain points in common, though on the other hand his version can be described as identical with none. Among the earliest extant versions are those of the Anglo-Latin *Romulus* (represented by *Romulus Treverensis*) and Marie de France's *Ysopet*, both of which belong to the latter half of the 12th century. Yet these works, which are presumably earlier than *The Owl and the Nightingale*, do not account for all the details of our poet's version, so that neither of them can have been the only source used by the poet. Thus certain elements which are wanting in those earlier fables, are to be found

[1] For the part played by these fables in English medieval literature generally, see J. A. Mosher, *The Exemplum in the Early Religious and Didactic Literature of England*, New York, 1911.

[2] *Cabinet de Fées*, XVII. 78 ff.; see also Warnke, *Die Quellen des Esope der Marie de France*, pp. 233–6.

[3] Cf. Odo of Cheriton, *Narrationes*, 4ᵃ (De cucula et burneta).

in one or other of the later texts, in Odo of Cheriton's *Narrationes* (1st half of 13th century) for instance, in the *Contes Moralisés* (c. 1320) of Nicole Bozon, in the *Fabulae* (c. 1350) of John of Sheppey and the Latin translation (c. 1350–1400) of Bozon's *Contes*. From which it would seem that our poet, together with the later fabulists, probably drew his material from certain 12th century sources other than those already mentioned. And this is borne out by a closer examination of the various texts[1], in which two main versions of the fable may be clearly detected.

A	B
(1) The fable concerns an Owl and a Falcon. (*Rom. Mar. O. and N.* Boz.)	(1) A Buzzard takes the place of the Owl. (Odo. John.)
(2) A close friendship exists between the two birds as a result of which the eggs of both are laid in the Falcon's nest. (*Rom. Mar.* Boz.)	(2) The Buzzard (Owl) drops an egg by stealth in the Falcon's nest. (*O. and N.* Odo. John.)
(3) The Falcon is said to go in search of food for its young. (Mar. *O. and N.* Boz.)	(3) Wanting. (*Rom.* Odo. John.)
(4) Wanting. (Mar. Odo. Boz.)	(4) When the Falcon reproaches the young birds for defiling the nest, the reply is that the culprit is "our brother, yonder fellow with the big head." (*Rom. O. and N.* John.)
(5) Wanting. (*Rom.* Mar. Boz.)	(5) The culprit is forthwith thrown out of the nest and its neck is broken. (*O. and N.* Odo. John.)
(6) The Falcon points out that although she could hatch the young Owl she could not change its nature. (*Rom.* Mar. Odo. John.)	(6) Wanting. (*O. and N.* Boz.)
(7) Proverb quoted as moral: "Though an apple roll ever so far, the tree which bore it can always be known." (Mar. *O. and N.* Boz.)	(7) Wanting. (*Rom.* Odo. John.)
(8) Wanting. (*Rom.* Mar. Boz. Odo. John.)	(8) Reference to the foul bird that defiles its own nest. (*O. and N.* Lat. tr. Boz.)

From this comparison it would appear that while one version (A) of the fable is roughly represented by the Anglo-Latin *Romulus*, Marie de France and Bozon, and another version (B) by Odo of Cheriton and John of Sheppey, the account given in *The Owl and the Nightingale* embodies elements of both traditions (A (1), (3), (7); B (2), (4), (5)), and thus represents a version of a composite and eclectic kind. The actual sources used by our poet,

---

[1] See Appendix III.

however, must still remain uncertain. Perhaps they were separate versions of the primitive *Romulus* collection of Aesopic fables, of which at least two distinct forms had appeared before the end of the 12th century[1]. On the other hand, he may have used other texts, such as that lost collection of fables in English verse attributed to a 12th century Alfred of England[2], as well as that *Anonymus Neveleti*[3] (c. 1175) due to Walter of England, a chaplain of Henry II. At all events, it was from Alfred of England's collection that Marie de France claimed to have taken the material for her *Ysopet*[4]: while the presence of English proverbs in the Latin text of Odo and in the Anglo-Norman version of Bozon also suggests borrowings from an English source. That the *Anonymus Neveleti*, too, was well known at the time is the inference that must be drawn from the traces of that collection found in French and Italian fables[5], while Jacobs further describes that collection as "the standard Aesop of medieval Christendom." So that it may well be that our poet was indebted for his version of the Owl and Falcon fable to both of these collections, and that he drew from each what his special purpose seemed to require.

(ii) The other animal-fable worked into the poem is that of the Cat and the Fox; and this, too, is a story of world-wide popularity,

---

[1] Some 83 fables (based on the Latin Phaedrus) were turned into prose in the ninth century, probably at the schools of Charlemagne, and were attributed to a fictitious Romulus. Another prose collection by Ademar de Chavannes appeared before 1030, consisting of 67 fables (first published by Nilant in 1709) and known as *Anonymus Nilant*. See J. Jacobs, *Fables of Aesop*, I. p. xx; also P. Harry, *Comparative Study of Aesopic Fable in Bozon* (Univ. Press, Cincinnati, 1903), p. 14.

[2] According to J. Jacobs (*Fables of Aesop*, pp. xviii ff.) a collection of 164 fables (based on Babrius and Bidpai) reached England after the third crusade of Richard I, and was translated into Latin by an Englishman named Alfred, with the aid of an Oxford Jew named Berachyah (Benedictus le Puncteur), who himself translated a number of fables into Hebrew rhymed verse (*Fox Fables*, c. 1200). Part of Alfred's *Aesop* was afterwards translated into English alliterative verse, and this again was translated into French by Marie de France, who attributed the collection to King Alfred. It is further notable that Alfred the Englishman is mentioned by Roger Bacon as an earlier translator (see Roger Bacon, *Compendium Studii*, ed. Brewer, p. 471). Cf. also J. Jacobs, *Jews in Angevin England*, pp. 165–73, 278–81.

[3] It consisted of 60 fables in Latin verse. See Wells, *Manual of the Writings in Middle English*, p. 180.

[4] Cf. Marie de France, *Ysopet* (Epil. 16–18): "Li reis Alvrez, kimult l'ama | le translata puis en Engleis | ej eo l'ai rimé en Franceis." See Warnke, *Die Fabeln der M. de F.* p. 328.

[5] See Jacobs, *Fables of Aesop*, I. p. 179.

which has assumed many forms throughout the centuries[1]. Its main theme is the overweening pride of some animal or other in the numerous tricks which it has at its disposal. It despises another animal who is capable of but one trick: but in time of need that one trick proves more effective than all the devices of the other. The story is already found in Indian fable, where it is a fish that boasts of its skill in eluding the fisherman. The latter, however, empties the pond, and the fish is caught: whereas the frog, innocent of all tricks, escapes safely to land. In the Mahâbhârata, again (Benfey, i. 311), an arrogant crow boasts to the flamingo of its hundred and one tricks in the air: but it is hopelessly overcome in the contest that follows. In ancient Greece, too, the fable was probably known, though no version of the story has actually come down. But the proverb of Archilochus (πόλλ᾽ οἶδ᾽ ἀλώπηξ, ἀλλ᾽ ἐχῖνος ἓν μέγα) seems to point to the existence of some such story, as do also the popular fairy tales of the Balkan peninsula[2]. The fable naturally varied in different parts of Europe. The boastful animal is generally the fox: but its fellow might be the hedgehog (Greece), the crane (Russia), the squirrel (Armenia), the cock, or the dove: while in Western Europe it is always the cat. And in the West the fable is generally as follows. A cat and a fox enter upon a discussion, in which the fox boasts of its many devices, whereas the cat has to confess that she possesses but one. Soon afterwards the hunter comes with his dogs, and the animals take to flight: whereupon the cat escapes by climbing a tree, but the fox is captured and maltreated by the hounds[3].

This, then, is the form of the fable as current in the 12th and following centuries. It appears, for instance, in the Anglo-Latin *Romulus*, in Marie de France's *Ysopet*, as well as in the fable-collections of Odo of Cheriton and John of Sheppey: and in each case the version will be found to be practically the same[4]. In *The Owl and the Nightingale* the fable appears in a slightly altered form: it is alluded to by way of illustration, and the tricks of the fox come in for a more specific treatment. Some amount of variation in this detail, indeed, is seen in the different versions of the fables: the fox is credited with two (Marie de F.), seventeen (Odo of C.) or eighty (Anglo-Lat. Rom.) devices in addition to a bagful

---

[1] See Warnke, *Die Quellen des Esope der Marie de France*, pp. 249–52.

[2] See *ibid.* p. 250.

[3] Warnke (*ibid.*) mentions an extension of the story which occurs in a Finnish fable (Schreck, *Finnische Märchen*, Weimar, 1877, p. 231). The wolf boasts of his 100 tricks, the fox of his 1000, the hare of his swiftness in flight; but the cat has only one trick, by which he escapes.

[4] See Appendix iv.

of tricks: but nothing definite is said as to the nature of those tricks. The treatment of our poet is, however, of a more concrete kind: he describes the three main stratagems of the fox with some amount of detail, and for that purpose he has drawn upon the natural history of the time—possibly upon Neckam's *De Naturis Rerum*. For instance, he refers to the feints and devious courses of the fox when pursued:

> Vor he can paþes riȝte ꞇ woȝe.
>
> .   .   .   .   .   .
>
> þe uox kan crope bi þe heie,
> an turne ut from his forme weie,
> an eft sone kume þarto:
> þonne is þe hundes smel fordo;   (ll. 815–22.)

with which might be compared the statement of Neckam: "Est enim [vulpes] volubilis pedibus, et nunquam rectis itineribus, sed tortuosis amfractibus, incedens[1]." So far, of course, there is nothing in the illustration which could not be regarded as common knowledge, or, at least, the result of personal observation. But one other detail there is which cannot be described as such. It consists of the statement that the fox, when hard-pressed, would take to a tree, and throw the hounds off the scent by hanging down from a bough, i.e.:

> An he kan hongi bi þe boȝe,
> an so forlost þe hund his fore,
> an turnþ aȝen eft to þan more.   (ll. 816–18.)

But the plain fact is that the fox cannot climb and would therefore be incapable of the trick described. So that what we have here is a piece of unnatural natural history, palpably derived, not from observation, but from some work of a pseudo-scientific kind. And the actual source is most probably Neckam, in whose work occurs the same surprising statement, viz.: "Venatoris quandoque [vulpes] evadit insidias......dum ramo alicujus arboris suspensa canes errare cogit, quae vestigia sequi habeant incertos[2]." In introducing in this fashion the familiar fable into his work, the poet has given a fresh colour to the tale: he has added certain details, which, however fanciful in kind, go to make his illustration more picturesque and realistic.

(c) But apart from this Aesopic material, the poet has also made use of certain points taken from the popular natural history of the time, and has drawn in no slight measure upon the legends and the bird-lore handed down by tradition.

In the first place, further borrowings from Neckam are perhaps seen in other passages where statements are made as to the habits

---

[1] *De Nat. Rerum*, ii. ch. 125, p. 205.   [2] *Ibid.* p. 204.

and qualities of birds. For instance, the charge brought by the Owl against the Nightingale, that she avoided the colder countries of the North, might well have been derived from the pages of Neckam, e.g.: "Loca multo frigori obnoxia, dum amoris vacat illecebris, avicula ista [i.e. philomena] reformidat, quae si interim aliquo casu visitat, modulationibus dulcissimis operam non impendit[1]." Or again, the reference to the singing quality of the wren (ll. 1721–2): this might also have been due to a passage in Neckam, i.e. "sed et in tam exili corpore garritum tantae sonoritatis quis non miretur[2]?" Then, too, the respect accorded to the wren, and the dignified part she plays towards the close of the debate (ll. 1717 ff.), might also have been suggested by a passage due to the same author: for he relates the "fabulosam narrationem," according to which the wren "qua vero astutia...regiam dignitatem inter aves visa est sibi adquisivisse," though he is careful to add that the story "vulgo notum est[3]." The indebtedness of our poet in such cases as these is clearly open to question: but in view of the unmistakable use of Neckam's work in at least two other places in the poem, it is not unlikely that further borrowing may have occurred where the evidence is less decisive. And among such borrowings we may reasonably include the passages mentioned above —as well, perhaps, as the curious illustration found in ll. 1021–2 (see note).

It is, however, in developing the characters of his two protagonists that the poet has drawn most freely upon medieval bird-lore. Many traditions connected with both the owl and the nightingale were in existence, and the poet has utilised most of them for his particular purpose. Thus his conception of the Owl will be found to embody three distinct ideas: (i) the Owl as a bird of filthy habits (ll. 91 ff.), (ii) the owl as a bird that avoided the light (ll. 227 ff.), (iii) the Owl as a prophet of evil (ll. 1145 ff.). According to contemporary learning the first of these characteristics was applied to the short-eared owl (*noctua*), concerning which Alanus de Insulis wrote: "tantae deformitatis sterquilinio sordescebat ut in ejus formatione Naturam crederes fuisse somnolentam[4]": though this feature is also mentioned in the contemporary Aesopic fable "de accipitre et noctua" (see Appendix III.). The other qualities, on the other hand, had reference to the long-horned owl (*bubo*). Thus Odo of Cheriton in one of his fables (*De Rosa et Volatilibus*) gives the tradition explaining why the owl was condemned to fly at

---

[1] *De Nat. Rerum*, I. ch. 51.   [2] *Ibid.* I. ch. 78.   [3] *Ibid.* I. ch. 78.
[4] *De Planctu Naturae*, ed. T. Wright (Anglo-Latin Satirical Poets, Rolls Series), II. 438.

night[1]: while Alanus de Insulis further states in connection with the same bird that it was "propheta miseriae, psalmodias funereae lamentationis praecinebat[2]." Hence the Owl of the poem may be said to combine all three traditional qualities, each quality being brought to bear on the allegorical theme. And a similar treatment is visible in connection with the Nightingale, the main characteristics of which are also drawn from contemporary lore. The Nightingale appears in one place as the herald of spring (ll. 433 ff.): elsewhere she appears as the minstrel of love (ll. 1339 f.): in yet another passage she stands for the songstress of the divine praises (ll. 735 ff., 1036): and each description belongs to a separate tradition. In the first place, the nightingale had not always been connected with the coming of spring. The cuckoo, in the earlier medieval period, had been associated with that season: and references to that effect are common in Latin[3] and Old English[4] verse. In Pliny, however, the nightingale takes the place of the cuckoo as the bird that announces the spring: "the nightingale chaunteth continually, namely at that time as the trees begin to put out their leaues thicke[5]": and this tradition is utilised by the author of our poem, doubtless under French influence[6]. The second function of the nightingale—the minstrel of love—was of a more conventional kind. It had been handed down from classical fable: the story of Philomela and Procne was familiar to all: and Alanus de Insulis writes in connection with that bird, that "deflorationis querelam reintegrans, harmoniaca tympanizans dulcedine, puritatis dedecus excusabat[7]." The third attribute, again, may be traced back to the Carolingian era, when the nightingale was praised, not for her love-song, but for her skill in chanting the glory of God. Thus Alcuin in his *De Luscinia* (ll. 15–20) writes:

> Felix o nimium, Dominum nocteque dieque
> Qui studio tali semper in ore canit!
>
> .   .   .   .   .   .
>
> Hoc natura dedit, naturae et conditor almus,
> Quem tu laudasti vocibus assiduis[8].

---

[1] See note, l. 227.   [2] *De Planctu Naturae (loc. cit.)*.

[3] Cf. *Conflictus veris et hiemis* (*Anth. Lat.* ed. Riese, ii. 687); also Alcuin, *De Cuculo* (Migne, *Pat. Lat.* 101).

[4] Cf. O.E. *Wanderer, Seafarer*, and M.E. *Cuckoo Song*.

[5] Holland, *Trans. of Pliny*, x. 29.

[6] "In France, the coming [of the nightingale], like that of the swallow in Greece, the stork in Germany, and the cuckoo in England, is the signal to the folk that summer is at hand." (Chambers and Sidgwick, *Early English Lyrics*, p. 270.)

[7] *De Planctu Naturae (loc. cit.)*.   [8] Migne, *Pat. Lat.* 101, pp. 803–4.

And this tradition is preserved by Neckam where he writes in connection with the nightingale: "Quid quod noctes tota ducit insomnes, dum delicioso garritui pervigil indulget? Nonne jam vitam claustralium prae oculis cordis constituis, noctes cum diebus in laudem divinam expendentium [1]."

(*d*) Our poet has therefore drawn freely upon the bird-lore of his day. But equally important are the borrowings of a still more popular kind, e.g. those reminiscences of folk-songs sung by dancers at the *fêtes du mai* in France, and preserved for us in the *chansons* of the jongleurs. These folk-songs had dealt with one conventional theme, according to which, marriage, from the woman's standpoint, was an odious form of slavery, while the husband was a jealous tyrant, who ill-treated his wife by beating her, locking her up and clothing her badly [2]. Such was the common motive of the *chansons dramatiques* of the jongleurs, and a trace of their influence is, for instance, seen in the modification introduced into the nightingale episode (ll. 1077–82), where the Nightingale explains that the Knight was "so gelus of his wiue" that

> He hire bileck in one bure,
> þat hire was boþe stronge ꝛ sure.   (ll. 1081–2.)

This particular detail was apparently added to the story by our poet: at all events, it forms no part of the *Laustic* version. Or again, there is the later passage (ll. 1523 ff.) which is still more clearly reminiscent of these *chansons de mal mariées*, for it embodies the theme in a yet more detailed form. There the Owl condones the sins of married women as being mostly due to the jealousy and cruelty of their husbands. Thus she complains of the neglect that such wives experience. The husband, in pursuit of pleasure abroad,

> haueþ attom his riȝte spuse,
> wowes weste, ꝛ lere huse,
> wel þunne ischrud ꝛ iued wroþe,
> an let heo bute mete ꝛ cloþe.   (ll. 1527–30.)

On his return home he behaves like one demented: everything that is done or said by his wife enrages him:

> an oft hwan heo noȝt ne misdeþ,
> heo haueþ þe fust in hire teþ.   (ll. 1537–8.)

---

[1] *De Nat. Rerum*, I. ch. 51; see also note, l. 736, for a similar reference in one of Odo of Cheriton's fables and elsewhere.

[2] See G. Paris, *Mélanges de Littérature française du moyen âge*, p. 549.

And throughout it all, he remains *le jaloux*:

> Ne mot non mon wiþ hire speke:
> he ueneð heo wule anon tobreke
> hire spusing, ʒef heo lokeþ
> oþer wiþ manne faire spekeþ.
> he hire bilukþ mid keie ꝗ loke:
> þar-þurh is spusing ofte tobroke.   (ll. 1553–8.)

Here the correspondence with the *mal mariée* theme is too close to admit of any doubt. The poet is evidently adapting the motive to his particular purpose. And while his acquaintance with the theme may have been due to the French *chansons*, it is not impossible that his knowledge may have been derived from a source nearer home. "The village summer festival of England seems to have closely resembled that of France[1]": and it is not unlikely that similar folk-songs may have been sung at the May-day rites in England.

But if popular origin may be suspected in the passages mentioned above, the case is even clearer when we turn to the proverbs of the poem, which may safely be attributed to a popular source. Of the eighteen proverbial utterances, however, which occur in the poem[2], no less than eleven are ascribed to King Alfred. To him is given the credit of their original utterance, and this claim is apparently supported by the existence of the 12th century *Proverbs of Alfred*, a collection of wise sayings which has come down in recensions of the following century. Moreover there is the further statement also connected with the 12th century, i.e. "Eluredus in proverbiis ita enituit ut nemo post illum amplius[3]": all of which seems to point to Alfred as the author of this proverbial wisdom. Yet no definite evidence in support of this claim is forthcoming: there is no trace of any such proverbs in the writings connected with his name. How far they may be traced to Alfred's lost *Handbook* must also remain uncertain, though the description of that work as "multimodos divinae scripturae flosculos[4]" does not point to any great probability. On the other hand, it is highly significant that three[5] at least of the sayings attributed to Alfred in our poem are connected later on with the name of Hending; and moreover, that similar proverbial sayings had previously been

---

[1] See E. K. Chambers, *Medieval Stage*, I. 72.

[2] See ll. 98–100; 135–8; 176; 235–6; 289–92; 294–7; 299–302; 349–52; 569–72; 637–8; 685–8; 761–2; 942–4; 1037–42; 1074; 1223–6; 1269–74; 1275–80.   [3] *Ann. Min. Winton. Anglia Sacra*, I. 289.

[4] *Asser's Life of Alfred*, ed. W. H. Stevenson, cap. 88. Oxford, 1904.

[5] See proverbs, ll. 687–8, 762, 1271.

attributed to Salomon and Marcolf, the former being the representative of Jewish wisdom, the latter, the supposed ruler of a race called the Hundings. And just as there is no reason for taking too seriously the authorship of Salomon or Marcolf or Hending, so the use of Alfred's name in connection with 12th century proverbs is probably nothing more than a literary device, a means of adding to the sayings the authority of a great name[1]. Alfred's name at that date was sufficiently remote to carry with it the dignity that comes from age: and it can therefore hardly be doubted that in the Alfredian proverbs of the poem we have elements of popular wisdom, of that shrewd communal philosophy that ever springs from the lips of the people[2].

(e) There yet remains to mention certain elements which our poet has taken from the works of Latin Christianity. Owing to the popular character of the poem, such details are less common than in some of the other contemporary works, in the Latin debates for instance, where classical references and phrases are abundantly found. At the same time, here and there in the poem, we do find passages reminiscent of earlier patristic teaching and scholarship: and among these must be included the reference to the Seven Deadly Sins (ll. 1395–1416). From the earliest period of Western monasticism the Christian Fathers had attempted to regulate the way of life by expounding the principal vices that beset mankind: and early in the 5th century, the eight chief vices were categorically set forth by Cassian[3], pride being regarded as the worst of sins. After the time of Benedict, the Deadly Sins (reduced to seven) became an integral part of Christian teaching, and formed one of the most common themes in medieval literature. The reference which occurs in the poem is one of the earliest treatments of the theme in English literature: and there the seven sins are mentioned—sins of the flesh and sins of the spirit—while pride is described as the most deadly of all[4].

Then, too, there are grounds for thinking that the description of Norway and the barbarous North (ll. 999–1014) is partly

---

[1] "The desire to refer institutions to a deified or canonised legislator is shown in England as late as the 14th century by the attribution to King Alfred of everything supposed to be specially national and excellent." (Pollock and Maitland, *History of English Law*, I. p. xxviii.)

[2] The antithesis between the owl and the nightingale, upon which the whole poem is based, also seems to have been of a proverbial kind. See note, ll. 411–16.

[3] See H. O. Taylor, *Classical Heritage of Middle Ages*, p. 162.

[4] See l. 1416, note.

based on a similar description found in the O.E. translation of Orosius' *History*. The most popular school-history in 12th century England was that of Orosius[1]: moreover, fragments of the O.E. translation in handwriting of the 11th century have recently been discovered[2]: and it is therefore possible that our poet may have been acquainted, not only with the Latin text, but also with the O.E. version of that popular work. At all events, there are details in the poet's description (ideas as well as phrases), which seem to point to some knowledge of Alfred's account (see note, l. 999).

And lastly, there is the association of the lily and the rose with the oncoming of spring (ll. 439–43), and the choice of those flowers as typical of the spring-time and love (see note, l. 439). This can hardly have been the result of observation: it would rather seem to rest upon some earlier literary convention, characteristic probably of the post-classical period, and existent already in the literature of the 9th century, where we find the debate of Sedulius Scotus entitled *De rosae liliique certamine*.

§ 9. THE POEM AS LITERATURE

It now remains to inquire what use our poet has made of his various materials: how far he has succeeded in giving to his work artistic quality and life: and further, what are the particular features that make the poem what it is—one of the finest achievements in English medieval literature. The main purpose of the writer, it has been suggested, was to commend himself (or one Nicholas) to the favourable notice of his contemporaries. He complains of neglect: a case for recognition is made out: and the real business is done in the eulogies so artfully placed near the beginning and the end of the poem. But for the plea to be effective, it was necessary above all that the work should be widely read: and no effort has therefore been spared in making the appeal as general as possible. Thus a poem in the popular "debate" form, dealing in allegorical fashion with a live question of the day, was a device well calculated to serve the particular object in view. But when into the poem was poured a mass of subsidiary detail drawn from the favourite reading of the time, the appeal must surely have been greatly increased. At every turn the reader would be met

---

[1] See Traill, *Social England*, I. 336; Schofield, *English Literature from the Norman Conquest*, p. 49.

[2] See Napier, *M.L.R.* VIII. i. 59–63.

by some delectable detail. The very title would prove alluring
to a generation brought up on animal-fables: while there was
matter also to suit every taste—natural history and bird-lore,
proverbs and *exempla*, reminiscences of French love-poetry, fragments of patristic learning, and above all, the legal atmosphere and
procedure so cunningly counterfeited. The poem is, in short,
a triumph of practical wit. The elements have been well mingled
with an eye to the main object: and the result is a tribute to the
shrewdness of the poet, to the subtle insight he possessed into
men and their ways.

But the work is something more than a successful occasional
poem, or a clever advertisement deserving of respect even in a
modern age. It is a piece of art amazingly put together: full of
striking effects, amusing, bizarre, and picturesque: with a well-
defined plot, a consistent allegory, a variety of incident, colour,
and tone, as well as the animation that comes from lively and
well-drawn characters. The poem is, in fact, as ingeniously wrought
as it is shrewdly planned. It is free from the formlessness of so
much of the medieval art: and here lies the miracle in connection
with a work of this period.

Of its actual form something has already been said. In many
ways, the poem is representative of the vernacular "debates" of
the time, which stood for a development of the earlier and more
conventional Latin type: so that elsewhere may be found hints
for many of the structural features of our poem, and the author's
debt to his predecessors was doubtless of no negligible kind.
But whatever that debt may have been, as to the artistic value of
the result there can be no doubt. If the poet has borrowed
liberally, he has made his borrowings his own; and earlier devices
are handled with a freedom and an originality that distinguish
this poem from all the rest of its kind.

In the first place, it will be conceded that the poem has been
provided with an excellent framework, one well adapted for the
purpose in hand. There is an exposition, to begin with, in which
the background is sketched, and the case is stated: this is followed
by a conflict of wits, which reaches a sort of crisis when the assembly of birds acclaims the Nightingale as victor; and after that
the action moves on as if to a *dénouement*, though no solution of
the conflict is actually given. The dispute is thus constructed on
dramatic lines: the arguments are marshalled in effective fashion:
and the reader need never be in doubt as to where the main issue
lies. But this is by no means all. More remarkable still is the

way in which this outline is filled in with a variety of detail, and with devices which serve artistic ends: for of the varied material that enters into the structure, there is but little that can be termed really superfluous, or that fails to contribute something to the general plan. The nightingale-episode, for instance, is no mere idle insertion: it has the effect of emphasising the main contention of the Owl—that the love-songs of her opponent often lead to grave abuse and disaster. The animal-fables, again, are introduced to illustrate certain moral truths: in the Owl and the Falcon fable we have an illustration of a well-known Horatian maxim, in the fable of the Cat and the Fox, an illustration of the fact that tricks are valuable only in so far as they are successful. Then, too, there are the proverbs that lend authority to the various statements: the scraps of natural history and bird-lore, which are utilised in developing the principal characters and in illustrating certain points of popular wisdom. Even the daring introduction of legal procedure must be regarded as something more than a mere *tour de force*: for it is a piece of machinery that introduces method into the argument, and gives a firmer outline to the course of the debate.

But while the poet has thus woven into his fabric a variety of material with unusual skill, not less remarkable are his structural devices for giving to the action increased verisimilitude, and for making the dispute more life-like and real. It was, for instance, a happy and original thought, that of making the time-duration of the quarrel the period of one night. The Owl waits until night-fall (l. 41) before taking up the Nightingale's challenge; and in the dawn (l. 1718) the thrush, the wren, and the rest of them appear on the scene, by which time the dispute of the two night-birds is over. By this touch of Nature an air of realism is given to the scene: the action is proper to a June night in an English valley, when the hoot of the brown owl and the screech of the white one are almost alone in replying to the notes of the nightingale. And something of the same effect is obtained by the varying length and tone of the utterances of the two disputants. In most of the Latin "debates" the dialogue is carried on with a dull monotonous formality, each statement being limited to a fixed number of lines. In our present poem, however, the dialogue is conducted with a vivacity and a freedom that do away with all formality, while suggesting as well the vicissitudes of an actual dispute. Yet it is, after all, in the narrative element so freely worked into the poem, that the author's constructive genius is most palpably seen. There is, first, the preliminary skirmishing, when the Owl suggests a decision by trial by combat; later on, there is much ado caused by the gathering of the birds; and such incidents as these may perhaps be paralleled in some of the other debates, in that of *Phillis and Flora*, for instance. But action of this kind is not confined to the framework of our present poem. It forms an integral part of the dialogue as well: in fact, the short interludes, which break the argument at frequent intervals, are among the most effective features of a well-constructed poem. As the dispute proceeds, we have visibly brought before us the changing moods of the two protagonists, confidence giving way to perplexity or vexation, a note of triumph creeping in before the launching of some weighty argument. We see the Owl, again, with her sullen demeanour, with downcast eyes that on occasion can blaze with fury; we note, too, her more timorous opponent, high-spirited but cautious, flying aloft at the end to announce her victory. Such passages are, of course, the natural breaks in the report of a heated conversation, made by one who had been present at the whole affair. But they discharge important functions in the structure of the poem as well. Obviously something more than mere links between the several arguments, they afford relief, first of all, from the long bout of pleading, by adding variety and animation to the work; they serve also a dramatic purpose by throwing light on the personalities of the two disputants; and at the same time, they supply a running commentary, chorus-fashion, on the various situations, in a way that illuminates the whole course of the dispute.

The poem has therefore been skilfully put together: it is characterised throughout by a nice proportion of parts, by a subordination of details to the main idea; and these qualities reveal unmistakably a true sense of form. Yet more went to the making of the poem than a well-designed structure, or a complicated machinery giving simple results. The work consists of an allegory with birds as the actors: it is an attempt to give human interest to an abstract question by means of a symbolical treatment; and it is here, in what is after all the essential aspect of the poem, that the real test of the poet's workmanship may be said to lie. And admirably has the poet discharged this part of his task, though his success is perhaps the less surprising, seeing that the medieval man thought and felt in symbols, so that allegory came naturally to 12th century minds. Yet the poet has chosen wisely in taking his material from the animal world; for in so doing he has based his allegory on the Aesopic fable, the symbolism of which would be intelligible to all his readers. He has also made good use of that particular material, and of the analogies it offered ready-made for allegorical purposes. And, as a result, he has presented his subject in picturesque and convincing fashion: his work has a lucidity and a force not excelled by any other writer of the kind in English.

For the setting of his allegory the poet has, first of all, taken a simple story. An owl and a nightingale meet at dusk in the coverts of birdland, and fall a-quarrelling over the merits of their songs. From the first it is clear that it is to be a serious business, and it is agreed to refer the decision to an independent judge, to one of good repute among the race of men. Throughout the whole night the dispute goes on with varying fortune, until in the dawn the nightingale claims to have won: and her claim is taken up by the newly-awakened birds, who enrage the owl by their joyful chirpings. The owl straightway threatens to call together her friends, and to avenge herself on those who have applauded her rival. When, however, the wren reminds them of the penalty for breaking the peace, the nightingale states her willingness to abide by the earlier agreement, and to go with the owl to the home of the appointed judge. And this accordingly is done, though the sequel is not told.

This, then, is the fable created by the poet, into which he was to read his allegorical meaning. And a delightful fable it is, of the doings of the birds in a world of their own, amidst the silence and darkness of the English country-side. A suitable fable, as well, with a meaning plain to all: for who could fail to see in the quarrel about the bird-songs a discussion relating to the songs of men? Nor could that interpretation be said to be either too far-fetched or too obvious, though at the same time sufficiently veiled to give the reader the delight of discovery. In short, the fable was well adapted to serve its particular purpose—to present its theme in effective fashion, and to do so with a racy directness that would come home to all.

It is, however, in the handling of this material that the skill of the poet most clearly appears: and that skill is seen in the life-like precision and truth with which the main characters are drawn, in the realism with which the poet has invested his mysterious bird-world, and in the consistency with which he has maintained the illusion necessary for the working out of his allegorical purpose. The figures of the two birds, in the first place, are unmistakably drawn: we recognise them at once from the descriptions given of their outward forms and habits. The details are all there, though they are never obtrusive, so neatly are they placed in the mouth of one or other of the birds. The Owl, for instance, is depicted as short of body, with a large head, a hooked bill, sharp claws, dark staring eyes, and with fluffy feathers that give her when angry a swollen appearance. Her haunt is a hollow tree covered over with ivy: she lives on mice and snails and such-like creatures. Blind and silent by day, she sings only at night: and her weird harsh cry is everywhere regarded as the forerunner of evil. The Nightingale, on the other hand, is a smaller bird, with dull brownish plumage—"a little dirty ball," as the Owl is pleased to call her. She frequents the woodlands of damp low-lying districts, but only during the summer months and in certain parts of England: for in Scotland and Ireland her presence is quite unknown. Her song is as delightful as the Owl's is discordant: it is heard day and night during May and June, though early in June it is apt to cease, when the mating season is over. The birds, as drawn by the poet, are therefore taken directly from life: there are touches which reveal the hand of the naturalist; and we are thus presented not with mere stock figures, but with life-size pictures of living creatures that compel our attention by their sheer reality.

But the poet has done yet more than this: he has made his creatures live by endowing them with human personality, and by ascribing to them thoughts and feelings characteristic of men. And, indeed, this was the only way of giving them life—it is La Fontaine's method at a later date—for we can never know much more than the outside of animals, the only inner life we can imagine being, after all, our own. To some extent, the moral qualities of the birds may be inferred from the physical characteristics depicted: the Owl, for example, is sullen and gloomy, as is natural in one who is unsightly and something of a recluse: whereas the Nightingale, a frail songstress who loves the sun, is of a gayer temperament, a milder and more lovable nature than her opponent. But the poet does not leave here the delineation of his characters: far more is done by the dramatic method, by the inferences to be drawn from what is said and done by the birds themselves. In this way we learn that the Owl is a dour fighter, with an overbearing manner and keen reasoning powers, given to coarse invective when provoked, and apt to prove surly and violent when worsted in argument: all of which is borne out by the fierce hatred she inspires, especially in the breasts of the weaker members of her tribe. As for her views on life, they are of the narrow ascetic kind: life to her is at best a bad business, and he lives best who sheds most tears. Hence her pride in the dismal nature of her songs, which are a perpetual reminder of the terrors to come, and aim at inducing men to leave their evil ways. Throughout the dispute she is conscious of her own rectitude: of her services to mankind she speaks at length. But for the frailties of others she has no sympathy, for she stands aloof from the lighter side of life. She is, in brief, a creature of gloom, a Puritan before her time, and her type is permanent in human nature. In marked contrast with her stands the Nightingale—a gentler creature, who holds her own against her brow-beating opponent, by her daring thrusts, her happy retorts, and the self-control she displays throughout the dispute. The cause she pleads is that of sweetness and light; the songs she sings are of love and the joy of life. Her mission is simply to spread happiness around; and she is therefore beloved by all her fellows; even Nature smiles at her approach. Nor is she without a more serious purpose in life, though she claims for her songs a value of their own. For the love-stricken soul she has a message of hope: her charity is as wide as humanity itself. Spiritual pride is to her the most deadly of sins: and with all her urbanity and art, she is a tender rebel against harsh unfeeling authority. An early humanist, with a touch of the modern spirit, she represents a brave "soldier in the Liberation War of humanity."

The personalities of the two protagonists thus stand out clear and distinct. They are birds obviously enough: but they are human beings as well. They are birds with the minds that human beings would possess, could we imagine them transformed, for the time being, into birds: and it is in this dual character that their fascination really lies. But this fascination is by no means confined to the two main actors: it is characteristic as well of the world to which they belong—that queer elusive world of the poet's own making, born as it were of some midnight fancy. There indeed we see a strange community of creatures, removed from the haunts of men, living a primitive life of their own full of factions and feuds, and yet not so very different after all from life as we know it. Of the members of that community some take part in the action of the poem: these are the thrush, the throstle, the wood-pecker and the wren. Concerning others, again, we hear only in passing, through references made by the Owl and the Nightingale; and thus it is that we learn of the tiny titmouse and the bellicose cock, of hedgesparrows and magpies waging war on the young corn, and of crows in large flocks attacking hawks in the marshes. It is therefore a seemingly substantial world that the poet has created: a community representative of the bird-life with which we are familiar. Nor is there anything incongruous or out of keeping in this fanciful world of the poet's: for the birds, for the most part, act in conformity with their nature, they remain true to the laws of their own being[1]. It is not without its significance, for example, that they discuss only such matters as birds might reasonably be supposed to discuss, namely, their songs, their habits and the like; or that when the Owl threatens violence, it is with her claws and the claws of her friends that she attempts to frighten her opponent[2]; or again, that the images which come naturally to the minds of the disputants, are taken, in general, from the animal world, and have reference either to the birds already mentioned, or to such animals as the cat, the fox, the hare and the horse. The truth is that the poet has preserved his fiction with extraordinary skill: neither the action nor the debate ever leaves the animal plane of being. The reader is never puzzled, as he is in reading Dryden's *Hind and the Panther*, with the bewildering changes that come over the actors, which at one time are rational creatures, capable of discussing abstruse doctrines like transubstantiation, while at other times they revert to the brute creation, one of them drinking at the "common watering-place" for animals, the other pacifying her tail and licking her frothy jaws. In *The Owl and the Nightingale*, on the other hand, the illusion is never destroyed: the fable as it stands is consistent throughout, and all of a piece. If we can suppose such beings as the poet creates, to exist at all, then from his treatment of them we must add, what Hazlitt said of the characters of the *Tempest*, that "they could not act or speak or feel otherwise than as [the poet] makes them."

The fable has therefore been handled with wonderful tact: everything is clearly outlined, concrete and convincing; and the workmanship throughout points to a master of his craft. But something of the same skill has also been shown in connection with the allegory, which the fable has been designed to bring before its readers. Running throughout the narrative is a secondary meaning, which brings the story into intimate connection with life; and this side of the work shows the same originality of treatment, the same effective handling, and the same insight into the requirements of

---

[1] See, however, note, ll. 303–8.
[2] Cf. ll. 1687–8, also ll. 1067–71.

art. Of the nature of that allegorical theme something has already been said. It has been shown to relate to contemporary songs and singers, to the challenging of religious poetry of the old tradition by the secular love-poetry of the new; and it only remains to suggest the quality of the treatment. The allegory, to begin with, is plain to the simplest of souls. With a mind well versed in contemporary fable, no one could fail to read what was meant into the dispute of the birds, or to see in their quarrel a reference to the struggle then beginning, between the different types of poetry in the world of men. Nevertheless, the poet has left but little to chance: from the opening scene the antithesis is clear, and the contrast is afterwards developed by a number of strokes—by the claims and counter-claims of the birds, their charges and countercharges—until the reader is convinced of what the poet was about. If, as is indeed the case, the success of an allegory largely depends upon the ingenious development of analogies between the symbols and the things symbolised, then *The Owl and the Nightingale* must surely rank high among works of its kind. Yet the poet has not exhausted his resources in the working out of his many analogies. All the while he has been telling an interesting story, a story which, like *Gulliver's Travels*, can be read for itself; and in his skill as a story-teller lies no small part of his art as an allegorist, for it is by this means that he manages to bring home his subject. Apart from the realism with which he endows his story, there are the subtlety and the restraint with which he has veiled his meaning. In some allegories, for instance, the story obscures the figurative sense; in others, the figurative sense destroys the story. But in our present poem a perfect balance has been attained: the allegory never obtrudes into the literal narrative, though it is there all the same as a sort of undertone. The bird-world we know is but a pendant of human society; and the imagination is, as it were, fired by the device. As for the originality of the treatment, we have only to turn to some of the earlier narratives, to the Owl and the Falcon fable, for instance, contained in the poem, which forms a good example of the type in question. And there we shall find a narrative of bare facts, with the moral appended: the birds mere automata, dull, lifeless, mechanical—little more than pegs for human attributes. The moral, in short, has stifled the story, which is wanting in life as well as in reality. Compared with such narratives our allegory assumes its just value and proportions, the difference being one of quality not merely of scale. Our poet, it is true, has enlarged the scope of the fable: but he has also breathed fresh life into all its details, while bringing to his work a fine sense of proportion and balance. Both the fable and the allegory have been changed beyond all recognition: what was mechanical and impersonal before, has felt the quickening touch of the poet's genius.

Leaving now the allegory, we approach the work from another standpoint, with a view to inquiring what claims may be advanced for the work as poetry, and whether the author has gifts, in the matter of expression, at all comparable with those he possessed as fabulist and allegorist. Is there anything, for instance, to be said for the style in which he has presented his work? Does his manner add anything to the total effect? What command has he shown of the instruments at his disposal,—of the diction and the verse he has chosen for his purpose? Are there any colours or tones that give special delight, or that help to vitalise the theme of his work? These are questions that arise when we turn to this side of the work: and they call for some sort of answer, if we are to appreciate at all adequately the appeal of its art. From the very nature of things, little enough would be expected from work of this date. The English genius, we are wont to say, was inarticulate as yet: and we point to the fumbling efforts of contemporary writers, as work which, while valuable for historical reasons, requires also some allowance to be made for crude and imperfect workmanship. But *The Owl and the Nightingale* does not ask to be tried by any mere historical standard: it has qualities that will stand a test of a more absolute and searching kind. In a multitude of different ways has the poet commended his fable by his manner of presenting it; and indeed, when all things are considered, his technique must be described as masterly—a marvel of literary art before our medieval art was born.

Nothing, to begin with, is more remarkable—though the point has hitherto almost escaped notice[1]—than the particular style in which the poem is written. An apparently artless vein, in which things are said simply and directly, without any straining for effect, any torturing of the syntax for the sake of the metre, but with word following word as in ordinary well-bred speech, the simple structure and diction of prose gliding naturally into verse without ever becoming prosaic—this is the style in which our poet has written, and the fact in itself is not without its significance. For what we have here is clearly the first example of the "familiar" style in English, that style which, according to Cowper, is "of all styles the most difficult to succeed in." Later on, in Chaucer, the same

---

[1] See, however, Ker, *English Literature Medieval*, pp. 181–2.

vein occurs: in Swift and Prior too, though with them there is a
refinement due to further literary practice. But to our poet belongs
the honour of originating the style in English: he first attempted
to build up the poetic idiom on a colloquial basis.

And in this he has succeeded to an astonishing degree: for nowhere does his tone rise above the conversational level, nowhere
does it fall beneath the dignity of art. Everywhere he writes in
irresistible effortless fashion, depending for his effects upon the
simplest forms of expression, upon a vocabulary drawn from the
lips of the people, and consisting of words full of colour and life. For
him there existed no poetic diction: the most trivial and commonplace
words came alike to his pen. Yet the words he uses are never out of
place or lacking in dignity; his colloquialisms he handles with
unfailing moderation and taste; and in so doing he has added a new
power to expression. But in other ways as well is this conversational tone maintained, and notably in the absence of conventional
stylistic devices. The poem, for one thing, contains no passages of
fine writing, none of the glitter or elevation derived from classical
allusions and the like. All tricks, in fact, are practically avoided:
our poet writes with the gay good-humour of one with a good
story to tell: and he writes to be understood—by the plain man,
most of all. And so the effect throughout is simplicity itself, the
simplicity that results from a well-concealed art, and wanting in
neither energy nor charm. Yet of the art underlying there can be
no doubt, as a comparison with contemporary work will plainly
reveal. The truth would seem to be that our poet's style grew
partly out of his subject-matter. Dealing with a theme that called
for no pretentious treatment, he has hit upon a vein that gives
just the light and whimsical touch required, while imparting to
the narrative an air of naturalness, almost capable of persuading
us that such things could be. But much was also due to the poet's
own personality, the style really being but an expression of himself. If there is present the *naïveté* of one dealing in fables, there
is also the easy familiarity of a wit indulging in a *jeu d'esprit*;
and these are the qualities, more than anything else, that give to
the poem its peculiar character and tone.

It would, however, be idle to deny that the "familiar" style of
our poet has features of its own, that distinguish him from later
writers in the same vein. There is, for example, his fondness for
synonyms[1], and for repeating his ideas—traces perhaps of the exu-

---

[1] E.g. *stif ꝥ starc ꝥ strong* (l. 5); *bischricheþ ꝥ bigredet* (l. 67); *tosvolle ꝥ ibolwe*
(l. 145); *chauling ꝥ chatere* (l. 284); *unnepe ꝥ ouerdede* (l. 352); also ll. 488,
526, 703, 757, 842, 865, 1005, 1083, 1103, 1137, 1160, 1347, 1521, 1647.

berance of the earlier poetic manner, or more particularly of the oral literary tradition which up to then had prevailed. Or, again, there is the element of alliteration[1], which runs throughout his work like veins in marble. Never obtrusive in its effects, it serves, notwithstanding, to emphasise the important words in a line, while adding an incidental charm to the poet's expression. But most striking of all is the poet's use of similes, which heighten the vitality of the work as a whole, in a way unprecedented in our native literature. Scattered throughout the poem are quite a number of images of this kind, which add an element of fine surprise to the style, while they also strike home by their daring and unexpected quality. When, for instance, the bill of the Owl is likened to a crooked awl (l. 80), or the persistent song of the Nightingale to an Irish priest's chattering (l. 322); when the Owl is said to sing as lugubriously as a hen in the snow (l. 413), or the twittering of the birds, on the supposed defeat of the Owl, is said to recall the excitement that follows a gambler's overthrow (ll. 1664–5)[2]—the figures may be described as unconventional perhaps, but they must also be said to be fresh and original. They present in arresting fashion the various points they are designed to illustrate; and here, without a doubt, the influence of the Troubadours may indirectly be felt.

But the poet does not depend upon similes alone for the colouring of his poem: in developing his argument he makes use of a number of illustrations, which, apart from their function of presenting the abstract in concrete fashion, supply also a wealth of imagery, which adds very materially to the picturesque quality of the work. And what we have here are no reprints of orthodox scenes: they are reflections caught from the world around, fleeting reminiscences of contemporary life, its manners and customs, its common sights and sounds. Inspired by Troubadour song, our poet, it is true, may depict in glowing but conventional fashion, the familiar scene of the oncoming of spring (ll. 437–44),—when trees and meadows are decked with blossom, with lilies and with roses that burst from the blackthorn; or again it may be the season of autumn, when the sheaves are being garnered and the leaves are stained with brown (ll. 455–6). But these are by no means his characteristic effects. His scenes are more often taken

---

[1] E.g. *wis an war of worde* (l. 192); *wile of bore wurchen bareȝ* (l. 408); *þrusche ȝ þrostle ȝ wudewale* (l. 1659); also ll. 296, 335, 396, 437, 495, 524, etc.

[2] Cf. also similes relating to the use of woad (l. 86), the music of the harp (l. 142), an envious man (l. 421), a useless well (l. 917).

first-hand from the country life of the people: they are the results of his own observation, as when reference is made to the hare flying hot-foot down forest glades, to the fox pursued in open chase, to the horse standing patiently beside the mill-door, or to the owl hunted down and hung as a scarecrow amidst the corn. Elsewhere, again, glimpses may be caught of other aspects of contemporary life: we hear incidentally of the fondness for wrestling and cock-fighting, of the dance-songs that formed part of the Christmas festivities, and of certain other features of the religious life of the time—the canonical hours, the different orders of clerks, monks and canons, and the rampant injustice that prevailed in the bestowal of livings. The effect of it all is to add very considerably to the appeal of the bird-fable. Not only are fresh colours worked into the poetic style, but a substantial historical background is also created, the familiarity of which would appeal to contemporary readers, while arousing in later readers that imaginative sympathy, ever needed for the appreciation of a work that has come down from out of the past.

Such, then, is the manner in which our poet has presented his story, though there are yet other factors that contribute to the total effect—the skill, for example, he displays in dialogue, his power of handling argument in verse, his piquant humour, his urbanity as well as his sane common-sense. But above all, there is the elusive personality that peers through the pages, and is all the more notable in an age of impersonal art. From first to last this personality dominates the work, making it the expression of an individual soul, with its own peculiar utterance and its own outlook upon life. And these are the things that ultimately determine the quality of the work. The poet has spoken to his generation of things of the mind: and he has done so in a way that is entirely his own. Rich in fancy, in humanity, and in the wisdom drawn from life, the poem is, in short, an intimate revelation of the poet himself.

Something must however be added as to our poet's verse, and his skill in handling that octosyllabic couplet, of which he is the first efficient exponent in English. The verse-form was one which was familiar in France, where it appeared in the popular romances, and indeed in much else besides. But its introduction into English marked the beginning of a new system of verse; and it remains to inquire how far our poet has succeeded in acclimatising the measure, and adapting it to the purpose in hand. That there were obstacles to his success is obvious enough: for he was attempting to run English words into a foreign mould, in spite of the persistence of the native accentual tradition, and without the guidance of earlier models. Yet the poet may be said to have triumphed over most of his technical difficulties: he has reconciled the English word-accent with the rhythm required, and has greatly enhanced by his metrical effects the artistic value of the story he tells.

With surprising skill, to begin with, has the poet impressed upon his readers the metrical pattern upon which he works. By far the greater proportion of his verses consists of normal octosyllabic iambic lines, with the sense complete in couplets: so that there can never be any doubt as to the controlling rhythm, or the metrical effects he has primarily in mind. And so the narrative proceeds in easy uninterrupted fashion, the short line harmonising with the *naïveté* of the theme; while arguments and descriptions fall naturally into couplet form, which is also well suited to the redundancy of the style.

Equally surprising, however, is the skill with which the poet has rung the changes upon his chosen rhythm, with the result of bringing about the necessary variety of movement. Sometimes the change is made by the omission of a syllable, either at the beginning[1], or in the middle of a line[2]. And the first of these devices, originally a means of avoiding displacement of the word-accent, has ultimately the effect of emphasising a particular word, or of introducing into the movement a delightful trochaic variety; while the second, though less pleasing in its metrical effects, is nevertheless a licence found in Anglo-French poems like Chardry's. Variation of a different kind again results when two syllables are included under a light accent[3]. And while here the influence of the native tradition would seem to have been at work, the effect produced is of an anapaestic kind—the trisyllabic foot coming as a welcome relief to the quick recurrence of the accent in an iambic line. But the poet has yet other devices for modifying his pattern: and specially notable is the way in which he, from time to time, breaks up the unity of his couplet[4], or by his use of *enjambement*[5] brings release from the monotony to which octosyllabics above all are apt to tend. Chrétien de Troyes seems to have been the first

---

[1] Cf. ll. 87, 116, 1130, 1628, etc.

[2] Cf. ll. 21, 568, 681, 923, etc.

[3] Cf. ll. 70, 355, 870, 875, etc.

[4] Cf. ll. 97, 173, 175, 257, 325, etc.

[5] Cf. ll. 23, 151, 337, 409, 425, 428, etc.

to break up the couplet, in terminating a phrase with the first line of the couplet, and commencing a new phrase with the line that followed. But what was with him a licence became later a mark of elegance; and our poet adds considerably to his freedom of movement by adopting the same device. Moreover the same effect results from his use of run-on lines, which occur frequently throughout the poem: and the poet, employing them with unvarying skill, has cleverly adapted his verse to the narrative purpose he had in view.

Nowhere, however, is the poet's metrical art more clearly displayed than in his handling of the rhymes with which he adorns his poem, thus adding a new music to English verse. From the first he appears as a master of this branch of his craft: for the rhymes throughout are wonderfully correct, and this in spite of the frequency with which they occur in an octosyllabic poem, and the severe demands made in consequence upon his resources. Thus he understands the value of variant forms[1], and dialect forms[2], in supplying him with the particular words he requires: he helps out his resources with self-rhyming forms[3], though he uses for this purpose only words that differed in meaning; and whereas occasionally he is content with assonant forms[4], it is but rarely that his rhymes can be said to break down. On the other hand, the excellence of the great majority of those rhymes is beyond all dispute: he carefully discriminates in his choice of rhyming sounds[5], and links together only vowels identical in quality and quantity. Then, too, he varies his effects by the introduction of masculine and feminine rhymes; and, naturally enough, it is the latter that predominate[6]; for in rhyming words in English, there would often occur, after the accented or rhyming syllable, an inflexional ending which would constitute a sort of extra syllable, and go to form a rhyme of a double or feminine kind. But whatever the cause, this variation of rhymes is not without its effect upon the harmony of the poem: the feminine rhymes bring about a "delaying grace of movement"; and for a greater artist in this vein we have to wait until Chaucer comes.

Such, then, is the poet's handling of this "light and lewed rhyme"

[1] Cf. *ilike* (l. 157), *iliche* (l. 316); *wailawai* (l. 220), *wolawo* (l. 412); *schame* (l. 50), *schome* (l. 363).

[2] For occasional use of Kentish forms see Appendix i. (a) (i).

[3] Cf. ll. 153–4, 391–2, 425–6, 603–4, 895–6; see, however, ll. 267–8.

[4] Cf. ll. 505–6, 987–8, 1531–2.

[5] See Appendix i. (c) (iv) for discrimination between $\bar{e}$ (O.E. $\bar{æ}$) and $\bar{e}$ (O.E. $\bar{e}a$).

[6] The proportion of masculine to feminine rhymes is nearly 1 to 4 (190 : 707).

of his: and his treatment in this respect is but in keeping with the many-sided art of the rest of the poem, with its well-designed form, its picturesque allegory, its clever character-drawing, and the manner and style in which the story is presented. If the test of a poem is its completeness, its unity of effect, then *The Owl and the Nightingale* must surely rank high in the annals of our literature: for, viewed from what standpoint we will, the work has qualities, arresting in themselves, yet contributing, each in its own way, to the harmony of the whole. What, in fact, we admire in the poem is not its lack of art, but the way in which art has made use of the homely and the familiar, turning what was commonplace to artistic ends. Out of such things as fables, debates and bird-lore, our poet has created a striking and an original phantasy, into which he has worked a symbolism of Nature's own devising, together with images drawn from contemporary life and likely to find a mirror in every mind. And since the principal ornament of fables was to have none, he has set forth his phantasy in artless colloquial fashion, requiring in his readers little more than a knowledge of common words and things, and ears that were attuned to the simple rhythm of the octosyllabic line. Throughout the work, in short, he has maintained contact with the commonplace, with reality; and, like the giant Antaeus, he has gained strength in touching mother Earth.

How the poem appealed to earlier readers can only be guessed, though the two MSS. that have come down— neither of which can have been the original—unmistakably point to some degree of popularity[1]. To modern readers, however, the poem has yet more to offer: for when placed in its true perspective, it presents new lights and shades, countless overtones and undertones, that could have existed for neither the poet nor his original readers. Faults in the workmanship, it is true, may here and there be found: occasionally a line limps with defective rhythm: or the native force of the expression may at times develop a crudity, that seems to modern readers a virtue overdone. Yet, even so, such lapses from good taste may be condoned when viewed in a historical light: they are blemishes upon which it would be fatuous to insist.

And for the rest, we cannot but be conscious of the abounding merits of the poem and of what it really stands for. A medieval poem with a colouring distinctly English, it enshrines in singular

---

[1] For the probable influence of the poem on the later *strif*, known as *The Throstle and the Nightingale*, see note, l. 1109.

fashion the intellectual energies of an age, that marked a new phase in the civilisation of Western Europe, and the beginnings of much of our modern English culture. In it may be heard echoes of that spirit of criticism, which was then for the first time challenging the old traditions in literature and life; in it, too, may be found traces of the literary conditions of the time—the fondness for such things as allegories, debates and fables, the insistent call of the new love-poetry, the move in the direction of a new system of verse-making. And as such it is a product of 12th century Western Europe: it looks back to the Troubadours, and on to Dante and Chaucer.

Yet it would be equally true to say that the poem is also a reflection of 12th century England: for its colouring is taken from English life and scenes, its form is influenced by legal activities under Henry II, while its idiom and vocabulary are reminiscent of the homely speech of Dorsetshire or Kent. Moreover, written, as in all probability it was, in the reign of King John, the poem also preserves traces of the growing spirit of independence among Englishmen, of the broadening intellectual sympathies of such men as John of Salisbury or Giraldus Cambrensis: and last, but not least, it is a silent witness to the gradual fusion of two races, in its fascinating blend of the French and English geniuses. To this mixture of racial qualities must indeed be attributed much of the charm of the poem: for if it is manifestly English, it is French as well,—French in its formal excellence and its unity of plan, in its urbanity, its good sense, its logic, and, above all, in the delightful vein of mockery that pervades the whole.

Other qualities there are of interest to the modern reader: for the poet has extended the scope of both fable and debate, he has introduced new effects into the native literature: and while he has revealed unexpected resources in the vernacular, he has also made use of popular material, out of which was subsequently to emerge the great animal epic of the Middle Ages. Yet it is, after all, as the expression of a unique personality, that the poem appeals finally to modern readers: for in it we have the authentic utterance of one who lived under the early Plantagenets, and whose ambitions and fancies, whose thoughts and moods are therein set down for all to read. That the work gives proof of genius as well as the highest art is a fact that will be conceded by all who know the poem. But what attracts us most is the rich humanity of the work, its freshness of utterance, its simple sincere handling of one of the great problems—the age-long contest between asceticism and pleasure. From out of that distant past the voices are few : though Abbot Samson yet lives in the pages of Jocelin, and tells us of things we would not readily forget. Another reading of life is presented by our poet, who comes to remind us of the joy of living. Both readings are true; they are equally the product of the men and their age: and to that age we may return in *The Owl and the Nightingale*, and catch again the accents of one who spoke in the dawn.

ABBREVIATIONS EMPLOYED IN THE NOTES

Ang. = *Anglia.*

B. T. = Bosworth-Toller, *Anglo-Saxon Dictionary.*

C. = MS. Cotton *Caligula* A ix.

E.D.D. = *English Dialect Dictionary.*

E. St. = *Englische Studien.*

G. = *Eule und Nachtigall*, ed. W. Gadow.

H. = *Selections from Early Middle English* (2 vols.), by Joseph Hall.

J. = MS. Jesus College, Oxford, 29.

J.E.G.P. = *Journal of English and Germanic Philology.*

M. = Mätzner, *Altenglische Sprachproben.*

M.L.N. = *Modern Language Notes.*

M.L.R. = *Modern Language Review.*

Morsbach = Morsbach, *Mittelenglische Grammatik.*

N.E.D. = *New English Dictionary.*

P.B.B. = Paul u. Braune, *Beiträge.*

Sievers = Sievers, *Angelsächsische Grammatik.*

Sk. = Morris & Skeat, *Specimens of Early English.*

St. = *The Owl and the Nightingale*, ed. J. Stevenson.

Str. = *The Owl and the Nightingale*, ed. Stratmann.

Str.-Br. = Stratmann, *Middle English Dictionary*, ed. Bradley.

W. = *The Owl and the Nightingale*, ed. J. E. Wells.

Wr. = *The Owl and the Nightingale*, ed. T. Wright.

THE OWL AND THE NIGHTINGALE

THE OWL AND THE NIGHTINGALE

MS. Cott. (C.)
Fol. 233 r. col. 1.

ICH was in one sum*ere* dale,
in one su*þe* di3ele hale,
iherde ich holde grete tale
an hule and one ni3tingale.

5 þat plait was stif 7 starc 7 strong,
sum wile softe 7 lud among;
an aiþer a3en oþer sval,
7 let þat [vue]le mod ut al.
7 eiþer seide of oþeres custe

10 þat alre-worste þat hi wuste:
7 hure 7 hure of oþere[s] songe
hi holde plaiding suþe stronge.
þe ni3tingale bigon þe speche,
in one hurne of one breche,

2. *þ* dotted (see note).   7. margin *eiþer*.   8. *wole*.   10. *alere*, first *ə* deleted.   11. *oþere*.

---

1. *sumere*=O.E. *sumere*, the L.W.S. form (fem. d. sg.) of *sum* (a certain): see Sievers § 293, a 4. Hence Sturmfels' suggestion (*Ang.* IX. 563) that *sumere* here is equivalent to *somere* < O.Fr. *sombre* with parasitic *e* before *r*, is unnecessary: nor is Gadow's rendering, "a summer" (valley), at all a likely one. (Cf. also H. *s.v.* and Kenyon, *J.E.G.P.* XII. 572.)

dale="valley." H. notes that "north of Portisham is a valley now called Mystecomb, formed by Hampton and Ridge Hills, and on the east side of the former are some pits, where the hundred courts were formerly held" (Hutchins, *Dorsetshire*, I. 556), and queries whether this is the scene of the dispute.

2. *suþe*=*swiþe* (very). As a rule a dotted *þ* in MS. C. stands for *w*: but here it is evidently a scribal error for *þ*. W. notes the occurrence of this error some nine times in this MS., e.g. ll. 171, 638, 758, etc.

hale < O.E. *healh* (corner, cranny): cf. the phrase "from hale to hurne" quoted by Sedgefield from an early M.E. Psalter. For the existence of this form in Mod. Eng. place-names (e.g. Hale, Hailes, etc.) see Sedgefield, *M.L.R.* IX. ii. 240–1.

4. *an...one*="an...a." The difference of form is due to difference of sentence-accent.

ni3tingale (J. *nyhtegale*). The word appears 16 times in C. with medial *n*, 5 times without: the latter forms occur all in (β) sections of the MS. In J. the invariable form is *nyhtegale* except in l. 203, where *Nihtingale* is found. In *Laustic*, by Marie de France, the Breton word *laustic* (l. 6) is glossed as *nihtegale*, showing that the late 12th century form did not necessarily contain medial *n*. Logeman (*E. St.* 34, 249) however maintains that similar cases of intrusive *n* are found in O.E. and quotes O.E. *þolenden*,

THE OWL AND THE NIGHTINGALE

Incip*it* alteroacio inter filomenam *et* Bubonem

ICH wes in one sumere dale,　　MS. Jes. Coll. (J.)
　In one swiþe dyele hale,　　Fol. 229 r. col. 1.
Iherde ich holde grete tale
An vle and one nyhtegale.

5　þat playd wes stif ꞇ starc ꞇ strong
Sum hwile softe ꞇ lud among;
And eyþer ayeyn oþer swal,
And let þat vuele mod vt al.
And eyþer seyde of oþres custe

10　þat alre-w[u]rste þat hi ywuste:
ꞇ hure ꞇ hure of oþres songe
Hi holde playding swiþe stronge.
　þe Nihtegale bigon þo speke
In one hurne of one beche,

Latin heading in red.

---

halantunge (*A.S. Chron.*) in support of his assertion. But as Mr W. H. Stevenson points out, these forms are probably scribal errors : see *N.E.D.*

8. *vuele* (C. *wole*, J. *vuele*). The C. scribe has evidently written *w* for *vu*, *uv* of his original; cf. C. ll. 31, 236. "The *o* may be due to careless writing of *e* in C. or in the original" (W.).

13. *speche* (J. *speke*). The C. reading is evidently correct, as is shown by the rhyme. The word means "law-suit, plea" : see note l. 398.

14. *breche* (J. *beche*). Most of the earlier editors including Str., Sk. and W., prefer the J. form. Sk. for instance adopts *beche* (= valley) and quotes *bæche* (*La ʒ* 5644), *baches* (*P. Plow.* C. viii. 159). W. emends to *beche* apparently accepting the rendering of Sk., while Hempl (*E. St.* 29, 411 ff.) again, explains *beche* as being derived from O.E. loc. *bece* (< *bec*, stream).

Kenyon (*J.E.G.P.* xii. 572), on the other hand, takes *beche* to mean "beech-tree" (< O.E. *bēce*), and with some reason objects to the interpretation "valley" as being ruled out by the context. He further points out that the other two birds are definitely located, the owl in an "old tree-stump" (l. 25), the wren in a lime-tree (l. 1750): and he argues that the poet is here associating the nightingale in like manner with one particular tree (cf. however "hawthorn" associated with N. in Clanvowe's *Cuckoo & Nightingale*, l. 287, and 15th century *Court of Love*, l. 1354)., Nor does he regard the irregular rhyme resulting from his reading as a serious obstacle. He claims that it is paralleled elsewhere in the poem (e.g. in ll. 988, 1041, 1413, and possibly 225). But this claim must in any case be modified as regards l. 1041 (see note), and probably in the case of two (if not all) of the other instances as well.

On the whole, however, there does not seem to be sufficient ground for rejecting the reading of C. which is the earlier and the more trustworthy of

15   ꝺ sat up one vaire boȝe,
—þar were abute blosme inoȝe,—
in ore waste þicke hegge
imeind mid spire ꝺ grene segge.
Ho was þe gladur uor þe rise,

20   ꝺ song auele cunne wise:
[b]et þuȝte þe dreim þat he were
of harpe ꝺ pipe þan he nere:
bet þuȝte þat he were ishote
of harpe ꝺ pipe þan of þrote.

25   [Þ]o stod on old stoc þar biside,
þar þo vle song hire tide,
ꝺ was mid iui al bigrowe;
hit was þare hule earding-stowe.
[Þ]e niȝtingale hi iseȝ,

30   ꝺ hi bihold ꝺ ouerseȝ,
ꝺ þuȝte wel [vu]l of þare hule,
for me hi halt lodlich ꝺ fule.
"Vnwiȝt," ho sede, "awei þu flo!
me is þe w[u]rs þat ich þe so.

35   Iwis for þine [vu]le lete,   Fol. 233 r. col. 2.
wel [oft ich] mine song forlete;

21. *het.*   23. *is hote.*   25, 29. omission of rubric capital: light þ
(directing letter) in margin.   31. *wl.*   34. *wrs.*   35. *wle.*   36. *oftich.*

---

the two MSS. On the contrary, *breche* may be safely retained as giving quite
a suitable reading. The word is preserved in Mod. Devon. dial. where *breach*
= "coarse, furzy or heathy ground on which the turf has been cut or
burnt" (*E.D.D.*). It is probably connected with O.E. *bræc, brec* which
(according to H.) "occurs in the boundaries of charters, and appears to mean
land left untilled among cultivated fields, such as would be covered with
underwood": while traces of it exist in such place-names as Norbreck, War-
brick, Scarisbrick (Lancs.), Haverbreck (Westmoreland). The form would
therefore seem to mean a small thicket or spinney. But apart from this, it
may be urged that *breche* thus interpreted would suit the context as well as
beche (beech-tree) and certainly better than *beche* (valley): while again it is
preferable to *beche* (beech-tree) as providing a normal rhyme in a poem in
which the rhyming technique is wonderfully correct. Thus the scene of the
poem is placed (l. 2) "in a corner (*hale*) of a valley (*dale*)": and if l. 14 be
anything more than a superfluous repetition of this statement the word at
the end of the line must mean something other than "valley." Moreover if
"valley" were really intended, one would expect the definite (not the indefinite) article before the word *beche*. On the other hand, when the line is
taken as an extension of the earlier description, indicating a patch of underwood in the valley (with hedges around, in flower), then there is no difficulty

15 ꝺ sat vp one vayre bowe,
    þat were abute blostme ynowe,
    In ore vaste þikke hegge
    I[m]eynd myd spire ꝺ grene segge.
    He wes þe gladder vor þe ryse,
20 ꝺ song a veole cunne wyse:
    Bet þuhte þe drem þat he were
    Of harpe ꝺ pipe þan he nere:
    Bet þuhte þat heo were ishote
    Of harpe ꝺ pipe þan of þrote.
25   þo stod on old stok þar byside,
    þar þe vle song hìre tyde,
    And wes myd ivi al bigrowe:
    Hit wes þare vle erdingstowe.
      þe Nihtegale hi iseyh,
30 ꝺ hi bi[hold] and ouerseyh,
    ꝺ þuhte wel ful of þare vle,
    For me hi halt lodlich ꝺ fule.
    "Vnwyht," heo seyde, "awey þu fleo! Fol. 229 r. col. 2.
    Me is þe wurs þat ich þe iseo.
35 Iwis for þine [vu]le lete
    Wel ofte ich my song furlete;

18. *IMeynd.*   30. *biholdeþ.*   35. *vle.*

about the use of the indefinite *one*, while the opening description is made to gain greatly in vividness and picturesque quality.

The rhyme *breche* ($\bar{e}$) : *speche* ($\bar{e}$) is quite regular.

17. *waste.* J. reads *vaste* (< O.E. *fæst*, firm, thick) which gives the better reading. The C. form *waste* is a different word < O.Fr. *wast*, "deserted, solitary." H. suggests that *waste* is written for *vaste* (*faste*) = "close, thick."

18. *imeind* (< O.E. *gemengd*, mingled). For palatal insertion *i* before *ngd* with subsequent loss of *g* see Morsbach § 107, a 4. Instances of a similar process (pal. *i* inserted before *nct*) are found in 12th century forms, cf. Napier, *O.E. Glosses*, xxvii., *aseint* (829), *adreintum* (832), *acweinte* (4125).

mid = "with." Throughout the poem the forms *mid* and *wiþ* are kept distinct, their respective W.S. meanings being preserved, viz. *mid* (with), *wiþ* (against): cf. ll. 801–2. There are but few exceptions, e.g. ll. 131, 1419. In the latter the phrase is "*wiþ þe maide holde*," where *wiþ* = "with": but in the parallel construction in l. 1517 the regular form *mid* occurs. A similar preservation of W.S. characteristics is seen in the use of the preposition *on* (= in), see note l. 54.

26. *þo* (J. *þe*) = "the": < L.O.E. *þēo* for *sēo*: see Sievers § 337, a 2.

hire tide = "her hours": see B.T. *tid* i c.: cf. also notes ll. 323–8, 1658 ff.

31. Trans. "it seemed (to her) foul with regard to the owl," i.e. "she thought but badly of the owl." Impersonal constructions are common at this date: cf. similar idioms in ll. 85, 114, 212, 609, 881, etc.

32. *halt*, see *falt* (l. 37).

lodlich (< O.E. *lāðlic*), "loathsome." The *dl* (< O.E. *ðl*) probably dates from the L.O.E. period, see Sievers § 201, 3.

min horte atfliþ ꝛ falt mi tonge,
wonne þu art [to me] iþrunge.
Me luste bet speten þane singe
40   of þine fule ʒoʒelinge."

þos hule abod fort hit was eve,
ho ne miʒte no leng bileue,
vor hire horte was so gret
þat wel neʒ hire fnast atschet,
45   ꝛ warp a word þar-after longe;
"Hu þincþe nu bi mine songe?
We[n]st þu þat ich ne cunne singe,
þeʒ ich ne cunne of writelinge?
Ilome þu dest me grame,
50   ꝛ seist me [boþe tone] ꝛ schame.
ʒif ich þe holde on mine uote,
(so hit bitide þat ich mote!)
ꝛ þu were vt of þine rise,
þu sholdest singe an oþer w[i]se."
55   þe niʒtingale ʒaf answare:
"ʒif ich me loki wit þe bare,
ꝛ me schilde wit þe blete,
ne reche ich noʒt of þine þrete;

38. *tome.*   47. *west.*   50. *bo þe to ne.*   51. *uote or note.*   54. *wse.*

---

37. *falt* < L.W.S. *fealt*, earlier *fielt*, pr. 3 sg. of O.E. *fealdan* (to fold): see
Sievers § 371, a 3. Sk. translates the word *falt* as "falters" (so also W.),
and derives it from O.Fr. *falte, faute* (a fault): G. regards it as the pr. 3 sg.
of *falle(n)* (to fall). The literal meaning of the word is however "folds up":
the tongue is, as it were, paralysed and unable to give utterance.

40. *ʒoʒelinge* (J. *howelynge*) = "howling, shrieking." Str. suggests a parallel
with M.H.G. *gogeln* (= *ululare*) (cf. also Germ. *johlen*), from which might be
inferred an O.E. **gogelian*, possibly a sound-formation. The J.-form, on the
other hand, is probably a scribal variant for the unfamiliar colloquial C.-form:
while the C.-form occurs elsewhere as *ʒuhelinge* in the passage *Quoð Eleusius,*
" *haldest tu ʒetten up o þi ʒuhelinge* " (Dost thou still keep up thy senseless
outcry?) (*St Juliana,* p. 57, E.E.T.S. 1872). That the word was unfamiliar
may be gathered from a further variant which occurs in another MS. (Royal
MS. 17, A. xxvii.) of the same work, where the French word *gencling* (jan-
gling) is found.

41. *fort* (J. *for*). The word *fort* = *for* + *to* (until), gives better sense than
the J.-form *for* (because).
eve = "evening." Both disputants were night-birds, see note l. 1688.

48. *writelinge* (C. and J.). A word of considerable interest: not in Str.-Br.
Both Sk. and W. correctly translate the word as "trilling," but neither gives
its origin. The earlier form of the word is probably an O.E. **writelian*
frequentative of O.E. *writian, wreotian* (to chirp, chatter): the latter forms

Min heorte atflyhþ ⁊ falt my tunge,
Hwenne þu art to me iþrunge.
Me luste bet speten þane singe
40   Of þine fule howelynge."
Þeos vle abod for hit wes eve,
Heo ne myhte no leng bileue,
Vor hire heorte wes so gret
Þat wel neyh hire fnast atset,
45   ⁊ warp a word þar-after longe;
"Hw þynk þe nu bi [m]ine songe?
Wenestu þat ich ne kunne singe,
Þe ich ne cunne of wrytelinge?
Ilome þu dest me grome,
50   ⁊ seist me boþe teone ⁊ schome.
If ich þe heolde on myne vote,
(So hit bitide þat ich mote!)
⁊ þu were vt of þine ryse,
Þu scholdest singe on oþer wise."
55   Þe Nihtegale yaf onsware:
"If ich me loki wiþ þe bare,
⁊ me schilde [w]it þe blete,
Ne recche ich nouht of þine þrete:

46. *Mine.*   57. *yit.*

occurring in Wright-Wülcker, *A.S. and O.E. Vocabularies*, 377³⁵ *crepitat* = *wreotað*, and in Napier's *O.E. Glosses*, 37, 3, *garrulantes* = *wri[tiende]*. This root-word has however been subject to misunderstanding. Elsewhere in Wright-Wülcker the gloss *pipant* = *pritigeað* (for *writigeað*) 516²⁶ is found: whence the ghost-word *pritigian* (to chirp) in Sweet's *A.S. Dictionary*. Other forms of the word occur elsewhere, but have been wrongly assigned in Bos.-Toller, *A.S. Dictionary* to a supposed *writian* (to draw, write, compose): see Napier, *O.E. Glosses*, 37³ (note); Kluge, *E. St.* xi. 512: cf. also *rittle* (*E.D.D.*).

As to the "trilling" of nightingales, Gilbert White writes that "their notes are so short, and their transitions so rapid that [one] cannot well ascertain their key" (*Natural History*, Letter x. to Hon. Daines Barrington).

52. *So* with opt. denotes a wish. Trans. "may it so happen."

53. *And* (⁊). The word *ȝif* (l. 51) is to be understood after ⁊, so that Sk.'s interpretation of *an* (= if) < O.N. *enda* is unnecessary.

54. *an.* The use of *an*, *on* (= in) together with *in* in this poem points to the preservation of W.S. characteristics (see note l. 18). In the earlier stages of the language W.S. *on* = Angl. *in* (see Miller, *O.E. Version of Bede's Eccles. History*, Intro. xxxiii ff. E.E.T.S. 1890).

56. *loki* < O.E. *lōcian*. Trans. "If I can avoid coming into (protect myself against) the open." For this L.O.E. meaning of *lōcian* cf. *A.S. Chron.* 1129, *ealle þa þæt Cristendome hæfdon to begemen and to locen*.

57. *blete* (O.E. *blēat*), adj. used as noun = "bleak weather": cf. Mod. Kent. dial. "You catch the full bleat [of the wind]" (*E.D.D.*).

ȝif ich me holde in mine hegge,
60 ne recche ich neu*er* what þu segge.
Ich wot þat þu art unmilde
wiþ hom þat ne muȝe fro*m* [þ]e schilde;
⁊ þu tukest wroþe ⁊ vuele,
whar þu miȝt, over smale fuȝele.
65 Vorþi þu art loþ al fuel-kunne,
⁊ alle ho þe driueþ honne,
⁊ þe bischricheþ ⁊ bigredet,
⁊ wel narewe þe biledet;
⁊ ek forþe þe sulue mose,   Fol. 233 v. col. 1.
70 hire þonkes, wolde þe totose.
þu art lodlich to biholde,
⁊ þu art loþ in monie volde;
þi bodi is short, þi swore is smal,
grett*ere* is þin heued þan þu al;
75 þin eȝene boþ col-blake ⁊ brode,
riȝt swo ho were*n* ipei*n*t mid wode;
þu starest so þu wille abiten
al þat þu mi[ȝ]t mid cliure smiten:
þi bile is stif ⁊ scharp ⁊ hoked,
80 riȝt so an owel þat is croked;
þar-mid þu clackes[t] oft ⁊ longe,
⁊ þat is on of þine songe.
Ac þu þretest to mine fleshe,
mid þine cliures woldest me meshe.
85 þe were icundur to one frogge
      *   *   *   *   *

62. *se.*   78. *mist.*   81. *clackes.*   86. line omitted.

62. *muȝe*=pr. opt. 3 pl. of O.E. *mæg*, corresponding to L.W.S. *mugen* (see Sievers § 424). Similar opt. forms are found in ll. 1117, 1581.
69. *þe sulue mose*, "the very titmouse," i.e. the smallest of birds.
70. *hire þonkes*="willingly, readily": a common idiom in O.E.: cf. *Godes þonces, here þances* (*A.S. Chron.* 897, A. 1140).
72. *in monie volde*="in many respects." The phrase is derived not from O.E. *manigfeald* but from *manig, feald*, as is shown by the inflected *monie*; cf. l. 696, *in one uolde*; also *Squire of Low Degree*, 745: *Your chaynes* [shall be] *enameled many a folde.*
73. *smal*, "thin, slender." A thin neck is characteristic of the owl.
74. J. *ne* (C. *þan*). Mr B. Dickins suggests the retention of *ne* (cf. *N.E.D.* ne conj.²)="nor"="than," as in certain modern dialects, cf. *E.D.D.* nor.
78. *miȝt* (C. *mist*, J. *myht*) < O.E. *miht* pr 2 sg. ind. of *mæg* (may). Str. reads *miht*, W. *mist*, G. *miȝt*. The C. reading is due to scribal error, the graph *st* being substituted for *ȝt*, cf. *nustest* (over *miȝtest*) l. 1300: *nuȝte* (for *nuste*) l. 1751.

If ich me holde in myne hegge,
60 Ne recche ich neuer hwat þu segge.
Ich wot þat þu art vn[m]ilde,
Wiþ heom þat ne [m]uwe from þe schilde:
And þu tukest wroþe ꝺ vuele,
Hwar þu myht ouer smale vowele.
65 Vorþi þu art loþ al fowel-cunne,   Fol. 229 v. col. 1.
ꝺ alle heo þe dryueþ heonne,
ꝺ þe biscrycheþ ꝺ bigredeþ,
ꝺ wel narewe þe byledeþ:
ꝺ ek forþe þe sulue mose,
70 Hire þonkes, wolde þe totose.
þu art lodlich to biholde,
And þu art loþ in monye volde:
þi body is scort, þi swere is smal,
Gretture is þin heued ne þu al;
75 þin eyen beoþ colblake ꝺ brode,
Ryht so hi weren ipeynt myd wode;
þu starest so þu wille abyten
Al þat þu myht myd clyure smyten;
þi bile is stif ꝺ sarp ꝺ hoked,
80 Riht as on ewel þat is croked;
þarmyd þu clechest euer among,
And þat is on of þine song.
Ac þu þretest to myne vleysse,
Mid þine cleures woldest me [m]eysse.
85 þe were icundere to one frogge
þat sit at [m]ulne vnder cogge:

61. *vnMilde.*   62. *Muwe.*   84. *Meysse.*   86. *Mulne.*

81. *oft ꝺ longe* (J. *euer among*). The C. reading is to be preferred for reasons of rhyme, *songe* (d. pl.) being required in the following line.

85. Trans. "a frog would be more suitable (natural) to thee for food." Kenyon (*J.E.G.P.* XII. 576) suggests the possibility of taking *þe* as rel. pro. and reading "thou wouldst crush me with thy claws which were more suitable for a frog." Better sense is however obtained by the translation given above: and besides, the construction is closely parallel to other impersonal forms found frequently in the poem, in which cases the *to* understood in the dative of the pronoun is repeated before the following noun: cf. *Ov nas neuer icunde þarto*, l. 114; *ne lust him nu to none unrede*, l. 212; *vor me is lof to Cristes huse*, l. 609.

[86.] *mulne.* The mill, found on every large manor in the 12th and 13th centuries, played an important part in the life of the time, cf. l. 778.

cogge. The "cogge of a mylle" is glossed in *Promp. Parv.* 85 = *scarioballum* (see *N.E.D. cog*): and *scariobala* is defined (D. P. Carpentier, *Glossarium*

snailes, mus, ꝛ fule wiȝte,
boþ þine cunde ꝛ þine riȝte.
þu sittest adai˙ꝛ fliȝ[s]t aniȝt,
90 þu cuþest þat þu art on vnwiȝt.
þu art lodlich ꝛ unclene,
bi þine neste ich hit mene,
ꝛ ek bi þine fule brode,
þu fedest on hom a wel ful fode.
95 Vel wostu þat hi doþ þarinne,
hi fuleþ hit up to þe chinne:
ho sitteþ þar so hi bo bisne.
þarbi men segget a uorbisne:
"Dahet habbe þat ilke best
100 þat fuleþ his owe nest."
þat oþer ȝer a faukun bredde;
his nest noȝt wel he ne bihedde:
þarto þu stele in o dai,
ꝛ leidest þaron þi fole ey.   Fol. 233 v. col. 2.
105 þo hit bicom þat he haȝte,
ꝛ of his eyre briddes wraȝte;
ho broȝte his briddes mete,
bihold his nest, iseȝ hi ete:

89. *fliȝt*, *s* written before *ȝ* and then erased.   99. *da het.*   106. The *wen* undotted in *wraȝte* looks like *y*.

Novum, Paris, 1766) as "quidam fusi sive nodi fixi in rota inferiori qui movent fusum molendini. Gallice, les nous de la roe" (Gloss. Lat.-Gall. ex Cod. reg. 7679). The reference is therefore to the projections (cogs) on the lower wheel of a mill which turns the upper wheel and hence the mill-stones.

88. Trans. "are thy natural and proper food. (lit. are [suitable] to thy nature and thy deserts (*riȝte*)."

99. *Dahet* (J. *dehaet*) < O.Fr. *dahet* (misfortune, bad luck). The word is not uncommon in M.E. and is derived originally from Merovingian Fr. **deu hat* (God's hate). According to Gaston Paris (*Romania* (1889) 469) a distinction has to be made between the sb. *dahet* and the somewhat similar word *daþeit* which is really a sb. + a vb. = O.Fr. *dahet ait* (May he receive God's curse), cf. *Daþeit hwo it hire yeue* (*Hav.* 300), *dait þat him wolde bymene* (*Metr. Jul.* 202). In the present instance the verbal form correctly follows so that *dahet habbe* = O.Fr. *dahet ait*. In ll. 1169, 1561, however, where the expression recurs, the verb *habbe* is omitted and the form *dahet* seems to have been confused with *daþeit* (see *N.E.D. dahet*).

99-100. This proverb occurs in the version of the "Owl and Falcon" fable found in the Latin translation (1350—1400) of Bozon's *Contes Moralisés*, viz. "hyt ys a fowle brydde that fylyth hys owne neste" (see Appendix III.). Later instances are found in Skelton, *Poems against Garnesche* (1520):

olde proverbys say
That byrd ys nat honest
That fylyth hys owne neste,

Snayles, [m]us, and fule wihte,
Beoþ þine cunde ꞇ þine rihte.
Þu sittest aday, and flyhst aniht,
90   Þu cuþest þat þu art on vnwiht.
Þu art lodlich and vnclene,
Bi þine neste ich hit mene,
And ek bi þine fule brode,
Þu vedest on heom a wel ful vode.
95   Wel wostu þat hi doþ þar-ynne,
Hi fuleþ hit vp to þe chynne:
Heo sytteþ þar so hi beo bysne.
Hwarbi men seggeþ a vorbysne:
"Dehaet habbe þat ilke best   Fol. 229 v. col. 2.
100 Þat fuleþ his owe nest."
Þot oþer yer a faukun bredde:
His nest nowiht wel he ne bihedde:
Þarto þu stele in o day,
ꞇ leydest þaron þi fule ey.
105 Þo hit bycom þat he hayhte,
ꞇ of his eyre briddes wrauhte;
Heo brouhte his briddes mete,
Biheold his nest, iseyh hi ete:

---

87. *Mus.*

---

also in the *Proverbs of Heywood* (1546), "the foul bird that fyled his own nest," and in Lodge's *Rosalind*, "Is it not a foule bird that defiles his own nest"; cf. also Ray's *Proverbs* (p. 79), "it's an ill bird that bewrays its own nest," and Shakespeare, *As You Like It*, IV. i. 216. French forms of the proverb are also found, e.g. "Malvais est li oisels qui son niu conchie," or,
"Cel oysel ait mal encombrer
Que foule soun demeine ny"
(in an Anglo-Norm. *dit*, see *Romania*, XV. 318, v. 147): while in Latin it runs "Est avis ingrata quae defoedat sua strata."
101-38. For a detailed treatment of the origin and form of this "Owl and Falcon" fable see Intro. § 8, p. lxiii, and Appendix III.
103. *stele.* The final *e* of the O.E. pret. 2 sg. (cf. *stǣle*) is consistently retained throughout the poem: cf. *bede* (l. 550), *come* (l. 1058). For the significance of the deceit implied on the part of the Owl, see Intro. § 7.
106. *eyre*=d. pl. of *ey* (l. 104). For the *r* in the plural forms of this word (O.E. *ǣg*) see Sievers § 290.
wraȝte (J. *wrauhte*). St. and Wr. both read *yraȝte* (taking the þ (wen) of the MS. for *y*), a form which is adopted in *N.E.D.* (see *hatch*). W. and G. describe *wraȝte* as pt. 3 sg. of *wurchen* (O.E. *wyrcean*): whereas the form=*wreahte* < L.O.E. *wreccean*, variant of *weccean* (arouse, awake), see Sievers § 407, a 9. That the J.-text has been modernised is suggested by the rhyme *hayhte* : *wrauhte*, which cannot represent the original (see Intro. § 3, p. xxviii.).

      he iseȝ bi one halue
110   his nest ifuled uthalue.
      Þe faucun was wroþ wit his bridde,
      ꝛ lude ȝal ꝛ sterne chidde:
      "Segget me, wo hauet þis ido?
      Ov nas neuer icunde þarto:
115   hit was idon ov a loþ[e] [cu]ste.
      Segge[þ] me ȝif ȝe hit wiste."
      Þo quaþ þat on ꝛ quad þat oþer:
      "Iwis it was ure oȝer broþer,
      þe ȝond þat haue[þ] þat grete heued:
120   wai þat hi[t] nis þarof bireued!
      Worp hit ut mid þe alre-[vu]rste
      þat his necke him to-berste!"
      Þe faucun ilefde his bridde,
      ꝛ nom þat fule brid amidde,
125   ꝛ warp hit of þan wilde bowe,
      þar pie ꝛ crowe hit todrowe.
      Herbi men segget a bispel,
      þeȝ hit ne bo fuliche spel;
      al so hit is bi þan ungode
130   þat is icumen of fule brode,

115. *loþ wiste.*   116. *Segge.*   119. *haued.*   120. *hi nis* with erasure
      between *i* and *n*.   121. *-wrste.*   127. *abi spel.*

---

114. Trans. "You were never wont to do this (this was not natural to you)."
The construction is an impersonal one, cf. l. 85 (note).
115. *custe* (C. *a loþ wiste*, J. *a loþe custe*). Here J. supplies the better
reading: the C. reading is probably accounted for by the fact that *wiste* in
l. 116 caught the eye of the scribe while copying.
116. *seggeþ* (C. *segge*, J. *seggeþ*). The imper. pl. form is needed here: cf.
segget (l. 113).
wiste. Morsbach suggests *wuste* on the ground that *i* and *ü* forms do not
give a good rhyme (Morsbach § 133, a 3): cf. however *wite : utschute* (ll. 1467–8),
oftigge : bugge (ll. 1505–6).
118. *oȝer* (J. *owe*). The C.-form "is probably influenced by neighbouring
[r]-sounds" (W.).
Falcons, hawks and owls are related in the common possession of hooked
bills, strong talons, strong wings and preying habits.
119. This line is a literal translation of a phrase which occurs in two separate
versions of the "Owl and Falcon" fable: cf. *Rom. Trev.* "frater noster ille cum
magno capite solus hoc fecerit": and John of Sheppey, *Fabulae*, "iste est
cum magno capite, ostenso filio Busardi" (where the passage also points to a
confusion between Owl and Buzzard), see Appendix III. For the bearing of

He iseyh bi one halue
110 His nest ifuled in þe vt halue.
þe faukun wes wroþ wiþ his bridde,
ꝛ lude yal and sturne chidde;
"Seggeþ me hwo haueþ þis ido?
Eu nas neuer icunde þerto:
115 Hit wes idon eu a loþe custe.
Seggeþ me if ye hit wiste."
þo queþ þat on and queþ þat oþer:
"Iwis hit wes vre owe broþer,
þat yeonde þat haueþ þat grete heued:
120 Way þat he nys þarof byreued!
Werp hit vt myd þe vyrste
þet his nekke him toberste!"
þe faukun leuede his ibridde,
ꝛ nom þat fule brid amydde,
125 ꝛ warp hym of þan wilde bowe,
þat pie and crowe hit todrowe.
þerby men seggeþ a byspel,
þeyh hit ne beo fulliche spel;
Al so hit is bi þan vngode
130 þat is icumen of fule brode,

this line upon the source from which the poet drew his account of the fable, see Intro. § 8, p. lxiv.

ӡond (J. *yeonde*) < O.E. *geon* (yon), see Sievers § 338, a 6. The final *d* is either excrescent or due to analogy with the O.E. adv. and prep. *geond*.

121. *alre-vurste* (C. *alre-wrste*, J. *vyrste*). The C.-text here gives the better reading as regards both metre and sense. The phrase may be taken to mean "first of all": *wrste* (MS. reading) = *vurste*, cf. *wl* = *vul* (l. 31). W. however takes *wrste* as = *wurste* (worst) and is followed by G. who reads *worste*: but the reading thus obtained, viz. "Cast it out among the worst of all," can scarcely be regarded as satisfactory. The form *alre-fyrst* is previously found in *A.S. Chron.* 1135: *Alrefyrst Balduin de Reduers* etc., while the idiom *mid þe furste* occurs elsewhere in M.E., e.g. *mid þe furste he* (a)*manseþ me* (*Beket*, 1942, Percy Soc. xix.); *schenk us mid þe furste* (*Horn*, 1154).

121–2. These details are peculiar to the versions of the fable given by Odo of Cheriton and John of Sheppey. In the former the statement is as follows: "accipiter cepit filium Buzardi et extra nidum proiecit"; in the latter it runs: "per capud arripiens proiecit extra nidum." See Intro. § 8, p. lxiv, and note l. 119.

125. *wilde bowe*. See additional notes, p. 202.

127. *a bispel* = "a parable." W. suggests that the construction here is similar to *a-bisemar* = "in scorn" (l. 148), where *a-* = "in": but the cases are not parallel and the word *hit* (l. 128) requires an antecedent sb. in this line, i.e. a *bispel*.

128. *fuliche spel* (J. *fulliche*) = "(not) a complete story" (i.e. the analogy is incomplete). W. reads *fuliche* as an adv.

ꝑ is meind wit fro monne,

euer he cuþ þat he com þonne,

þat he com of þan adel-eye,

þeȝ he a fro nest[e] leie.

135 þeȝ appel trendli fro[m] þon trowe,

þar he ꝑ oþer mid growe,

þeȝ he bo þar-from bicume,

he cuþ wel whonene he is icume."   Fol. 234 r. col. 1.

Þos word aȝaf þe niȝtingale,

140 ꝑ after þare longe tale

he song so lude ꝑ so scharpe,

riȝt so me grulde schille harpe.

Þos hule luste þiderward,

ꝑ hold hire eȝe noþerwa[r]d,

145 ꝑ sat tosvolle ꝑ ibolwe,

also ho hadde one frogge isuolȝe:

for ho wel wiste ꝑ was iwar

þat ho song hire a-bisemar.

ꝑ noþeles ho ȝa[f] andsuare,

150 "Whi neltu flon into þe bare,

---

134. *nest.* 135. *fron.* 144. *-wad.* 149. *ȝas*, with *f* in margin.

135–8. This proverb occurs in an A.-N. form in the version of the fable due to Marie of France:

> Pur ceo dit hum en repruvier
> de la pume del dulz pumier,
> s'ele chiet sur un fust amer,
> ja ne savra tant ruëler
> qu'al mordre ne seit cuneüe,
> desur quel arbre ele est creüe.
>
> De accipitre et noctua (ll. 33–8)

also in an English form in the version due to Bozon, viz.: "Trendle the appel nevere so fer, he conyes fro what tree he cam" (*Les Contes Moralisés* p. 23); and in the Latin translation of that version as: "Trendul an appull never so ferr, hyt wyll be know fro wheyne he comyth" (*Les Contes Moralisés*, p. 205). See Appendix III.

Elsewhere the proverb is found as a Latin-English "sentence," written at the back of Aelfric's *Glossary* (MS. Cott. Faust. A IX. Brit. Mus.), and quoted by Zupitza in *Ang.* I. 285. The "sentence," which occurs in a later form in *Guy of Warwick*, ll. 1301–3 (ed. Zupitza), runs as follows:

> Pomum licet ab arbore (MS. igitur unde?) reuoluitur tamen prodit (MS. prouidit) unde nascitur.
> Se æppel næfre þæs feorr ne trendleð (MS. trenddeð), he cyð hwanon he com.

The fact that the forms *trendli* (O. & N.), *trendle, trendul* (Bozon) occur in the proverb as quoted above, establishes beyond all doubt Zupitza's conjecture of *trendleð* (O.E. (ā)*trendlian*) in place of the MS. reading *trenddeð*

ꝧ is ymeynd wiþ freo monne,

Euer he cuþ þat he com þenne,

þat he com of þan adel-eye,   Fol. 230 r. col. 1.

þeyh he a freo neste leye.

135 þeyh appel trendli from þe treo,

þar he and oþer myde grewe,

þeyh he beo þar-from bicume,

He cuþ hwenene he is icume."

þeos word ayaf þe nihtegale,

140 And after þare longe tale

Heo song so lude ꝧ so scharpe,

Ryht so me *grulde* schille harpe.

þeos vle luste þider-ward,

ꝧ heold hire eyen neþer-ward,

145 ꝧ sat toswolle ꝧ tobolewe,

So heo hedde one frogge iswolwe:

For heo wel wiste ꝧ was iwar

þat heo song hire a-bysemar.

ꝧ naþeles heo yaf ondsware,

150 "Hwy neltu fleon in-to [þe] bare,

150. *to bare.*

(cf. also *Guy of Warwick*, ed. Zupitza, l. 3712, " þe hedde trendild on þe borde "), in spite of Napier's defence of the MS. reading on the ground that an O.E. **trendan* might be inferred from *sintrendende* and *fortrendon*, quoted in his *O.E. Glosses* (114), (see *Athenæum*, June 17, 1905, p. 758).

For a similar proverbial utterance see Wright, *Political Songs* (Camd. Soc. 1839), p. 15, l. 2: "Et radici consonat pomum in sapore" (the flavour of the apple depends on the root from whence it sprang).

140. *tale*, the technical term (Lat. *narratio*, Fr. *conte*) for the charge made by the plaintiff in a contemporary lawsuit. From Fr. *conte* is derived the Mod. Eng. "count" (charge in an indictment), see Pollock and Maitland, *History of English Law*, II. 605.

148. *a-bisemar* = "in mockery," cf. *a-bisemere* (l. 1311). The dat. usually ends in *e*: but an O.E. dat. without inflexion is found, cf. *on his bismer* = "in mockery of him" (see B.T. under *bismer*). The *-ar* (O.E. *-er*) is due to exigencies of rhyme.

150. *neltu*. In E.W.S. forms in *y* (*nylle*, etc.) are more common, but in L.W.S. *e*-forms (*nelle*, etc.) prevail. See Sievers § 428, a 2.

There is a reference here to the ordeal by battle or judicial combat which was introduced by the Normans and remained in force until 1219. It had already been condemned as a mode of judgment at the Lateran Council of 1215: but previous to this, it had been viewed by the clergy with marked disfavour, and this attitude, characteristic of the opening years of the 13th century, is reflected in this passage where the Nightingale refuses to accept the ordeal. The allusion would therefore seem to suggest 1200—1215 as the approximate date of the poem.

ꝥ sewi [w]are unk*er* bo
of briȝt*er* howe, of uairur blo?"
"No, þu hauest wel scharpe clawe,
ne kepich noȝt þat þu me clawe.

155 þu hauest cliuers suþe stronge,
þu tuengst þar-mid so doþ a tonge.
Þu poȝtest, so doþ þine ilike,
mid faire worde me biswike.
Ich nolde don þat þu me raddest,

160 ich wiste wel þat þu me misraddest.
Schamie þe for þin unrede!
Vnwroȝen is þi svikelhede!
Schild þine svikeldom vram þe liȝte,
ꝥ hud þat woȝe amon[g] þe riȝte.

165 þane þu wilt þin unriȝt spene,
loke þat hit ne bo isene:
vor svikedom haue[þ] schome ꝥ hete,
ȝif hit is ope ꝥ underȝete.
Ne speddestu noȝt mid þine unwrenche,

170 for ich am war ꝥ can wel blenche.
Ne helpþ noȝt þat þu bo to [þ]riste:
ich wolde viȝte bet mid liste   Fol. 234 r. col. 2.

151. *þare.*   164. *amon.*   167. *haued.*   171. *wriste* (see note *suþe*, l. 2).

---

151. *ware* (J. *hweþer*) < O.E. *hwæþer*, "which of two." Sk. reads *wheþer*,
G. *hweþer*; but other instances of the contracted form are found, cf. Str.-Br.
whær (*Laȝ* 20877), *wer* (*R. of Gl.* ed. Hearne, p. 352).
154. *ne kepich noȝt* = "and I do not wish." For a similar use of *kepen*
(O.E. *cēpan*), cf. *he dysigra manna herunga cepþ* (desires). See B.T. under
cēpan. The double negative in the line stands for "not."
157. *ilike* (J. *ilyche*). Here the J. scribe has clearly altered his original
and has spoilt the rhyme (with *biswike*) in so doing.
162. *Vnwroȝen* (J. *Vnwryen*). The C. and J. variants represent O.E.
-wrogen and *-wrigen* respectively. See Sievers § 383.
   svikelhede = "deceit." The M.E. abstract suffix *-hede* (L.O.E. *-hed*) by the
side of M.E. *-hode* (O.E. *-hād*), has not yet been satisfactorily explained.
It was first used with adjectives (cf. *druncenhed*, *A.S. Chron.* 1070) at
a later date with substantives (cf. Mod. Eng. "Godhead"). In the *O. & N.*
it occurs only with adj. forms: cf. *boldhede* (l. 514), *fairhede* (l. 581), *wrechede*
(l. 1219), *sikerhede* (l. 1265).
165. *þane* (J. *hwanne*) = "when." Str. reads *hwanne*, Sk. *þane*, W. and G.
wane. But in spite of the J. reading, which is probably modernised, it is
safer to retain the C.-form *þane* < O.E. *þanne* which was commonly used in
O.E. in a relative sense (= when), cf. ll. 453, 463, etc. for similar instances.
The form *þane*, in this relative sense, was probably becoming archaic at the
date of the poem, for the alternative *wane* is also frequently found in C. (cf.

And schewi hweþer vnker beo
Of brihter hewe, of fayrur bleo?"
"No, þu hauest scharpe clawe,
Ne kepe ich noht þat þu me clawe.

155 Þu hauest clyures swiþe stronge,
Þu twengest þar-mid so doþ a tonge.
Þu þoutest, so doþ þine ilyche,
Mid fayre worde me biswike.
Ich nolde don þat þu me raddest,

160 Ich wiste wel þat þu me misraddest.
Schomye þe vor þine vnrede!
Vnwryen is þi swikehede!
Schild þi swike-dom from þe lyhte,
And hud þat wowe among þe ryhte.

165 Hwanne þu wilt vnriht spene,
Loke þat hit ne beo isene:
Vor swikedom haueþ schome and hete,　　　Fol. 230 r. col. 2.
If hit is ope and vnder-yete.
Ne spedestu nouht mid þin vnwrenche,

170 For ich am war and can blenche.
Ne helpeþ noht þat þu bo to þriste:
Ich wolde vyhte bet myd liste

---

ll. 455, 459, etc.), while the *hw-* form appears regularly in all those places in J.

spene (spend, perform). Pabst (*Ang.* XIII. 227 § 40) explains *spēne* as = *spēnde* (O.E. *spendan* with lengthened *e*) and as being due to analogy with M.E. *wēne*, *wēnde* (O.E. *wēnan*, *wēnde*)—an explanation apparently accepted by Morsbach (see Morsbach § 58, a 1). More probably however what we have in *spene* is a new infin. based on the pr. ind. 3 sg. form *spenð*, *speneð* (cf. ll. 362, 1525), from which an O.E. *d*, being the medial of three consonants (*spendð*), is consequently dropped (see Napier, *O.E. Glosses*, XXXIX. § 8). The form without *d* is not uncommon in M.E.: and for similar formations of new M.E. infinitives from pr. indic. 3 sg. forms cf. *lie(n) < liþ : seie(n) < seiþ*, *segeþ*, etc.

The form *spene* is however capable of another explanation: it may have been due to a fairly common process by which final *d* was lost after *n*. The process was not confined to verbal forms (cf. *an* (for *and*), frequently in *O. & N.*). At a later date the omission of *d* became yet more common: cf. L.M.E. *sene* (for *senden*), *lan* (for *land*), *blyn* (for *blynd*): while it is especially characteristic of the S.W. dialects of Mod. Eng., see Wright, *Eng. Dial. Gram.* § 307, and also Barnes' *Poems*, where the forms *win'*, *groun'*, *roun'*, *han'*, etc. are found.

166. *isene < O.E. gesīene* (adj.) = "visible." W. incorrectly describes it as a p. p. of *iseo* (O.E. *gesēon*, to see), for which however it is sometimes used: see Sievers § 391, a 7.

A.　　　　　　　　　　　　　　　　　　　　　　　　2

þan þu mid al þine strengþe.
Ich habbe, on brede ꝥ eck on lengþe,
175   castel god on mine rise:
"Wel fiȝt þat wel fliȝt," seiþ þe wise.
Ac lete we awei þos cheste,
vor suiche wordes boþ unw[re]ste;
ꝥ fo we on mid riȝte dome,
180   mid faire worde ꝥ mid ysome.
þeȝ we ne bo at one acorde,
we m[a]ȝe bet mid fayre worde,
witute cheste, ꝥ bute fiȝte,
plaidi mid foȝe ꝥ mid riȝte:
185   ꝥ mai hure eiþer wat h[e] wile
mid riȝte segge ꝥ mid sckile."
    þo quaþ þe hule "[W]u schal us seme,
þat kunne ꝥ wille riȝt us deme?"
    "Ich wot wel" quaþ þe niȝtingale,
190   "Ne þaref þarof bo no tale.
Maister Nichole of Guldeforde,
he is wis an war of worde:
he is of dome suþe gleu,
ꝥ him is loþ eurich unþeu.

174. *eck*, h altered into *k*, cf. *sckile* (186).   178. *-werste*.
        182. *muȝe*.   185. *hi*.   187. *þu*.

176. This proverb occurs in the *Proverbs of Hending*, 77, *Wel fyht þat wel flyhþ*; in *Li Proverbe au Vilain*, no. 64, *Mieuz vaut bone fuie que mauvaise atente*, and in the *Gesta Romanorum*, LVII. 420, "It is an olde sawe, He feghtith wele that fleith faste": cf. also Chaucer, *Parl. of F.* (140), "Theschewing is only the remedye," and Butler, *Hudibras*, III. 3. 243:
        For those that fly may fight again
        Which he can never do that's slain.
177. *lete we awei*="let us refrain from," cf. also l. 250. The idiom is found in O.E. *aweg lǣtan*: cf. *Alis*, 29, *Now pais holdith and leteth cheste*.
180. *ysome* (J. *some*). Str. and Wr. read *ylome*, confusing the symbols *l* and long *s*. The C.-reading *ysome* (O.E. *gesōm*, friendly) is preferable to the J.-reading *som* (O.E. *sōm*, harmony, concord) on metrical grounds, while the adj. form occurs again in ll. 1522, 1735. Nor does the reading "with fair words and friendly" offer any syntactical difficulty. The idiom occurs in O.E., cf. *hi habbaþ swyþe lytle scypa and swyþe leohte* (*Orosius*, ed. Sweet, p. 19, E.E.T.S. 79): see also Kenyon, *J.E.G.P.* XII. 576.
182. *maȝe* (C. *muȝe*, J. *mawe*). Earlier editors all read *muȝe*: but the *u*-form (*muȝe*) in this poem is used for the opt. (see note l. 62), and since the indic. is employed here, the *a*-form (preserved in J. *mawe*) is to be preferred.
184. *foȝe* (J. *soþe*)="order, decency." The J. scribe, evidently unfamiliar with *foȝe*, has altered it to *soþe*. No O.E. equivalent has yet been found: cf.

þan þu mid al þine strengþe.

Ich habbe, on brede ⁊ ek on lengþe,

175 Castel god on myne ryse:

"Wel fyht þat wel flyhþ," seyþ þe wise.

Ac lete [we] awey þeos cheste,

For suche wordes beoþ vnwreste:

And fo we on myd rihte dome,

180 Mid fayre worde ⁊ myd some.

þeyh we ne beon at one acorde,

We mawe bet myd fayre worde,

Wiþvte cheste, and bute vyhte,

Playde mid soþe ⁊ mid ryhte:

185 ⁊ may vr eyþer hwat he wile

Mid rihte segge ⁊ myd skile."

þo quaþ þe vle, "Hwo schal vs seme,

þat cunne ⁊ wille riht vs deme?"

"Ich wot wel" quaþ þe nyhtegale,

190 "Ne þarf þerof beo no tale.

Mayster Nichol of Guldeuorde,

He is wis and war of worde:

He is of worde swyþe glev,

And him is loþ eurich vnþeu.

177. *lete awey.*

---

however M.H.G. *vuoc*, Mod. Germ. *fug*, Sw. *fog*. In O.E. a form *gefōg* occurs = "a joining," whence, in a secondary sense, the idea of "fitness." The word also survives in certain Mod. Eng. dialects (Notts, Yorks), as *fog* = "first in order." Boys in those districts are said to claim precedence in their games by calling out "foggie" (see *E.D.D.*).

190. *þaref* (J. *þarf*) = "need" (vb). For similar instances of the insertion of *e* after *r*, cf. *mureʒþe* (l. 355), *areʒþe* (l. 404), *bareʒ* (l. 408). The insertion was probably due to French scribal influence, the *r* being more strongly trilled in English than in French words (see Skeat, *Trans. Phil. Soc.* 1897).

191. *Maister Nichole of Guldeforde.* The full designation of Nicholas is not without its interest, pointing as it does to certain changes characteristic of the 11th and 12th centuries. Under Norman influence the single personal names of the O.E. period had become supplemented by surnames denoting, amongst other things, place of birth. Thus in the later sections of the *A.S. Chron.* such names as Rotbert de Bælesne (1104), Willelm of Curboil (1123), Hugo of Mundford (1123) are found. The addition of *Maister*, moreover, conveyed the notion of academic status. Rashdall (*Universities of Europe in Mid. Ages*, I. 291-2) refers to "the enormous multiplication of Masters" in the 12th century, and mentions "the custom which grew up in the course of this century of prefixing the title of 'Master' as an honourable designation."

For the claims of Nicholas to the authorship of the poem see Intro. § 5, pp. xli ff.

195　He wot insiȝt in eche songe,

wo singet wel, wo singet wronge:

Ꞇ he can schede vrom þe riȝte

þat woȝe, þat þuster from þe liȝte."

þo hule one wile hi biþoȝte,

200　Ꞇ after þan þis word upbroȝte:

"Ich granti wel þat he us deme,

vor þeȝ he were wile breme,

Ꞇ lof him were niȝtingale,

Ꞇ oþer wiȝte gente Ꞇ smale,

205　ich wot he is nu suþe acoled.

Nis he vor þe noȝt afoled,　　　　　　Fol. 234 v. col. 1.

þat he, for þine olde luue,

me adun legge Ꞇ þe buue:

ne schaltu neure so him queme,

210　þat he for þe fals dom deme.

He is him ripe Ꞇ fast-rede,

ne lust him nu to none unrede:

nu him ne lust na more pleie,

he wile gon a riȝte weie."

215　þe niȝtingale was al ȝare,

ho hadde ilorned wel aiware:

"Hule," ho sede, "seie me soþ,

wi dostu þat unwiȝtis doþ?

þu singist aniȝt Ꞇ noȝt adai,

220　Ꞇ al þi song is wailawai.

207. *loue*; *u* above *o*; *o* deleted.

199. *biþoȝte* (J. *bihouhte*) = "bethought (herself), i.e. pondered." The J. reading is probably a scribal error since *h* and *þ* are confused elsewhere by the scribes (see Intro. § 3 (*d*) (*β*)). It is unlikely (as W. seems to suggest) that *bihouhte* is the pt. form of O.E. *behycgan*, *behogian*: the form required would be *bihoȝode*.

201. *granti* (J. *graunti*). The J. form occurs in one place in C. (l. 745): but *granti* is the usual spelling before 1250, the *u* (denoting O.Fr. nasal quality) being inserted after that date.

203–4. The reference here may well be to the light love-verses which many sober scholars of the age deplored as lapses of their youth. To Hilarius, for instance, is attributed a Latin love-lyric addressed to an English maiden named Rose: while *nugae amatoriae* of the same kind are claimed by Henry of Huntingdon, Abelard, Peter of Blois and other learned Latinists (see Schofield, *Eng. Lit.* p. 67).

204. *wiȝte* = O.E. *wihte*, fem. pl.; cf. however *wiȝtes*, l. 431; *unwiȝtis*, l. 218.

205. *nu suþe* (J. *nu þe*). W. suggests that the J. reading points to the

195 He wot insyht in euche songe,
Hwo singeþ wel, hwo singeþ wronge:
And he con schede from þe rihte
þat wowe, þat þuster from þe lyhte."
þe vle one hwile hi bihouhte
200 And after þan þis word upbrouhte:
"Ich graunti wel þat he vs deme,   Fol. 230 v. col. 1.
For þeyh he were hwile breme,
⁊ leof hym w[e]re Nihtingale,
And oþer wyhte gent ⁊ smale,
205 Ich wot he is nu [su]þe acoled.
Nis he vor þe nouht afoled,
þat he, vor þine olde luue,
Me adun legge ⁊ þe abuue:
N[e] schaltu neuer so him queme,
210 þat he for þe fals dom deme.
He is nv ripe ⁊ fastrede,
Ne luste hym nv to non vnrede:
Nv him ne lust namore pleye,
He wile gon a rihte weye."
215   þe Nihtegale wes al ware,
Heo hedde ileorned wel ihware:
"Vle," heo seyde "seye me soþ,
Hwi dostu þat vnwihtes doþ?
þu singest anyht ⁊ nouht aday,
220 And al þi song is waylaway.

205. *nu þe.*   209. *N.*

---

presence of *suþe* in the common original, as was probably the case, the scribal error in J. being an instance of haplography (see Intro. § 3 (*d*) ii).
210. *fals dom* = "false judgment": legal term. The complaint of "false judgment" was the method by which a judgment given by an inferior court could be questioned. See Pollock and Maitland, *Hist. of Eng. Law*, II. 666.
211. *him* (J. *nu*). W. regards *nu* as the more probable reading and suggests that the scribe's eye may have fallen on *him* in the following line. On the other hand, *him* gives a good reading, for, as H. points out, "the dative pronoun mostly in the 3rd pers. is used with intrans. verbs to reinforce the subject" (see H. p. 279).
215. *ȝare* (J. *ware*). The J. scribe (with one exception, l. 1222) consistently reads *ware*, *vare*, in place of *ȝare* (C.), as if the latter form was becoming unfamiliar and archaic.
220. For the bearing of this passage on the theme of the poem see Intro. § 7, p. lvii: cf. also l. 412.

þu miȝt mid þine songe afere
alle þat ihereþ þine ibere:
þu sch[ri]chest ꞇ ȝollest to þine fere,
þat hit is grislich to ihere:

225 hit þinche[þ] boþe wise ꞇ snepe
noȝt þat þu singe, ac þat þu wepe.
þu fliȝst aniȝt ꞇ noȝt adai:
þarof ich w[u]ndri ꞇ wel mai.
vor eurich þing þat schuniet riȝt,

230 hit luueþ þuster ꞇ hatiet liȝt:
ꞇ eurich þing þat is lof misdede,
hit luueþ þuster to his dede.
A wis word, þeȝ hit bo unclene,
is fele manne a-muþe imene,

235 for Alured King hit seide ꞇ wrot:
"He schunet þat hine [vu]l wot."
Ich wene þat þu dost also,
vor þu fliȝst niȝtes euer mo.
An oþer þing me is a-wene,

240 þu hauest aniȝt wel briȝte sene;   Fol. 234 v. col. 2.
bi daie þu art stare-blind,
þat þu ne sichst ne bov ne strind.

---

223. *schirchest.*   225. *þinchest.*   228. *wndri.*   236. *schunet*, insertion of *t* or *i* after *n*, probably by later hand: *wl.*   242. *bos, s* deleted, *v* above *s* : *strind, st* deleted.

221–4. W. (note l. 1) erroneously describes these four lines as a quatrain with one rhyming sound. But the rhyming vowel in the first couplet is [ę̄], while in the second it is [ę̆].

222. *ibere* = "outcry, voice" (< O.E. *gebǣru*). W. glosses this word, here and elsewhere, as "behaviour"; but this is hardly likely in view of the word *ihereþ*. See also ll. 925, 1348.

223. *ȝollest* (J. *yollest*). The verb *ȝolle* (cf. l. 972) is probably derived from O.E. **geollan* variant of *giellan* (yell): cf. O.E. *gierran* alongside **georran* (see Sievers § 388, a 1).

225. Trans. "It seemeth both to the wise and to the foolish (i.e. to all) that thou dost not sing but weep." For similar constructions in which the preposition is wanting cf. *Ich am loþ smale foȝle* (l. 277), also l. 910.

snepe = W.S. *snǣp*, Angl. *snēp*, cf. O.N. *snāpr*, "stupid." The word "sneep" is also found in the Mod. Lincs. dial. meaning "foolish" (see *E.D.D.*). The rhyme *snepe : wepe* must however be regarded as faulty (i.e. [ę̄] : [ę̆]) unless the Anglian form (*snēp*) is to be assumed here.

226. *ac þat* (J. *at*). The J. scribe has evidently read *at* for *ac*, confusing *c* and *t* in his original, and then omitted the following *þat*—another instance of haplography.

227. The traditional reason why the Owl does not fly by day is supplied by one of the *Narrationes* of Odo of Cheriton, according to which the birds

Þu miht mid þine songe afere
Alle þat hereþ þine ibere:
Þ[u] scrichest ꝥ yollest to þine fere,
þat hit is gryslich to ihere:
225 Hit þincheþ boþe wise ꝥ snepe
Nouht þat þu singe [ac þat] þu wepe.
Þu flyhst anyht and noht aday:
Þarof ich wundri ꝥ wel may.
For vych þing þat schonyeþ riht,
230 Hit luuyeþ þuster ꝥ hateþ lyht;
ꝥ euych þing þat luueþ misdede,
Hit luueþ þuster to his dede.
A wis word, þeyh hit beo vnclene,
Is fele monne a-muþe imene,
235 For Alured King hit seyde ꝥ wrot: Fol. 230 v. col. 2.
"He schuneþ þat hine ful wot."
Ich wene þat þu dost al so,
For þu flyhst nyhtes euer mo.
[An] oþer þing me is a-wene,
240 Þu hauest anyht wel bryhte sene:
Bi daye þu art stare-blynd,
Þat þu ne syst bouh of lynd.

223. *þ.*   226. *singe at þu.*   239. *ꝥ.*

---

in council discuss as to whom they are to give the rose they have found. The Owl puts forward his claims and is laughed at: but the final decision is postponed. Meanwhile (the narrative goes on), "in nocte clare uidet Bubo, et aliis auibus dormientibus, rosam furata est. Quo comperto, mane dederunt aues sentenciam quod Bubo nunquam uolaret de die, nec inter alias aues habitaret, et in tenebris clarius uideret et si die appareret omnes aues ipsum clamore et lesione infestarent" (*Narrationes*, 55, *De Rosa et Volatilibus*: see Hervieux, *Les Fab. lat.* IV. 226).

231. *is lof* (J. *luueþ*). Trans. "Everything that loves evil-doing" (i.e. to which evil-doing is dear), cf. ll. 281, 609.

236. Trans. "a man (he) shuns that which knows him to be foul."

241. *stare-blind* = "blind." W. takes it to mean "purblind, partly blind." The word occurs in O.E. *stærblind*, O.Fris. *stareblind*, O.H.G. *starablind*, etc. In O.E. it means both "blind" and "purblind" (see B.T.): cf. Dan. *stær-blind* (purblind), Sw. *starrblind* (quite blind). From the context in the present poem, *stareblind* is apparently synonymous with *blind* and *bisene* (l. 243) and therefore means "blind, stone-blind."

242. *sichst* (J. *syst*) = "seest," cf. *isihst* (l. 1225). The *ch* here probably represents the scribal attempt to denote the sound-value of medial *h* (*g*), cf. *A.S. Chron.* 1137, *halechen* (O.E. *halgan*). W.'s suggestion is that *-ch* may have been an error for *-eh* (*e* and *c* being easily confused) and that *siehst* (instead of *sichst*) was the reading of the original. But this is unlikely as O.E. *ie* (in O.E. *siehst*) was not preserved as *ie* at this date.

bov ne strind. A difficult passage. The original C. reading *bos ne strind* is

Adai þu art blind oþer bisne,
þarbi men segget a uorbisne:
245 "Riȝt so hit farþ bi þan ungode
þat noȝt ne suþ to none gode,
'T is so ful of vuele wrenche
þat him ne mai no man atprenche,
'T can wel þane þu[str]e wai,
250 'T þane briȝte lat awai."
So doþ þat boþ of þine cunde,
of liȝte nabbeþ hi none imunde."

Þos hule luste suþe longe,
'T was oftoned suþe stronge:
255 ho quaþ "Þu [h]attest niȝtingale,
þu miȝtest bet hoten galegale,

249. *þurste.* 255. *attest, h* added later.

---

corrected to *bov ne rind*, probably by a later scribe. J., on the other hand, has *bouh of lynd* (=a lime-tree bough) which gives good sense, though in all probability the phrase represents, as frequently in J., an attempt to get over a difficult reading in the common original, by means of substitution. What the poet actually wrote seems therefore to be best represented by C.: and in the first place, the corrected form *bov* must probably be accepted as = *bow* (bough), cf. *bowe* (l. 125). G. however reads *boȝ* (bough), writing ȝ for original *s*: a similar confusion between *s* and ȝ being found in *nuste* (MS. *nuȝte*), l. 1751. But it is not so clear that the correction of *strind* need be accepted. It is true that *ne bov ne rind* gives an intelligible reading (i.e. thou seest neither bough nor bark < O.E. *rind*): and it may be that the eye of the scribe as he was about to write the word was caught by *stare*—in the preceding line, so that he commenced with *st*—which he afterwards deleted. On the other hand the correction may have been due to a later scribe who failed to recognise a somewhat unfamiliar form : and on the whole, *strind* would seem to give better sense than *rind*. The word occurs, for instance, in *Ancren Riwle* (Titus MS. Camd. Soc.), p. 188, *strundes streamden* (streams poured down), and in *Patience*, l. 311, *þy stryvande stremeȝ of stryndeȝ so mony* (thy clashing floods of streams so many): cf. also Mod. Eng. dial. *strine, stryne* (water-channel), see *E.D.D.* Hence if *strind* be retained, as on the whole seems advisable, the passage would read "thou seest neither tree (bough) nor stream."

243. *bisne.* The exact meaning of this word is not easy to define. Str.-Br. gives it as "blind," Mätzner as "blind, dim-sighted," while W. takes it to mean "purblind," apparently on the assumption that *oþer* (=or) which preceded it, implied some sort of distinction (see also *N.E.D.*). But in a parallel quotation in the *Lindisfarne Gospels* (Matt. ix. 27), *Tuoege bisene vel blinde* (*duo caeci*), the words are clearly synonymous. Nor does the sentence (also quoted in *N.E.D.*) in *Rel. Ant.* ii. 239, *Now the bysom ledys the blynde*, give evidence as to any such distinction, in view of the Biblical phrase (Matt. xv. 14) "if the blind lead the blind" (τυφλὸς...τυφλὸν). In the passage *Quo made bisne and quo lockende* (*Gen. & Ex.* 2822) the contrast is clearly between the blind and those who see: while the word, as used by Shakespeare, "bisson rheum" (blinding tears), *Ham.* ii. ii. 529, and "bisson conspectuities" (*Cor.* ii. i. 70), affords no further information on the point. On the other hand, in

Aday þu art blynd oþer bisne,
þarby men seggeþ a vorbisne:
245 "Riht so hit farþ bi þan vngode
þat nouht ne isyhþ to none gode,
ꝗt is so ful of vuele wrenche
þat him ne may no mon aprenche,
ꝗt con wel þene þustre way,
250 ꝗt þane bryhte lat away."
So doþ þat beoþ of þine cunde,
Of lihte nabbeþ hi none imunde."
þeos vle luste swiþe longe,
ꝗt wes ofteoned swiþe stronge:
255 Heo quaþ "þu hattest Nihtegale,
þu [m]ihtest bet hote galegale,

246. *isyhþ* in different hand; see note.   256. *Mihtest.*

---

the following passage of Udall's *Para. of Erasmus* (quoted by *E.D.D.*): "Thys manne was not purblynde or a lyttle appayred and decayed in syght, but as bysome as was possible to be," the word "bysome" is clearly distinct from "purblind." And this is further suggested by two other quotations made in *E.D.D.*, viz. *Beesen, bison vel beezen, caecus, vox agro Lincoln. usitatissima*: and again "the poor owd man's aumust bisson" (Mod. Lincs. dial.). On review of all the evidence therefore, there seems to be no adequate reason for interpreting *bisne* as "purblind." The present passage is certainly not sufficient to establish any difference of meaning between *blind* and *bisne*: and in l. 366 where the substance of this line is repeated, the statement is plain. What we have therefore in l. 243 are two of the synonyms characteristic of the poem: and the use of the second synonym *bisne* is sufficiently explained by the exigencies of rhyme.

246. *suþ* (J. *isyhþ*) = "seeth." This unusual form < O.E. *syhþ, siehþ* (with omission of *h*), is possibly a Southern dial. variant of *isiþ, isihþ* (l. 407). Owing to its rarity, it seems to have puzzled the J. scribe who left a blank space in which a later hand inserted the normal *isyhþ*: cf. also *isoþ* (= *iseoþ*), l. 424 note. On the other hand it is also possible that *siiþ* may have been the original form, and that the C. reading (*u*) is but a careless reproduction of *ii* (double *i*).

Trans. "who seeth nothing to any good purpose."

248. *atprenche* (J. *aprenche*) = "deceive, escape." Str. adopts the reading *atwrenche*, on the ground that it would not have been difficult for a scribe to have read the O.E. *w* (*wen*) as *p*. But both MSS. read *p* in this word and in l. 814 *atprenche* occurs in both C. and J. No O.E. form, however, has been found to correspond to this word, though Mod. dial. *prink* = "to trim" (Nares) and Mod. Eng. *prank* go to suggest a root form *prinkan*, with secondary form *prencan*. The root idea would be "to prick" (= unnasalised form of *prink*) with the meaning "to bedeck, to make a show." Hence in all probability M.E. *prenchen* (to deceive): cf. Shak. *Winter's Tale*, ii. i. 51, "a pinch'd thing(?)"

256. *galegale* = "chatterbox," a coinage. The reduplication of the root (cf. O.E. *galan*) produces a pejorative and comic effect: cf. "sing-song."

vor þu hauest to monie tale.

Lat þine tunge habbe spale!

Þu wenest þat þes dai bo þin oȝe:

260　lat me nu habbe mine þroȝe:

bo nu stille ⁊ lat me speke,

ich wille bon of þe awreke.

⁊ lust hu ich con me bitelle,

mid riȝte soþe, witute spelle.

265　Þu seist þat ich me hude adai,

þarto ne segge ich nich ne nai:

⁊ lust ich telle þe wareuore,

al wi hit is ⁊ wareuore.

Ich habbe bile stif ⁊ stronge,

270　⁊ gode cliuers scharp ⁊ longe,

so hit bicumeþ to hauekes cunne;

hit is min hiȝte, hit is mi w[u]nne,

þat ich me draȝe to mine cunde,

ne mai [me] no man þareuore schende:　　Fol. 235 r. col. 1.

275　on me hit is wel isene,

vor riȝte cunde ich am so kene.

Vorþi ich am loþ smale foȝle

þat floþ bi grunde an bi þuuele:

272.　*wune*, see note.　　　274.　*mai no.*

---

258. *spale*. Sk. translates as "a spell, a turn of work" (cf. Du. *spelen*, to play), which is quite contrary to what one would expect from the context. Str.-Br. connects the word with M.H.G. *spale* (rung of a ladder) and O.N. *spölr* (plank), and translates it as "splinter." W. takes it to mean "splint, a cleft stick in which the tongue is caught," and translates: "let thy tongue have a splint" (i.e. be fastened and so held still). The most satisfactory explanation, however is obtained by connecting the word with O.E. *spala* (substitute), in which case the line would read "Let thy tongue have a substitute, i.e. take a rest." The form *spale* itself is rare, but the corresponding verbal form (O.E. *spelian*, to act as a substitute) is more frequently found; cf. *Orm*, 10133, *Al þat tu miht spelen*; *P. Plow.* C. xiv. 77, *spele and spare*; also the old Dorsets. dial. *speal* (to spare one and take his place), see E.D.D.

266. *nich ne nai* (J. *nyk no nay*) = "no nor nay." Str. (followed by G.) did not improve this line when he omitted *nich*. The C. reading is supported by that of J.: and while *nich* is metrically necessary it is interesting as well from the etymological point of view. Sk. reads *nich* = "not I," and translates "To that I say (not I) no nay." But a better reading is obtained by taking *nich* = "no" (O.E. *nic* = "no," cf. Sievers § 332, a 2) and translating "To that I say neither no nor nay." This use of synonyms especially in the rhyming position is characteristic of the poet (cf. l. 243), while similar phrases with M.E. *nikken* (to deny, say no) are fairly common: cf. *Sir*

Vor þu hauest to monye tale.

Let þine tunge habbe spale!

Þu wenest þat þes day beo þin owe:

260 Let me nv habbe myne þrowe:

Beo nv stille ꝛ let me speke,

Ich wile beo of þe awreke.

ꝛ lust hw ich con me bitelle,

Mid rihte soþe wiþvte spelle.

265 Þu seyst þat ich me hude aday,

Þarto ne segge ich nyk no nay:

ꝛ lust ich telle hwervore,

Al hwi hit is ꝛ hwarevore.

Ich habbe bile stif ꝛ stronge,   Fol. 231 r. col. 1.

270 ꝛ gode cleures scharp ꝛ longe,

So hit bycumeþ to hauekes cunne

Hit is myn hyhte ꝛ my [wu]nne

Þat ich me drawe to mine cunde,

Ne may me no mon þarfor sende;

275 On me hit is wel isene,

For rihte cunde ich am so kene.

Vorþi ich am loþ smale vowele

Þat fleoþ bi grunde ꝛ bi þuuele:

272. *ynne.*

Gawayne and the Grene Knight, 706, "*nikked him with nai.*" Moreover in Scott's *Abbot* (ch. 38) Adam Woodcock says "I trust you will not nick me with nay."

272. *wunne* (C. *wune,* J. *ynne*) = "delight." Str. reads *wunne,* Sk. W. and G. retain *wune.* The different readings of the two MSS. suggest some difficulty in the common original. The C.-reading *wune* in the first place does not rhyme regularly with *cunne* (l. 271), secondly it does not give the synonym with *hiȝte* that the context seems to require: while the J.-reading admits of no sense at all. Both scribes, it would seem, have made the best of an obscure reading but without success. If however we take *wnne* as the reading of the common original, all difficulties vanish. This form *wnne = wunne,* the omission of *u* after *w* being common: cf. *w*[*u*]*rs* (l. 34), *w*[*u*]*nest* (l. 589). And *wnne* is copied by the C. scribe as *wune* (confusing *n* and *u*), while the J. scribe wrote *ynne,* reading *w* as *y,* cf. *yit, yest* (l. 689).

273. *to mine cunde* = (obey the laws) "of my kind." In medieval law appeal was sometimes made to the "law of Nature" as well as to the law of the land. See Pollock and Maitland, *History of English Law,* I. 466, 514 *n.*

276. Trans. "From my very nature [it is that] I am so keen"; see note l. 273.

277 ff. For the attacks made upon the Owl by the rest of the birds, see l. 227 note, *ad fin.*

hi me bichermet ⁊ bigredeþ,

280   ⁊ hore flockes to [m]e ledeþ.

Me is lof to habbe reste

⁊ sitte stille in mine neste:

vor nere ich neuer no þe betere,

[ȝ]if ich mid chauling ⁊ mid chatere

285   hom schende ⁊ mid fule worde,

so herdes doþ oþer mid schit-worde.

Ne lust me wit þe screwen chide;

forþi ich wende from hom wide.

Hit is a wise monne dome,

290   ⁊ hi hit segget wel ilome,

þat me ne chide wit þe gidie,

ne wit þan ofne me ne ȝonie.

At sume siþe herde [I] telle

hu Alured sede on his spelle:

295   "Loke þat þu ne bo þare

þar chauling boþ ⁊ cheste ȝare:

lat sottes chide ⁊ uorþ þu go."

⁊ ich am wis ⁊ do also.

⁊ ȝet Alured seide an oþer side

300   a word þat is isprunge wide:

"þat wit þe fule haueþ imene,

ne cumeþ he neuer from him cleine."

Wenestu þat haueck bo þe worse

þoȝ crowe bigrede him bi þe mershe,

280. *ne,* margin *me* later.   284. *þif.*   293. *itelle.*

---

281. Mr Coulton suggests here a reference to the cloistered monastic life. Cf. l. 89.

284. *chauling* (J. *changling*). The J.-reading represents a scribal attempt to substitute for an obsolescent form one that was more familiar: with *changling* (=jangling) cf. *gencling* (*St Jul.* p. 57). The form *chauling* (< O.E. *cēaft*, jaw) is paralleled in L.Ger. *kavelen,* Du. *kevelen* and Mod. Eng. colloquial "jawing."

292. Cf. Ray's *Proverbs* (p. 112), "No gaping against an oven."

295–7. Similar proverbial utterances are found in *A.S. Apophthegms* (quoted by Kemble, *Salomon and Saturn,* pp. 258 ff.), *ne beo ðu to ceastful* (23); *ne flyt ðu na wið anwilne man ne wið ofersprecenne* (5); in the *Distichs of Cato* (see *Ang.* VII. pp. 170, 172):

        (a) *A ȝeynes men ful of wordes*
             Stryue þow riht nouht.
        (b) *Beo corteis and jangle not*
             þer þou art set at bord.

Also in the *Proverbs of Alfred: ne chid þu wyþ none sotte* (412) and *Be thou*

Hi me bichirmeþ ꝛ bigredeþ,
280   ꝛ heore flockes to me ledeþ.
Me is leof to habbe reste
And sitte stille in myne neste:
Vor nere ich neuer þe betere,
Þeyh ich mid changling and myd chatere
285   Heom schende ꝛ myd fule worde,
So herdes doþ oþer [m]id sit-worde.
Ne lust me wiþ þe screwen chide;
Forþi ich wende from heom wide.
Hit is a wise monne dome,
290   ꝛ hi hit seggeþ wel ilome,
Þat me ne chide wiþ þe gidie,
Ne wiþ þan ofne me ne yonie.
At sum syþe herde I telle
Hw Alured seyde on his spelle:
295   "Loke þat þu ne beo þare
Þar changling beoþ ꝛ cheste vare;
Let sottes chide ꝛ forþ þu go."
ꝛ ich am wis, ꝛ do al so.
ꝛ yet Alured seyde an oþer syde
300   A word þat is isprunge wide,
"Þat wiþ þe fule haueþ imene,
Ne cumeþ he neuer from him clene."
Wenestu þat hauek beo þe w[u]rse   Fol. 231 r. col. 2.
Þe crowe bigrede him bi þe mersche,

286. *Mid.*   303. *wrse.*

---

never too bold | To chide against any scold, | nor with many tales | To chide against all the foolish (sect. XXVI.), and in *The Wise Man's Proverbs* (ed. Furnivall):

> Evermore fle discorde and hate,
> Wyth þi neighbour make no debate.

299. *side* (C. and J.). The form *siþe* would normally be expected here (cf. *at sume siþe* (l. 293)), and may have appeared in the original; in which case the rhyme *siþe : wide* would find a parallel in *itrede : iqueþe* (ll. 501–2). Both MSS. however agree in reading *side* which has therefore been retained. Trans. "in another place."

301. Trans. "he that hath to do with what is foul," cf. the O.E. idiom *gemæne habban wiþ* = "to have to do with" (an adversary).

303–8. A piece of unnatural natural history, probably of the same origin as the idea of the young owl fouling the nest of the hawk (cf. also l. 227 note). The hawk, as Mr G. G. Coulton points out, "is not baited by carrion crows (which are solitary birds) but by rooks, and swallows and even sparrows."

305 ꞇ goþ to him mid hore chirme
rיʒt so hi wille wit him schirme?
þe hauec folʒeþ gode rede,
ꞇ fliʒt his wei ꞇ lat him grede."   Fol. 235 r. col. 2.
      "ʒet þu me seist of oþer þinge,
310 ꞇ telst þat ich ne can noʒt singe,
ac al mi rorde is woning,
ꞇ to ihire grislich þing.
þat nis noʒt soþ, ich singe efne,
mid fulle dreme ꞇ lude stefne.
315 þu wenist þat ech song bo grislich,
þat þine pipinge nis ilich.
Mi stefne is [bold] ꞇ noʒt unorne,
ho is ilich one grete horne,
ꞇ þin is ilich one pipe,
320 of one smale wode unripe.
Ich singe bet þan þu dest:
þu chaterest so doþ on Irish prost.
Ich singe an eue a riʒte time,
ꞇ soþþe won hit is bed-time,
325 þe þridde siþe a[t] middel-niʒte:
ꞇ so ich mine song adiʒte
wone ich iso arise vorre,
oþer dai-rim oþer dai-sterre.
Ich do god mid mine þrote,
330 ꞇ warni men to hore note.
Ac þu singest alle longe niʒt,
from eue fort hit is dai-liʒt,
ꞇ eure seist þin o song
so longe so þe niʒt is long:

308. *him, i* altered to *e.*   312. *hire, i-* later.   317. *blod*, margin later
bold.   320. *wode, e* inserted after and above *o* later.   322. *prost*, after
and above *r*, later *e* inserted.   325. *ad.*

308. "*him* (C.) illustrates the displacing of acc. form *hi* (J.) by the
dat." (W.).
309. Note the word-order: "*ʒet þu seist of me.*"
313. *efne*="smoothly," i.e. without trills. Cf. l. 48.
322. *on Irish prost.* Irish priests, according to Mr G. G. Coulton, were
proverbially of the lowest type: see *P. Plowman*, B. xx. 220; *Reg. of St
Osmund* (R.S.), I. 304–6 (two illiterates ordained in Ireland); Giraldus Cambrensis, *Opera* (R.S.), I. 60, IV. 78, V. 172. See additional notes, p. 202.
323–8. The Owl refers here to the canonical hours observed by the regular

305 ꞇ goþ to him myd heore chyrme
Riht so hi wille wiþ him schirme?
Þe hauek foleweþ gode rede;
He flyhþ his wey, ꞇ let hi grede."

"[Y]et þu me seyst of oþer þinge,
310 ꞇ tellest þat ich ne can nouht singe,
Ac al my reorde is wonyng,
And to ihere gryslych þing.
Þat nis nouht soþ, ich singe efne,
Mid fulle dreme ꞇ lude stefne.

315 Þu wenest þat eoch song beo *gr*islich
Þat þine pipinge nis ilich.
Mi stefne is bold ꞇ nouht vnorne,
Heo is ilich one grete horne,
ꞇ þin is iliche one pype,
320 Of one smale weode vnripe.
Ich [singe] bet þan þu dest:
Þu chaterest so doþ on Yris *pr*est.
Ich singe an efne a ryhte time,
ꞇ seþþe hwenne hit is bed-time,

325 Þe þridde syþe a middel-nyhte:
ꞇ so ich myne songe adihte
Hwenne ich iseo arise veorre
Oþer day-rewe oþer day-steorre.
Ic do god myd myne þrote,
330 And warny men to heore note.
Ac þu singest alle longe nyht,
From eue þat hit is day-liht,
ꞇ euer lesteþ þin o song
So longe so þe nyht is long:

309. *þet* (small blue *þ*).   321. *Ich bet.*

clergy for prayer and devotion. The services alluded to are Vespers, at sunset
(l. 323); Compline, just before retiring to rest (l. 324); Matins, soon after
midnight (l. 325); and Lauds at sunrise (l. 328). The other hours or services
belonged to the day-time and are therefore not mentioned by the Owl. (See
Gasquet, *English Monastic Life*, ch. VI.)   See also note ll. 1658 ff.

331 ff. Curious legends have existed with regard to the nocturnal singing
of the nightingale. According to one story, the sightless nightingale had
borrowed the eyes of the glow-worm in order to attend a fairy wedding.
After the ceremony she refused to give them back, but wishing to soothe her
injured friend, she promised to continue her song by night as well as by day (see
Prov. Names and Folklore of British Birds, C. Swainson, E. Dial. Soc. XVIII.).

335   ꝛ eure croweþ þi wrecche crei,
þat he ne swikeþ niȝt ne dai.
Mid þine pipinge þu adunest
þas monnes earen þar þu wunest,
ꝛ makest þine song so unw[u]rþ
340   þa[t] me ne telþ of þar noȝ[t] w[u]rþ.
Eurich murȝþe mai so longe ileste
þat ho shal liki wel unwreste: Fol. 235 v. col. 1.
vor harpe, ꝛ pipe, ꝛ fuȝeles [song]
mislikeþ, ȝif hit is to long.
345   Ne bo þe song neuer so murie,
þat he ne shal þinche wel unmurie
ȝef he ilesteþ ouer unwille:
so þu miȝt þine song aspille.
Vor hit is soþ, Alured hit seide,
350   ꝛ me hit mai ine boke rede:
"Eurich þing mai losen his godhede
mid unmeþe ꝛ mid ouerdede."
Mid este þu þe miȝt ouerquatie,
ꝛ ouerfulle makeþ wlatie:

339. *-wrþ.*   340. *þat, noȝt*, the *t* in each case later: *wrþ.*
343. *songe.*   349. *seidde*, first *d* deleted.

---

335. *crei.* This word presents much difficulty. Sk. and G. translate it as "cry" (O.Fr. *cri*), but this correspondence between *ei* and *i* seems scarcely possible. Str.-Br. interprets it as "crowing," W. as "crying" without further comment. The form is perhaps derived from an O.N. **krei* (=O.E. *crā*, the croaking of frogs or crows, cf. *wailawai* (l. 220), *wolawo* (l. 412), in which case the line would mean "Thy wretched croaking ever goes on." A more satisfactory solution, however, would be to read *crei*="throat," the word suggested by the context as the subject of *croweþ*. The Mod. Eng. *crag* (=M.E. *crawe*<O.E. *craga*, neck or throat) is clearly not the word, but an O.E. variant **cræg* would give the form and meaning required. A Northern variant *craig* occurs in Dunbar's *Flyting Poem* (169), "Thy lang lene craig, Thy pure pynit thrott": the form is also found in Mod. Scots dial. (see *E.D.D.*), and the corresponding Southern form would seem to give the best meaning to the line, viz. "And ever croweth thy wretched throat."
340. *of þar*="*þar-of*, not *of þare* (f.): O.E. *song* is masc." (W.). Trans. "that one reckons nothing of it" (=reckons thereof nothing of worth). H. suggests that "the construction is of a mixed kind, combining (1) one esteems nothing of thy song, and (2) thy song is worth nothing."
343. *song* (C. *songe*, J. *song*). The J. form is preferable for both grammatical and metrical reasons.
345. *neuer so murie.* Instance of an irrational negative in a concessive clause—a construction found in O.E. and other Teutonic languages (see W. E. Collinson, *M.L.R.* x. 3, pp. 349–65) as well as occasionally in A.-Norman, where it is apparently due to English influence (see J. Vising, *M.L.R.* xi. 2, pp. 219–21): cf. *A.S. Chron.* (1087), *nan man ne dorste slean oðerne man, næfde he næfre swa mycel yfel gedon.*

335 ꝛ euer croweþ þi wrecche crey,
    Þat he ne swikeþ nyht ne day.
    Mid þine pipinge þu adunest   Fol. 231 v. col. 1.
    Þas monnes eren þar þu wunest,
    ꝛ makest þi song so vnwiht
340 Þat me ne telleþ of þe nowiht.
    Eurych mureþe may so longe leste,
    Þat heo schal liki wel vnwreste:
    For harpe, ꝛ pipe, ꝛ foweles song
    Mislikeþ, if hit is to long.
345 Ne beo þe song ne so murie,
    Þat he ne sal þinche vnmurie
    If he ilesteþ ouer vnwille:
    So þu myht þi song aspille.
    For hit is soþ, Alured hit seyde,
350 ꝛ me hit may in boke rede:
    "Eurich þing may lesen his godhede
    Mid vnmeþe and ouerdede."
    Mid este þu þe maist ouerquatie,
    ꝛ ouerfulle makieþ wlatie:

345–7. Trans. "Be the song ever so merry, it will seem quite unpleasant, if it lasts beyond the proper time" (i.e. what is desirable).

ouer unwille (C. and J.). Various explanations of this phrase have been made. Sk. glossed *unwille* as "displeasure" (< O.E. *unwilla*) and then, somewhat illogically, explained the phrase *ouer unwille* as meaning "beyond what is desirable." Egge (*M.L.N.* I. 14) suggested an O.E. *unwille* (pleasant): but while this would undoubtedly give the sense required, no such form is found. W., again, takes *unwille* as an adv. = "unpleasantly" (< O.E. *unwillum*, against one's will), and the phrase he translates as "over or too unpleasantly": cf. *ouerlonge* (l. 450), *ouerswiþe* (l. 1518). It is however worth noting that *unwille* occurs in two other places (ll. 422, 1535) in the poem and in each case it represents an adj. = "displeasing" (O.E. *unwilla*). There would seem to be no reason for interpreting it differently here: so that the literal rendering of the phrase would be "beyond what is displeasing," i.e. not pleasing. And if the "not" herein implied be regarded as another instance of the redundant negative (cf. *ne*, l. 346), the actual interpretation becomes "beyond what is (not) pleasing or desirable," which is the sense required by the context.

351–2. Cf. *The Wise Man's Proverbs* (Bodl. MS. 9, lf. 99), ll. 32–3:
    Whan game ys best, is tyme to lete:
    Measure is a mery mele:
also Ray's *Proverbs* (p. 75), "Measure is a treasure"; *Piers Plowman*, B I. 35, "Measure is medcyne"; Camden's *Remains* (p. 310), "Measure is a merrie meane"; also μηδὲν ἄγαν of the Seven Sages.

353. *ouerquatie.* According to Str. the word means "to cram to excess" and is connected with Prov. Eng. *quat* (Str. *Beit.* 425), O.Fr. *quatier* (Roquef. *Gloss.* 2. 414). The word is found in Mod. Somer. dial. *aquat, quat* (full,

A. 3

355　an eurich mureȝþe mai agon
　　ȝif me hit halt eure forþ in on,
　　bute one, þat is Godes riche,
　　þat eure is svete ꝼ eure iliche:
　　þeȝ þu nime eure o[f] þan lepe,
360　hit is eure ful bi hepe.
　　Wu*nder* hit is of Godes riche,
　　þat eure spenþ ꝼ eu*er* is iliche.

　　　ȝut þu me seist an o*þer* shome,
　　þat ich a[m] on mine eȝen lome,
365　an seist, for þat ich flo bi niȝte,
　　þat ich ne mai iso bi liȝte.
　　þu liest! on me hit is isene
　　þat ich habbe gode sene:
　　vor nis non so dim þuster*nesse*
370　þat ich eu*er* iso þe lasse.
　　þu wenest þat ich ne miȝte iso,
　　vor ich bi daie noȝt ne flo.
　　þe hare luteþ al dai,
　　ac noþeles iso he mai.
375　ȝif hundes urneþ to him-ward,
　　[h]e gengþ wel suiþe awai-ward,　　Fol. 235 v. col. 2.
　　ꝼ hokeþ paþes sviþe narewe,
　　ꝼ haueþ mid hi*m* his blenches ȝarewe,
　　ꝼ hupþ ꝼ star[t] suþe coue,
380　an secheþ paþes to þe groue:
　　ne sholde he uor boþe his eȝe
　　so don, ȝif he þe bet niseȝe.

359. *oþ.*　364. *an. n* deleted, stroke (for *m*) over *a.*　376. *He.*　379. *stard.*

---

sated) < O.Fr. *quaitir, quatir* (to force in, press down): cf. Lyly, *Euphues*
(ed. Arber, p. 44), "To the stomach quatted with dainties, al delicates
seeme queasie." (See *N.E.D.* and *E.D.D.*)
　362. *spenþ,* see note l. 165.
　364. *am* (C. and J. *an*). The presence of *an* (for *am*) in both MSS.
points to a common original, see Intro. § 3, p. xxv.
　370. *lasse,* probably a scribal alteration. The rhyme requires *lesse,* a
Kentish form (cf. J. reading). See ll. 1227–8, 1405–6, also Appendix I (a) (i).
　375. *to him-ward,* a common construction in early English: cf. O.E. *to
þære sunnan weard, til heuene ward* (*Gen. & Ex.* 3025); *to me ward* (*Horn,*
1118); also "his power to us-ward who believe" (*Ephesians* i. 19).

355 ⁊ euerich mureþe may agon,
If me hit halt euer in on,
Bute one, þat is Godes riche,
Þa[t] euer is swete ⁊ euer iliche:
Þeyh þu nyme of þan lepe,

360 Hit is euer ful by hepe.
Wunder hit is of Godes ryche,
Þat euer spenþ ⁊ euer is iliche.
    Yet þu me seyst an oþer schome,
Þat ich a[m] on [m]yne eye lome,

365 ⁊ seyst, for þat ich fleo bi nyhte,
Þat ich ne may iseo bi lyhte.
Þu liest! on me hit is isene
Þat ich habbe gode sene:
Vor nys no so dym þesternesse

370 Þat ich euer iseo þe lesse.
Þu wenest þat ich ne m[u]we iseo,
Vor ich bi daye nouht ne fleo.   Fol. 231 v. col. 2.
Þe hare luteþ al day,
Ac noþeles iseo he may.

375 If hundes eorneþ to him-ward,
He gencheþ swiþe awey-ward,
⁊ hokeþ paþes swiþe narewe,
⁊ haueþ mid him blenches yarewe.
He [hupþ] ⁊ start swiþe cove,

380 ⁊ secheþ paþes to þe groue:
Ne scholde he vor bo his eye
So do, if he þe bet ne iseye.

358. *þa.*   364. *an, Myne.*   371. *mwe.*   379. *huphþ.*

379. *hupþ* (< M.E. *huppen*, O.E. * *hyppan*, alongside M.E. *hoppen*, O.E. *hoppian*) = "hops, leaps," cf. *hypped* (*Gaw. and Gr. Kt.* l. 2232), *hippit* (*Kingis Quair*, st. 35). This form in *-u* occurs together with an *-o* form in M.E. as well as in other Teutonic languages: cf. O.N. *hoppa*, M.H.G. *hopfen*; M.L.G. *huppen*, M.H.G. *hüpfen*. For similar variants in *o, u* cf. *folȝeþ* (l. 307), *fulieþ* (l. 1239): *soleþ* (l. 1276), *sulieþ* (l. 1240): *hoȝeþ* (l. 455), cf. O.E. *hycgan: tolli* (l. 1627), cf. O.E. *tyllan*. See also Morsbach § 126, a 2; and O.E. *dor, duru: spora, spura: cnocian, cnucian.*
    start (C. *stard*, J. *start*) = *starteþ* < *sterteþ* (leaps), cf. Ritson's *Anc. Songs,* iv., *bulluc sterteþ.* For change of *e* to *a* before *r* cf. *barnde* (< *bernde*), *Laȝ,* 3824.

3—2

Ich mai ison so wel so on hare,
þeʒ ich bi daie sitte an dare.

385 Þar aʒte men [boþ] in worre,
an fareþ boþe ner an forre,
an oueruareþ fele [þ]ode,
an doþ bi niʒte gode node,
ich folʒi þan aʒte manne,

390 an flo bi niʒte in hore banne."
     Þe niʒtingale in hire þoʒte
athold al þis, ꝺ longe þoʒte
wat ho þarafter miʒte segge:
vor ho ne miʒte noʒt alegge

395 þat þe hule hadde hire ised,
vor he spac boþe riʒt an red.
An hire ofþuʒte þat ho hadde
þe speche so for uorþ iladde,
an was oferd þat hire answare

400 ne w[u]rþe noʒt ariʒt ifare.
Ac noþeles he spac boldeliche,
vor he is wis þat hardeliche
wiþ is uo berþ grete ilete,
þat he uor areʒþe hit ne forlete:

---

385. *boþe*, cf. *boþe* in next line.   387. *þode* or *wode*. *e* inserted above *o* in later hand.   388. *node. e* inserted above *o* in later hand.   400. *wrþe.*

---

384. *an dare* (J. *a dare*) = "and lurk." The form *dare* is < O.E. *darian* (lurk, lie hidden) quoted by Sweet (*A.S. Dict.*) as occurring once: cf. Swed. *darra*. The word however occurs frequently in M.E.: cf. *droupe and dare* (*Met. Morte Arthur*, 2575), also *at þat syʒt uche douthe con dare* (*Pearl*, 839), and it is this verbal form that occurs in l. 384. Str. however, influenced by the J. reading (i.e. *a dare*), suggested *an* = prep. *dare* = sb., and W. in support of this suggestion, noted Cornish *dar* (oak) in Williams' *Dict. of Anc. Lang. of Cornwall* (not in *E.D.D.*). But this explanation is not convincing and the J.-reading is probably a scribal error.

387. *þode* (C. *þode*, J. *þeode*) = "peoples." W. reads C. as *wode*, apparently taking the undotted *wen* (þ) as *w* instead of *þ* (see note l. 2). He would therefore translate the line as: "(They) pass over many forests (*wode*)," an interpretation which, applied to *aʒte men...in worre* (l. 385), does not give clear sense. There are however other reasons for rejecting *wode*, apart from the facts that it does not suit the context and is not the actual reading of C.: (1) the J.-form is *þeode*, which suggests a þ-form in C. (2) The word *node* (*neode*) occurs in two other places (ll. 906, 1584) in the rhyming position and in each case it rhymes with *þeode*. (3) The form *wode* (O.E. *wudu*) cannot possibly rhyme with *node* (O.E. *nēode*). There is consequently but little doubt that *þode* is the correct reading: while *oueruareþ* (W. = "pass over") probably means "overrun, come into conflict with," cf. *A.S. Chron.* 1016, *Hi slogon ꝺ bærndon swa hwæt swa hi oferforon.*

Ich may iseo so wel so on hare,
Þeyh ich bi daye sytte a dare.

385 Þar auhte men beoþ in worre,
⁊ fareþ boþe neor ⁊ feorre,
⁊ ouervareþ veole þeode,
⁊ doþ bi nyhte gode neode,
Ich folewi þane ahte manne,

390 ⁊ fleo bi nyhte *in* heore barme."
Þe nyhtegale *in* hire þouhte
Atheold al þis, ⁊ longe þouhte
Hwat heo þarafter myhte segge:
Vor heo ne myhte noht alegge

395 Þat þe vle hedde hire iseyd,
Vor ho spak boþe riht ⁊ red.
⁊ hire ofþuhte þat heo hadde
Þe speche so feor uorþ iladde,
⁊ wes aferd þat hire answare

400 Ne w[u]rþe nouht ariht ivare.
Ac noþeles heo spak boldeliche,
Vor heo is wis þat hardeliche
Wiþ his fo berþ grete ilete,
[Þ]at he for arehþe hit ne forlete:

400. *wrþe*.   404. *Hwat*.

The passage is therefore best translated as "When bold men are at war...
and come into conflict with (or overrun) many peoples, and perform by night
brave deeds, then I follow...." The idea is possibly reminiscent of that O.E.
epic convention according to which the raven, the wolf, and the eagle are
represented as hovering around the scenes of battle (cf. *Beowulf*, 3025 ff.).
Mr B. Dickins, further, points out that in the O.N. *Sigrdrifumál* the phrase
á nefi uglu occurs in st. 17, beside *á ulfs klóum ok á arnar nefi* in the preceding stanza—which looks as though the owl were also reckoned among the
"properties" of the battlefield.

390. *banne* < O.Fr. *ban*, troop: of Teutonic origin, cf. O.E. *gebann* = "edict,
summons"—the more usual meaning of the word in M.E. (see *N.E.D.*). The
J.-reading *barme* is clearly a scribal emendation, see Intro. § 3, p. xxviii.

398. *speche* < O.E. *spræc*, *spæc*, a legal term = "suit, plea." Cf. O.E. *he
draf his spræce* (= he prosecuted his suit), *Chart. Th.* 376, 11; also *Ær he
clæne sy of ælcre spæce ðe he ær beclyped wæs* (= before he be clear of every
suit, etc.), *L.C.S.* 28. See B.T. s.v. *spræc* x (6), *N.E.D.* s.v. *speech* (10).

400. *ifare* = O.E. *gefaren* (p.p.). W. makes the unnecessary suggestion
that "*ifare* < O.E. *ferian* (wk. I) is a strong p.p. form by analogy with strong
faran." In O.E. the verb *weorþan* was frequently used as pret.-aux., cf. O.E.
wearþ gefeallen (he fell): hence *wurþe ifare* (= O.E. *wurde gefaren*) would
be equivalent to O.E. *gefōre* (pt. opt. sg.) = "had gone." Trans. "She was
afraid that her answer had not gone aright."

404. *areȝþe* = "cowardice" (cf. O.E. *iergþu*). The M.E. form is due to

405 vor suich worþ bold ȝif þu [fliȝst],

þat w[u]lle flo ȝif þu [n]isvicst;

ȝif he isiþ þat þu nart areȝ,

he wile of [bore] w[u]rchen bareȝ.

˥ forþi, þeȝ þe niȝtingale

410 were aferd, ho spac bolde tale.   Fol. 236 r. col. 1.

"[H]ule" ho seide "wi dostu so?

þu singest a-winter wolawo!

þu singest so doþ hen a-snowe,

al þat ho singeþ hit is for wowe.

415 A-wintere þu singest wroþe ˥ ȝomere,

an eure þu art dumb a-sumere.

Hit is for þine fule niþe

þat þu ne miȝt mid us bo bliþe,

vor þu forbernest wel neȝ for onde

420 wane ure blisse cumeþ to londe.

þu farest so doþ þe ille,

evrich blisse him is unwille:

grucching ˥ luring him boþ rade,

ȝif he isoþ þat men boþ glade.

---

405. *fliȝste.*   406. *wle, isvicst* with *is* deleted.   408. *boreȝ,* with line
through *o*: later altered to *a*. Possibly the line through *o* may have stood
for an attempt to change *o* to *e,* cf. stroke across *o* in *bo* (l. 418). *wrchen.*
411. rubric *þ* (direction letter *h*).   416. *an, d* added by later hand.   418. *bo*
with oblique stroke across *o*.

---

analogy with the M.E. adj. *areȝ* (O.E. *earg*), and it affords an example of
M.E. levelling of O.E. mutated forms.

405. *fliȝst* (C. *fliȝste,* J. *flyhst*) = "dost flee." The C. form (with final -*e*)
is evidently a scribal error, the *e* being unnecessary from both the grammatical and the rhyming points of view.

406. *nisvicst* (C. *isvicst* with *is* deleted, J. [*ne*] *swykst*), Str. and Sk.
niswicst, W. and G. *vicst.* The actual C. reading *vicst* is adopted and explained by W. and G. as = *viȝt(e)st* (pr. 2 sg. of *viȝte,* to fight): but this seems
unlikely, since (i) the *is* was probably deleted by a later hand, (ii) both MSS.
agree in reading *svic-* (*swyk-*), (iii) and on metrical grounds a syllable is
probably wanting between the two last words of the line. But if the *sv-* (*sw-*)
forms be retained, the sense evidently would require a negative (viz. "who
will flee if thou dost (not) fail"), and this negative would supply the missing
syllable. Hence, the C. and J. readings are on the whole best accounted
for by supposing that *n* was omitted from the common original, that the
omission was faithfully repeated by the C. and J. scribes, and that some
later scribe, puzzled by the reading which resulted, attempted to improve the
C. text by the deletion of -*is.*

408. Trans. "From being (out of) a boar, he will become (make) a barrow-
pig (= *porcus castratus*)," i.e. he will lose all his fierceness. Sk. reads *wurthen*
(= become) for *wurchen* (C. and J.), but it is unlikely that *th* (instead of *þ*)
appeared in the common original.

405 Vor suych worþ bold if þu flyhst,
Þat wile fleo if þu [ne] swykst;
If he isihþ þat þu [n]art areh,
He wile of bore wurche bareh.
⁊ forþi, þey [þe] nyhtegale
410 Were aferd, heo spak bolde tale.
"[H]vle" heo seyde "hwi dostu so?
Þu singest a-wynter wolawo!
Þu singest so doþ hen a-snowe,
Al þat heo singeþ hit is for wowe.
415 A-wintre þu singest wroþe ⁊ yomere,
⁊ euer þu art dumb a-sumere.
Hit is for þine fule nyþe
Þat þu ne myht myd vs be bliþe,
Vor þu forbernest neyh for onde
420 Hwenne vre blisse cumeþ to londe.
Þu farest so doþ þe ille,
Euerich blisse him is vnwille:
Grucching ⁊ luring him beoþ rade,
If he iseoþ þat men beoþ glade.

406. *þu swykst.*   407. *art.*   409. *þey nyhtegale*: margin *þe.*
411. *þvle*, direction letter *þ.*

411. "Pointing to a common original is the odd coincidence that both rubricators wrote *þ* for probable original ? H: this in C. in spite of direction *h*" (W.).

411–6. It has been pointed out (see H. B. Hinckley, *Mod. Phil.* XVII. No. 5, p. 73 n.) that the antithesis between the owl and the nightingale was apparently proverbial. Thus Map's *Epistle of Valerius to Rufinus* begins: "Loqui prohibeor et tacere non possum. Grues odi et uocem ulule, bubonem et aues ceteras que lutose hiemis grauitatem luctuose preululant: et tu subsannas uenturi uaticinia dispendii, uera, si perseueras. Ideo loqui prohibeor, ueritatis augur, non uoluntatis. Lusciniam amo et merulam que leticiam aure lenis concentu placido preloquuntur, et potissimum philomenam, que optate tempus iocunditatis tota deliciarum plenitudine annulat, nec fallor." See also Walter Map, *De Nugis Curialium*, ed. James (Oxford, 1914), p. 143.

Hinckley also (*loc. cit.*) quotes the Low German proverb, *Wat dem eenen sin Uhl ist dem andern sin Nachtigall* (= "One man's owl is another man's nightingale").

413. *hen* (C. and J.): Str. and Sk. read *henne*, an unnecessary emendation, cf. O.E. *henn* (f.).

417–9. *niþe...onde*, see note l. 1096.

420. *cumeþ to londe* = "comes among us."

421. *þe ille* = "the churlish man": H. however explains it as = "the evil one, the devil."

424. *iso þ* (J. *iseoþ*) = "sees." A new form (pr. ind. 3 sg.) due to analogy with the infin. and formed by adding *þ* to the infin. root: cf. however *suþ* (l. 246), *isiþ* (l. 407), *iseʒþ* (l. 1465).

425   He wolde þat he iseȝe
        teres in evrich monnes eȝe:
        ne roȝte he þeȝ flockes were
        imeind bi toppes ꝼ bi here.
        Al so þu dost on þire side:
430   vor wanne snov liþ þicke ꝼ wide,
        an alle wiȝtes habbeþ sorȝe,
        þu singest from eue fort a-morȝe.
        Ac ich alle blisse mid me bringe:
        ech wiȝt is glad for mine þinge,
435   ꝼ blisseþ hit wanne ich cume,
        ꝼ hiȝteþ aȝen mine kume.
        Þe blostme ginneþ springe ꝼ sprede,
        boþe ine tro ꝼ ek on mede.
        Þe lilie mid hire faire wlite
440   wolcumeþ me, þat þu hit w[i]te,
        bit me mid hire faire blo
        þat ich shulle to hire flo.

440. *wte.*   441. *bit, t* altered to *d*, cf. however l. 445.

427–8. Sk. trans. *flockes* (<O.E. *flocc*) as "companies," *toppes* (<O.N. *toppr*) as "tufts of hair": and the passage, as a whole, as "He cared not though companies were mingled (huddled together) by heads and by hair, i.e. were fighting and pulling one another by the hair." Str.-Br. trans. *flockes* as "flocks of wool" (=M.Du. *vlocke*, O.H.G. *floccho*?, Lat. *floccus*), and *toppes* (=O.E. *topp*) as "tufts of hair, heads."

The word *flockes* in this passage undoubtedly stands for "tufts or flocks of wool" (<O.Fr. *floc*, Lat. *floccus*), while *toppes* = "threads," cf. Napier, *O.E. Glosses*, 23, 45. O.E. *toppa* = Lat. *pensa*: ibid. 26, 74. Lat. *serica pensa* = O.E. *seolcen ðræd*. The metaphor is therefore taken from the weaver's craft, a knowledge of which was widespread at a time when all large landowners made their cloth at home (cf. Neckam, *De Nat. Rerum*, II. 71). And the passage is best translated as "He would not care though the tufts of wool were mingled with (i.e. made up of a mixture of) threads and hairs," the reference being to those impurities in the raw wool which made the combing process necessary. The object of that process was to comb out from the tufts of wool the short fibres or hairs (mod. tech. "noil"), leaving the long fibres (mod. tech. "top") ready for the drawing and spinning operation. And so the metaphor here is as follows: the evil or envious man, to whom the owl is likened, is said to be careless of the trouble to which the weavers were put in preparing their material.

The word *toppe* (=thread) occurs again in *Sir Gawayne and the Grene Knight*, l. 191, viz.: *þe tayl and his toppyng twynnen of a sute* ("the tail and its plaiting were braided in the same fashion"). In Str.-Br. *toppyng* is glossed as "mane? head?": but this does not suit the context, for the mane and its plaiting had already been described in the preceding lines.

435. *blisseþ* (J. *blesseþ*). The C. reading is probably the original one: it not only suits the context better than that of J., but it also provides a synonym

425 He wolde þat he iseye
    Teres *in* eu*er*iche monnes eye:
    Ne rouhte [h]e þeyh flockes were
    Imeynd bi toppes ⁊ bi here.
    Al so þu dost on þire syde:
430 For hwanne snouh liþ þikke ⁊ wid*e*,
    ⁊ alle wihtes habbeþ sorewe,
    Þu singest from eue to a-morewe.
    Ac ich mid me alle blisse bringe:
    Ech wiht is glad for myne þinge,
435 ⁊ blesseþ hit hwenne ich cume,
    ⁊ hihteþ ayeyn myne cume.
    Þe blostme gynneþ spr*i*nge ⁊ spred*e*,
    Boþe *in* treo ⁊ ek in mede.
    Þe lilie myd hire fayre wlite
440 Welcomeþ me, þeyh þu hit wite,
    Bid me myd hire fayre bleo
    Þat ich schulle to hire fleo.   Fol. 232 r. col. 2.

         427. þe þeyh.

---

with *hiȝteþ* (rejoices) in the following line, in accordance with the usage of the poet.

For the Nightingale as herald of the Spring see Intro. § 8, p. lxviii.

437 ff. This passage of Nature description is reminiscent of many similar sketches in the Troubadour poetry, cf.

> Quan la vertz fouilla s'espan,
> E par flors blanqu'el ramel
> Per lo dolz chan del auzel
> Si va mos cors alegran,
> Lanquant vei los arbres florir,
> Et aug lo rosignol chantar
> Adonc se deu ben alegrar
> Qui bon' amor saup chausir

(quoted by Diez-Bartsch, *Die Poesie der Troubadours*, pp. 108–9).

439–43. For the literary convention underlying this association of the lily and the rose see Intro. § 8, p. lxxiii. The two flowers are frequently mentioned together in later medieval literature, e.g.

> Equitabant pariter duae domicellae,
> vultus verecundi sunt, et genae tenellae :
> Sic erumpunt lilia, sic rosae novellae,
> sic decurrunt pariter duae coeli stellae.
>   *De Phillide et Flora*, 229–32

(Wright, *Poems attrib. to W. Map* (Cam. Soc. 1841), p. 265) ; also

> þe rose rayleþ hire rode,
> .   .   .
> þe lilie is lossom to see.   (*Spec. Early Eng.* II. p. 48.)
> Lylie whyt hue is,
> Hire rode so rose on rys.   (*Ibid.* II. p. 45.)

440. C. reading = "as thou dost know." H. however prefers the J. reading = "though thou mayst blame her action."

Þe rose also mid hire rude,
þat cumeþ ut of þe þorne wode,   Fol. 236 r. col. 2.
445   bit me þat ich shulle singe
vor hire luue one skentinge:
ꞇ ich so do þurȝ niȝt ꞇ dai,
þe more ich singe þe more I mai,
an skente hi mid mine songe,
450   ac noþeles noȝt ouerlonge;
wane ich iso þat men boþ glade,
ich nelle þat hi bon to sade:
þan is ido vor wan ich com,
ich fare aȝen ꞇ do wisdom.
455   Wane mon hoȝeþ of his sheue,
an falewi cumeþ on grene leue,
ich fare hom ꞇ nime leue:
ne recche ich noȝt of winteres reue.
wan ich iso þat cumeþ þat harde,
460   ich fare hom to min erde,
an habbe boþe luue ꞇ þonc
þat ich her com ꞇ hider swonk.
Þan min erende is ido,
sholde ich bileue? nai, [w]arto?
465   vor he nis noþer ȝep ne wis,
þat longe abid þar him nod nis."
    Þos hule luste, ꞇ leide an hord
al þis mot, word after word,
an after þoȝte hu he miȝte
470   ansvere uinde best mid riȝte:
vor he mot hine ful wel biþenche,
þat is aferd of plaites wrenche.
    "Þv aishest me," þe hule sede,
"wi ich a-winter singe ꞇ grede.

446. *one one* (dittography), former *one* deleted.
    449. *an*, later *d* above.   464. *þarto*.

---

452. *sade* = "sated, surfeited"; see Gloss.
453. *þan* (J. *hwenne*) = "when": see note l. 165. Cf. also ll. 463, 482.
456. *falewi* (C. and J.) < O.E. *fealu, fealw-* (fallow). The O.E. adj. suffix
-*ig* has been added by analogy with the numerous O.E. adj. forms in -*ig*:
cf. *iredi* (O.E. *rǣde*), l. 488, also M.E. *heri* (hairy) < O.E. *gehǣre*.

Þe rose also myd hire rude,
Þat cumeþ of þe þorne wode,
445 Bit me þat ich schulle singe
For hire luue one skentynge:
˥ ich so do þureh nyht ˥ day,
Þe more ich singe þe more ich may,
˥ skente hi myd myne songe,
450 Ac noþeles nouht ouerlonge:
Hwenne ich iseo þat men beoþ glade,
Ich nelle þat hi beon to sade:
Hwenne is ido for hwan ich com,
Ich vare ayeyn ˥ do wisdom.
455 Hwanne mon howieþ of his sheue,
˥ falewi cumeþ of grene leue,
Ich fare hom ˥ nyme leue:
Ne recche ich nouht of wyntres teone.
Hwanne ich iseo þat cumeþ [þat] harde,
460 Ich fare hom to myn erde,
˥ habbe boþe luue ˥ þonk
Þat ich her com ˥ hider swonk.
Hwanne myn erende is ido,
Scholde ich bileue? nay, hwarto?
465 Vor he nys noþer yep ne wis,
Þat longe abid þar him no neod is."
Þeos vle luste, ˥ leyde an hord
Al þis mot, word after word,
And after þouhte hw heo myhte
470 Onswere vynde best myd rihte:
Vor he mot ful wel him biþenche,
Þat is aferd of playtes wrenche.
"Þv ayssest me," þe vle seyde,
"Hwi ich a-winter singe ˥ grede.

459. *þat de harde.*

---

458. *reue* (J. *teone*). The J. scribe in substituting the more familiar word *teone* for original *reue* has spoilt the rhyme, see Intro. § 3, p. xxviii.
466. *þar* = "where." The O.E. relative sense of *þar* (O.E. *þǣr*) is here preserved, see note l. 165.
472. *plaites wrenche* = "tricks of debate." See Intro. § 6, p. liv.

475 Hit is gode monne iwone,
   an was from þe worlde frome,
   þat ech god man his frond icnowe,
   an blisse mid hom sume þrowe   Fol. 236 v. col. 1.
   in his huse at his borde,
480 mid faire speche ꞇ faire worde.
   ꞇ hure ꞇ hure to Cristesmasse,
   þane riche ꞇ poure, more ꞇ lasse,
   singeþ cundut niȝt ꞇ dai,
   ich hom helpe what ich mai.
485 ꞇ ek ich þenche of oþer þinge
   þane to pleien oþer to singe.
   Ich habbe herto gode ansuare
   anon iredi ꞇ al ȝare:
   vor sumeres-tide is al to [w]lonc,
490 an doþ misreken monnes þonk:
   vor he ne recþ noȝt of clennesse,
   al his þoȝt is of golnesse:
   vor none dor no leng nabideþ,
   ac eurich upon oþer rideþ:
495 þe sulue stottes ine þe stode
   boþ boþe wilde ꞇ mere-wode.
   ꞇ þu sulf art þar-among,
   for of golnesse is al þi song,
   an aȝen þet þu w[i]lt teme,
500 þu art wel modi ꞇ wel breme.
   Sone so þu hau[e]st itrede,
   ne miȝtu leng a word iqueþe,
   ac pipest al so doþ a mose,
   mid chokeringe, mid steune hose.

489. *þlonc.*   499. *an,* later *d* above.   501. *hauest,* *e* inserted in different
ink before *s.*   502. *iqueþe,* *d* placed above in later hand.

483. *cundut* (=*conductus,* 11th century) was a medieval dance-song which
had much in common with the *motet* from which indeed it is hard to
distinguish. Both consisted of part-songs in which the tenor took the melody,
while the other voices (generally two) sang in harmony with the tenor. The
main difference between the two forms was, that, while in the *cundut* the
melody was invented by the composer, in the *motet* it was generally borrowed
either from "plain-chant" or some popular air. These *cunduts* could be sung
with or without words, and Latin texts of liturgical as well as secular forms
are extant. The name was probably applied in the first instance to the

475 Hit is gode monne ywune,
˥ was from þe worlde frume,
Þat ech god mon his frend iknowe, Fol. 232 v. col. 1.
˥ blissi myd heom sume þrowe
In his huse at his borde,
480 Mid fayre speche ˥ fayre worde.
˥ hure ˥ hure to Cristesmasse,
Hwenne riche ˥ poure, more ˥ lasse,
Singeþ cundut nyht ˥ day,
Ich heom helpe hwat ich may.
485 ˥ ek ich þenche of oþer þinge
Þane to pleye oþer to singe.
Ich habbe herto god onsware
Anon iredi and al ware:
Vor sumeres-tyde is al wlonk,
490 ˥ doþ mysreken monnes þonk:
Vor he ne rekþ noht of clennesse,
Al his þouht is of golnesse:
Vor none dor no leng nabideþ,
Ac euerich vp oþer rideþ:
495 Þe sulue stottes yne þe stode,
Beþ boþe wilde and mare-wode.
˥ þu sulf art þar-among,
Vor of golnysse is al þi song,
˥ ayeyn [þet þu wilt teme],
500 Þu art wel modi ˥ wel breme.
Sone so þu hauest itrede,
Ne myht þu leng a word iqueþe,
Ac pipest al so doþ a mose,
Mid cokeringe, mid stefne hose.

499. [þu wilt teme þet.]

---

leading melody in the part-song, and then to the song itself. Concerning
the composition of the *cundut* Walter Odington writes in his *De Speculatione
musicae* (c. 1228) and his work is quoted at length in Coussemaker's *Scriptores
de Musica medii Ævi*, I. 247: see also Petit de Julleville, *Hist. de la Litt.
française*, vol. I. pp. 402 ff.: cf. *Sir Gawayne and the Grene Knight*, l. 1655.

490. *misreken* = "(cause to) go astray." W. trans. = "reach wrongly" as if
from O.E. *rēcan*. Str.-Br. regards its origin as doubtful, but the word is < O.E.
recan (go, rush), quoted by Sweet (*St. Dict. of A.S.*).

501–2. *itrede* : *iqueþe*. Note the *-ed* : *-eþ* rhyme: cf. ll. 631–2, also note
l. 1588.

504. *chokeringe* (J. *cokeringe*). Str. adopts the J. reading, which Str.-Br.

505 Ʒet þu singst worse þon þe heisugge,
[þ]at fliʒþ bi grunde among þe stubbe:
wane þi lust is ago,
þonne is þi song ago also.
A-sumere chorles awedeþ

510 ꝛ uorcrempeþ ꝛ uorbredeþ:
hit nis for luue noþeles,
ac is þe chorles wode res;
vor wane he haueþ ido his dede,   Fol. 236 v. col. 2.
ifallen is al his boldhede,

515 habbe he istunge under gore,
ne last his luue no leng more.
Al so hit is on þine mode:
so sone so þu sittest a-brode,
þu forlost al þine wise.

520 Al so þu farest on þine rise:
wane þu hauest ido þi gome,
þi steune goþ anon to shome.
Ac [w]ane niʒtes cumeþ longe,
ꝛ b[r]ingeþ forstes starke an stronge,

525 þanne erest hit is isene
war is þe snelle, [w]ar is þe kene.
At þan harde me mai auinde
[w]o geþ forþ, wo liþ bihinde.
Me mai ison at þare node,

530 [w]an me shal harde wike bode;

506. ʒat.   515. *istunge*, after *is* a long *s* inserted, probably later.
516. *leng* with crook after *g* denoting *er*, probably later. (Str. reads *lenger*.)
523. *þane.*   524. *bingeþ*, *r* added later.   526. *þar.*   528. *þo.*   530. *þan.*

explains = "warming" (cf. M.E. *cokerin*, to keep warm = Lat. *fotio*, Pr. P. 85):
the form is preserved in M.E. *cocker* (= pamper) and in Shak. *K. J.* v. i. 70, "a
cocker'd silken wanton." But this J. reading does not suit the context and
it is clearly a scribal emendation. The original is represented by *chokeringe*
< M.E. *chokeren*, a sound-word, frequentative of M.E. **chok(k)en, chukken*
(cluck, chuck): cf. Chau. *C.T.* B. 4372, "Chaunticleer chukketh whan he
hath a corn yfounde," also Mod. Eng. "chuckle." The Mod. dialect form
"chokkered" (= obstructed, choked up) quoted by W. is derived from O.E.
(a)*cēocian* (choke) and stands for a different word.
      hose < O.E. *hās*, **hārs* (hoarse). Forms with and without *r* occur in M.E.
(see Str.-Br. under *hās*): for Mod. dial. (Som. and Dev.) form *hose*, see
E.D.D.
      With regard to the voice of the titmouse (*mose*, 1. 503) White (*Nat. Hist. of
Selborne*, Letter 60) states that "early in February [the titmouse] begins to
make two quaint notes like the whetting of a saw."

505 Yet þu singest w[o]rse þan þe heysugge,
Þat flyhþ bi grunde among þe stubbe:
Hwenne þi lust is ago,
Þenne is þi song ago al so.
A-sumere chorles aweydeþ
510 ⁊ uorcrempeþ ⁊ uorbredeþ:
Hit nys for luue noþeles,   Fol. 232 v. col. 2.
Ac is þeos cherles wode res;
Vo[r] hwanne he haueþ ido his dede,
Ifalle is al his boldhede,
515 Habbe he istunge vnder gore,
Ne last his luue no leng more.
Al so hit is on þine mode;
So sone so þu sittest a-brode,
Þu forleost al þine wise.
520 Al so þu varest on þine ryse:
Hwenne þu hauest ido þi gome,
Þi stefne goþ anon to schome.
Ac hwenne nyhtes cumeþ longe,
⁊ bryngeþ forstes starke ⁊ stronge,
525 Þanne erest hit is isene
Hwar is þe snelle, hwar þe kene.
At þan harde me may avynde
Hwo goþ forþ, hwo lyþ bihynde.
Me may iseon at þare neode,
530 Hwan me schal harde wike beode;

513. *Vo.*

---

505. *heisugge* = " hedgesparrow ": cf. *haysuck*, Worc. and Glo. dialects: see E.D.D.

506. *stubbe* = dat. pl. of *stubb* (stump of a tree), cf. Mod. Eng. *stubble*. According to Morsbach (§ 133, a 2) this word is derived not from O.E. *stybb* but from O.E. **stubbe* on the ground that M.E. *u* (< O.E. *u*) cannot rhyme with M.E. *ü* (< O.E. *y*), cf. however O.N. *stubbi*.

508. The song of the male nightingale is heard only until the young birds are hatched in June.   509. *chorles*, see note l. 1507.

510. *uorcrempeþ* (C. and J.). Str.-Br. = "contract": W. = "twist convulsively." The latter seems preferable in view of the context: the word is < O.E. **crempan* < O.E. **crimpan*, cf. O.E. *crompeht* = crumpled, wrinkled (Hessels, *Corp. Gloss.* 67): also Mod. Eng. "crimp," "cramp," "crumple."

523. *wane* (C. *þane*, J. *hwenne*). The C. reading would give quite good sense (cf. note l. 165), but since *wane* appears in the parallel phrase (l. 521) the form with *w* is probably intended here (cf. ll. 526, 528 for similar confusion between *þ* and *w*).

530. *wan* (C. *þan*, J. *hwan*) = " to whom " (W. trans. = " when "). As Kenyon

þanne ich am snel ⁊ pleie ⁊ singe,
⁊ hiȝte me mid mi skentinge:
of none wint*ere* ich ne recche,
vor ich nam non asv[u]nde wrecche.
535 ⁊ ek ich frouri uele wiȝte
þat mid hom nabbe[þ] none miȝtte:
hi boþ hoȝfule ⁊ uel arme,
an secheþ ȝorne to þe warme;
oft ich singe uor hom þe more
540 for lutli sum of hore sore.
Hu þincþ þe? artu ȝut inume?
Artu mid riȝte ouercume?"
     "Nay, nay!" sede þe niȝtingale,
"þu shalt ihere anoþ*er* tale:
545 ȝet nis þos speche ibroȝt to dome.
Ac bo wel stille, ⁊ lust nu to me   Fol. 237 r. col. 1.
ich shal mid one bare worde
do þat þi speche [wurþ] forworþe."
     "Þat nere noht riȝt" þe hule sede,
550 "þu hauest bicloped al so þu bede,

534. *asvnde.*   536. *nabbed.*
541. *inune,* second *n* altered later to *m.*   548. *wrht.*

(*J.E.G.P.* **XII.** 577–8) points out, a more coherent reading is obtained by
taking *wan* as dat. sg. of "who," a parallel construction being found in
ll. 527–8. Moreover the J. form *hwan* goes to support this view, since *hwenne*
(not *hwan*) is the usual form of "when" in that text.
     bode (J. *beode*) = "to command, enjoin." W. suggests that the word is
< O.E. *bodian* (foretell, bode). But apart from the evidence of the J. reading
beode, this is impossible on account of the rhyme, which would then be
node [$\bar{e}$] : *bode* [ð]. On the other hand *bode* < O.E. *bēodan* would give a correct
rhyme and the passage should therefore read: "One can see in times of
hardship to whom one may assign hard duties."
     535 ff. Mr Coulton suggests that the reference here is to the works of charity
connected with monastic life. Cf. also ll. 603–4.
     537. *hoȝful* = "anxious, full of care." According to Hulme (*Mod. Phil.* **I.**
586) this word, together with *hoȝe* (l. 701), *hohful* (l. 1292) and L.O.E. *hoge-
lease,* illustrates "a general tendency in L.O.E. and E.M.E. to discard umlaut forms and to return to the stems of the primitive words." He is wrong,
however, in deriving *hogelēase* from O.E. *hygelēas,* for all the above forms
come from O.E. *hogu* (care, solicitude) and not from O.E. *hoga* (as in Str.-Br.).
The latter form *hoga* (not found in Sweet) means (1) "fear," (2) "struggle":
see Napier, *O.E. Glosses,* **VIII.** 283. For the existence of this root (O.E. *hogu*)
in Mod. dial. cf. Barnes, *Poems,* p. 19, "An' have noo ho vor any thing."
     544. *tale.* See note l. 140.
     545. *speche.* See note l. 398.
     546. *to me.* With the rhyme *dome* : *to me,* cf. *come* : *to me* (ll. 1671–2). The

Þanne ich am snel, ꝺ pleye ꝺ singe,
ꝺ hyhte me myd my skentinge:
Of none wyntre ich ne recche,
Vo[r] ich nam non aswunde wrecche.
535   ꝺ ek ich froueri fele wihte
Þat myd heom nabbeþ none [m]ihte:
Hi beoþ houhful ꝺ wel arme,
And secheþ yorne to þen warme;
Ofte ich singe for hem þe more
540   For lutly sum of heore sore.
Hw þinkþ þe? artu [inome]?
Artu myd rihte ouercume?"
      "Nay, nay!" seyde þe Nihtegale,
"Þu schalt ihere on oþer tale:
545   Yet nis þeos speche ibroht to dome.   Fol. 233 r. col. 1.
Ac be stille, and lust nv to me:
Ich schal mid one bare worde
Do þat þi speche w[u]rþ forwurþe."
      "Þat nere noht riht" þe vle seyde,
550   "Þu hauest bicleped al so þu bede,

534. *Vo.*   536. *Mihte.*   541. *inome*, later insertion.   548. *wrþ.*

---

vowel in *me* is weakened owing to the unaccented position of the word. This device for obtaining a feminine rhyme is found in Chaucer (cf. *Prol. C.T.* 671–2), also in Gower where the two words are joined together, cf. *Conf. Aman.* I. 232, *tome*, II. 2016, *byme.*

547. *bare worde* (= Fr. *nude parole*, Lat. *simplex dictum*) is the technical term for a mere assertion on the part of a plaintiff unsupported by witnesses: to such a statement no defendant was required to reply (see Pollock and Maitland, *Hist. of Eng. Law*, II. 605–6). The Nightingale here states in answer to the taunt of the Owl that the next charge to be brought forward would convict without need of further evidence.

548. *forworþe* (J. *forwur þe*). It is possible that an original *forworde* (O.E. *-worden*) has here been modernised (perhaps in the common original since both MSS. agree) to *forworþe*, in which case the earlier form might be restored to the improvement of the rhyme. That earlier form occurs for instance in l. 1491, e.g. *forwurde*. On the other hand, forms in þ and *d* appear elsewhere in the rhyming position, cf. *itrede : iqueþe* (ll. 501–2), *cradele : aþele* (ll. 631–2), and it may be that the poet himself used the later form *forworþe.*

550. *bicloped* = "made thy charge" < O.E. *becleopian* = "summon, sue at law": a technical legal term: cf. *Ær he clæne sy of ælcre spæce, ðe he ær beclyped wæs* (before he be clear of every suit in which he had previously been accused: see B.-T. s.v. *beclypian*); also, *a preost...That of manslaȝt was bicliped* (*Bek.* 365). For the legal procedure at this stage—the Owl's claim to the right of "exceptio" (l. 553) and the Nightingale's subsequent "replicatio" (ll. 707 ff.), see Intro. § 6, pp. liii–liv.

an ich þe habbe iȝiue ansuare.
Ac ar we to unker dome fare,
ich wille speke toward þe
al so þu speke toward me;
555   an þu me ansuare ȝif þu miȝt.
Seie me nu, þu wrecche wiȝt,
is in þe eni oþer note
bute þu hauest schille þrote?
Þu nart noȝt to non oþer þinge,
560   bute þu canst of chateringe:
vor þu art lutel an unstrong,
an nis þi regel noþing long.
Wat dostu godes among monne?
Na mo þe deþ a w[re]cche wranne.
565   Of þe ne cumeþ non oþer god,
bute þu gredest suich þu bo wod:
an bo þi piping ouergo,
ne boþ on þe craftes namo.
Alured sede, þat was wis:
570   (he miȝte wel, for soþ hit is,)
"Nis no man for is bare songe
lof ne w[u]rþ noȝt suþe longe:
vor þat is a forworþe man
þat bute singe noȝt ne can."
575   Þu nart bute on forworþe þing:
on þe nis bute chatering.
Þu art dim an of fule howe,
an þinchest a lutel soti clowe.

561, 562. *an*, with later addition of *d*.   564. *mo*, later addition of *re*:
wercche.   572. *wrþ*.

---

559. Trans. "Thou art useless (*noȝt*=adj.) for anything else."
564. *þe* (J. *þene*)="than." The J. scribe has substituted for the archaic
þe (=than) a form with *n* (viz. *þene*), although *þan* is the usual spelling in
both MSS. For earlier instances of this use of *þe* cf. *A.S. Chron.* 901 A,
læs þe xxx *wintra*; *ibid.* 1009 E, 1016 E, *þe ma þe* (any more than).
a wrecche wranne. For the significance of the epithet *wrecche* cf. White,
Nat. Hist. of Selborne (41), "The feeble little...wren, that shadow of a bird,
braves our severest frosts without availing himself of houses or villages."
Cf. however Shakespeare's reference to the songs of the wren and the nightingale in *M. of V.* v. i. 104 ff. For the dignity accorded to the wren in fable, see
note ll. 1727 ff.

And ich þe habbe iy[i]ue onswere.
Ac are we to vnker dome fare,
Ich wile speke toward þe
Al so þu speke toward me;
555 ꝥ þu me onswere if þu myht.
Sey me nv, þu wrecche wiht,
Is in þe eny oþer note
Bute þu hauest schille þrote?
Þu nart nouht to non oþer þinge,
560 Bute þu canst of chateringe:
Vor þu art lutel and vnstrong,
ꝥ nys þi ryel nowiht long.
Hwat dostu godes among monne?
Na mo þene doþ a wrecche wrenne.
565 Of þe ne cumeþ non oþer god,
Bute þu gredest swich þu be wod:
ꝥ beo þi piping ouergo,
Ne beoþ on þe craftes na mo.
Alured seyde, þat wes wis:
570 (He myhte wel, for soþ hit is,)
"Nis nomon for his bare songe
Leof ne w[u]rþ noht swiþe longe:
Vor þat is o furw[u]rþe man
Þat bute singe naht ne can."
575 Þu nart bute o furw[u]rþe þing:
On þe nys bute chateryng.
Þu art dym ꝥ of fule heowe,
ꝥ þinchest a lytel soty clewe.

551. *iyue.*   572. *wrþ.*   573, 575. *-wrþe.*

569. *wis : is.* The faulty rhyme [ĭ] : [ĭ] is due to the lack of words ending in *-is*; cf. ll. 1635–6.

571–2. It is not unlikely that this proverb gave rise to the modern idiom ("a mere song," i.e. a trifle) which appears in works of the 17th cent.: see *N.E.D. song* (5).

577. *fule howe* = "dirty colour": cf. Alcuin, *De Luscinia*, l. 7, "Spreta colore, tamen fueras non spreta canendo" (Migne, *Pat. Lat.* 101, p. 803).

The inconspicuous coloration of the plumage of the nightingale is a notable feature of that bird. It is of "a reddish brown above, and dull greyish white beneath, the breast being rather darker, and the rufous tail showing the only bright tint" (see *Encycl. Brit.* s.v.).

578. *clowe* < O.E. *clēowen* (ball). According to *N.E.D.* (see "clew") "the length of the vowel in the O.E. form is uncertain." The evidence of the

Þu nart fair, no þu nart strong,
580 ne þu nart þicke, ne þu nart long: Fol. 237 r. col. 2.
þu hauest imist al of fairhede,
an lutel is al þi godede.
An oþer þing of þe ich mene,
þu nart vair ne þu nart clene.
585 Wane þu comest to manne haȝe,
þar þornes boþ ⁊ ris idraȝe,
bi hegge ⁊ bi þicke wode,
þar men goþ oft to hore node,
þarto þu draȝst, þarto þu w[u]nest,
590 an oþer clene stede þu schunest.
Þan ich flo niȝtes after muse,
I mai þe uinde ate rum-huse;
among þe wode, among þe netle,
þu sittest ⁊ singst bihinde þe setle:
595 þar me mai þe ilomest finde,
þar men worpeþ hore bihinde.
Ȝet þu atuitest me mine mete,
an seist þat ich fule wiȝtes ete.
Ac wat etestu, þat þu ne liȝe,
600 bute attercoppe ⁊ fule ulige,
an wormes, ȝif þu miȝte finde
among þe uolde of harde rinde?
Ȝet ich can do wel gode wike,
vor ich can loki manne wike:
605 an mine wike boþ wel gode,
vor ich helpe to manne uode.
Ich can nimen mus at berne,
an ek at chirche ine þe derne:
vor me is lof to Cristes huse,
610 to clansi hit wiþ fule muse,
ne schal þar neure come to
ful wiȝt, ȝif ich hit mai iuo.

---

rhyme in this couplet *howe : clowe* suggests a long vowel: since an originally
(O.E.) long vowel or diphthong does not rhyme in this poem with a lengthened
vowel or diphthong, and the diphthong in *howe* (O.E. *hēow*) is long.

589. *wunest* (C. *wnest*, J. *wenst*). The C. reading gives the better sense
and the more accurate rhyme, and therefore represents the original form.
For similar scribal forms see 1. 272 note.

Þu nart fayr, ne þu nart stro*n*g,
580 Ne þu nart þikke, ne þu nart long;
Þu hauest ymyst of fayrhede,
ꞇ lutel is þi godhede.
An oþer þing of þe ich mene,
Þu [n]art feyr ne þu nart clene.
585 Hwanne þu cumest to mo*n*ne hawe,
Þar þornes beoþ ꞇ ris idrawe,
Bi hegge ꞇ bi þikke weode,
Þar men goþ to heore neode,
Þarto þu draust [þar]to þu w[u]nst
590 ꞇ oþer clene stude þu schunest.
Hwanne ich fleo nyhtes after muse,
Ich may þe vinde at þe ru*m*-huse:
Amo*n*g þe wede, amo*n*g þe netle,
Þu syttest ꞇ singst bihinde seotle:
595 Þar me þe may ilomest fynde,
Þar men worpeþ heore byhinde.
Yet þu atwitest me myne mete,
ꞇ seyst þat ich fule wyhtes ete.
Ac hwat etestu, þat þu ne lye,
600 Bute attercoppe ꞇ fule vlye,
ꞇ wurmes, if þu myht fynde
Amo*n*g þe volde of harde rynde?
Yet ich can do wel gode wike,
For ich can loki monne wike:
605 ꞇ mine wike beoþ wel gode,
For ich helpe to monne vode.
Ich can nyme [m]us at berne,
ꞇ ek at chireche in þe derne:
For me is leof to Cristes huse,
610 To clansi hit wiþ fule [m]use,
Ne schal þar neuer cume to
Ful wiht, if ich hit may ivo.

---

584. *þu art.*   589. *þartto: wenst.*   607. *Mus.*   610. *Muse.*

---

602. Trans. "Among the crevices of the hard bark (of the trees)," cf.
Barnes' *Poems* (95):

> True love's the ivy that do twine
> Unwith'ren roun' his mossy rine.

603 ff. See note l. 535.   609. *me is lof,* see note l. 85.

An ȝif me lust one mi skentinge
to wernen oþer w[u]nienge,　　　　Fol. 237 v. col. 1.
615　ich habbe at wude tron wel *grete*,
mit þicke boȝe noþing blete,
mid iui grene al bigrowe,
þat eure stont iliche iblowe,
an his hou neu*er* ne uorlost,
620　wan hit sniuw ne wan hit frost.
Þarin ich habbe god ihold,
a-wint*er* warm, a-sum*ere* cold.
Wane min hus stont briȝt ꝛ grene,
of þine nis noþing isene.
625　Ȝet þu me telst of oþer þinge,
of mine briddes seist gabbinge,
þat hore nest nis noȝt clene.
Hit is fale oþer wiȝte imene:
vor hors a-stable ꝛ oxe a-stalle
630　[d]oþ al þat hom wule þar falle.
An lutle children in þe cradele,
boþe chorles an ek aþele,
[d]oþ al þat in hore ȝoeþe
þat hi uorleteþ in hore duȝeþe.
635　Wat! can þat ȝongling hit bihede?
Ȝif hit misdeþ, hit mo[t] nede:
a uorbisne is of olde i[vu]rne,
[þ]at node makeþ old wif urne.

614. *wnienge.*　　630, 633. *boþ.*　　636. *mod.*　　637. *iwrne.*　　638. *wat.*

614. *wernen* (C. and J.). St. and Wr. *yernen*; Str., Sk. and W. *wernen*, though Sk. prefers *yernen*. The initial letter in C. may be read as either *y* or *w*; but J. has *w* quite distinctly, and moreover initial *y* (< O.E. *g*) instead of *ȝ* would be unusual in C.
wunienge (C. *wnienge*, J. *wunyng*). Str. *wuninge*, Sk. *wunienge*, W. *wnienge*. The C. reading again is preferable, for the metre requires the additional syllable, i.e. *wúniénge*. The J. scribe has altered the reading of the original: cf. l. 272 for similar change.
615. *tron* (J. *treon*) = "trees." An extension of the *-en* plural (characteristic of S. dial.) to a word in which it was etymologically incorrect, cf. *scheon* (*A.R.* 362), *lambren* (*Ayen.* 139), *children* (*O. & N.* l. 631): also *fëazen* (faces), *plëazen* (places), Barnes' *Poems* (24, 35).
616. *noþing* = "not at all." Probably formed on analogy with O.E. *nawiht*, *noht* (not), cf. *noþing* (J. *nowiht*) ll. 624, 1247.
620. *sniuw* (J. *snywe*) = "snow(s)." Str., Sk. and G. read here the indic. form *sniuþ* (though the *wen* has a dot above it in the MS.) possibly on account of the indic. *frost* which follows. The reading *sniuw* (= *sniwe*),

⁊ if me lust on my skenting
To wernen oþe[r] wunyng,
615 Ich habbe at wode treon grete,
Mid þikke bowe noþing blete,
Mid ivi grene al bigrowe,
Þat euer stont iliche iblowe,
⁊ his heou neuer ne uorleost,
620 Hwanne hit snywe ne [hwanne hit] frost.
Þarinne ic habbe god ihold,
A-wintre warm, a-sumere cold.
Þane myn hus stont briht ⁊ grene,
Of þine nys nowiht isene.
625 Yet þu me telst of oþer þinge,
Of myne briddes seyst gabbinge,
Þat heore [nest] nys nouht clene.
Hit is fale oþer wihte imene:
Vor hors a-stable, ⁊ oxe a-stalle
630 Doþ al þat heom wile þar valle.
⁊ lutle childre in þe cradele,
Boþe cheorles ⁊ ek aþele,
Doþ al þat in heore youhþe
Þat hi uorleteþ in heore duhþe.
635 Hwat! can þat yongling hit bihede?
Yf hit mys[d]eþ, hit mot nede:
A vorbisne is of olde iwurne,
Þat neode makeþ old wif eorne.

614. *oþe.*   620. *ne frost.*   627. *heore nys.*   636. *myskeþ.*

adopted by W., is however to be preferred, for not only is the opt. grammatically correct but it is also the reading of both MSS. The change of mood
in *frost* is due to rhyming exigencies.
630. *doþ* (C. *boþ*, J. *doþ*). W. retains *boþ*, but does not explain how he
would interpret the passage. The J. reading gives the better sense, and
boþ (C.) is probably a scribal error, the eye of the scribe having been caught
by *boþe* (l. 632).
631–2. For the rhyme, see note ll. 501–2.
637. *ivurne* (C. *iwrne*, J. *iwurne*) = "formerly." Str. reads *ifurne* which he
regards as a sb. < *ifurn* (O.E. *gefyrn*, adv. "formerly"): cf. Str.-Br. *ifurne* =
antiquity (?). W., on the other hand, retains *iwrne* (< O.E. *ge-urnen*, p.p. of
iernan) = "run, passed, come down," and the line he translates: "A parable
has come down from of old." But this is to regard *w-* (J. *wu-*) = *u-*, an
equivalence for which no parallel exists in the poem; and moreover, the
resulting rhyme *u* (O.E. *urnen*) : *ü* (O.E. *yrnan*) would be faulty. The most
satisfactory reading is that of G. who takes *iwrne* = *ivurne* (O.E. *gefyrn*,
formerly), adv. with inorganic *-e*, cf. *wl* = *vul* (l. 31). The J. scribe has

An ȝet ich habbe an oþer andsware:
640 wiltu to mine neste uare
an loki hu hit is idiȝt?
Ȝif þu art wis lorni þu [miȝt]:
mi nest is holȝ ᛏ rum amidde,
so hit is softest mine bridde.

645 Hit is broiden al abute,
vrom þe neste uor wiþute:
þarto hi go[þ] to hore node,
ac þat þu menest ich hom forbode. 　Fol. 237 v. col. 2.
We nimeþ ȝeme of manne bure,
650 an after þan we makeþ ure:
men habbet, among oþer i[h]ende,
a rum-hus at hore bures ende,
vor þat hi nelleþ to uor go,
an mine briddes doþ al so.

655 Site nu stille, chaterestre!
nere þu neuer ibunde uastre:
herto ne uindestu neuer andsware.
Hong up þin ax! nu þu miȝt fare!"
Þe niȝtingale at þisse worde
660 was wel neȝ ut of rede iworþe,
an þoȝte ȝorne on hire mode
ȝif ho oȝt elles understode,
ȝif ho kuþe oȝt bute singe,
þat miȝte helpe to oþer þinge.

642. *miȝst.*　　647. *god.*　　651. *iwende.*

---

evidently misread *iwrne* of the common original and wrongly inserted *u* after
w. The phrase *of olde ivurne* would thus mean "formerly of old," i.e. of
long ago. For similar redundancies cf. the common O.E. phrase *íu gēara,*
and *gefyrn ǣr* (=Lat. *jam*) (Napier, *O.E. Glosses,* 56, 93).
　638. This proverb is of frequent occurrence in medieval and later times:
cf. *Neode makad heald wif eorne—ut cito se portet uetule cogit oportet* (*Lat.-
Fr. Misc.,* Trin. Coll. Camb., Ο. ii. 45); *Nede makyth an olde wyf* [*runne*]—
currere non fesse vetulam dat sepe necesse (*Harl.* 3362, fol. 3, Kemble);
Neede maketh the old wife trot (Heywood's *Proverbs,* p. 169); *Besoin fait
vieille trotter* (*Rom. de Trubert,* 1300); "Need makes the old wife trot" (*Harl.*
MS. 2231, 16th century: *Rel. Ant.* i. 207); *Besoing si fet vieille troter* (*Rom.
de Renart,* 4905). It is found also in the works of Taylor the Water-poet and
in Brewer's *Scottish Proverbs*—in the latter it reads "Need gars naked men
run." In Ray's *Proverbs* (p. 139) the Italian form *Bisogno la trotter la
vecchia* is quoted, as well as another variant, "Need makes the naked queen
spin." In Dykes' *English Proverbs* (1709), p. 193, occurs "Need makes the
naked man run or the naked queen spin," with the comment, "I suppose,
to cover their nakedness"; cf. also Scott, *St Ronan's Well* (ch. xxxvi.) where

    ꞇ yet ich habbe an oþer onswere:

640 Wiltu to myne neste vare

    ꞇ loki hw hit is idiht?

    If þu art wis leorny þu mi[h]t:

    Mi nest is holeuh ꞇ rum amidde,

    So hit is softest myne bridde.

645 Hit is ibroyde al abute,

    Vrom þe neste ueor wiþvte:

    Þarto hi goþ to heore neode,

    Ac [hwat] þu menest ich heom forbode.   Fol. 233 v. col. 2.

    We yeme nymeþ of manne bure,

650 ꞇ after þan we makieþ vre:

    Men habbeþ among oþre i[h]ende,

    A rum-hus at heore bures ende,

    Vor þat hi nelleþ to veor go,

    ꞇ myne briddes doþ al so.

655 Syte nv stille, chaterestre!

    Nere þu neuer ibunde vastre:

    Herto ne vyndestu neuer answere.

    Hong up þin ax! nv þu miht fare!"

    Þe Nihtegale at þisse worde

660 Was wel neyh ut of rede iworþe,

    ꞇ þouhte yorne on hire mode

    Yf heo ouht elles vnderstode,

    If heo cuþe ouht bute singe,

    Þat myhte helpe to oþer þinge.

---

642. *mist.*   648. *ac þu.*   651. *iwende.*

Mr Touchwood quotes in his reply to Mowbray: "Necessity that makes the old wife trot." W. cites *Besoing fet ueille troter* from a collection of O.Fr. proverbs of the early 12th century (Cod. Voss. Lat. 31 F., Univ. Lib., Leiden) (Haupt, *Zeitschrift*, XI. 115).

    642. *miȝt* (C. *miȝst*, J. *mist*) = "mayst." The rhyme suggests that *miȝt* (cf. *diȝt*, l. 641) was the original form, see note l. 78.

    651. *ihende.* See additional notes, p. 202.

    658. *Hong up þin ax*, a colloquial expression = "cease from further efforts, confess thyself beaten," cf. *Ich mai honge vp min ax, febliche iche abbe agonne* (Robt. of Glou., *Chron.* 11771). The phrase occurs in its original sense in *Gaw. and the Gr. Knight*, ll. 476 ff.:

        "Now, sir, heng up þyn ax, þat hatȝ innogh hewen,"
          And hit watȝ don abof þe dece, on doser to henge,
          þer alle men for mervayl myȝt on hit loke.

    659–700. A lively commentary on the vicissitudes and tricks of pleading.

    660. *ut of rede.* Sk. trans. "out of patience." But from the context it is clear that *rede* has here its usual meaning, i.e. "counsel, plan." The Nightingale was almost at her wit's end to know what to do.

665   Herto ho moste andswere uinde,
oþer mid alle bon bihinde:
an hit is suþe strong to fiȝte
aȝen soþ ꝼ aȝen riȝte.
He mot gon to al mid ginne,
670   þan þe horte boþ on [w]inne:
an þe man mot on oþer segge,
he mot bihemmen ꝼ bilegge,
ȝif muþ wiþute mai biwro
þat me þe horte noȝt niso:
675   an sone mai a word misreke
þar muþ shal aȝen horte speke;
an sone mai a word misstorte
þar muþ shal speken aȝen horte.
Ac noþeles ȝut upe þon,
680   her is to red wo hine kon:
vor neuer nis wit so kene
so þane red him is a-wene.   Fol. 238 r. col. 1.
þanne erest kume[þ] his ȝephede
wone hit is alre-mest on drede:
685   for Aluered seide of olde quide,
an ȝut hit nis of horte islide:
"Wone þe bale is alre-hecst,
þonne is þe bote alre-necst";

670. *þinne.*   683. *kumed.*   686. *sut ȝut, sut* deleted.

---

671. *on oþer* (J. *oþer*) = "in other fashion, otherwise," i.e. so as not to let it appear that his heart is troubled; cf. l. 903, for a similar idiom; also *Laȝ.* 21005, *hit iwarþ on oþer*; *Hav.* 1395 H, *þouhte al an oþer.* In the present instance, the phrase clearly means "with dissimulation."

675. The Nightingale, as a cautious pleader, realises the danger of making the slightest technical error (*miskenning*) in her statement of her case. See Intro. § 6, p. liv.

677. *misstorte* (J. *myssturte*) = "go wrong." Str. reads *missteorte*, but other forms found in M.E. are *sturte, stirte, sterte* (see Str.-Br.), which point to an O.E. *styrtan, *sturtjan: see Skeat, *Concise Eng. Dict.* (*start*).

679. *upe þon* = O.E. *uppan þam* (as against that).

680. *her is to red = her is [him] to red*, i.e. "here is help for him" (who knows it), cf. O.E. *Hom.* I. 165, *hwat scal us to rede* (what shall help us); *Wm. of Pal.* 902–3, *i not...what is me to rede* (I know not...what will help me). Note the preservation of O.E. grammatical gender in *hine*, = *red* (< O.E. *rǣd* (m.)).

682. *a-wene.* W. (followed by G.) regards this form as = "in his thought," and the line he would translate "As when counsel (a sound plan) is in his thought." Better sense is, however, obtained by taking *a-wene* = O.E. *on wēne*

665 Herto heo moste answere vynde,
    Oþer mid alle beon bihinde:
    ꝉ hit is strong to vyhte
    Ayeyn soþe ꝉ ayeyn rihte.
    He mot gon to al mid gynne,
670 Hwan þe horte beoþ on winne:
    ꝉ þe man mot oþer segge,
    He mot bihemme ꝉ bilegge,
    If muþ wiþvte may biwreo
    Þat me þe horte nouht niseo:
675 ꝉ sone may a word mysreke
    Þar muþ schal ayeyn horte speke:
    ꝉ sone may a word myssturte
    Þar muþ schal speke ayeyn horte.
    Ac [noþeles hyet] upe þon,
680 Her is to red hwo hyne con:
    Vor neuer nys wit so kene
    So hwanne red him is a-wene.
    Þanne erest cumeþ his yephede   Fol. 234 r. col. 1.
    Hwenne hit is alremest on drede;
685 For Alured seyde of olde quide,
    ꝉ hyet hit nis of horte islide:
    "Hwenne þe bale is alre-hekst,
    Þenne is þe bote alre-nest."

        679. *noþeles þ. hyet.*

("in expectation, in doubt"), in which case the line would read "As when good counsel from it (i.e. the wit) is in doubt." The point of the passage evidently is that the wit is sharpened by an emergency, and the idea is characteristically repeated in ll. 683–4 (cf. ll. 675–8 for a similar repetition of ideas).

683–4. Cf. Shak. *Venus and Adonis*, l. 690, "Danger deviseth shifts: wit waits on fear."

687–8. This proverb is common in M.E.: it is also found in an Icel. form (see *N.E.D. bale*). Further instances occur in *A.S. Apophthegms* (quoted by Kemble, *Sal. and Sat.* p. 258), ðonne hit ðe frǣcnost þynce, wen ðe ðonne frofre; *O.E. Hom.* p. 277, þer þe bale was alre meast, swa was te bote nehest; *Prov. of Hending*, l. 176, *When þe bale is hest, þenne is þe bote nest*; *Flor. and Blanch.* (l. 821), *After bale comeþ bote*; Usk, *Testament of Love*, ii. ix. 143, *Whan bale is greetest, than is bote a nye-bore*; Ray's *Proverbs*, p. 75, "When bale is hext, boot is next"; Scott, *Pev. of Peak*, xlvi., "When bale is at highest, as the poet singeth, boot is at nighest." In *Spec. of E.E.* ii. p. 296, a parallel Jewish proverb is quoted, "When the tale of bricks is doubled, Moses comes" (cf. Ray's *Proverbs*, p. 75, Cum duplicantur lateres, venit Moses).

vor wit west among his sore,
690   an for his sore hit is þe more.
Vorþi nis neu*e*re mon redles
ar his horte bo witles:
ac ʒif þat he forlost his wit,
þonne is his red-purs al to-slit;
695   ʒif he ne kon his wit atholde,
ne uint he red in one uolde.
Vor Alur[e]d seide, þat wel kuþe,
eure he spac mid soþe muþe:
"Wone þe bale is alre-hecst,
700   þanne is þe bote alre-nest."

þe niʒtingale al hire hoʒe
mid rede hadde wel bitoʒe;
among þe harde, amo*n*g þe toʒte,
ful wel mid rede hire biþoʒte,
705   an hadde andsuere gode ifunde
among al hire harde stunde.

"[H]ule, þu axest me," ho seide,
"ʒif ich kon eni oþer dede
bute singen in sume tide,
710   an bringe blisse for ꝛ wide.
Wi axestu of craftes mine?
Betere is min on þan alle þine,
bet*e*re is o song of mine muþe
þan al þat eure þi kun kuþe:
715   an lust, ich telle þe wareuore.
Wostu to wan man was ibore?   Fol. 238 r. col. 2.
To þare blisse of houene-riche,
þar eu*e*r is song ꝛ murʒþe iliche:

697. *Alurd.*   707. *Nule*, rubric N.

697. *his red-purs al to-slit*, trans. "His pocket is picked of all its wisdom,"
or "his store of counsel is quite destroyed." The reference is possibly to the
practices of the cutpurse (*purs...to-slit*).
    to-slit. The absence of the *-e(n)* ending suggests that the word=p. p. of
wk. vb. *toslitten* (<O.E. **slitjan*), as distinct from str. vb. *tosliten* (<O.E.
-slitan). Possibly, however, we have here an instance of an O.E. str. vb.
which already by 1200 had become wk.: hence *sliten, slitte, slit,* cf. *banned*
(O.E. *bēonn*), l. 1668.
    702. *bitoʒe* (J. *bitowe*) = "employed" (p. p.): cf. *Anc. Riw.* p. 430, *Elles
ich heuede uvele bitowen muchel of mine hwile.*

Vor [w]it [w]est among his sore,

690　⁊ for his sore hit is þe more.

Vorþi nis neuer mon redles

Ar his horte beo witles:

Ac if he furleost his wit,

Þenne is his red-purs al to-slyt:

695　If he ne con his wit atholde,

N[e] vynt he red in none volde.

Vor Alured seyde, þat wel cuþe,

Euer he spak mid soþe muþe:

"Hwenne þe bale is alre-hekst,

700　Þenne is þe bote alre-nexst."

　　Þe Nihtegale al hi[re howe]

Mid rede hadde wel bitowe;

Among þe harde, among þe towehte,

Ful wel myd rede hire biþouhte,

705　⁊ hedde onswere god ifunde

Among alle hire harde stunde.

　　"[U]le, þu axest me," heo seyde,

"[I]f ich con eny oþer dede

Bute syngen in sume tyde,

710　⁊ bringe blisse veor ⁊ wyde.

Hwy axestu of craftes myne?

Beter is myn on þan alle þine,

Beter is o song of myne muþe

Þan al þat [evre] þi kun kuþe:

715　⁊ lust, ich telle þe hwarvore.

Wostu to hwan mon wes ibore?

To þare blisse of heueryche,

Þar euer is song ⁊ [m]urehþe ilyche:　Fol. 234 r. col. 2.

---

689. *yit yest.*　　696. *N.*　　701. *al hit*, rest omitted.
707. capital *u* omitted.　　708. capital *i* omitted.　　714. *þat þi.*
718. *Murehþe.*

---

704. *hire biþoȝte.* Note the use of dat. *hire*: an early instance of the dat. taking the place of the acc. Elsewhere the acc. form is found as in *hi biþoȝte* (l. 199), *hine biþenche* (ll. 828, 871): cf. also *A.S. Chron.* *hire* (used for acc.) 1127, 1140; *him* (used for acc.) 654 E, 963 E.
709. *sume.* Possibly a scribal misreading, as M. points out, of the intermediate text, for *sumere*; cf. l. 489.

þider fundeþ eurich man
720 þat eni þing of gode kan.
Vorþi me singþ in holi-chirche,
an clerkes ginneþ songes wirche,
þat man iþenche bi þe songe
wider he shal, ꞇ þar bon longe:
725 þat he þe murȝþe ne uorȝete,
ac þarof þenche ꞇ biȝete,
an nime ȝeme of chirche steuene,
hu murie is þe blisse of houene.
Clerkes, munekes, ꞇ kanunes,
730 þar boþ þos gode wicke-tunes,
ariseþ up to midel-niȝte,
an singeþ of þe houene-liȝte:
an prostes upe londe singeþ,
wane þe liȝt of daie springeþ.
735 An ich hom helpe wat I mai,
ich singe mid hom niȝt ꞇ dai,
an ho boþ alle for me þe gladdere,
an to þe songe boþ þe raddere.
Ich warni men to hore gode,
740 þat hi bon bliþe on hore mode,
an bidde þat hi moten iseche
þan ilke song þat euer is eche.
Nu þu miȝt, hule, sitte ꞇ clinge:
her-among nis no chateringe:
745 ich graunti þat [w]e go to dome
tofore þe [sulfe Pope] of Rome.

745. *þe.*   746. *sulfe þe Pope.*

---

719. *fundeþ* = "goeth," <O.E. *fundian*: cf. *fundieþ* (l. 850). W. confuses this word with *fondeþ* (l. 1581), *vonde* (l. 1063), both of which are <O.E. *fandian* (to try).

724. Verb of motion omitted after *shal*, as in O.E.

730. *wicke-tunes* (<O.E. *wic-tūnas*, courts, enclosures in a sacred place) = "sacred dwellings, religious communities." The O.E. word is used in the *O.E. Trans. of Psalms* 96, 8, *ingangeþ on his wictunas* (go into His courts), but at the date of our poem it was probably obsolescent; cf. Wicklif's rendering "Entre ȝe in to his porchis."

731. See note ll. 323–8.

733. *upe londe* <O.E. *uppan londe* = "up and down (or throughout) the country." The reference is to "the parish priests" whose services were confined to the day-time. See additional notes, p. 202.

Þider fundeþ euerich man
720 Þat eny þing of gode can.
For-þi me syngþ *in* holy-chireche,
⁊ clerekes gynneþ songes w[i]rche,
Þat mon yþenche bi þe songe
Hwider he shal, ⁊ þar ben longe:
725 Þat he þe murehþe ne voryete,
Ac þarof þenche ⁊ bige[t]e,
⁊ nyme yeme of chirche stefne,
Hw [m]urie is þe blisse of heuene.
Clerekes, Munekes, ⁊ canunes,
730 Þar beoþ þos gode wike-tunes,
Ariseþ vp to middel-nyhte,
⁊ singeþ of þon heuene-lyhte:
⁊ preostes vpe londe singeþ,

    *   *   *   *

735 ⁊ ich heom helpe hwat ic may,
Ich singe myd hem nyht ⁊ day,
⁊ heo beoþ alle for me þe gladd*ere*,
⁊ to þe songe beoþ þe raddure.
Ich warny men to heore gode,
740 Þat hi beon blyþe on heore mode,
⁊ bidden þat hi moten iseche
Þat ilche song þat eu*er* is eche.
Nu þu myht, vle, sitte and clynge:
Her-amo*n*g nys no chateringe:
745 Ich graunti þat þu go to dome
Tovore þe sulve Pope of Rome.

726. -*gethe.*   728. *Murie.*   734. line omitted.

736 ff. For the tradition according to which the Nightingale sang the praises of God, see Intro. § 8, p. lxix.
The tradition is also preserved in Odo of Cheriton's *Fables* (1200—1250), where it is explained that "Philomela significat religiosos super duros ramos, id est austeritates religionis habitantes et Deum in choris nocturnis laudantes" (*De Upupa et Philomena*), Hervieux, *Les Fabulistes latins*, IV. p. 214. See additional notes, p. 202.
745–6. The rhyme *dome* : *Rome* indirectly throws light on the well-known pun in Shak. *Jul. Caesar*, I. ii. 156: "Now is it Rome indeed and room enough." During the 13th—16th centuries the root-vowel in *Rome* had the same sound-value as *doom* or *room*, i.e. [ō], later [ū]. After the 16th century the sound-value in *Rome* reverted from [ū] to [ō], as in the pronunciation of to-day, owing to continental influence.

Ac abid ȝete, noþeles,
þu shalt ihere an oþer [h]es;
ne shaltu, for Engelonde,
750 at þisse worde me atstonde.   Fol. 238 v. col. 1.
Wi atuitestu me mine unstrengþe,
an mine ungrete ꞇ mine unlengþe,
an seist þat ich nam noȝt strong,
vor ich nam noþer gret ne long?
755 Ac þu nost neuer wat þu menst,
bute lese wordes þu me lenst:
for ich kan craft ꞇ ich kan liste,
an [þ]areuore ich am þus þriste.
Ich kan wit ꞇ song man[t]eine,
760 ne triste ich to non oþer maine:
vor soþ hit is þat seide Alured:
"Ne mai no strengþe aȝen red."

748. *þes.*   758. *ware-.*   759. *mani eine.*

---

748. *hes* (C. *þes*, J. *bles* inserted by later hand). The uncertain readings
of both MSS. are evidently the result of an obscure reading in the common
original (see Intro. § 3 (*a*) (iv)). It is hardly likely, in the first place, that *bles*
(J.) represents the reading of the original, for it is difficult to see how the
C. scribe (who always attempts to copy rather than to emend) could have
written *þ* for an original *bl.* The J. form is therefore a guess on the part of
a later scribe, which at least has the merit of suiting the context while
affording a normal rhyme. Thus *bles* (< O.E. *blǣs,* blast) gives good sense
as well as a correct rhyme with *-les* (O.E. *lǣs*). On the other hand, the
retention of the C. form *þes* (see Str. and G., also *E.St.* I. 212) involves
certain difficulty. G. takes it to be the neu. gen. of the def. art. (O.E. *þǣs*)
used as a demonstrative, and he quotes *fondi þas* (l. 1442) as a parallel construction. But the cases are somewhat different, and his interpretation of
l. 748, viz. "thou shalt hear something different" (etwas anderes hiervon), is
palpably forced. Other editors, including Sk., M. and W., adopt the reading
an oþer wes but without solving the difficulty. Neither of the two interpretations proposed, viz. (1) "in a different manner" (O.E. *wis, wise*), (2)
"in another strain" (O.N. *visa*) is satisfactory, on account of the defective
rhyme that would result. The most likely solution is obtained by regarding
þes as a scribal error for *hes* (cf. ll. 1256, 1267; for similar errors, see also
Intro. § 3 (*d*) (v)), and by interpreting *hes* (O.E. *hǣs*) as "judicial pronouncement, sentence"; cf. Napier, *O.E. Glosses,* 1294. *hǣse=prẹcepti* (for
prǣceptum="sentence judiciaire"), see Maigne D'Arnis, *Lexicon Med. et
Inf. Lat.* This reading gives the sense required as well as a correct rhyme:
it is also in keeping with the legal phraseology scattered throughout the
poem.
   It is curious, further, to note that in *The Throstle and the Nightingale*
(ed. F. Holthausen, *Anglia,* XLIII. (xxxi.), pp. 53–9) this same rhyme *les : þes*
occurs, viz. *Fowel, me þinkeþ, þou art les,* | *þey you be milde and softe of þes*
(ll. 67–8). Here, again, the meaning is obscure, unless *hes* (command) be

Ac abid yete, noþeles,

Þu schalt abyde on oþer [bles]:

Ne schaltu, vor Engelonde,

750　At þisse worde me atstonde.

Hwy atwitestu me myne vnstrengþe,

⁊ myne vngrete, ⁊ myn vnlengþe,

⁊ sayst þat ich am nouht strong,

Vor ic nam noþer gret ne long?　　Fol. 234 v. col. 1.

755　Ac þu nost neuer hwat þu menest,

Bute lese wordes þu me lenest:

For ic kan craft ⁊ ic kan lyste,

⁊ þarfore ic am þus þriste.

Ich kan wit ⁊ song mony eine,

760　Ne triste ic to non oþer mayne:

Vor soþ hit is þat seyde Alured:

"Ne may no strengþe ayeyn red."

748. *bles* inserted later.

---

read, in which case the interpretation would be "O bird! methinketh thou art false, though thou art mild and gentle of speech (command)." In the later poem, it is true, the rhyme is somewhat different from that in the *O. & N.*, where $\bar{e}$ (O.E. $\bar{æ}$) : $\bar{e}$ (O.E. $\bar{æ}$). In *The Throstle and the N.* the rhyme is $\bar{e}$ (O.E. *ēa*) : $\bar{e}$ (O.E. $\bar{æ}$); but at the later date these two O.E. values had fallen together, so that no difficulty arises with regard to the proposed interpretation (see also l. 1109, note).

759. *manteine* (C. *mani eine*, J. *mony eine*). Most of the earlier editors (St., Wr., Str. and M.) read *manteine*, whereas W. and G. retain *mani eine*, apparently on account of the agreement of the two MSS. W. explains *mani eine* as = "many a one": but *eine* must be regarded as a highly improbable form whether derived (as in W.) from O.E. $\bar{æ}nne$ or from O.N. *einn*. G., on the other hand, suggests *manieine* (infin.) < O.Fr. *manier*, "to manage, deal with"—also an unlikely reading. What we have here, in all probability, is an instance of a carelessly-made *t* in the common original, a form which was faithfully copied in C. (the stroke at the top of the *t* being possibly wanting) and taken for *i*. A similar obscurity in the common original occurs in ll. 763, 1322 (see notes, also Intro. § 3 (*d*) (v)). Hence the form *manteine* may safely be adopted here: see Gloss.

760. *triste* (C. and J.), cf. *truste* (l. 1273). The M.E. form *trust* (sb.) is derived from O.W. Scand. *traust*; and *tristen*, according to Björkman, is possibly the corresponding verb, as "analogical *i*-mutation may very well have taken place...in M.E. times": see Björkman, *Scand. Loan-words in M.E.* p. 249.

762. Similar sentences are found in *Laȝ*, 17210–3, *Betere is liste | þene ufel strengþe* : | *for mid liste me mai ihalden* | *þat strengþe ne mai iwalden*; *Anc. Riwle*, p. 268, *Betere is liste þen luþer strencþe*; *Prov. of Hending* (Oxf. Bodl., Digby 86), v. 34, *Betere is red þen res*. Giraldus Cambrensis (*Descriptio Kambriae*, ed. Dimock, Rolls Series, I. xii. p. 188) quotes from the English of his day *betere is red thene rap, and liste thene lither streingthe*: cf. also

A.　　　　　　　　　　　　　　　　　　　　　　　　5

Oft spet wel a lute liste,

þar muche strengþe sholde miste;

765 mid lutle strengþe, þurȝ ginne,

castel ꝸ burȝ me mai iwinne.

Mid liste me mai walle[s] felle,

an worpe of horsse kniȝtes snelle.

Vuel strengþe is lutel wurþ,

770 *   *   *   *   *

*   *   *   *   *

ac wisdom naueþ non euening.

An hors is strengur þan a mon;

ac for hit non iwit ne kon,

775 hit berþ on rugge grete semes,

an draȝþ biuore grete temes,

767. *walle.*   770, 771 omitted.

(quoted by Regel, *Angl.* I. 200):

Rois, dist Merlin, et ne ses tu

Qu'engiens sormonte vertu?

Bone est force et engins mius valt,

La vaut engins ou force falt:

Engins et ars font maint cose

Que force commeneheir ne n'ose.

(Wace, *Rom. de Brut,* 8261–6.)

Ja par force n'en seroit plus:

Or verres engin et savoir

mius que vertu del cors valoir.   (*Ibid.* 8350–2.)

G. quotes "Ingenio salso praeceps violentia cedit" (*Fecunda Ratis des Egbert von Lüttich,* ed. Voigt, Halle, 1889, p. 50), and O.Fr. "Engins vaut mielz que force."

763. *lute* (C. and J.). W. notes that the C. reading might be either *lute* or *litte,* the second stroke of *u* being written very much like a careless *t* (cf. ll. 759, 1322).

764. *sholde miste* (J. *solde myste*). Str., Str.-Br. and G. agree in adopting the J. reading and in taking *solde* (O.Fr. *solde,* wages) = "reward," and *miste* as pt. 3 sg. of *misse* (to miss). They would therefore translate the line as "Where great strength would have missed its reward." In l. 975 however both C. and J. have *solde=sholde*: and M. retained the C. reading, explaining *miste* as=*misse* (O.E. *missan,* infin.), the O.E. *-ss* having been changed to *-st* owing to the exigencies of rhyme. It may possibly be that *miste* represents a dialect variant of *misse* (cf. O.N. *missa,* Dan. *miste*), but neither explanation is quite convincing, and in either case the line would read "Where great strength would miss (its mark)." The most likely suggestion comes from Kenyon (*J.E.G.P.* XII. 580), who points out the existence elsewhere, in the rhyming position, of weak p.p. with inorganic final *-e,* e.g. *iladde* (ll. 398, 1294). Hence *miste* in the present instance may possibly be regarded as equivalent to the normal p.p. (*i)mist* (cf. l. 581). Kenyon further suggests that in *sholde miste* we have "one of the not infrequent instances in which unstressed *have* is phonetically reduced and absorbed in the *e* of *sholde,*" so that *sholde miste=sholde haue mist(e).* But his explanation here seems open to question. The omission of *haue* seems due, not to phonetic causes, but to that O.E. idiom in which an infin. after *sceal,*

Oft spet wel a lute lyste,
Þar muche strengþe solde myste;
765 Mid lutle strengþe, þureh ginne,
Castel ꞇ bureh me may winne.
Mid liste me may walles felle,
ꞇ werpe of horse knyhtes snelle.
Vuel strengþe is lutel w[u]rþ,
770 Ac wisdom ne w[u]rþ neuer vnw[u]rþ:
Þu myht iseo þurh alle þing,
Þat wisdom naueþ non euening.
An hors is strengur þan a mon;
Ac for hit non iwit ne kon,
775 Hit berþ on rugge grete semes,
ꞇ drahþ bi sweore grete temes,

769. *wrþ.*   770. *wrþ, vnwrþ.*

---

sceolde was often dropped; cf. *Beowulf*, 2255, "*sceal se hearda helm..fætum befeallen*" (the hard helmet shall [be] deprived of its plating). It is in accordance with this idiom that the auxiliary infin. is omitted from *sholde miste*, which therefore is best rendered as "would (should) have missed, or gone astray."

767. *walles* (C. *walle*, J. *walles*) = acc. pl. "walls." Kenyon (*J.E.G.P.* XII. 579) suggests that *walle* is the only instance in the poem of a form in which the d. pl. ending (O.E. *-um*) of an O.E. masc. *o*-stem has been substituted for the ending of the acc. pl. (O.E. *-as*). More probably, however, *walle* (C.) is a scribal error for *walles*. What we have here is a sort of haplography, the scribe having confused final *s* with the *f* at the beginning of the following word *felle*.

772. *ac wisdom* (J. *þat wisdom*). In explanation of the omission of ll. 770–1 from the C. text, W. suggests that "the scribe, having begun l. 770 correctly, was led into completing the verse from l. 772, his eye having fallen on *wisdom*, the second word of l. 772 as of l. 770." For the significance of this omission as regards the relation of the two texts see Intro. § 3 (*a*) (ii) (*a*).

euening. W. incorrectly translates as "evening." But the invariable form for Mod. Eng. "evening" in the poem is *eue* (5 times), and here *euening* clearly stands for "equal" (see *N.E.D. evening*). Mr B. Dickins quotes Thomas de Hales, *Love Rune*, vv. 19–20, *Absalon | þat nevede on eorþe non evenyng.*

776. *draȝþ biuore* (J. *drahþ bi sweore*). Str. adopts the reading of J. which undoubtedly gives the better sense, and which might well be taken as the reading of the original, were there any grounds for supposing that the C. scribe had omitted an *s*, thus reading *biuore* for *bi suore*. As things are, however, the C. reading, though not free from difficulty, is best retained. The form *draȝþ*, since it is followed by the prep. *biuore*, is intrans. and is probably best translated as "goes," cf. *drah to þe* (l. 1186). The line would therefore read, "it goes in front of great teams (of horses)": and according to Kenyon (*J.E.G.P.* XII. 581) the allusion is to a medieval team, which worked, not abreast, but tandem-wise, so that a special responsibility would fall on the leading horse. By way of illustration he quotes Chau. *Troil. and Cres.* I. 218 ff. and further recalls the picture from the Louterell Psalter (reproduced in Coulton's *Chaucer and his England*) in which "five horses are hitched, one ahead of another, to a four-wheeled travelling carriage" while a driver with a long whip sits on the last horse, and another driver with a short whip on the leader.

an þoleþ boþe ȝerd ⁊ spure,
an stont iteid at mulne dure.
An hit deþ þat mon hit hot:
780 an for þan þat hit no wit not,
ne mai his strenþe hit ishilde
þat hit nabuȝþ þe lutle childe.
Mon deþ, mid strengþe ⁊ mid witte,
þat oþer þing nis non his fitte.
785 Þeȝ alle strengþe at one were,
monnes wit ȝet more were;   Fol. 238 v. col. 2.
vor þe mon mid his crafte,
ouerkumeþ al orþliche shafte.
Al so ich do mid mine one songe
790 bet þan þu al þe ȝer longe:
vor mine crafte men me luuieþ,
vor þine strengþe men þe shunieþ.
Telstu bi me þe wurs for þan
þat ich bute anne craft ne kan?
795 Ȝif tueie men goþ to wraslinge,
an eiþer oþer faste þringe,
an þe on can swenges suþe fele,
an kan his wrenches wel forhele,
an þe oþer ne can sweng but anne,
800 an þe is god wiþ eche manne,
an mid þon one leiþ to grunde
anne after oþer a lutle stunde,
[w]at þarf he recche of a mo swenge,
þone þe on him is swo genge?

803. *þat.*

---

778. *mulne dure*="the doors of the mills"; see note l. 86.
784. *fitte*="equal, a match." The word is rare (cf. *Pr. P.* 163, *fit*=
"congruus"), but the root idea is that of "meeting" or "joining" (cf.
O.N. *fitja*="knit"); cf. Shak. *All's Well*, II. i. 93, "I'll fit you": also Lancs.
dial. "I'll fit you" (=I'll match you).
795. *wraslinge* (J. *wrastlinge*)="wrestling." The C. form affords an
instance of the dropping of the middle one of three consonants—a change
already found in 11th century MSS. (see Napier, *O.E. Glosses*, p. xxix); cf.
strenþe (l. 781), *sprinþ* (l. 1042).
803. *a mo swenge.* The meaning of the line is: "What need he care

ꝛ þoleþ boþe yerd ꝛ spure,
ꝛ stont iteyed at mulne dure.
ꝛ hit doþ þat mon hit hot:
780 ꝛ for þan þat hit no wit not,
Ne may his strengþe hit ischilde
Þat h[it] nabuhþ þe lutle childe.
Mon doþ, mid strengþe ꝛ mid witte,
Þat oþer þing nys non his fitte.
785 Þey alle strengþe at one [w]ere,
Monnes wit yet more were:
Vor þe mon myd his crafte,
Ouercumeþ al eorþliche shafte.   Fol. 234 v. col. 2.
Al so ic do myd myne one songe
790 Bet þan þu alle yer longe:
Vor myne crafte men me luuyeþ,
Vor þine strengþe men þe schunyeþ.
Telstu bi me þe w[u]rs for þan
Þat ic bute enne craft ne·kan?
795 If twey men goþ to wrastlinge,
ꝛ eyþer oþer vaste þringe,
ꝛ þe on can swenges swiþe fele,
ꝛ kan his wrenches wel forhele,
ꝛ þe oþer ne can sweng bute onne,
800 ꝛ þe is god wiþ eche manne,
ꝛ myd þan one leyþ to grunde
Anne after oþe[r] a lutle stunde,
Hwat þarf he recche of a mo swenge,
Hwenne þe on him is so genge?

782. *h. nabuhþ.*   785. *yere.*   793. *wrs.*   802. *oþe.*

---

about more (or further) strokes (or tricks).'' W. however translates: ''[What need he care] concerning a greater blow,'' which clearly misrepresents the passage. In the first place, that rendering is not in keeping with the context (cf. ll. 795—802), which consists of a comparison, not between one trick and a greater trick, but between many tricks and one that is sufficiently effective. Secondly, the form *mo* (O.E. *mā*) = ''more in number'' is confused by W. with *more* (O.E. *māra*) = ''greater in size.'' The adv. *mo* is here used as a sb. with *swenge* (g. pl.), dependent upon it: cf. *A.S. Chron.* 905 A, 1043 E, for similar examples: also Shak. *Merch. of Ven.* III. v. 66, ''a many fools,'' Tennyson, *Miller's Daughter*, ''a many tears.''

805 Þ[u] seist þat þu canst fele wike,
     ac euer ich am þin unilike.
     Do þine craftes alle togadere,
     ȝet is min on horte betere.
     Oft þan hundes foxes driueþ,
810 þe kat ful wel him sulue liueþ,
     þeȝ he ne kunne wrench bute anne.
     Þe fo[x] so godne ne can nanne,
     þe[ȝ] he kunne so uele wrenche,
     þat he wenþ eche hunde atprenche.
815 Vor he can paþes riȝte 't woȝe,
     an he kan hongi bi þe boȝe,
     an so forlost þe hund his fore,
     an turnþ aȝen eft to þan more.
     Þe uox kan crope bi þe heie,
820 an turne ut from his forme weie,   Fol. 239 r. col. 1.
     an eft sone kume þarto:
     þonne is þe hundes smel fordo:
     he not, þur[ȝ] þe imeinde smak,
     weþer he shal auorþ þe abak.
825 Ȝif þe uox mist of al þis dwole,
     at þan ende he cropþ to hole:

805. *þe.*   812. *for.*   813. *þe.*   823. *þurs.*

---

805. *þu* (C. and J. *þe*). The common scribal error points to the existence of an intermediate text as common original, see Intro. § 3, a, iii (*a*).

806. *unilike* (J. *vnyliche*). That C. gives the original reading and J. an emended form is shown by the rhyme.

808. *horte* (J. *heorte*). M. unnecessarily emends to *hore*="their, of them."

809 ff. The fable *The Cat and the Fox* is here introduced as an illustration of the argument in the preceding lines (795 ff.). For a discussion of its sources see Intro. § 8, pp. lxv ff. The fable is also referred to in Erasmus, *Adag.* I. 5. 18, and in Bacon's *Adv. of Learning*, Bk. VI. Ch. III.

810. *liueþ*. This word has been variously misinterpreted. M. trans. "trusts" (<O.E. *líefan*), which would result in an *i* : *ē* rhyme. W. prefers "keeps life," G. "lives": both from O.E. *libban* (live). But apart from the strained meaning assigned by W. the form *liueþ* cannot=O.E. *lifaþ* (*leofaþ*), where the root-vowel is short, for the rhyme with *driueþ* (l. 809) requires a long *i*, and M.E. *ĭ* is not lengthened in open syllables. The word is evidently derived from O.E. (*be*)*lífan*, "to remain," which would give a form *liueþ* in keeping with the sense and the demands of rhyme. The correct reading therefore is: "the cat remains all by himself," i.e. he escapes the hounds.

812. *fox* (C. and J. *for*). For the significance of this scribal error common to both MSS., see note l. 805.

814. *atprenche* (C. and J.), see note l. 248.

805 Þ[u] seyst þat þu canst fele wike,
Ac euer ich am þin vnyliche.
Do þine craftes alle togadere,
Yet is myn on heorte betere.
Ofte hwan hundes foxes driueþ,
810 Þe kat ful wel him sulue liueþ,
Þeh he ne cunne wreynch bute anne.
Þe fo[x] so godne ne can nanne,
Þey he cunne so vele wrenche,
Þat he weneþ eche hunde atprenche.
815 Vor he can paþes rihte and wowe,
ꝼ he can hongi bi þe bowe,
ꝼ so vorlest þe hund his fore,
ꝼ turnþ eft ayeyn to þe more.
Þe fox can crepe by þe heye,
820 ꝼ turne vt from his forme weye,
ꝼ eft sone cume þarto:
Þenne is þes hundes smel fordo: Fol. 235 r. col. 1.
He not, þurh þe [m]eynde smak,
Hweþer he schal vorþ þe abak.
825 If þe uox miste of al þis dwele,
At þan ende he [creopþ] to hole:

805. *þe.*   812. *for.*   823. *Meynde.*   826. *creophþ.*

---

815. *he,* i.e. the fox. W. suggests a change of subject here. He takes the word *he* to refer to the *kat,* on the grounds (1) that the fox can scarcely be said to *hongi bi þe boȝe,* (2) that the change of subject is suggested by the subsequent return to *uox* as subject in l. 819. Kenyon (*J.E.G.P.* xii. 583) however regards W.'s suggestion as unnecessary, and his view is evidently the correct one. He maintains (1) that "the hanging from the bough" has reference to "one of the many well-known tricks of the fox (as leaping to a fence, a reclining tree or low limb)": (2) that the "return to *uox* (l. 819) is a return, not from the *cat,* but from *hund* which is the subject of the two preceding lines": (3) that if ll. 815-8 referred to the cat, as W. suggests, then that creature would have, not one trick (cf. l. 831), but three, viz. the tricks of following devious paths, of hanging from boughs, and of climbing trees: and as a result the whole point of the illustration would be lost.
But whereas Kenyon is right in his main contention, his explanation of the phrase *hongi bi þe boȝe,* as applied to the fox, is still unconvincing, for the simple reason that the fox cannot climb trees. The real explanation lies in the fact that the poet is here drawing on Neckam's *De Naturis Rerum;* and it is from that source that he borrows the idea that the fox when hard-pressed will take to a tree: see Intro. §8, p. lxvii, for quotation from Neckam.
819. *heie.* Glossed by W. under *hegge.* But these two words are quite distinct, though both of the same meaning, viz. *heie* (O.E. *hege*), *hegge* (O.E. *hecg*). The form *heie* (hedge) is used here for reasons of rhyme: cf. *hegge* (ll. 17, 59), also *heisugge* (l. 505).

ac naþeles mid alle his wrenche,
ne kan he hine so biþenche,
þeȝ he bo ȝep an suþe snel,

830　þat he ne lost his rede uel.
Þe cat ne kan wrench bute anne
noþer bi dune ne bi uenne:
bute he kan climbe suþe wel,
þarmid he wereþ his greie uel.

835　Al so ich segge bi mi solue,
betere is min on þan þine twelue."
"Abid! abid!" þe ule seide,
"þu gest al to mid swikelede:
alle þine wordes þu bileist

840　þat hit þincþ soþ al þat þu seist;
alle þine wordes boþ isliked,
an so bisemed an biliked,
þat alle þo þat hi auoþ,
hi weneþ þat þu segge soþ.

845　Abid! abid! me shal þe ȝene.
[N]u hit shal w[u]rþe wel isene
þat þu hauest muchel iloȝe,
wone þi lesing boþ unwroȝe.
Þu seist þat þu singist mankunne,

850　't techest hom þat hi fundieþ honne
vp to þe songe þat eure ilest:
ac hit is alre w[u]nder mest,
þat þu darst liȝe so opeliche.
Wenest þu hi bringe so liȝtliche　　Fol. 239 r. col. 2.

855　to Godes riche al singin[d]e?
Nai! nai! hi shulle wel auinde

846. *þu, wrþe.*　　852. *wnder.*　　855. *singinge.*

---

838. *al to* < O.E. *eall to* (altogether too). The O.E. construction was used normally before adj. and adv.: cf. *A.S. Chron.* 1095, *eall to medumlice gewende* (all too little changed). In the present instance *mid swikelede* is equivalent to an adv. = "craftily." Trans. " Thou behavest in altogether too crafty a fashion."

For the omission of *h* (from -*hede*), cf. *godede* (l. 582), *wrechede* (ll. 1219, 1251).

841. *isliked* = "made sleek or specious." The word is probably of native origin (< O.E. *slician*), the O.E. form *slic* (cunning) being mentioned by Sweet (*Stud. Dict. of A.S.*) as occurring once. The word has been described as < O.N. *slikr*, though, according to Björkman, the existence of such a

Ac naþeles myd al his wrenche,
Ne can he hine so biþenche,
Þey he beo yep ⁊ swiþe snel,

830   Þat he ne leost his rede vel.
Þe kat ne can wrench bute anne,
Noþer bi dune ne bi venne:
Bute he can clymbe swiþe wel,
Þarmyd he wereþ his greye vel.

835   Al so ich segge bi my seolue,
Beter is myn on þan þine twelue."
   "Abid! abid!" þe vle seyde,
"Þu gest al to mid swikelhede:
Alle þine wordes þu bileyst

840   Þat hit þinkþ soþ þat þu seyst:
Alle þine wordes beoþ isliked,
⁊ so biseme[d] and bilike[d],
Þat alle heo þat hi auoþ,
Hi weneþ þat þu segge soþ.

845   Abid! abid! me schal þe yene!
Nu hit schal w[u]rþe wel isene
Þat þu hauest muchel ilowe,
Hwenne þi lesing beoþ vnwrowe.
Þu seist þat þu singest moncunne,

850   ⁊ techest heom þat hi fundeþ heonne
Vp to þe songe þat euer ilast:
Ac hit is alre w[u]ndre mest,
Þat [þu] darst lye so opeliche.
Wenestu hi bringe so lyhtliche

855   To Godes riche al singinde?
   Nay! Nay! hi schule wel avynde   Fol. 235 r. col. 2.

842. *bisemeþ, bilikeþ.*   846. *wrþe.*   852. *wndre.*   853. *þu* omitted.

---

word is not certain. He would however appear to be in error when he states that "the vowel of this M.E. *slike* was probably short": for the rhyme in the present instance points to *i*, cf. *isliked : biliked.*

841–2. Trans. "All thy words are so sleek, (they are made) so plausible and specious."

845. *ȝene* = "oppose, answer," probably from an O.E. equivalent of O.N. *gegna*, i.e. O.E. *gegnian (O.E. *gegn* = "direct"), which would give M.E. *ȝeine(n)* (to meet, oppose), the form usually found. In the present instance *ȝēne* = *ȝeine* with omission of *i*(ȝ) and lengthening of preceding vowel.

855. *singinde* (C. *singinge*, J. *singinde*). The C. spelling is probably a scribal alteration, for the rhyme requires *-inde*; cf. J. *cumynde* (l. 1220).

þat hi mid longe wope mote
of hore sunne*n* bidde bote,
ar hi mote eu*er* kume þare.

860   Ich rede þi þat men bo ȝare,
an more wepe þane singe,
þat fundeþ to þan houen-kinge:
vor nis no man witúte sunne.
Vorþi he mot, ar he wende honne,

865   mid teres an mid wope bete,
þat him bo sur þat er was swete.
Þarto ich helpe, God hit wot!
Ne singe i[c]h hom no foliot:
for al m[i] song is of longinge,

870   an imend sumdel mid woninge,
þat mon bi me hine biþenche
þat he gro[ni] for his unwrenche:
mid mine songe ich hine pulte,
þat he groni for his gulte.

875   Ȝif þu gest herof to disputinge,
ich wepe bet þane þu singe:
ȝif riȝt goþ forþ, 'ᴛ abak wrong,
bet*er*e is mi wop þane þi song.
Þeȝ sume men bo þurȝut gode,

880   an þurȝut clene on hore mode,
ho[m] longeþ honne noþeles.
Þat boþ her, [w]o is hom þes:
vor þeȝ hi bon hom solue iborȝe,
hi ne soþ her nowiȝt bote sorwe.

885   Vor oþ*er* men hi wepeþ sore,
an for hom biddeþ Cristes ore.

---

868. *ih.*   869. *me.*   872, 874. *grom.*   881. *hon.*   882. *þo.*

---

860 ff. "Here the Owl pleads that the kingdom of heaven is better won by weeping than by singing, and boasts his own frequent tears (l. 876). Is not this one of the many medieval echoes of that sentence of Jerome's, so dear to St Bernard, "Monachus non docentis sed plangentis habet officium"? cf. *Ancren Riwle*, p. 109 " (see G. G. Coulton, *M.L.R.* xvii. p. 70).

868. *foliot.* See additional notes, p. 202.

872. **groni** (C. *grom*, J. *grony*). The C. scribe has apparently misread *ni* for *m*—a common error of Carolingian scribes. St., Wr. and M. read *grom*.

873. *pulte* = "belabour, incite." W. translates = "pelt, thrust": but a figurative sense is clearly required. The word is < O.E. **pyltan* < Lat. *pul-*

Þat hi myd longe wope mote
Of heore sunnen bidde bote,
Ar hi mote eu*er* cume þare.
860 Ich rede þi þat men beo ware,
ꞇ more wepe þane singe,
Þat fundeþ to þan heuene-kynge:
For nys no mo*n* wiþvten sunne.
Forþi he mot ar he wende heonne,
865 Mid teres ꞇ myd wope bete,
Þat him beo sur þat er was swete.
Þarto ich helpe, God hit wot!
Ne singe ich heom no foliot:
Vor al my song is of longinge,
870 And ymeynd su*m*del myd woninge,
Þat mo*n* bi me hine biþenche
Þat he grony for his vnwrenche;
Mid myne songe ich hine [pulte],
Þat he grony for his gulte.
875 If þu gest herof to disputinge,
Ich wepe bet þan þu singe:
If riht goþ forþ, ꞇ abak wrong,
Bet*er*e is my wop þan þi song.
Þeyh su*m*me men beon þurhut god*e*,
880 ꞇ þurhut clene on heore mod*e*,
Heo*m* longeþ heonne noþeles.
Þat beoþ her, wo is hom þes:
Vor þeyh hi beo heo*m* selue iborewe,
Hi ne seoþ her nowiht bute serewe.
885 Vor oþer men hi wepeþ sore,
ꞇ for heom biddeþ Cristes ore.

873. *pulte* inserted later.

---

tare (to beat), and in M.E. all three forms *pulten, pilten, pelten* are found. In Mod. Eng. the Kentish "pelt" has survived, but the *u*-form occurs in the dialects: cf. Worcest. "polting apples"=knocking apples from the tree; Herefords. "polting lug"=the pole used for that purpose. In Hants "pulting"=a beating, and elsewhere "polt"=a blow: see *E.D.D.*

882. *þat boþ* (J. *þat beoþ*). Str. and M. both insert *hi* before *boþ*. But in view of the fact that both MSS. agree in reading *þat boþ* (*beoþ*), W. is probably correct in taking *þat*=rel. pro. "those who" (cf. l. 251), and in translating the line literally as "Those who are here, woe is it to them because of that" (i.e. because they are here).

Ich helpe monne on eiþer halue,

mi muþ haueþ tweire kunne salue: Fol. 239 v. col. 1.

þan gode ich fulste to longinge,

890   vor þan hi[m] longeþ, ich him singe:

an þan sunfulle ich helpe alswo,

vor ich him teche þare is wo.

ʒet ich þe ʒene in oþer wise:

vor þane þu sittest on þine rise,

895   þu draʒst men to fleses luste,

þat w[u]lleþ þine songes luste.

Al þu forlost þe murʒþe of houene,

for þarto neuestu none steuene:

al þat þu singst is of golnesse,

900   for nis on þe non holinesse,

ne wene[ð] na man for þi pipinge

þat eni preost in chir[ch]e singe.

ʒet I þe wulle an o[ð]er seggë,

ʒif þu hit const ariht bilegge:

905   [w]i nultu singe an o[ð]er þeode,

þar hit is muchele more neode?

Þu neauer ne singst in Irlonde,

ne þu ne cumest noʒt in Scotlonde.

Hwi nultu fare to Noreweie,

910   an singin men of Galeweie?

890. *hin.*   896. *wlleþ.*   901. *wened.*   902. *chircce,* cc written over g.
903. *oder.*   905. *þi, oder.*

---

888. *tweire* = "of two" (< O.E. *twēgra*): an interesting survival of the O.E. gen. pl. inflexion.

901. Here, half-way through the poem, a change takes place in the orthography of C., a different system being introduced (see α and β orthographies, Intro. § 3 (c)). The β orthography is maintained fairly regularly throughout ll. 902–60 and ll. 1184—end: but in ll. 961–1183, the α spelling (characteristic of ll. 1–901) is again adopted. For the significance of these spellings see Intro. § 3 (a) (iv).

weneð (C. *wened,* J. *weneþ*): cf. C. *oder,* J. *oþer* (l. 903). As W. suggests, the forms in *d* (for *þ*) which occur occasionally from now on are probably due to the fact that ð (instead of þ) appeared in these places in the intermediate text which formed the common original, and that the C. scribe, while attempting to copy the symbol, sometimes omitted to cross the d. In *beoð* (l. 911) the first actual use of ð occurs in C.: the J. scribe always uses þ.

902. *þat.* The first instance of the use of the contracted form. The fact that the abbreviation occurs simultaneously in both C. and J. points to the use of a common original. Occasionally the scribes write out the form in full where the common original used the contraction (cf. l. 918), and in such cases confusion sometimes arises between *þat* and *þar* (cf. C. *þar,* J. *þat* (l. 906)).

Ich helpe moɴne on eyþer halue,

Mi [m]uþ haueþ tweire kunne salue:

Þan gode ich fulste to longinge,

890 Vor hwenne him longeþ ic him singe: Fol. 235 v. col. 1.

ꝛ þan sunfulle ic helpe also,

Vor ic him teche hwar is wo.

Yet ic þe yene on oþer wise:

Vor hwenne þu sittest on þine rise,

895 Þu drahst men to fleyses luste,

Þat wil[l]eþ þine songes luste.

Al þu vorleost þe [m]urehþe of heuene,

For þarto nauestu none steuene:

Al þat þu singest is of golnesse,

900 For nys on þe non holynesse,

Ne weneþ no moɴ for þi pipinge

Þat eny preost in chirche singe.

Yet ic þe wile on oþer segge,

If þu hit const ariht bilegge:

905 Hwi nultu singe an oþer þeode,

Þa[r] hit is muchele more neode?

Þu neuer ne singest in Irlonde,

Ne þu ne cumest in Scotlonde.

Hwi nultu vare to Norweye,

910 ꝛ singen men of Galeweye?

888. *Muþ.*   896. *wileþ*, prob. for original *wlleþ*, cf. C. reading.
897. *Murehþe.*   906. *þat, r* written above *t*.

---

907 ff. The argument in this passage is based on information probably derived from Neckam, *De Naturis Rerum* (see Intro. § 8, p. lxviii), to the effect that the nightingale as a rule avoids cold countries, and that, if by any chance she visits such regions, she is unable to produce there her sweetest notes. Gilbert White's account of the matter is somewhat different. He writes "Nightingales not only never reach Northumberland and Scotland, but also, as I have been told, Devonshire and Cornwall. In these two last counties we cannot attribute the failure of them to the want of warmth: the defect in the West is rather a presumptive argument that these birds come over to us from the Continent at the narrowest passage, and do not stroll so far westward" (White, *Nat. Hist. of Selborne*, Letter IX).

910. *Galeweie* = "Galloway," a principality in the S.W. of Scotland which retained its independence almost up to the close of the reign of Henry II. Its mention as a separate country in the poem would therefore seem to suggest a writer acquainted with political conditions under Henry II. W. translates the form as "Galway" in Ireland—an unlikely interpretation: and he adds "the concern and activity of the Papal authorities to establish peace and some ecclesiastical discipline in disorganised Ireland between 1150 and 1200 is well known" (see Wells, Intro. p. xxiii): see however note l. 1016, and Intro. § 4, p. xxxvii.

Þar beoð men þat lutel kunne
of songe þat is bineoðe þe sunne.
Wi nultu þare preoste singe,
an teche of þire writelinge,
915 an wisi hom mid þire steuene
hu engeles singeð ine heouene?
Þu farest so doð an ydel wel
þat springeþ bi burne þa[t] is snel,
an let fordrue þe dune,
920 ꝛ flo[þ] on idel þar adune.
Ac ich fare boþe norþ ꝛ s[u]þ:
in eauereuch londe ich am cuuþ: Fol. 239 v. col. 2.
east ꝛ west, feor ꝛ neor,
I do wel faire mi meoster,
925 an warni men mid mine bere,
þat þi dweole-song heo ne forlere.
Ich wisse men mid min[e] songe,
þat hi ne sunegi nowiht longe:
I bidde hom þat heo iswike,
930 þat [heo] heom seolue ne biswike:
for betere is þat heo wepen here,
þan elles hwar [beon] deoulene fere."
    Þe niȝtingale was igr[amed]
an ek heo was sum del of[s]chamed,
935 for þe hule hire atwiten hadde
in hwucche stude he sat an gradde,
bihinde þe bure, among þe wede,
þar men goð to here neode:

918. *þar*.   920. *floh*.   921. *soþ*.   927. *min*, with *-e* added later.
930. *þat heom*.   932. *to beon*.   933. *igremet*.   934. *-chamed*.

---

920. *floþ* (C. *floh*, J. *flohþ*) = "flows." W. retains *floh*, Str. unnecessarily emends to *floweþ*, G. reads *floþ*, which is probably the original form (cf. *floweþ* l. 946). Since the *h* spelling occurs in both C. and J., the scribal error (*h* for *þ*, see Intro. § 3 (*d*) (v)) must have already appeared in the common original. The C. scribe as usual copies the error, while in J. an attempt is made at emendation.

925. *bere*. See note l. 222.

930. *heo* is required here for grammatical and metrical reasons. Its omission from both C. and J. points to omission from the intermediate text: an instance of haplography. See Intro. § 3 (*d*) (iv).

932. *beon* (C. *to beon*, J. *beo*). W. and G. retain *to*: but the construction

Þar beoþ men þat litel kunne
Of songe þat is vnder sunne.
Hwi nultu þare preoste singe,
⁊ teche of þire writelinge,
915 ⁊ wisi heom myd þire stefne
Hw engles singeþ in þe heuene?
Þu farest so doþ on an yde[l] wel
Þat springeþ bi burne þat is snel,
⁊ let fordruye þe dune,
920 ⁊ flohþ an ydel þar adune.
Ac ich fare norþ and souþ:
In euerich londe ich am cuþ;
East ⁊ west, souþ ⁊ norþ,
I do wel fayre my mester,   Fol. 235 v. col. 2.
925 ⁊ warny men mid myne bere,
Þat þi dwele-song heo ne forle[r]e.
Ich wisse men myd myne songe,
Þat hi ne sunegi nowiht longe;
Ich bidde heom þat heo iswike,
930 Þat heom seolue ne biswike:
For betere is þat heo wepe here,
Þan elles hwar beo deoulene yuere."
    Þe Nihtegale wes agromed
⁊ ek sum-del ofschomed,
935 For þe vle hire atwiten hedde
In hwiche stude ho sat ⁊ gradde,
Bihinde þe bure, among þe wed,
Þar men gon to heore ned;

---

917. *yde.*   924. above line 924 in top margin is the line (very indistinct)
þat men ihere fer and ner: possibly an attempt at emendation.   926. *forlete.*

---

is parallel with that in the preceding line, i.e. an opt. pl. form is required.
Hence the omission of *to* (as in J.) improves the line from both the grammatical and the metrical points of view.

deoulene=wk. gen. pl. of O.E. *dēofol.* The use of *-ena, -ana* in gen. pl. of
str. mas. and neu. sb. is not uncommon in certain L.O.E. MSS.: see Napier,
O.E. Glosses (1557 N), *applana* (3845), *baþena* (4777), *hergana* (1898), *stafena*
(2311).

933. *igramed* (C. *igremet*, J. *agromed*). The form *igramed* (cf. l. 1603) is
adopted for reasons of rhyme. Str. and G. read *agromed*: W. retains the
C. form.

an sat sum-del, ꝛ heo biþohte,
940 an wiste wel on hire þohte
þe wraþþe binimeþ monnes red.
For hit seide þe king Alfred:
"Sel[d]e endeð wel þe loþe,
an selde plaideð wel þe wroþe."
945 For wraþþe meinþ þe horte blod
þat hit floweþ so wilde flod,
an al þe heorte ouergeþ,
þat heo naueþ no þing bute breþ,
an so forleost al hire liht,
950 þat heo ni siþ soþ ne riht.
Þe niȝtingale hi understod,
an ouergan lette hire mod:
he mihte bet speken a-sele
þan mid wraþþe wordes deale.
955 "[H]ule," heo seide "lust nu hider:
þu schalt falle, þe wei is slider.　　　Fol. 240 r. col. 1.
Þu seist ich fleo bihinde bure:
hit is riht, þe bur is ure:
þar lauerd liggeþ ꝛ lauedi,
960 ich schal heom singe ꝛ sitte bi.
Wenstu þat uise men forlete,
for fule venne, þe riȝtte strete?
ne sunne þe later shine,
þeȝ hit bo ful ine nest[e] þine?
965 Sholde ich, for one hole brede,
forlete mine riȝte stede,

943. *sele.*　　　955. *þule*, rubric þ for H.　　　964. *nest.*

943. Similar sentiments occur in the *Distichs of Cato*, ɪɪ. 299–300 (quoted by Goldberg, *Angl.* vɪɪ. 172): *Wraþþe destruyeþ monnes wit | whon soþ may not beo seiȝene*: also in Icel. *Proverb Poem* ɪɪ. 15, l. 4, " *Eigi* " *spillir hyggins hiali* (Anger spoils the wise man's talk).
948. *breþ* (L.O.E. *brǣð*)="fury, passion," as in ll. 1454, 1461; cf. Napier, *O.E. Glosses*, 2511, feruorem, i, *ardorem*, wylm, brǣð, and the various meanings of Lat. *animus*: see also *N.E.D. breth, brath.*
952. *lette*="let." The meaning of the line is clearly: "she let her anger pass." Hence *lette*=a wk. pt. of O.E. *lǣtan* (allow): it is not derived from O.E. *lettan* (hinder), as G. suggests. The form is an instance of an O.E. str. vb. that had already become weak.

ꝉ sat sum-del ꝉ ho biþouhte,
940 ꝉ wiste wel on hire þouhte
Þe wraþþe binymeþ monnes red.
For hit seyde þe king Alured:
"Selde endeþ wel þe loþe,
ꝉ selde playdeþ wel þe wroþe."
945 For wraþþe meynþ þe heorte blod
Þat hit floweþ so wilde flod,
ꝉ al þe heorte ouergeþ,
Þat heo naueþ naþing bute breþ,
ꝉ so uorleost al his lyht,
950 Þat ho ne syhþ soþ ne riht.
Þe nyhtegale hi vnderstod,
ꝉ [o]uergan lette hire mod:
He myhte bet speken i-sele
Þan myd wraþþe wordes dele.
955 "[H]vle," [heo] seyde "lust nv hider:
Þu schalt falle, þi wey is slider.
Þu seyst ich fleo bihinde bure:
Hit is riht, þe bur is vre: Fol. 236 r. col. 1.
Þar louerd liggeþ and leuedy,
960 Ich schal heom synge ꝉ sitte bi.
Wenestu þat wise men forlete,
Vor fule venne, þe rihte strete?
Ne sunne þe later schyne,
Þeyh hit beo ful in neste þine?
965 Scholdich, for one hole brede,
Furlete myne rihte stede,

---

952. *auergan.*   955. *þe vle seyde*; in bottom margin *þe nystegale* is written.

---

953. *a-sele* (J. *i-sele*)="in joyous mood, in good humour." W. and G. translate "at a favourable time": but the context makes it plain that a contrast is here intended between speaking in anger (l. 954) and speaking with an unclouded mind: cf. *Beowulf* (l. 643), *on sǣlum.*

955. *Hule* (C. *þule,* J. *þe vle*), see note l. 411.

961-2. See additional notes, p. 202.

963. The phrase *wenstu þat* must be supplied from l. 961: the line then reads "[Dost thou suppose that] the sun no longer (lit. later) shines?"

965. *hole brede*="a hollow log" (see Glossary). The reference is to the dwelling-place of the Owl: cf. *old stoc* (l. 25), *an holʒ stok* (l. 1113). M. reads *bred* < O.E. *brād* and translates "a broad hole." But *bred* would be an abnormal development of O.E. *brād*: it would moreover contain a long vowel which would spoil the rhyme with *stede.*

A.   6

þat ich ne singe bi þe bedde,
þar louerd haueþ his loue ibedde?
Hit is mi riȝt, hit is mi laȝe,
970 þa[t] to þe he[x]st ich me draȝe.
Ac ȝet þu ȝelpst of þine songe,
þat þu canst ȝolle wroþe ᴉ stronge,
an seist þu uisest mankunne,
þat hi biwepen hore sunne.
975 Solde euch mon wonie ᴉ grede
riȝt suich hi weren unlede,
solde hi ȝollen al so þu dest,
hi miȝte oferen here brost.
Man schal bo stille ᴉ noȝt grede;
980 he mot biwepe his misdede:
ac þar is Cristes heriinge,
þar me shal grede ᴉ lude singe.
Nis noþer to lud ne to long,
at riȝte time, chirche-song.
985 Þu ȝolst ᴉ wones[t], ᴉ ich singe:
þi steuene is wop, ᴉ min skentinge.
Euer mote þu ȝolle ᴉ wepen
þat þu þi lif mote forleten!
an ȝollen mote þu so heȝe
990 þat ut berste bo þin eȝe!   Fol. 240 r. col. 2.
Weþer is betere of twe[n]e twom,
þat mon bo bliþe oþer grom?

970. *þar, herst.*   985. *wones.*   991. *twere.*

---

970. *hexst* (C. *herst*, J. *hexste*) = "highest." The C. scribe has almost certainly read *r* for *x* (cf. C. and J. 812 for a similar error): and the line is best taken to mean "that I follow the highest." W. tentatively suggests the retention of *herst* < O.E. *hyrst* (copse, wood). But this reading, besides presenting difficulty in the matter of form, does not supply quite a satisfactory sense: for the preceding line suggests that some guiding principle of the Nightingale's life is to be stated, and this is not given by *herst*. G. on the other hand queries the possibility of reading *þarto þe erst* (< O.E. *ǣrest*): but his argument is not convincing.

981. *þar* (C. and J.) = "where." W. reads *war*: see however note l. 165.

982. W. reads this line in an interrogative sense. But this is surely unnecessary, as ll. 981–2 merely complete the assertion begun in ll. 979–80, viz. that silence goes with repentance, and song with praise.

987. *mote* = opt. 2 sg. (of a wish), i.e. "may"; cf. *mote* (l. 989). Trans. "Ever mayest thou tearfully exclaim (in thy longing) to leave this life!"

wepen : forleten, one of the few defective rhymes in the poem, viz. [ẹ̄p] : [ẹ̄t].

Þat ich ne singe bi þe bedde,
Þar louerd haueþ his lauedi bedde?
Hit is my rihte, hit it my lawe,
970   Þat to þe hexste ich me drawe.
Ac if þu yelpst of þine songe,
Þat þu kanst yolle uroþe ⁊ stronge,
⁊ seyst þu wisest monkunne,
Þat hi biwepen heore sunne,
975   Solde eueruych mon wony ⁊ grede
Riht such hi weren vnlede?
Scholde hi yollen al so þu dest,
Hi myhten afere heore preost.
Mon schal beo stille ⁊ noht grede;
980   He mot biwepe his mysdede:
Ac þar is Cristes heriynge,
Þar me grede ⁊ lude singe.
Nis noþe[r] to lude ne to long,
At rihte tyme, chirche-song.
985   Þu yollest ⁊ wonest, ⁊ ic singe:
Þi stefne is wop, ⁊ myn skentinge.
Euer mote þu yolle ⁊ wepen
Þat þu þi lif mote forleten!
⁊ yolle mote þu so heye,
990   Þat ut tobersten bo þin eye!
Hweþer is betere of tweyre twom,
Þat mon beo bliþe oþer grom?   Fol. 236 r. col. 2.

983. *noþe.*

---

991. *twene twom* (C. *twere twom*, J. *tweyre twom*) = "of two doubtful things
(lit. doubts)." W. and G. retain *twere twom* and explain it as < O.E. *twēgra
twām*, a pleonastic expression possibly due to analogy with O.E. *bām twām*.
But the analogy is by no means complete, and the result gives no good sense.
M., on the other hand, emends to *þan twam*, or *þinge twam*; cf. the similar
phrase: *For oþer hit is of twam þinge* (l. 1477). But it is clear from the almost
identical readings of C. and J. that the reading of the common original is
to be sought for in those forms; the only difference between them being the
slight emendation of the J. scribe, who, reading *twere* (= O.E. *twegra*), altered
the spelling to the more normal *tweyre*. In fact, there can be no doubt that the
reading of the common original looked like *twere twom*. It is equally certain
that the form which looked like *twere* was in reality a badly written *twene*,
with the second stroke of the *n* either written short or coinciding with the
down stroke of the following *e*. (For scribal confusion between *n* and *r* see
Napier, *O.E. Glosses*, xxxi. note 3.) This original *twene* < O.E. *twēona*, gen. pl.
of O.E. *twēo* (doubt), and the line therefore reads "Which is the better of
two doubtful things?"

So bo hit euer in unker siþe,
þat þu bo sori ꝯ ich bliþe.

995 ꝫut þu aisheist wi ich ne fare
into oþer londe ꝯ singe þare?
No! wat sholde ich among hom do,
þar neuer blisse ne com to?
Þat lond nis god, ne hit nis este,

1000 ac wildernisse hit is ꝯ weste:
knarres ꝯ cludes houen[e]-tinge,
snou ꝯ haȝel hom is genge.
Þat lond is grislich ꝯ unuele,
þe men boþ wilde ꝯ unisele,

1005 hi nabbeþ noþer griþ ne sibbe:
hi ne reccheþ hu hi libbe.
Hi eteþ fihs an flehs unsode,
suich wulues hit hadde tobrode:
hi drinkeþ milc ꝯ wei þarto,

1010 hi nute elles þat hi do:

1001. *houen-*.

999–1014. This description of Norway and the barbarous North seems to be in some measure reminiscent of the account of the voyages of Ohthere and Wulfstan given in the O.E. translation of Orosius' *History*; see *King Alfred's Orosius*, ed. H. Sweet, E.E.T.S. 1883, pp. 17–21, *passim*. The details which seem to suggest a borrowing from that source are as follows: (i) with ll. 999–1000, cf. O.E. *Oros.*: "þæt land...is eall weste buton on feawum stowum." (ii) with l. 1001, cf. O.E. *Oros.*: "þæt land is on sumum stowum swiþe cludig." (iii) with ll. 1004–5, cf. O.E. *Oros.*: "hie ne dorston forð bi þære ea siglan for unfriþe." (iv) with ll. 1006–13, cf. O.E. *Oros.*: "And þær biþ swyþe mycel hunig and fiscnaþ: and se cyning and þa ricostan menn drincaþ myran meolc, and þa unspedigan and þa þeowan drincaþ medo, ...and ne biþ þær nænig ealo gebrowen...ac þær biþ medo genoh:......berenne kyrtel oþþe yterenne." Further evidence of the survival of these ideas is supplied by Mr B. Dickins, who refers to the account of the mission of Cardinal Williams to Hakon the Old in 1247 and quotes: "it was told him by the Englishmen for envy's sake against the men of Norway that he would get no honour there and hardly any meat, and no drink but sour whey: and the Englishmen dissuaded him...against going to Norway and frightened him both with the sea and the grimness of the folk" (Dasent, *Trans. of Saga of Hakon*, c. 249 (R.S. 1894)). At Hakon's coronation feast, moreover, the Cardinal said "It was told me that I should see few men,...[and] they would be more like to beasts in their behaviour than men" (*ibid.* c. 255).
   See also Intro. § 8, p. lxxii.
   1001. *knarres* = "rocks, crags," cf. M.Du. *knorre*, Mod. Eng. "gnarled." The original meaning was "a knot" in a piece of wood: but the word could also stand for "a rugged eminence, rock, or crag," cf. *Gaw. and the Gr. Knight* (l. 1434): *þay umbekesten þe knarre and þe knot boþe* ("They looked around the rock and the crag as well").
   houene-tinge < O.E. *heofone getenge* = "heaven-touching, reaching to the sky." For similar O.E. compounds cf. *grunde getenge* (*Beow*. l. 2758); *eorþan*

So beo hit euer in vnker siþe,
Þat þu beo sori ⁊ ich bliþe.
995 Yet þu ayschest hwi ic ne vare
Into oþer londe ⁊ singe þare?
No! hwat scholdich among heom do,
Þar neuer blisse ne com to?
Þat lond nys god, ne hit nys este,
1000 Ac wildernesse hit is ⁊ weste:
Knarres ⁊ cludes houenetinge,
Snov ⁊ hawel hom is genge.
Þat lond is grislich ⁊ vnuele,
Þe men beoþ wilde ⁊ vnsele,
1005 Hi nabbeþ noþer griþ ne sibbe:
Hi ne reccheþ hw hi libbe.
Hi eteþ fys ⁊ fleys vnsode,
Suych wolues hit hadde tobroude;
Hi drinkeþ mylk ⁊ hwey þarto,
1010 Hi nuteþ elles hwet hi do:

---

getenge (*Alf. Metr.* 31, 7); *lyfte getenge*, *Runic Poem*, v. 54, also Shak. *Hamlet*, III. iv. 59, "a heaven-kissing hill."

1005. While the poet possibly drew upon the O.E. trans. of Orosius' *History* for his highly-coloured description of the conditions which prevailed in the North, those countries, even in his own day, were not free from disorder. During the 12th century, Scotland (including Galloway) was the scene of perpetual warfare and misgovernment. The principality of Galloway under its turbulent chiefs was in a permanent state of unrest, though it retained its independence until 1160, when Fergus its lord was conquered by Malcolm IV. Then in 1173 the sons of Fergus expelled the Scots, but only to have William King of Scotland thrust upon them as their overlord by Henry II of England, owing to their internal quarrels. This, in its turn, led to frequent revolts. The rising of 1176 under Gilbert of Galloway was successfully put down: but rebellion broke out once more some eight years later. And similar ravages and slaughters prevailed in the Norway of this period. After Magnus Bareleg had been slain in 1103, Harold Gilli obtained the throne by treacherous means, and was killed in turn by Sigurd Sham-Deacon. Subsequently Ingi and Hakon met with violent ends: while Magnus, who was elected king in 1164, was subsequently overthrown by Sverri (1180), and was driven out of the kingdom. These conditions prevailed until 1240 when Hakon Hakonson slew his father-in-law Duke Skuli. See Morris and Magnússon, *Heimskringla*, vol. III.; J. Sephton, *Saga of King Sverri* (London, 1899); G. W. Dasent, *Saga of Hakon* (R.S. 1894).

1007. *fihs, flehs*. It is possible that these forms are due to scribal error, *hs* being written for *sh* (see Intro. § 3 (d) iii). On the other hand, they may represent dialectal forms of the more usual *fish* and *flesh*: cf. O.E. *fix, fisc*, Wycl. *flehs, fleixh* (see B.T. 8, *flǣse*).

1010. *nute* (J. *nuteþ*) = "they know not." Str. adopts the J. reading, though the C. form is grammatically correct, i.e. O.E. *nyton* (=*ne witon*). In J. the ending of the pr. pl. indic. (-*eþ*) has been wrongly added to a str.-wk. verb, cf. C. *schule*, J. *schulleþ*, l. 1703.

hi nabbeþ noþ[er] win ne bor,
ac libbeþ al so wilde dor:
hi goþ bitiȝt mid ruȝe uelle,
riȝt suich hi comen ut of helle.
1015   Þeȝ eni god man to hom come,
so wile dude sum from Rome,
for hom to lere gode þewes,
an for to leten hore unþewes,
he miȝte bet sitte stille,
1020   vor al his wile he sholde spille:
he miȝte bet teche ane bore
to weȝe boþe sheld ꞇ spere,
þan me þat wilde folc ibringe
þat hi [me] wolde ihere singe.   Fol. 240 v. col. 1.
1025   Wat sol[d]ich þar mid mine songe?
ne sunge ich hom neu*er* so longe,
mi song were ispild ech del:
for hom ne mai halt*er* ne bridel
bringe vrom hore w[o]de wise,
1030   ne mon mid stele ne mid i[s]e.

1011. *noþ*.   1024. *me segge wolde*.   1025. *sol ich*.   1029. *wude*.
1030. *ire*.

1011. *noþer* (C. *noþ*, J. *noht*) = "neither." The MS. readings point to an error in the common original; the contraction for *-er* was probably omitted.
1013. *bitiȝt* (J. *bytuht*) = "clad." Str. reads *bituht*. The form represents a p. p. < O.E. **be + tyhtan* (cf. O.E. *beteon*, to cover): the *i* in *bitiȝt* = unstable *i* (< O.E. *y*), before palatals (see Sievers § 31).
1014. H. B. Hinckley (*Mod. Phil.* xvii. 251 note) points out that this phrase was proverbial, and quotes *Richard Cœur de Lion*, ed. Brunner (ll. 6703–4), where it is said of the Saracens,
   "No tungge," he seide, "may hem telle:
   I wene þey comen out of helle."
1016. The Papal mission referred to in this line is somewhat uncertain. Börsch (*Ueber Metrik u. Poetik*, see Bibliog.) hints at the embassy of Cardinal Guala "who was to divert King Alexander II of Scotland from his alliance with France and to make peace with England; and who, when the king did not obey, pronounced excommunication and interdict of 1218" (quoted by W.). But, as W. points out, "it is not Scotland alone that is referred to here" (cf. ll. 907–10): and moreover to accept this suggestion would be to regard the middle of the 13th century as the approximate date of the poem (cf. *wile*, "formerly," l. 1016)—a date out of keeping with the rest of the evidence. In all probability an allusion is here made to the embassy of Cardinal Vivian (1176), for which see Intro. § 4, p. xxxvii.
1018. *leten* (J. *lete*) = "prevent." As is seen from the context, the meaning of *leten* here is not that of O.E. *lætan* (permit), but of O.E. *lettan* (hinder). The fact is that the two forms have been confused by the poet, the former being used with the meaning of the latter, cf. *lette* (l. 952), *lete* (l. 1445).

Hi nabbeþ noht wyn ne beor,

Ac libbeþ al so wilde deor:

Hi goþ bytuht myd rowe felle,

Riht suych hi come vt of helle.

1015 Þey eny god man to heom come,

So hwile dude sum from Rome,

For heom to lere gode þewes,

꒵ for to lete heore vnþewes,

He myhte be[t] sytte stille,

1020 Vor al his hwile he scolde spille:

He myhte bet teche ane beore

To bere scheld and spere,

Þane þat wilde volk ibringe

Þat hi me wolde ihere singe.

1025 Hwat scholdich þar mid myne song[e],

Ne singe ic heom neuer so longe, Fol. 236 v. col. 1.

Mi song were ispild vych del:

For heom ne may halter ne bridel

Bringe from here wode wyse,

1030 Ne mon mid stele ne mid i[s]e.

1019. *be.* 1025. *song.* 1030. *ire.*

1021. *bore* (J. *beore*)="bear." M. and W. read *bōre*<O.E. *bār* (boar): but this reading is impossible, because the rhyme requires short *e* (*eo*), i.e. *b(e)ore*:*spere*, so that the C. form stands for *beore*<O.E. *bera* (bear), cf. J. *beore*. Moreover a variant *beore* alongside *bere* is frequently found in M.E. (see Str.-Br.) though a corresponding W.S. *beora* is not found (see Sievers § 107), and its existence in M.E. is therefore probably due to scribal confusion between *e* and *eo*: cf. *leot, seonde* (*A.S. Chron.* 852 E, 656 E).

1021–2. This rather fantastic illustration may have been suggested by the poet's reading of Neckam's *De Naturis Rerum* (II. ch. 129) where an account is given of a jongleur who trained two apes to fight in a mimic tournament, armed with shield, sword and spear. In the chapter immediately following, the bear is described as a type of cruelty ("per ursum accipe crudelitatem"), and this idea may have suggested itself as adding point to the illustration.

1025. *soldich* (C. *sol ich*, J. *scholdich*)="should I." The C. form is probably due to scribal carelessness. Trans. "What should I [do] there...?" For omission of infin. after *solde* (*sholde*) see *Beow.* 2584–5, *guðbill geswac, nacod æt niðe, swa hyt no sceolde*: also l. 764 of this poem.

1026. *neuer so longe*, see note l. 345.

1030. *ise* (C. and J. *ire*)<O.E. *isen, iren* (iron). The rhyme shows that the poet originally wrote *ise* which was changed to *ire* probably in the intermediate text. According to the evidence of *Vesp. Ps.* and *Cura Past.* the form *iren*=Anglian, while *ise(r)n*=W.S. (see Sievers, *P.B.B.* IX. § 205). Professor Craigie suggests that, as "the form *yzen, yse, ise* is distinctly S.E. whereas *ire* is S.W., consequently this is an instance in which S.W. scribes have altered the author's dialect in spite of rhyme": cf. also l. 1725.

Ac war lon[d] is boþe este ꝛ god,
an þar men habbeþ milde mod,
ich noti mid hom mine þrote,
vor ich mai do þar gode note:

1035 an bringe hom loue tiþinge,
vor ich of chirche-songe singe.
Hit was iseid in olde laȝe,
an ȝet ilast þilke soþ-saȝe,
þat man shal erien an sowe,

1040 þar he wenþ after sum god mowe:
for he is wod þat soweþ his sed
þar neuer gras ne sprinþ ne bled."

Þe hule was wroþ, to cheste rad,
mid þisse worde hire eȝen abrad:

1045 "Þu seist þu witest manne bures,
þar leues boþ ꝛ faire flores,
þar two iloue in one bedde
liggeþ biclop[t] ꝛ wel bihedde.
Enes þu sunge, ic wo[t] wel ware,

1050 bi one bure, ꝛ woldest lere
þe lefdi to an uuel luue,
an sunge boþe loȝe ꝛ buue,

1031. *long.*   1048. *biclop.*   1049. *wod.*

1036. For the consistency of this statement with the view that the Nightingale represents the love-poet, see Intro. § 7, p. lviii.

1037. *olde laȝe* (J. *olde lawe*)="ancient law." M. reads *daȝe*. In O.E. the expression is used for "the old Dispensation": cf. *saga me hwylc bisceop wære ærest on þære ealdan æ ær Cristes tocyme* (quoted by Kemble, *Sal. and Sat.* p. 200).

1039 ff. This seems to be an adaptation of
  Hwych so þe mon soweþ
  Al swuch he schal mowe. (*Prov. of Alf.* 52–4.)
Cf. also Galatians vi. 8.

1041-2. Breier (*Eule und Nacht. eine Untersuchung*, p. 73, a 2) describes the rhyme *sed* : *bled* as irregular, i.e. =open *ē* (W.S. *ǣ*) : close *ē* (O.E. *ē*). He has however confused O.E. *blēd* with O.E. *blǣd*, both of which have much the same meaning. The form *bled* (l. 1042) is < O.E. *blǣd* (flower), which gives a regular rhyme with *sed* (l. 1041) < O.E. *sǣd*, the rhyming vowel in each case being [ę̄]. G. also incorrectly derives *bled* < O.E. *blēd*. W. glosses the word as = Mod. Eng. "blade," thus apparently connecting it with yet another O.E. form, viz. *blæd* (blade, leaf).

1044. *abrad* (J. *abraid*)="moved (or rolled) rapidly." The C. form is derived from O.E. *ābrǣd* (< O.E. *ābrægd*, pt. sg. of *ābregdan*) with shortening. Str.-Br. and W. translate "broadened, dilated," apparently connecting the word with O.E. *ābrǣdan*, but in that case the form would be *abradde*.

        Ac þar lond is este and god,

        ꝉ þar men habbeþ mylde mod,

        Ic notye myd heo*m* [m]ine þrote,

        For ic may do þar gode note:

1035   ꝉ bringe heom leue tydinge,

        For ic of chirche-songe singe.

        Hit wes isayd in olde lawe,

        Þat yet ilast þilke soþ-sawe,

        Þat mo*n* schal eryen ꝉ sowe,

1040   Þar he weneþ after god mowe:

        For he is wod þat soweþ his sed

        Þar neu*er* gras ne springþ ne bled."

        Þe vle wes wroþ, to cheste rad,

        Mid þisse word*e* hire eyen abraid:

1045   "Þu seyst þu witest mo*n*ne bures,

        Þar leues beoþ ꝉ fayre flures,

        Þar two yleoue in one bedde

        Liggeþ iclupt ꝉ wel bihedde.

        Enes þu sunge, ic wot wel hware,

1050   Bi one bure, ꝉ woldest lere

        Þe leuedi to an vuel l[u]ue,

        ꝉ s[u]nge boþe lowe ꝉ buue,

     1033. *Mine.*   1051. *lyue.*   1052. *singe.*

     1045. *witest* = "watchest over, guardest"—a reference to the Nightingale's assertion in ll. 958–60. Hence the form is not (as in W., see Gloss.) the pr. 2 sg. of *witen* (O.E. *witan*, to know), which throughout the poem assumes a form equivalent to O.E. *wast*: cf. *wostu* (l. 95), *nost* (l. 755). Str.-Br. quotes other instances of the word (e.g. *þet wit* (= "guards") *and wereþ us* (*Anc. Riw.* l. 312) and derives it from O.E. *witan* (see also G.). This O.E. word *witan* however has a different meaning and is represented in the present poem by *witestu* (= "dost thou reproach"), l. 1356. The real origin of *witest* (l. 1045) would therefore seem to be O.E. *witian* (watch over, guard), cf. O.E. (*be*)-*witian* and *Beow.* l. 2212, (*be*)*weotian*.

     1048. *biclopt* (C. *biclop*, J. *iclupt*) = "clasped, embraced" < O.E. *beclyppan*. J. gives the normal form. The C. form is possibly due to an O.E. variant *cloppian, see note l. 379: otherwise it may be a rare example of *o* written for *u*.

     1049. *enes* = "once." The regular O.E. form was *æne* (cf. *ēne*, l. 1107), but *ǣnes* (adv. gen.) is found in *A.S. Chron.* 1120, and from this later form *enes* is derived.

     sunge, see note l. 103.

     1049–62, 1076–1104. Reference is here made to a nightingale story which seems to have been widely known towards the end of the 12th century. For probable sources and later versions of the story, see Intro. § 8, p. lxii, and Appendix II.

　　an lerdest hi to don shome
　　an vnriȝt of hire licome.
1055　Þe louerd þat sone underȝat,
　　liim ꝛ grine [ꝛ] wel eiwat,
　　sette ꝛ le[i]de þe for to lacche.
　　Þu come sone to þan hacche,　　　Fol. 240 v. col. 2.
　　þu were inume in one grine,
1060　al hit aboȝte þine shine:
　　þu naddest non oþer dom ne laȝe,
　　bute mid wilde horse were todraȝe.
　　Vonde ȝif þu miȝt eft misrede,
　　waþer þu wult, wif þe maide:
1065　þi song mai bo so longe genge
　　þat þu shalt wippen on a sprenge."
　　　Þe niȝtingale at þisse worde,
　　mid sworde an mid speres orde,
　　ȝif ho mon were, wolde fiȝte:
1070　ac þo ho bet do ne miȝte,
　　ho uaȝt mid hire wise tunge.
　　"Wel fiȝt þat wel specþ," seiþ in þe songe.
　　Of hire tunge ho nom red:
　　"Wel fiȝt þat wel specþ" seide Alured.
1075　　"Wat! seistu þis for mine shome?
　　þe louerd hadde herof grame.
　　He was so gelus of his wiue,
　　þat he ne miȝte for his liue
　　iso þat man wiþ hire speke,
1080　þat his horte nolde breke.
　　He hire bileck in one bure,
　　þat hire was boþe stronge ꝛ sure:

　　　　1056. *grinew*, see note.　　1057. *ledde.*

1056. *grine* (C. *grinew*, J. *grune* ꝛ) = "traps, snares." W. retains *grinew* which he describes as < O.E. *grinu* (plu.) (cf. Sievers § 267), the O.E. -*u* being written as -*ew*. This however would be unusual, and more probably *grine* is the original form, the *w* being a scribal misreading of a badly-written ꝛ in the intermediate text: cf. J. reading.

1057. *leide* (C. *ledde*, J. *leyde*) = "laid." W. and G. retain *ledde* (as pt. sg. of *legge*, to lay)—an unlikely form, probably an instance of dittography: cf. *leidest* (l. 104), *leide* (l. 467).

1058. *hacche* < O.E. *hæc(c)* = "half-door, gate or wicket" (*N.E.D.*). The meaning here is, probably, as suggested by Mr B. Dickins, "the casement" of the lady's bower (*bure*, l. 1050).

꒑ leredest hi to don schome
꒑ vnriht of hire lichome.
1055 Þe louerd þat sone vnderyat,
Lym ꒑ grune ꒑ wel ihwat,
Sette ꒑ leyde þe for to lacche.
Þu come sone to þan hacche,
Þu were ynume in one grune,
1060 Al hit abouhte þine schine: Fol. 236 v. col. 2.
Þu neddest non oþer dom ne lawe,
Bute myd wilde hors [were] todrawe.
Vonde if þu myht eft mysrede,
Hweþer þu wilt, wif þe meyde:
1065 Þi song mai beo so longe genge
Þat þu schalt hwippen on a sprenge."

Þe Nihtegale at þisse worde,
Mid swerde ꒑ myd speres orde,
If heo mon were, wolde vyhte:
1070 Ac þo heo bet do ne [m]ihte,
Heo vauht myd hire wise tunge.
"Wel viht þat wel spekþ" seyþ in þe songe.
Of hire tunge heo nom red:
"Wel viht þat wel spekþ" seyde Alured.
1075 "Hwat! seystu þis for myne schome?
Þe louerd hadde herof grome.
He wes so gelus of his wyue,
Þat he ne myhte vor his lyue
Iseo þat mon wiþ hire speke,
1080 Þat his heorte [n]olde breke.
He hire bilek in one bure,
Þat hire was stronge ꒑ sure:

1062. *were* omitted.   1070. *Mihte.*   1080. *wolde.*

1062. For the origin of this detail see Intro. § 8, p. lxii.
1066. *wippen* (J. *hwippen*) = "tremble, flutter." Str. adopts the J. reading, but parallel forms in other Teutonic languages suggest the *w*-form (see Str.-Br.).
1081 ff. This passage is in some measure reminiscent of *Yonec*, one of the *lais* of Marie de France, according to which, a young wife, shut up in a tower by her jealous husband, is consoled by a lover, who flies into her chamber in the form of a falcon.
1082. *stronge ꒑ sure* = "harsh and bitter." Prof. Craigie notes "adv. here used for adj. as in *Judith*, *torne* (l. 93), *hāte* (l. 94), *rūme* (l. 97)."

ich hadde of hire milse an ore,

an sori was for hire sore,

1085 an skente hi mid mine songe

al þat ich miȝte, raþe an longe.

Vorþan þe kniȝt was wiþ me wroþ,

vor riȝte niþe ich was him loþ:

he dude me his oȝene shome,

1090 ac al him turnde it to grome.

Þat underyat þe king Henri:

Jesus his soule do merci!   Fol. 241 r. col. 1.

He let forbonne þene kniȝt,

þat hadde idon so muchel unriȝt

1095 ine so gode kinges londe;

vor riȝte niþe ʔt for fule onde

let þane lutle fuȝel nime

an him fordeme lif an lime.

Hit was w[u]rþsipe al mine kunne;

1100 forþon þe kniȝt forles his wunne,

an ȝaf for me an hundred punde:

an mine briddes seten isunde,

1091. *underþat* or *underyat*.   1099. *wrþsipe*.

1088. The Nightingale, in this particular case, pleads an "exception," i.e. the plea of "spite and hate" (see note l. 1096), stating that the charge of the knight is no *bona fide* appeal but a malicious prosecution.

1091. *underyat* (C. and J.) = "perceived." Str., W. and G. read *underwat*, which W. translates as "perceived" without giving any further explanation. Str.-Br. also adopts *underwat*, and quotes as cognate O.L.G. *undarwitan*. But this explanation seems unlikely: for *underwat*, if it means "perceived" (as required by the context), must surely be related, not to an O.E. *witan* but to O.E. *witan* (to know). Moreover, no such form as *underwitan* exists in O.E., nor does any instance of such a verb appear in M.E. So that, altogether, the form *underwat* is probably not genuine. The reading, on the other hand, which we should have expected in C. would be *underȝat*, and this form actually occurs in l. 1055. Occasionally however in C. the symbol *y* is found for the more normal *ȝ*: cf. *ey* (l. 104), *eyre* (l. 106) (also in *nay* (l. 543), *ydel* (l. 917) where *y* = *i*): and in each case the *y* is written very much like a dotted *þ*, i.e. *w*. This then would account for the reading of *underwat* (instead of *underyat*) by Str., W. and G. That the correct reading is *underyat* is confirmed by the J. form (*vnderyat*).

King Henri, an allusion to Henry II of England, whose reign "initiated the rule of law as distinct from the despotism of the earlier Norman kings." G. however suggests (see ed. p. 14) that the poet may have had special reasons for bearing Henry in grateful memory, since that monarch transferred Godalming (near Guildford) to the diocese of Salisbury (1158). For the bearing of this allusion on the date of the poem see Intro. § 4, p. xxxv.

1093. *let forbonne* = "caused (the knight) to be outlawed." This sentence, at the date of the poem, does not necessarily mean "banishment or exile,"

Ic hadde of hire [m]ilce ⁊ ore,
And sori was for hire sore,
1085 ⁊ skente hi mid myne songe
Al þat ic mihte, raþe ⁊ longe.
Vorþan þe knyht wes wiþ me wroþ,
Vor rihte nyþe ic wes him loþ:
He dude me his owe schome,
1090 Ac al hit turnde him eft to grome.
Þat vnderyat þe kyng Henri:
Jesu his soule do mercy!
He let forbonne þene knyht,
Þat hadde ido svich vnriht   Fol. 237 r. col. 1.
1095 In so gode kynges londe;
For rihte nyþe ⁊ ful onde
Let þane lytel fowel nyme
⁊ him fordeme lif and lyme.
Hit wes w[u]rþsipe al myne kunne;
1100 Forþon þe kniht furles his w[u]nne,
⁊ yaf for me an hundred punde:
⁊ myne briddes seten ysunde,

1083. *Milce.*   1099. *wrþsipe.*   1100. *wnne.*

---

i.e. a substantive punishment, but merely a criminal process, a means of com-
pelling accused persons to stand their trial (see Pollock and Maitland, *Hist.
of Eng. Law*, I. 459). For Hall's suggestion as to the reference here, see
Intro. § 4, p. xxxv note.

For the causative use of *let* in L.O.E. cf. *A.S. Chron.* 963 E, *D. leot wircen
þa þæt mynstre.*

þene=O.E. *þæne*, variant of *þone* (mas. acc. sg.): cf. *þane*, ll. 249, 1097, see
Sievers § 337, a 2.

1096. *niþe ⁊...onde*="spite and hate," a legal formula=Lat. *odium et
atia*, cf. also ll. 417–9, 1401.

Other legal phrases occur in *lif ⁊ lime*, l. 1098 (see note); *bedde ⁊...borde*,
l. 1492 (see note). See also Intro. § 6, p. liii note 2.

1098. *fordeme lif an lime*="to condemn, life and limb" (cf. "condemnari in
vitam suam vel membra"), i.e. the severest of penalties for what was therefore
a most serious crime. Under the new criminal law instituted by Henry II,
as contrasted with the *Leges Henrici*, only a few crimes, with wide defini-
tions, placed life and limb at the king's mercy, other crimes being punishable
by money penalties. Thus "quisquis enim in regiam maiestatem deliquisse
deprehenditur, uno trium modorum...regi condemnatur: aut enim in uni-
verso mobili suo reus iudicatur, pro minoribus culpis; aut in omnibus im-
mobilibus, fundis scilicet et redditibus, ut eis exheredetur; quod si pro
maioribus culpis, aut pro maximis quibuscunque vel enormibus delictis, in
vitam suam vel membra," *Dial. de Scac.* II. 16 (quoted by Pollock and
Maitland, *History of Eng. Law*, II. 457 footnote).

1101. *an hundred punde* would represent an excessive fine or wergild. "In
the books of the Norman age the *wer* of the mere ceorl or *villanus*...is

an hadde soþþe blisse ꝛ hiȝte,

an were bliþe, ꝛ wel miȝte.

1105 Vorþon ich was so wel awreke,

euer eft ich dar[r] þe bet speke:

vor hit bitidde ene swo,

ich am þe bliþur euer mo.

Nu ich mai singe war ich wulle,

1110 ne dar me neuer eft mon agrulle.

Ac þu, eremi[n]g! þu wrecche gost!

þu ne canst finde, ne þu nost,

an holȝ stok þar þu þe miȝt hude,

þat me ne twengeþ þine hude.

1115 Vor children, gromes, heme ꝛ hine,

hi þencheþ alle of þire pine:

ȝif hi muȝe iso þe sitte,

stones hi doþ in hore slitte,

an þe totorue[ð] ꝛ toheneþ,

1120 an þine fule bon tosheneþ.

Ȝif þu art iworpe oþer ishote,

þanne þu miȝt erest to note.

Vor me þe hoþ in one rodde,

an þu, mid þine fule codde,

1125 an mid þine ateliche s[w]ore,

biwerest manne corn urom dore.   Fol. 241 r. col. 2.

1106. *dart.*   1111. *eremig.*   1119. *totorued.*   1125. *spore.*

---

reckoned at £4, that of the thegn or the *homo plene nobilis*...is £25 "
(Pollock and Maitland, *Hist. of Eng. Law*, II. 458): while "the London
citizens of the thirteenth century claimed as a chartered right that none of
them could be compelled to pay a higher fine than his *wer* of a hundred
shillings" (*ibid.* II. 457).

1104. ꝛ *wel miȝte* = "and well they might." This is a favourite expression
of the poet's, and is probably the correct rendering here, cf. ꝛ *wel mai*, l. 228;
he miȝte wel, l. 570; ꝛ *ful wel miȝte*, l. 1292. Otherwise it might be possible
to take *miȝte* as an adj. = "powerful, influential, of good standing." But
this, while giving good sense, is in all probability not what the poet intended.

1109. The later *strif* known as *The Throstle and the Nightingale* (ed.
Holthausen, *Anglia*, XLIII. (xxxi.), pp. 53–60) has details that are reminiscent
of the *O. & N.*, e.g. (1) The boast of the N. in the present passage, that she
is free to sing where she will, under royal protection, finds a parallel in the
T. and N. (ll. 97–9), where the N. exclaims *Ich habbe leue to ben here | In
orchard and ek in erbere | Mine songes for to singe.* (2) The expression *And
temeþ al þat is wilde* (*T. and N.*, l. 174) recalls *þat of so wilde makeþ tome*
(*O. & N.*, l. 1444). (3) The vocabularies etc. of the two poems contain
certain common elements, e.g. *T. and N., wrowe* (l. 31), *þes* (*hes*) (l. 68),
daþeit (l. 135), *niȝttegale*, *niȝtingale* (ll. 5, 13), *hoe* (l. 15); *O. & N.*,

ꝶ hedde seþþe blisse and hihte,
ꝶ were bliþe, ꝶ wel myhte.

1105   Vorþan ic wes so wel awreke,
Euer eft ich dar þe bet speke:
For hit bitydde ene so,
Ich am þe bliþure euer mo.
Nu ic may singe hwar ic wile,
1110   Ne dar me neuer eft mon agrulle.
Ac þu, ermyng! þu wrecche gost!
Þu ne canst fynde, ne þu nost,
An holeh stoc hwar þu þe mist hude,
Þat me ne twenge þine hude.
1115   Vor children, gromes, heme ꝶ hine,
Hi þencheþ alle of þine pine:
If hi mowe iseo þe sitte,
Stones hi doþ in heore slytte,
ꝶ þe totorueþ ꝶ toheneþ,
1120   ꝶ þine fule bon toscheneþ.
If þu art iworpe oþer iscote,
Þenne þu myht erest to note.
Vor me þe hoþ in one rodde,
ꝶ þu, myd þine fule codde,
1125   ꝶ myd þine ateliche sweore,
Biwerest monne corn from deore.

---

wrouehede (l. 1400), *þes, hes* (l. 748), *dahet* (l. 99), *nihtegale, niʒtingale* (ll. 1635, 13), *ho, heo* (ll. 19, 934). It would therefore seem probable that the later poem was in some measure influenced by the *O. & N.*

1115. *children*="girls," the sense in which the word is used in ll. 1453, 1463, also in certain modern dialects (*chiel, chield*, W. Corn., Dev., W. Som., see *E.D.D.*) and in one place in Shakespeare, viz. *Wint. T.* III. iii. 71, "a boy or a child, I wonder." Elsewhere in this poem (see Gloss.) the word occurs in its modern sense: but here the contrast implied in the phrase that follows (*heme ꝶ hine*) renders probable a similar contrast between *children* and *gromes* (girls and boys).

heme ꝶ hine="masters and servants." The form *heme* < O.E. -*hǣme* [*hūm*], cf. O.E. -*hǣmingas* (inhabitants): also *hemma* (housewife), quoted by W. from *Glossary of Shetland and Orkney Words* (Edmondston, 1866). For *hine* < O.E. **hina*, see Skeat, *Ety. Dict.* under *hind*.

1123. *rodde*="rod." According to Sk. and Str.-Br. this form was originally the same as *rode* (<O.E. *rōd*). The word however is distinct: <O.E. *rodd*, cf. O.N. *rudda* (see *N.E.D.*).

1125. *swore* (C. *spore*, J. *sweore*)="neck." W. (also St. and Wr.) reads *spore* (claw), Str. *sweore*, G. *swore*. The form *swore* is preferable, not only because it is supported by J., but also because of the rhyme: for while *spore* (O.E. *spora*): *dore* (O.E. *dĕor*) presents obvious difficulties, a normal rhyme is obtained with *swore* (O.E. *swĕora*) : *dore* (O.E. *dĕor*).

Nis noþer noȝt, þi lif ne þi blod:
ac þu art sh[e]ueles suþe god.
Þar nowe sedes boþe isowe,
1130　pinnuc, golfinc, rok, ne crowe
ne dar þar neuer cumen ihende,
ȝif þi buc hongeþ at þan ende.
Þar tron shulle aȝere blowe,
an ȝunge sedes springe ꝛ growe,
1135　ne dar no fuȝel þarto uonge,
ȝif þu art þarouer ihonge.
Þi lif is eure luþer ꝛ qued,
þu nar[t] noȝt bute ded.
Nu þu miȝt wite sikerliche
1140　þat þine leches boþ grisliche
þe wile þu art on lifdaȝe:
vor wane þu hongest islaȝe,
ȝut hi boþ of þe ofdradde,
þe fuȝeles þat þe er bigradde.
1145　Mid riȝte men boþ wiþ þe wroþe,
for þu singist euer of hore loþe:
al þat þu singst, raþe oþer late,
hit is euer of manne unwate:
wane þu hauest aniȝt igrad,
1150　men boþ of þe wel sore ofdrad.

1128. *shueles.*　　　　1138. *nard.*

1128. *sheueles* (C. *shueles*, J. *sheules*) = "a scarecrow." The word is derived
from O.E. **sciewels*, one of several earlier forms (O.E. *byrgels*, *fætels*, *gyrdels*,
græfels, *rǣdels*, *riecels*), each of which ended in *s* in the sg.　In each instance
the ending was -*els* (= O. Teut. -*isloz*, forming abstract sb.): and O.E. **sciewels*
therefore < earlier O.E. **scēow* + *isl* (cf. O.E. *byrgels*, O. Sax. *burgisli*: O.E.
gyrdels, Ep. *gyrdisl*), the *sl* > *ls* in O.E. after unaccented syllables.　See Sievers,
§ 183 (2).　With this Prim. O.E. **scēowisl* may be compared M. Du. *schouwsel*,
M.H.G. *schūsel*, Mod. Ger. *scheusal*, where metathesis has not taken place;
while, corresponding to O.E. **sciewels* is M.L.G. *schūwelse*, where metathesis
is visible.　Moreover the original meaning of O.E. **scēowisl*, **sciewels* (= "an
object of horror") is suggested by the root-form, viz. O.E. *scēoh(w)* = "shy."
In M.E., later forms of O.E. **sciewels* appear only in this poem (viz. *sheueles*,
l. 1128, and *schawles*, l. 1648, see note): and it is noteworthy that the *s* ending
of the sg. is as yet retained.　At a later date the *s* was dropped (cf. *burial*, *girdle*,
riddle), and the word is found (without the *s*) in mod. dial. forms like *shewell*,
sewell.　In Berks and Oxford dial. *shewell*, *shool* = "scarecrow"; in Northants

Nis nouþer nouht, þi lif ne blod:

Ac þu art sheules swiþe god.   Fol. 237 r. col. 2.

Þar newe sedes beoþ isowe,

1130 Pynnuc, goldfynch, rok, ne crowe

Ne dar neuer cumen ihende,

If þi buk hongeþ at þan ende.

Þar treon schulleþ ayer blowe,

˄ yonge sedes springe ˄ growe,

1135 Ne dar no fuoel þarto fonge,

If þu art þarouer ihonge.

Þi lif is euer luþer and qued,

Þu nart nouht bute ded.

Nv þu myht wite sikerliche

1140 Þat þine leches beoþ grisliche

Þe hwile þu art on lyfdaye:

Vor hwenne þu hongest islawe,

Yet hi beoþ of þe atdradde,

Þe foweles þat þe er bigradde.

1145 Mid rihte men beoþ wiþ þe wroþe,

For þu singest of heore loþe:

Al þat þu singest, raþe oþer late,

Hit is euer of mannes vnhwate:

Hwanne þu hauest anyht igrad,

1150 Men beoþ of þe wel sore aferd.

---

a "*sewell*" = "a line of feathers on twine placed a foot or two from the ground...to keep the deer within bounds": elsewhere the phrase "to break sewell" = "to forsake an old habit" (see *E.D.D. sewell, N.E.D. shewell*).

1133. *shulle* (J. *schulleþ*) = "shall." The C. form is etymologically correct (< O.E. *sculon*), the J. form is modernised: see note l. 1010, also l. 1703.

a ȝere. W. trans. "in the year, at the appropriate yearly season." Mr Bruce Dickins, with greater probability, suggests, "in the spring, in the warm season." The word *gear* originally meant "the warm part of the year," as opposed to *winter*: and this meaning is occasionally found in O.E., cf. *Runic Poem* (l. 32), Ger byþ gumena hiht (summer is a joy to men), also *Beowulf* (l. 1134), *Guðlac* (l. 716). Subsequently both *gear* and *winter* were used for the whole year, though at a later time, winter was restricted to its original significance. (See Dickins, *Runic and Heroic Poems*, p. 16, also B.T. Suppl. s. *gear*, III (b).)

1140. *leches* = "looks, appearance," < O.E. *lēc* [cf. *lōcian*]. For instances of O.E. *lēc* in compounds, see Napier, *O.E. Glosses*, 3462 n.

1150 ff. See additional notes, p. 202.

A.   7

Þu singst þar su*m* man shal be ded:
euer þu bodest sumne qued.
Þu singst aȝen eiȝte lure,
oþer of summe frondes rure:

1155 oþer þu bodes[t] huses brune,
oþer ferde of manne, oþer þoues rune;
oþer þu bodest cualm of oreue,
oþer þat londfolc wurþ idorue,
oþer þat wif lost hire make;

1160 oþer þu bodest cheste an sake.   Fol. 241 v. col. 1.
Euer þu singist of manne hareme,
þurȝ þe hi boþ sori ꞇ areme.
þu ne singst neuer one siþe,
þat hit nis for sum unsiþe.

1165 Heruore hit is þat me þe shuneþ,
an þe totorueþ ꞇ tobuneþ
mid staue, ꞇ stoone, ꞇ turf, ꞇ clute,
þat þu ne miȝt nowar atrute.
Dahet euer suich budel in tune

1170 þat euer bodeþ unwreste rune,
an euer bringeþ vuele tiþinge,
an þat euer specþ of vuele þinge!
God Almiȝti w[u]rþe him wroþ,
an al þat werieþ linnene cloþ!"

1175   Þe hule ne abo[d] noȝt swiþ[e] longe,
ah ȝef ondsware starke ꞇ stronge:
"Wat," quaþ ho, "hartu ihoded?
oþer þu kursest al unihoded?

1155. *bodes.*   1173. *wrþe.*   1175. *abot, swiþ.*

1166. *tobuneþ* = "beats" < O.E. **to-bynian* or **tobunian.* It is uncertain whether the *u* or the *y* form is to be inferred in O.E.: and the rhyme with *shuneþ* (l. 1165) does not help, since both O.E. *scunian* and *scynian* are found. The word also occurs in Shoreham's *Poems* (l. 85), *So tobete and so toboned,* where Str.-Br. reads *tobōned* (and in the present instance *tobūneþ*). In that case however the Shoreham form would be *tobouned*: and as against the long vowel in *tobūneþ* there is the rhyme with *shuneþ,* where the vowel is short. Hence the respective forms most probably are *tobūneþ* and *tobŏned* (*o* = a later variant of *ŭ*). Then, too, the origin of the word remains obscure. W. connects it apparently with O.E. and M.E. *bune* (hollow stem) and explains the verb as "to beat with sticks or reeds."
1167. *turf* < O.E. *tyrf,* mutated dat. of O.E. *turf.*
1169. *Dahet,* see note l. 99.
1174. W. interprets this as = "the clergy": Mr G. G. Coulton as "all

Þu singst þar sum man sal beo ded:
Euer þu bodest sumne qued.
Þu singst ayeyn ayhte lure,
Oþer of summe vrendes rure:
1155 Oþer þu bodest huses brune,
Oþer ferde of manne, oþer þeues run[e]:
Oþer þu bodest qualm of orue,
Oþer þat londfolc w[u]rþ idorue,
Oþer þat wif leost hire make:
1160 Oþer þu bodest cheste and sake.
Euer þu singest of manne harme,
Þurh þe hi beoþ sorie ꞇ arme: Fol. 237 v. col. 1.
Þu ne singest neuer one syþe,
Þat hit nys for summe vnsyþe.
1165 Hervore hit is þat me þe suneþ,
ꞇ þe totorueþ ꞇ tobuneþ
Mid staue, ꞇ stone, ꞇ turf, ꞇ clute,
Þat þu ne myht noware atrute.
Dahet euer budel in tune
1170 Þat bedeþ vnwreste rune,
ꞇ euer bringeþ vuele tydinge,
ꞇ þat spekeþ of vuele þinge!
God Almyhti w[u]rþe him wroþ.
ꞇ al þat wereþ lynnene cloþ!"
1175   Þe vle nabod noht swiþe longe,
Ac ȝef answere stark ꞇ stronge:
"Hwat," queþ heo, "ertu ihoded?
Oþer þu cursest vnihoded?

1156. *run.*   1158. *wrþ.*   1173. *wrþe.*

---

decent unmonastic folk." The latter points out (see *M.L.R.* xvii. p. 69),
(1) that "the usual meaning of *linen cloth* in medieval English, as in French,
is that of *underclothing*" (see *N.E.D.* s.v. *linen*, Godefroy, s.v. *linge*), (2) that
"this specification of linen cloth cannot be referred to the outer garments of
the clergy (who appeared in linen only for a few hours of the day) in preference to the large class who were distinguished by the linen shirt," (3) that a
large section of the community were without the linen shirt: "the peasant
and the poor man by necessity, many others, for religion's sake," (4) that
if *linen cloth* is used in *O. & N.* in its commonest sense, the phrase would
therefore roughly connote all socially respectable people except the monk and
his congeners, and that here the N. is invoking upon the O. "the malison of
all decent unmonastic folk."
1177 ff. For the meaning of these lines see Intro. § 7, p. lvii note.

For prestes wike ich wat þu dest.

1180 Ich not ȝef þu were ȝaure prest:

ich not ȝef þu canst masse singe:

inoh þu canst of mansinge.

Ah hit is for þine alde niþe,

þat þu me akursedest oðer siðe:

1185 ah þarto is lihtlich ondsware;

"Drah to þe!" cwaþ þe cartare.

Wi attwitestu me mine insihte,

an min iwit ꞇ mine miȝte?

For ich am witi ful iwis,

1190 an wo[t] al þat to kumen is:

ich wot of hunger, of hergonge:

ich wot ȝef men schule libbe longe:

ich wat ȝef wif lus[t] hire make:

ich wat þar schal beo niþ ꞇ wrake; Fol. 241 v. col. 2.

1195 ich wot hwo schal beon [an]honge,

oþer elles fulne deþ afonge.

Ȝef men habbeþ bataile inume,

ich wat hwaþer schal beon ouerkume:

ich wat ȝif cwalm scal comen on orfe,

1200 an ȝif dor schul ligge [a]storue;

1190. *wod.* 1193. *luste.* 1195. *ꞇ honge.* 1200. *ꞇ storue.*

1180. *ȝaure.* J. omits this form as unusual. It is probably a variant of *eauere* (l. 1282) = " ever." W. and G. however trans. = "certainly, fully," and the former quotes Mätzner, *Wb.* (335), *ȝeare* (adv.) < O.E. *gear(w)e.* But this seems an unlikely derivation, as it is difficult to see how O.E. *-earwe, -eare* could give M.E. *-aure:* moreover O.E. *gear(w)e* in the poem regularly > *ȝare* (cf. l. 860).

1184. Here the (β) orthography begins again, and the contractions for *þat, þer* are used.

1186. *Drah to þe,* apparently a colloquial expression used here derisively. English carters of to-day have definite commands for the guidance of their horses when walking without the help of the reins. Among these commands are "come up!," "gee (go) away!": and in accordance with the command, the horses move to left or to right. The form *drah* = "go" (cf. ll. 274, 776): the phrase = "go to!" with *þe* as ethical dative: and the expression is one of contempt and derision. Cf. Barnes, *Poems,* 119:

> An' ev'ry hoss do know my feäce
> An' mind my 'mether ho! an' whug!

where "'mether ho!" = "come hither" and "whug" = "go off!"

1189. *witi* (J. *þin*), scribal error, *n* written for *ti*: cf. similar confusion between *u* and *it* (Intro. § 3 (*d*) (v) (η)).

1193. *lust* (C. *luste,* J. *lust*). W. retains *luste* and translates = "has joy in" (opt. sg.). Str. and G. adopt the J. reading, and G. suggests that *lust* here = *lüst* (O.E. *lȳst, líest*) "shall lose," which is probably the correct inter-

For prestes wike ich wat þu dest.
1180 Ich not if þu were preost:
Ich not if þu canst masse singe:
Inouh þu canst of Mansynge.
Ac hit is for þine olde nyþe,
Þat þu me acursedest oþer siþe:
1185 Ac þarto is lihtlych answere:
"Drah to þe!" queþ þe kartere.
Hwi atwitestu me myne insihte,
ꝛ [m]in iwit ꝛ myne myhte?
For ich am [witi] ful iwis,
1190 ꝛ wo[t] al þat to comen is.
Ich wot of hunger, of heregonge;
Ich wot if men sulle libbe longe;
Ich wot if wif lust hire make;
Ich wot hwar sal beo niþ ꝛ wrake:
1195 Ich wot hwo sal beo anhonge,
Oþer elles fulne deþ avonge.
If men habbeþ batayle inume,
Ic w[o]t hwaþer sal beo ouercume;
Ic wot if qualm sal cumen on orve,   Fol. 237 v. col. 2.
1200 ꝛ if deor schulle ligge astorue:

1188. *Min.*   1189. *þin.*   1190. *wod.*   1198. *wt.*

---

pretation. As Kenyon (*J.E.G.P.* XII. 584) pointed out, this line (1193) is virtually a repetition of l. 1159 where the form *lost* (=O.E. *lēost* pr. 3 sg. of *lēosan*) appears: and of this form, *lust* (O.E. *liest*) is the more regular variant.

1195. *anhonge* (C.ꝛ *honge*, J. *anhonge*)="hung." Since ꝛ *honge* gives no sense, the C. scribe has evidently misread *an* of his original as *and*, and has employed the corresponding symbol (ꝛ): see Intro. § 3 (*a*) (ii) (*β*).

1196. *afonge*="receive." This word=an infin. (after *schal*, l. 1195), and is formed either from the p.p. of O.E. *onfon*, or from O.E. *a*+O.N. *fanga*: cf. *misfonge* (l. 1374).

1200. *astorue* (C. ꝛ *storue*, J. *astorue*)=(p.p.) "dead." The J. reading is undoubtedly correct, the C. scribe having fallen into an error similar to that of l. 1195. W. however retains the C. reading which involves certain difficulties. In the first place, if the C. reading be adopted, *storue* must obviously be read as an infin. (<O.E. *steorfan*, to die), and in this section of the text (see note l. 1184) the form would ordinarily have been written as *steorue*, not *storue*. Moreover certain difficulties are incurred with regard to the rhyme. Sweet (*History of English Sounds*, § 657) maintained in this connection that "the rhyme *storfe* : *orfe* is an exceptional one on O.E. *eo* which is perhaps due to some change of pronunciation (**eorf* for *orf*)." But this suggestion is unnecessary: a normal rhyme on *o* is obtained by reading *astorue* (<O.E. *āstorfen*, p.p. of *āsteorfan*) which is also the form required for orthographical reasons. Trans. "I know whether beasts shall lie dead."

ich wot ȝef treon schule blowe:

ich wat ȝef cornes schule growe:

ich wot ȝef huses schule berne:

ich wot ȝef men schule eorne oþer erne:

1205 ich wot ȝef sea schal schipes drenche:

ich wot ȝef snuw[e] schal uuele clenche.

An ȝet ich con muchel more:

ich con inoh in bokes lore,

an eke ich can of þe Goddspelle

1210 more þan ich nule þe telle:

for ich at chirche come ilome,

an muche leorni of wisdome:

ich wat al of þe tacninge,

an of oþer feole þinge.

1215 Ȝef eni mon schal rem abide,

al ich hit wot ear hit itide.

1206. *snuwes.*

1204. *eorne oþer erne.* W. trans. "run or cause to run," without further comment. G. regards the phrase as a legal formula meaning "to seek refuge," and he quotes in support of his view from the A.S. Law, "*gif hie* (i.e. refuge) *fahmon geierne oððe geærne*" (see B. T. s.v. *fahman*) = "if a foeman shall obtain refuge by running or riding." A simpler explanation however is obtained by translating: "I know whether men shall run (on foot) or ride," i.e. whether they shall be poor or not. Later on, the phrase occurs with the meaning "under all circumstances," cf. Chaucer, *C.T.* A 2251-2, "Thy temple wol I worshipe evermo...wher I ride or go." And possibly that is the meaning here, i.e. "I know of men under all circumstances." Cf. also Usk, *Testament of Love*, II. i. 62, *ryder and goer.*

1206. *snuwe* (C. *snuwes* or *smiþes,* J. *smithes*) = "snow." St. and Wr. read *snuwes,* Str. *smiþes,* W. *snuwes,* G. *snuwes schule.* It is evident from the C. and J. readings that this passage in the common original was somewhat obscure and presented difficulty to both of the scribes. In the first place, whichever of the two readings be adopted it would seem likely that in either case the final *s* is due to a scribal error (i.e. dittography) in the intermediate text. This is suggested by the form *schal* (pres. 3 sg.) which immediately follows. In the second place it will be noted that the passage ll. 1199-1206 deals with the various disasters of which the Owl claims to have foreknowledge and the list is fairly systematic. First come the plagues on cattle and wild beasts (ll. 1199-1200), then the blights on trees and crops (ll. 1201-2), thirdly, social calamities (ll. 1203-4), and lastly, disasters due to Nature itself (ll. 1205-6). Under this last heading come the tempests at sea (l. 1205), and it is clear that, in view of this context, the reading *snuwe* is preferable to *smiþe;* so that l. 1206 would read, "I know if snow shall bind [the earth] in evil fashion (or with harsh fetters)." The only difficulty arises from the undoubtedly irregular form *snuwe,* which elsewhere occurs in the poem as *asnowe* (l. 413), *snov* (l. 430), *snou* (l. 1002) (=O.E. *snāw*). G. suggests that it may be due to the influence of the *w:* but such instances of that influence as occur have initial *w* (cf. *wude* (l. 1029) alongside *wode* (l. 444) and *wu* (l. 187)

Ic wot if tren schulle blowe:
Ic wot if corn schulle growe:
Ic wot if huses schulle berne:
Ic wot if men sulle eorne oþer erne:
1205   Ic wot if sea sal sch[i]pes drenche:
Ic wot if [smithe] sale vuele clenche.
ꝛ ic con muchele more:
Ic con ynouh in bokes lore,
ꝛ ek ic can of þe Godspelle
1210   More þan ic wile þe telle:
Vor ic at chireche cume ilome,
ꝛ muchel leorny of wisdome:
Ic wot al of þe toknynge,
ꝛ of oþer vale þinge.
1215   If eny mon schal rem abide,
Al ic hit wot ar hit ityde.

1205. *schpes.*   1206. *sMithes.*

---

alongside *wo* (l. 113)), and thus do not offer a parallel to *snuwe* where the *w* follows the root vowel. More probably the *u* in *snuwe* must be regarded as a scribal variant of *o* (rare at this date) irrespective of quality or quantity: and instances of this change occur in *hu* (l. 1230), *ho* (*heo*) (l. 33), *wude* (l. 1029), *wode* (l. 444).

But while the C. reading is most probably that of the original, the reading of the J. scribe is not without its interest. In the first place, it represents an attempt to emend an obscure passage in the common original in the light of *clenche*, a word generally associated in M.E. with the work of smiths: so that the J. reading becomes "I know if smiths shall rivet badly, i.e. make defective arms and armour." This reading, though palaeographically possible (C. *snuwes* might easily be read as *smiþes*), must however be dismissed in view of the context. Secondly, the reading of the J. scribe is possessed of considerable value as illustrating the errors to which copyists of that time were liable. Thus, in writing *smith*—for *snuw*—he reads *n* of his original for *m* (see Intro. § 3 (*d*) (v) (ε)), *u* for *it* (see Intro. § 3 (*d*) (v) (η)), and *þ* (= w) for *h* (see Intro. § 3 (*d*) (v) (a)): and a knowledge of these possibilities is of great help in elucidating the text (cf. ll. 763, 1322, 1256, 1257).

1213. *tacninge* = "symbolism." The 12th century not only adopted the allegorical interpretation of Scripture elaborated by the Fathers of the Church (cf. *Ormulum*, *Bestiary*, etc.), but they also exalted the symbolical principle into an ultimate explanation of the Universe. For an account of such works as Hugo de St Victor, *De Sacramentis Christianae fidei*, Alanus de Insulis, *Anticlaudianus*, and of the symbolism underlying the architecture and sculpture of that period see H. O. Taylor, *The Medieval Mind*, II. ch. XXVII—XXVIII.

1215. *rem* (< O.E. *hrēam*) = "hue-and-cry": cf. *uthest* (l. 1683). G. points out that both expressions were legal terms for the outcry raised in pursuit of a thief or murderer. All who heard the "hue-and-cry" had to join in the pursuit (see Pollock and Maitland, *Hist. of Eng. Law*, II. 578), cf. ll. 1264, 1683.

Ofte, for mine muchele iwitte,
wel sori-mod ꞇ w[ro]þ ich sitte:
wan ich iseo þat sum wrechede
1220 is manne neh, innoh ich grede:
ich bidde þat men beon iwar[r]e,
an habbe gode reades ȝar[r]e.
For Alfred seide a wis word,
euch mon hit schulde legge on hord:
1225 "ȝef þu isihst [er] he beo icume,
his str[e]ncþe is him wel neh binume."
An grete duntes beoþ þe lasse,   Fol. 242 r. col. 1.
ȝef me ikepþ mid iwarnesse,
an [flo] schal toward misȝenge,
1230 ȝef þu isihst hu fleo of strenge;
for þu miȝt blenche wel ꞇ fleo,
ȝif þu isihst heo to þe teo.
Þat eni man beo falle in [e]dwite,
wi schal he me his sor atwite?
1235 Þah ich iseo his harm biuore,
ne comeþ hit noȝt of me þaru[o]re.
Þah þu iseo þat sum blind mon,
þat nanne rihtne wei ne con,
to þare diche his dweole fulie[ð],
1240 an falleþ, and þarone sulie[ð],

1218. *worþ.*	1221. *iwarte.*	1222. *ȝarte.*	1225. *er* omitted.
1226. *strncþe.*	1229. *fleo,* see note.	1233. *odwit.*	1237. *þaruare.*
	1239. *fulied.*	1240. *sulied.*	

1221. *iwarre* (C. *iwarte,* J. *warre*) = "aware, cautious." For similar scribal errors of *t* written for *r,* cf. l. 1222, also ll. 1106, J. 1260.

1225. Trans. "If thou seest [trouble] before it comes, it is deprived of almost all its force." For similar sentiments cf. Icel. *Proverb Poem,* III. 27, *Fýsa man-ek ins fyrra vara* (Forewarned is forearmed).

1229-30. A passage of considerable difficulty. W. takes *duntes* (understood from l. 1227) as the subject of *fleo schal* and translates "And [*duntes,* i.e. "blows"] shall fly towards misfaring, if thou seest how [they] fly from the string." But, apart from the awkward ellipsis of [they] in l. 1230, this interpretation involves the reading of a nom. pl. *duntes* with a sg. vb. *schal;* while the connection of "blows" with "a string" is not free from ambiguity. G. therefore reads *fleo* (l. 1229) = *flo* (< O.E. *flā,* arrow) as the nom. of *schal.* And this seems to be quite plausible: for, as Kenyon (*J.E.G.P.* XII. 584) points out, "since each scribe was copying from a MS. that in different parts had both *o* and *eo* (for O.E. *eo*), it is not surprising that *flo* (< O.E. *flā*)

Ofte, vor myne muchele witte,
Wel sori-mod ꞇ wroþ I sytte:
Hwanne ic iseo þer su*m* wrecchede
1220 Is cumynde neyh, inoh ic grede:
Ic bidde þer men beon warre,
ꞇ habbe gode redes yare.
Vor Alu*r*ed seyde a wis word,
Vych mo*n* hit schold*e* legge on hord:
1225 "If þu isyst her heo beo icume,
His strengþe is him wel neyh binume."
ꞇ grete duntes beoþ þe lasse,
If me ikepeþ myd iwarnesse,
ꞇ [flo] schal toward misyenge,
1230 If þu isihst hw fleo of strenge:
For þu myht blenche ꞇ fleo,
If þu isihst heo to þe teo.
Þauh eny mo*n* beo falle i*n* edwite,
Hwi schal [he] me his sor atwite?
1235 Þauh ic iseo his harm bivore,
Ne cumeþ hit nouht of me þarfore.   Fol. 238 r. col. 1.
Þah þu iseo þat su*m* blynd mon,
Þat nanne rihtne wey ne con,
To þare diche his dwele voleweþ,
1240 ꞇ falleþ, ꞇ þaronne sulieþ,

1229. *fleo.*   1234. *he* omitted.

should be changed to *fleo* in the neighbourhood of two occurrences of *fleo*"
(cf. ll. 1230, 1231). This suggestion may therefore be adopted, with the additional remark that the alteration of *flo* to *fleo* had in all probability taken
place in the intermediate text which stood for the common original, since
the spelling *fleo* is characteristic of both C. and J. Line 1229 will therefore
read "And an arrow shall miscarry (fly towards miscarriage)": the verb of
motion (viz. "fly") having been omitted after *schal*. There yet remains the
difficulty of the ellipsis in l. 1230. But this may be avoided by taking *hu*
as = *heo* (*ho*), which occurs in l. 1232, where the construction is closely
parallel and *heo* is used for O.E. fem. acc. sg. *hie*. The reading of l. 1230
would then be "if thou dost see it fly from the string": and this on the
whole would seem to be the most satisfactory interpretation. It is not necessary
to take *an* (l. 1229) as = indef. article (see Kenyon): for J. reads ꞇ, and moreover *an* (indef. article) occurs, as a rule, only before vowels in this poem.
1239–40. *fulieð...sulieð*, cf. *folȝeþ* (l. 307), *soleþ* (l. 1276). For these
variants see note l. 379.
Trans. "he follows his uncertain (erratic) course to the ditch."

wenest þu, þah ich al iseo,

þat hit for me þe raþere beo?

Al swo hit fareþ bi mine witte:

hwanne ich on mine bowe sitte,

1245   ich wot 'l iseo swiþe brihte

an summe men kume[ð] harm þarrihte.

Schal he, þat þerof noþing not,

hit wite me for ich hit wot?

Schal he his mishap wite me,

1250   for ich am wisure þane he?

Hwanne ich iseo þat sum wrechede

is manne neh, inoh ich grede,

an bidde inoh þat hi heom schilde,

for toward heom is [harm unmilde].

1255   Ah þah ich grede lude an stille,

al hit itid þur[h] Godes wille.

Hwi wulleþ men of me hi mene,

þah ich mid soþe heo awene?

Þah ich hi warni al þat ȝer,

1260   nis heom þerfore harem no þe ner:

ah ich heom singe for ich wolde   Fol. 242 r. col. 2.

þat hi wel understonde schulde

þat sum unselþe heom is ihende,

hwan ich min huing to heom sende.

1265   Naueþ no man none sikerhede

þat he ne mai wene 'l adrede

þat sum unhwate ne[h] him beo,

þah he ne conne hit iseo.

Forþi seide Alfred swiþe wel,

1270   and his worde was Goddspel,

1246. *kumed.*   1254. *harm unmilde* omitted.   1256. *þurþ.*
1264. *huing*, u altered to o.   1267. *neþ.*

1246. *men*=dat. sg. Trans. "on some man."
1255. *lude an stille*=either "loud and low" (W.) or "under all circumstances" (Str.-Br.).
1256. *þurh* (C. *þurþ*, J. omits). The omission of the word from J. suggests that the reading of the common original was *þurþ*. For similar scribal confusion between *h* and *þ* see Intro. § 3 (d) (v) (a).

Wenestu, þah ic al iseo,
Þat hit for me þe raþer beo?
Al so hit fareþ bi [m]ine witte:
Þanne ic on myne bowe sitte,
1245 Ic wot ꞇ iseo swiþe brihte
Þat summe men cumeþ harm þarrihte.
Sal he, þar he nowiht not,
Hit wite me vor ic hit wot?
Sal he his myshap wyten me,
1250 Vor ic am wisure þan he?
Hwanne ic iseo þat sum wrechede
Is manne neyh, inouh ic grede,
ꞇ bidde inouh þat hi heom schilde,
Vor toward heom is harm vnmylde.
1255 Ac þah ic grede lude and stille,
Al iwurþ Godes wille.
Hwi wulleþ men of me mene,
Þah ic mid soþe heo awene?
Þah ic hi warny al þat yer,
1260 Nis heom þarvore [harem] þe ner:
Ac ich singe vor ich wolde
Þer hi wel vnderstonde scholde
Þat sum vnsel heom is ihende,
Hwen ic myn huyng to heom sende.
1265 Naueþ mon no sikerhede
Þat he ne may wene ꞇ adrede
Þat sum vnhap neih him beo,
Þah he ne cunne hit iseo.
Forþi seyde Alured swiþe wel,
1270 ꞇ his word was Godspel,

1243. *Mine.*   1260. *atem.*

1260. harem (J. *atem*), scribal confusion between *t* and *r*, see Intro. § 3
(d) (v) (δ).
1264. *huing* = "outcry." St. *soing*, Wr. *song*, Str. *hoing*. Str.-Br. trans. =
"clamour" (< O.Fr. *huer*, to cry out), cf. Mod. Eng. "hue-and-cry." W.
connects the word with "hooing, whooing," imitative of the owl's cry.
1267. *neh* (C. *neþ*, J. *neih*). W. reads *ney*, with *y* written very much like
dotted *þ*. The reading of the intermediate text was doubtless *neþ* in error for
neh of the original, see note l. 1256. Note also C. *unhwate*, J. *vnhap*.

       þat "euereuch man, þe bet him beo,
       eauer þe bet he hine beseo:"
       "ne truste no mon to his weole
       to swiþe, þah he habbe ueole."
1275   "Nis [nout] so hot þat hit nacoleþ,
       ne noȝt so hwit þat hit ne soleþ,
       ne noȝt so leof þat hit ne aloþeþ,
       ne noȝt so glad þat hit ne awroþeþ:
       ac eauereeu[c]h þing þat eche nis,
1280   agon schal, ⁊ al þis worldes blis."
       Nu þu miȝt wite readliche,
       þat eauere þu spekest gideliche:
       for al þat þu me seist for schame,
       euer þe seolue hit turneþ to grome.
1285   Go so hit go, at eche fenge
       þu fallest mid þine ahene swenge;
       al þat þu seist for me to schende,
       hit is mi wurschipe at þan ende.
       Bute þu wille bet aginne,
1290   ne shaltu bute schame iwinne."
       Þe niȝtingale sat ⁊ siȝte,
       ⁊ hohful was, ⁊ ful wel miȝte,
       for þe hule swo ispeke hadde,
       an hire speche swo iladde.   Fol. 242 v. col. 1.
1295   Heo was ho[h]ful, ⁊ erede
       hwat heo þarafter hire sede:

1276. *nou* with *t* written above.   1279. *-euh.*
            1295. *hoþful* or *howful.*

1271. Trans. "Let every man, the better his condition be, all the more carefully look to himself." Cf. *Prov. of Hending* (160), *þe bet þe be, þe bet þe byse*: *Prov. of Alfred* (131), *ne ilef þu nouht to fele·uppe þe see þat floweþ*: Cato 218, 18, *Cum fueris felix, quae sunt adversa caveto.*

1273-4. Cf. *Prov. of Alfred* (181-4), "Yf þu seoluer and gold ȝefst | and weldest in þis world | neuer vpon eorþe to wlonk | þu ny-wurþe."

1275-82. This passage is an adaptation of certain Lat.-Eng. "sentences" found by Zupitza at the back of Aelfric's *Glossary* (see note l. 135). The "sentences" are as follows:

   (i) *Ardor frigescit, nitor squalescit, amor abolescit, lux obtenebrescit.*
       Hat acolað, hwit asolað, leof alaðað, leoht aðystrað (MS. *ad*).
  (ii) *Senescunt omnia, quae aeterna non sunt.*
       Æghwæt forealdað, þæs þe ece ne byð.
Cf. also O.E. *Rhyme Song*, l. 67, *Searohwit solað, sumur-hat colað.*

1276. *soleþ*, cf. *sulieð*, see note l. 1240.

1285-6. The metaphor here is connected with wrestling, cf. ll. 795 ff.

Þat "euerich mon, þe bet [him] beo,
Euer þe bet he him biseo":
"Ne triste no mon to his wele   Fol. 238 r. col. 2.
To swiþe, þa[h] he habbe uele."

1275 "Nis noht so hot þat hit nacoleþ,
Ne noht so hwit þat hit ne soleþ,
Ne noht so leof þat hit naloþeþ,
Ne noht so glad þat hit nawreþeþ:
Ac euerich þing þat eche nys,

1280 Agon schal, ℸ al þis worldes blis."
Nu þu miht witen redeliche,
Þat euer þu spekest gidiliche:
For al þu me seyst vor schame,
Euer þe [solue] hit turneþ to grome.

1285 Go so hit go, at eche fenge
Þu vallest myd þin owe swenge;
Al þat þu sayst for me to schende,
Hit is my w[u]rþsipe at þan ende.
Bute þu wille bet agynne,

1290 Ne schaltu bute schame iwynne."
Þe nyhtegale sat and syhte,
ℸ hauhful was, ℸ wel myhte,
For þe vle so ispeke hadde,
And hire speche so iladde.

1295 Heo wes houhful, and erede
Hwat heo þarafter hire seyde:

1271. *him* omitted.   1274. *þat.*   1284. *soule.*   1288. *wrþsipe.*

1290. Trans. "Thou shalt win [nothing] but shame."
1291. *siʒte* = "sighed" (O.E. *sican*). This form together with *sihð* (l. 1587) helps to explain the development of the word from O.E. *sican* to Mod. Eng. *sigh.* In E.M.E. -*kþ* (-*cþ*) = -*hþ* (cf. *sikeþ* (l. 1352), *sihð* (l. 1587): *rekþ, recþ* (l. 491), *rehþ* (l. 1404)): and from the form *sihð* (pr. 3 sg.) a new infin. and pret. were formed, viz. *siʒen, siʒte*, which afterwards became Mod. Eng. "sigh." For similar new formations of verbs based on the pr. 3 sg. cf. *spene* (note l. 165).
1292. *hohful* = "thoughtful, anxious," see note l. 537.
1295. *hohful* (C. *hoþful* or *howful*, J. *houhful*). Str. and G. read *hohful*, W. *howful.* Since -*ow* (< O.E. -*og*) is unusual in C., the form with -*h* is probably correct, the scribe having misread original *h* as *þ*: see Intro. § 3 (*d*) (v) (*a*).
erede. W. incorrectly takes this word to be pt. sg. of *arede* (O.E. *ārǣdan*) = "made ready, took counsel": but the form in that case would have been *aradde* (cf. *raddest* (l. 157)). Str.-Br. rightly explains it as "devoid of counsel, at a loss" (< O.E. *ǣrǣde*).

ah neoþeles heo hire understod.

"Wat!" heo seide, "hule, artu wod?

þu 3eolpest of seolliche wisdome,

1300 þu nustest wanene he þe come,

bute hit of wicchecrefte were.

Þarof þu, wrecche, mos[t] þe skere

3if þu wult among manne b[eo]:

oþer þu most of londe fleo.

1305 For alle þeo þat [þ]erof cuþe,

heo uere ifurn of prestes muþe

amanset: swuch þu art 3ette,

þu wiecche-crafte neauer ne lete.

Ich þe seide nu lutel ere,

1310 an þu askedest 3ef ich were

a-bisemere to preost ihoded.

Ah þe mansing is so ibroded,

þah no preost a-londe nere,

a wrecche neoþeles þu were:

1315 for eauereuch chil[d] þe cleopeþ fule,

an euereuch man a wrecche hule.

Ich habbe iherd, Ᵹ soþ hit is,

þe mon mot beo wel storre-wis,

[þat] wite inno[h] of wucche þinge kume,

1320 so þu seist þ[e] is iwune.

1300. *nustest*, altered from *mi3test*.   1302. *moste*.   1303. *boe.*
1305. *wer-*.   1306. *uere, u* deleted: marg. *w* later.   1315. *chil.*
1319. *an: innoþ* or *innoy*.   1320. *þat*.

1297. *hire understod* = "bethought herself, took thought," cf. *hi understod*
l. 951. In the present instance the dat. *hire* has taken the place of *hi* (acc.):
cf. note l. 704.

1300. *nustest* (C. *nustest* over *mi3test*, J. *nustest*), see note l. 78.

1302. *skere* = "cleanse, purify," cf. O.Sw. *skæra* (purify). W. (*Gloss.*)
connects it with O.E. *scēran* (for *sceran, scieran*?). But this does not explain
sk-, and even if the O.E. equivalent were *scēran* its derivative *skere* [ē] could
not rhyme with *were* [ẹ̄]. For the connection of this word *skere* with N.E.
dial. *skeer* and with *Scereþorsday* (=Maundy Thursday) found in *Judas*, the
oldest of the English ballads, see E. Björkman, *Scandinavian Loan-Words in
M.E.* I. 125 (Halle, 1900).

1305–8. Trans. "For all those who were skilled in witchcraft were cursed
of old by the mouth of the priest: as thou art still, (for) thou hast never
forsaken witchcraft."

The form *lete* (l. 1308) = pt. 2 sg. < O.E. *lēte*, which thus gives a regular
rhyme on [ẹ̄] with *3et(t)e* < O.E. *gieta*.

1309. Trans. "I said to thee just now [that thou wert accursed]: and thou
didst ask in mockery if I had been ordained as priest," cf. ll. 1169 ff., 1177 ff.

Ac noþeles heo hire vnderstod.

"Hwat!" heo seyde, "vle, artu wod?

Þu yelpest of selliche wisdome,

1300 Þu nustest hwenne hit þe come,

Bute hit of wicchecrafte were.

Þarof þu, wrecche, most þe skere

If þu wilt among manne beo:

Oþer þu most of londe fleo.

1305 Vor alle þeo þat þerof cuþe,

Heo weren ifurn of prestes muþe

Amansed: such [þu] art yette.

*   *   *   *   *

Ic þe seyde nv lutel ere,

1310 ꝥ þu askedest if ich were

A-bysemare to preoste ihoded.   Fol. 238 v. col. 1.

Ac þe mansyng is so ibroded,

Þauh no preost a-londe nere,

A wrecche naþeles þu were:

1315 For euerich chi[l]d þe clepede fule,

ꝥ euerich man a wrecche vle.

Ich habbe iherd, ꝥ soþ hit is,

Þe mon mot beo wel sturre-wis,

ꝥ wite inoh of hwiche þinge cume,

1320 So þu seyst þat is iwune.

1307. *þu* omitted.   1308. line omitted.   1315. *chid.*

1315. *child* (C. *chil*, J. *chid*), the defective readings of both MSS. point to error in the intermediate text: otherwise the C. reading might possibly have been correct, cf. mod. dial. *chiel*, quoted in note l. 1115.

1317–20. One of the most obscure passages in the poem. Neither of the MSS. gives real sense, while the interpretations hitherto offered are all of an unsatisfactory kind. Str. suggests *þat* for *an* (l. 1319), and *inoh* for *innoþ* (l. 1319): he inserts *þin* before *iwune* (l. 1320) and translates: "The man must be well starwise who know (*sic*) enough of the coming of such things, as thou sayst (*sic*) that is thy custom." W., on the other hand, retains the C. reading, takes *innoþ* (< O.E. *innoþ*, bowels, heart) to mean "the hidden source of things," and translates: "(The man must be wise in star-lore) and know quite well from what things come, as thou sayest, what (that which) is usual (in the regular course of nature)": or "and know the hidden source from which thing (source) comes, as thou sayest, what is in the course of nature."

But as a statement of a general truth (cf. l. 1317, "I have heard and true it is (that)...") no one of these interpretations can be described as coherent: and to obtain sense some amount of emendation is necessary. Both MSS., it will be noted, agree almost exactly in their readings, so that the obscurity doubtless arose from errors already existing in the intermediate text.

(1) In the first place, the general sense of the passage requires that

Hwat canstu, wrecche þing, of storre,
bute þat þu biha[u]est hi feorre?
Alswo deþ mani dor ⁊ man,
þeo of [swucche] nawiht ne con.

1325   On ape mai a boc bih[o]lde,
an leues wende*n* ⁊ eft folde:
ac he ne con þe bet þaruore
of clerkes lore top ne more.   Fol. 242 v. col. 2.

Þah þu iseo þe steorre alsw[o],
1330   nartu þe wisure neau*er* þe mo.
Ah ȝet þu, fule þing, me chist,
an wel grimliche me atwist
þat ich singe bi manne huse,
an teache wif breke spuse.

1335   Þu liest iwis, þu fule þing!
þ[urh] me nas neau*er* ischend spusing.
Ah soþ hit is ich singe ⁊ grede
þar lauedies beoþ ⁊ faire maide;
⁊ soþ hit is of luue ich singe:
1340   for god wif mai i[n] spusing

1322. *bihaitest.*   1324. *hswucche.*   1325. *bihalde.*   1329. *alswa.*
1336. *þ*, cross line omitted.   1340. *i.*

---

l. 1319 should be in some way descriptive of *mon* (l. 1818): and Str.'s suggestion to read *þat* in place of *an* at the beginning of the line provides a clue to the solution. The emendation is palaeographically easy. The scribe of the intermediate text may well have written ⁊ (C. *an*) in mistake for an abbreviated *þat* of the original version, with which the symbol ⁊ would easily be confused.

(2) Secondly the C. reading *innoþ* must undoubtedly be emended to *innoh* (cf. J. *inoh*): see also Intro. § 3 (*d*) (v) (*a*).

(3) Then again, with regard to l. 1320 (C. and J. *So þu seist* (J. *seyst*) *þat is iwune*) here too the general sense of the passage requires an emendation, viz. the reading of *þe* in place of *þat*. In both C. and J., it will be noticed, the contracted form of *þat* appears, and this abbreviation may easily have been written in the intermediate text by mistake for original *þe*.

Hence the passage, as emended, would seem to be coherent and to fit in with the context: and it would run as follows: "I have heard, and true it is, (that) the man who really knows what things are coming, must be wise in star-lore: as thou sayest is true (i.e. usual) of thee." The rhyme *is* : *·wis* (l. 1317–8) is probably correct since the vowel in *is* was lengthened in O.E. before final consonant (see Sievers § 122). Cf. also *þis* : *ris* (ll. 1635–6), *is* : *wis* (ll. 1745–6).

1322. *bihauest* (C. and J. *bihaitest*). Various suggestions have been made with regard to this obscure reading of the MSS. Str. emended to *biwaitest* (< O.Fr. *waiter*, to watch): W. retained *bihaitest*, which he explained as "due to analogy with O.E. *beheht* < O.E. *behātan*, 'to promise, threaten'" (cf. *beheyhte, Moral Ode,* 238): G. suggested a connection with O.E. *behātest* (= "thou dost worship"): while Kenyon (*J.E.G.P.* xii. 586) proposed to substitute *behaldest*, a form involving serious palaeographical difficulties. Of

Hwat constu, wr[e]cche þing, of stor[r]e,
Bute þat þu biha[u]est hi ferre?
Al so doþ mony deor and man,
Þeo of suyche nowiht ne can.

1325   On ape may on bok biholde,
'Ꞇ leues wende and eft folde:
Ac he ne con þe bet þarvore
Of clerkes lore top ne more.
Þey þu iseo þe steorre al so,
1330   Nertu þ[e] wisere neuer þe mo.
Ac yet þu, fule þing, me chist,
'Ꞇ wel grimlyche me atwist
Þat ic singe bi manne huse,
'Ꞇ theche wyue breke spuse.

1335   Þu lyest iwis, þu fule þing!
Þurh me nes neuer isend spusing.
Ac soþ hit is ich singe 'Ꞇ grede
Þar leuedis beoþ 'Ꞇ feyre meide:
'Ꞇ soþ hit is of luue ich singe:
1340   For god wif may in spusinge

1321. *wrcche*; *storie*, later *r* above *i*.   1322. *bihaitest*.   1330. *þu*.

the proposed emendations *biwaitest* is the most probable. The scribe of the intermediate text may have misread original *w* (*þ*) as *h* (see Intro. § 3 (*d*) (v) (*β*)). At the same time, *biwaitest* must be regarded as an unusual form; according to Str., it is not found elsewhere, though the form *wayted* occurs in Chau. *Sq. T.* 121.

The simplest and most likely emendation, however, would be *bihauest* (< O.E. *behawian*, to gaze at). This would give the sense required, viz. "thou beholdest them from afar": and at the same time it would be palaeographically easy, for the scribe of the intermediate text might easily have read a badly-written original *u* as *it* (see Intro. § 3 (*d*) (v) (*η*)), an error subsequently copied by the scribes of C. and J. For *u=w* (in *behauest*), cf. *andsuare* (l. 149), *atuitestu* (l. 751).

1325. *On ape.* The ape appears to have been a favourite domesticated animal in medieval times: and Neckam in two chapters (*De Nat. Rerum*, II. ch. 128–9) which he devotes to that animal, illustrates its natural talent for mimicry: cf. "Simia non solum gestibus sed et lineamentis hominem mentiens, ipsum in multis imitari satagit."

1328. *top ne more* = "top nor bottom" (< O.E. *moru*, "root") = "nothing at all": cf. Mod. Eng. "from top to toe, head to tail."

This word *more* is preserved in Mod. Dorsets. dial., cf. Barnes, *Poems, The Clote* (Water-lily), p. 16:

How proud wer I when I vu'st could zwim
Athirt the deep pleace, where thou bist growen
Wi' thy long more vrom the bottom dim.

1340–2. A commentary on the doctrine of the Courts of Love, according to which, love in marriage was impossible.

A.   8

bet luuien hire oȝene were,
þane awe[r] hire copenere;
an maide mai luue cheose
þat hire wurþschipe ne forleose,
1345 an luuie mid rihte luue
þane þe schal beon hire buue.
Swiche luue ich itache � lere,
þerof beoþ al mine ibere.
Þah sum wif beo of nesche mode,
1350 for wumm[e]n beoþ of softe blode,
þat heo, þurh sume sottes lore
þe ȝeorne bit � sikeþ sore,
mis[r]empe � misdo sumne stunde,
schal ich þaruore beon ibunde?
1355 Ȝif wimmen luuieþ unrede,
[w]itestu me hore misdede?
Ȝef wimmon þencheþ luuie derne,
[ne] mai ich mine songes werne.
Wummon mai pleie under cloþe,
1360 weþer heo wile, wel þe wroþe:
� heo mai do bi mine songe,
hwaþer heo wule, wel þe wronge.   Fol. 243 r. col. 1.
For nis a-worlde þing so god,
þat ne mai do sum ungod,
1365 ȝif me hit wule turne amis.
For gold � seoluer, god hit is:
an noþeles þarmid þu miȝt
spusbruche buggen � unriȝt.
Wepne beoþ gode *griþ* to halde:
1370 ah neoþeles þarmide beoþ men acwalde

1342. *awet.*   1350. *wummon.*   1353. *-tempe* or *-rempe*: marg. *steppe.*
1356. *hwitestu.*   1358. *ne ne.*   1366. *For* deleted. marg. *euere.*

1350. *wummen* (C. *wummon*, J. *wymmen*)="women." The J. reading
(i.e. the plu. form) is required here by the pl. vb. *beoþ*. For occasional scribal
confusion between *o* and *e* see Napier, *O.E. Glosses*, xxxi.
  1353. *misrempe* (C. *mistempe*, J. *misnyme*)="go astray." There is a
marginal reading in C. (in later hand)=*missteppe*, a form adopted by St.
and Wr. Str.'s suggestion (adopted by W. and G.) of *misrempe* is however

Bet luuyen hire owe were,
Þan on oþer, hire copinere;
Ꞇ mayde may luue cheose
Þat hire trevschipe ne forleose,
1345 Ꞇ luuye mid rihte luue
Þane þat schal hire beo boue.
Suyche luue ic theche Ꞇ lere,
Þerof beoþ al myne ilere.   Fol. 238 v. col. 2.
Þauh sum wif beo of neysse mode,
1350 Vor wymmen beoþ of softe blode,
Þat heo, vor summe sottes lore
Þe yorne bit and sykeþ sore,
Misnyme Ꞇ misdo sume stunde,
Schal ic þarvore beo ibunde?
1355 Yef wymmen luuyeþ for vnrede,
Witestu me heore mysdede?
If wymmon þencheþ luuye derne,
[Ne] may ic myne songes werne.
Wymmon may pleye vnder cloþe,
1360 Hweþer heo wile, wel þe wroþe:
Ꞇ heo may do bi [m]yne songe,
Hweþer heo wile, wel þe wronge.
Vor nys a-worlde þing so god,
Þat ne may do sum vngod,
1365 If me hit wile turne amys.
Vor gold Ꞇ seoluer, god hit is:
Ꞇ naþeles þarmyd þu myht
Spusbruche bugge Ꞇ vnryht.
Wepne beoþ gode griþ to holde:
1370 Ꞇ naþeles þarmyd beoþ men aqolde

1358. *Ne ne.*   1361. *Myne.*   1370. *aqᵒld'.*

---

probably correct, cf. *misrempe* C. and J. (l. 1787). For other instances of *t*
written by mistake for *r* see Intro. §3 (*d*) (v) (δ). The error was probably due
to the scribe of the intermediate text, for the J. scribe, not understanding
mistempe, has substituted an entirely different form, viz. *misnyme*.
   1356. *witestu* (C. *hwitestu*, J. *witestu*) = "blamest." The C. form affords
another instance of scribal confusion between *h* and þ (w) (cf. l. 1256): the
scribe corrected himself in time but forgot to mark the elision.

aȝeines riht [an] fale londe,
þar þeoues hi bereð an honde.
Alswa hit is bi mine songe,
þah heo beo god, me hine mai misfonge,
1375 an drahe hine to sothede,
an to oþre uuele dede.
Ah [schaltu] wrecch, luue tele?
Bo wuch ho bo, vich luue is fele
bitweone wepmon ⁊ wimmane:
1380 ah ȝef heo is atbroide, þenne
he is unfele ⁊ forbrode.
Wroþ wurþe heom þe holi rode
þe rihte ikunde swo forbreideþ!
W[u]nder hit is þat heo nawedeþ.
1385 An swo heo doþ, for heo beoþ wode
þe bute nest goþ to brode.
Wummon is of nesche flesche,
an flesches [lust] is strong to cwesse:
nis wunder nan þah he abide.
1390 For flesches lustes hi makeþ slide,
ne beoþ heo nowt alle forlore,
þat stumpeþ at þe flesches more:
for moni wummon haueþ misdo
þat aris[t] op of þe slo.
1395 Ne beoþ nowt ones alle sunne,
forþan hi beoþ tweire kunne: Fol. 243 r. col. 2.

1371. ⁊.   1377. *sch altu.*   1381. *forbroide* with *i* deleted.
        1384. *winder.*   1388. *lustes.*   1394. *aris.*

1371. *an* (C. ⁊, J. *of*) = "in." Probably another error in the intermediate
text, copied by the C. scribe and modified by the scribe of J., cf. l. 1195.
1372. *hi* = "them." As W. points out, *hi* here refers to *wepne* (l. 1369), and
the phrase *bereð an honde* must be interpreted literally: cf. however the
later idiom *bere on hand* = "to accuse."
1378. *Bo wuch ho bo* = "whichever it be," i.e. all love is natural (pure).
vich = "each." According to W. and G. this word is connected with *euch*,
ech. The more correct derivation is however given in Str.-Br., viz. < O.E.
gehwilc (each), cf. *wilch, uiche* also J. *vych* (l. 1592).
1380. *þenne.* See additional notes, p. 202.
1381. *forbrode* (C. *forbroide* with *i* deleted, J. *forbroyde*). The readings of
both MSS. point to error in the intermediate text, for the rhyme with
rode [ǭ] requires *forbrode*: the error is however corrected in C.
1388. *lust* (C. and J. *lustes*). Str. reads *lust* which gives the better reading
because of the following *is* (sg.) (cf. also the sg. pro. *he* l. 1389) and of the more

Ayeynes riht of alle londe,
Þar þeoues hi bereþ an honde.
Al so hit is bi myne songe,
Þah heo beo god, me hine may mysfonge,
1375 ꝼ drawe hine to sothede,
ꝼ to oþre vuele dede.
Ah schaltu, wrecche, luue tele?
Beo hwich heo beo, vich luue is fele
Bitwene þe mon ꝼ wymmone:
1380 Ah if heo is abroyde, þeonne
He is vnvele and forbroyde.
Wroþ wurþe him þe holy rode
Þe rihte icunde so forbreydeþ!
Wunder [hit is] þat heo ne awedeþ.
1385 ꝼ so heo doþ, vor heo beoþ wode,   Fol. 239 r. col. 1.
Þat bute neste goþ to brode.
Wymmon is of neysse fleysse,
ꝼ fleysses [lust] is strong to queysse:
Nis wunder non þah he abide.
1390 Vor fleysses lustes hi makeþ slide,
Ne beoþ heo nouht alle forlore
Þat stumpeþ at þe fleysses more:
Vor mony wymmon haueþ mysdo
Þat aryst vp of þe slo.
1395 Ne beoþ noht ones alle sunne,
Vorþan hi beoþ tweire ikunne:

1384. *his.*   1388. *lustes.*

---

regular scansion thus obtained. If *lustes* be retained (as in W.) the line must be translated: "it is hard to overcome the lusts of the flesh"; but in that case *he* (1389) = "they" is an unusual form. On the whole it would seem probable that in this section of the MSS. where scribal errors abound, we have here another error of the intermediate text: viz. either an instance of dittography or else an error due to the fact that the eye of the scribe was caught by *flesches lustes* (l. 1390).

1391–2. *forlore* : *more.* This rhyme is wrongly quoted by Morsbach (§ 64, a 1) as illustrating M.E. lengthening of O.E. ŏ in open syllables. He has apparently taken the *o* in *more* as long (as if < O.E. *mōr*) whereas it is short (< O.E. *moru*); and the word therefore affords no evidence as to the lengthening process. For *more* = "root, stumbling-block," see note l. 1328.

stumpeþ = "stumbles" (see *N.E.D.*), with which the M.E. form is connected: cf. Barnes, *Poems* (45), "An' then they stump'd along vrom there," where "stump'd" describes the tottering gait of two old people.

1395. Trans. "Nor are all sins of one (kind)."

1396 ff. Kenyon (*J.E.G.P.* xii. 587–9) was the first to notice the reference

su[m] arist of þe flesches luste,

an sum of þe gostes custe.

Þar flesch draheþ men to drunnesse,

1400 an to [wrouehede] ꝛ to golnesse,

þe gost misdeþ þurch niþe an onde,

ꝛ seoþþe mid murhþe of [monne shonde,]

1397. *sun.*   1400. *wronchede.*   1402. *monnes honde.*

---

to the Seven Deadly Sins in this passage (see Intro. §8, p. lxxii). He points out that the sins are divided, in accordance with the medieval classification, into sins of the flesh and sins of the spirit (ll. 1397–8), the former being described in further detail in ll. 1399–1400, the latter in ll. 1401–6. As to the identification of the respective sins, five of them at least present no great difficulty. Thus *drunnesse* (l. 1399) stands for Gluttony or *Gula*: *golnesse* (l. 1400) for Lechery or *Luxuria*: *niþe an onde* (l. 1401) for Wrath or *Ira*: *ȝeoneþ after more* ꝛ *more* (l. 1403) for Avarice or *Avaritia*: while *modinesse* (l. 1405) represents Pride or *Superbia*.

With regard to the more obvious readings, the C. form *drunnesse* (l. 1399) has been retained (as in W.) in preference to J. *drunkenesse* (adopted by Str.) since the *k(e)* may well have been dropped as the medial of three consonants (cf. *wraslinge*, l. 795). In l. 1403, the C. form *ȝeoneþ* (J. *wunneþ*) was emended to *ȝeorneþ* by Str., W. and G.: but Kenyon rightly defends the C. reading as giving good sense (cf. *ȝonie*, l. 292), as well as a picturesque touch characteristic of the poet's style: and the C. reading has therefore been retained. In l. 1405, on the other hand, C. *heþ, þurþ* are obvious scribal errors for *heh* (W. prefers *hey*) and *þurh* (see notes to ll. 1267, 1256).

Of the two remaining Sins which present rather more difficulty, Kenyon detected one after a skilful emendation of l. 1402. Both C. and J. read here *of monnes honde* which gives no sense at all. Kenyon therefore proposed to read *of monne shonde*, suggesting that the *s* of *shonde* in "some previous copy" had been crowded on to the preceding word owing to the length of the line, and had thus led both the C. and J. scribes astray. The line, as emended, would therefore run: *mid murhþe of monne shonde* = "with joy at another's shame"—an obvious reference to Envy or *Invidia*.

For other instances of Envy representing Joy at other men's harm cf. Chau. *Parson's Tale*, 490: "The seconde spece of envye is joye of oother mannes harm," also *Rom. of Rose*, ll. 252 ff.:

No thyng may so moch hir (i.e. Envy) plese

    .   .   .   .   .   .

[As] whan she seeth discomfiture

Upon ony worthy man falle.

Also *P. Plow.* B. v. 91–2.

In attempting to identify the remaining Sin, i.e. Sloth or *Accidia*, Kenyon is less successful. He is inclined to accept neither of the readings of the texts: and indeed, neither C. *wronchede* (= "wrongness, wickedness") nor J. *wlonkhede* (= "pride") can well supply a possible reading. He therefore suggests that "the author, not intending to make a complete list of the Sins, omitted Sloth as less distinctly a sin of the flesh": and he goes on to add that if we accept J. *wlonkhede* as the original reading, "the poet may have intended to refer among the sins of the flesh to *Luxuria* in its three manifestations: *drun(ke)nesse, wlonkhede, golnesse*." But this is not altogether satisfactory: it would be surprising to find that one of the familiar Deadly Sins was omitted from such an account. And in aiming at a new solution we must start from the assumption that in *wronchede* (*wlonkhede*) we have two attempts at copying the unfamilar or badly-written form of the intermediate text, and that, according to the scribal practices, the C. scribe

Sum arist of fleysses luste,
ꞇ sum of þe gostes custe.
Þar fleys drahþ nv men to drunkenesse,
1400 ꞇ to [wrouehede] ꞇ to golnesse,
Þe gost mysdoþ þurh nyþ and onde,
ꞇ seþþe myd [m]urehþe of [monne shonde,]

1400. *wlonkhede.*   1402. *Murehþe*; *monnes honde.*

---

has aimed at reproducing, the J. scribe at emending, the reading of that intermediate text. It is therefore the form *wronchede* that will be found the safer guide to the reading of the original, and it may well be that in writing that form, the scribe of the intermediate text had confused *n* with *u*, and *c* with *e* (see Intro. § 3 (*d*) (v) (*e*)) and that the form of the original was in reality *wrouehede.*

In seeking to connect this word with Sloth or *Accidia*, it is important in the first place to remember that in the Middle Ages a free interpretation was given to the Deadly Sins, and that each of those Sins was divided into many varying subdivisions and branches, each of which, on occasion, might stand for that particular Sin (see J. L. Lowes, *Chaucer and the Seven Deadly Sins*, Publications of Mod. Lang. Assoc. of America, New Series XXIII. No. 2, pp. 243 ff.). Thus *Sloth* in the *Aȝenbite of Inwit* covered Slackness, Timidity, Tenderness, Idleness, Heaviness, Forgetfulness, Weariness, Sorrow, Despair and other things besides: so that the medieval connotation of Sloth was something very different from that of to-day, when its meaning has been limited to "laziness, indolence" and such like. This tendency, it might be noted, was already present in Cassian's *De institutis Coenobiorum et de octo principalium vitiorum remediis*, libri XII. of the early 5th century, where *acedia* is defined as "anxietas sive taedium cordis" (see H. O. Taylor, *Classical Heritage of Mid. Ages*, p. 162): and something of the same interpretation seems to be present in the account given of *Accidia* or Sloth in Chaucer's *Parson's Tale*, 678–728. There for example we find that "Bitternesse" is said to be "mooder (mother) of accidie": and that "accidie" is defined as "the angwissh of troubled herte." *Accidia*, again, it is said "maketh (a man) hevy (i.e. sad), thoghtful (i.e. anxious) and wrawful (i.e. irritable)"......(so that) "he dooth alle thyng with anoy (i.e. annoyance) and with wrawnesse (i.e. irritation), slaknesse, and excusacioun, and with ydelnesse, and unlust." It would therefore appear that one at least of the accepted meanings (indeed, if we may judge from Cassian, the original and fundamental meaning) of *Accidia* or Sloth was that vexed and irritable state of mind which prevented a man from doing deeds of goodness. And this sinful state of mind Chaucer describes by the words *wrawnesse* and *wrawful* (cf. Chau. *C.T.* I. 677, Ellesmere MS. *wrawful*; Petworth MS. *wrowe*; rest of MSS. *wrawe*) which suggest some connection with *wrouehede* above: and in that case *wrouehede*="irritation, that anguish of a troubled heart, or anxietas sive taedium cordis" which in the Middle Ages stood for *Accidia* or Sloth. The word *wroue* (*wrowe*), it might be added, occurs in *The Throstle and the Nightingale* (ll. 31–2): *Hy gladieþ hem þat beþ wrowe,* | *Boþe þe heye and þe lowe*, see note l. 1109.

Concerning the origin of the word *wrouehede* (=*wrowehede*, cf. *siueþ*, l. 1526; *snov*, l. 430) there must remain some doubt. Skeat gives no derivation of *wrawnesse* or *wrawful*, though Str.-Br. notes *wraw, wrau, wroȝe, wrowe* (plu.), *wraȝed, wrawid* (p.p.) as connected with Swed. *vrå* (perverse). But these forms, together with *wrouehede*, would seem to point to an O.E. root **wrāg-*: for the change of O.E. *-āg* to M.E. *-ōw* in the present poem (C. text) cf. *þrowe* (O.E. *þrāgu*) l. 478, *wowes* (O.E. *wāhas*) l. 1528, *owe* (O.E. *āgen*) l. 100.

an ʒeoneþ after more ⁊ more,
an lutel rehþ of milce ⁊ ore;

1405 an stiʒþ on he[h] þur[h] modinesse,
an ouerhoheð þanne lasse.
Sei [me sooþ], ʒef þu hit wost,
hweþer deþ wurse, flesch þe gost?
Þu miʒt segge, ʒef þu wult,

1410 þat lasse is þe flesches gult:
moni man is of his flesche clene,
þat is mid mode deouel-imene.
Ne schal non mon wimman bigrede,
an flesches lustes hire upbreide:

1415 swuch he may te[l]en of golnesse,
þat sunegeþ wurse i[n] modinesse.
[ʒ]et ʒif ich schulde a-luue bringe
wif oþer maide, hwanne ich singe,
ich wolde wiþ þe maide holde,

1420 ʒif þu hit const ariht atholde:
Lust nu, ich segge þe hwaruore,
vp to þe toppe from þe more.
ʒef maide luueþ dernliche,
heo stumpeþ ⁊ falþ icundeliche:

1425 for þah heo sum hwile pleie,
heo nis nout feor ut of þe weie;
heo mai hire guld atwende
a rihte weie þur[h] chirche-bende,
an mai eft habbe to make

1430 hire leofmon wiþute sake,   Fol. 243 v. col. 1.

1405. heþ, þurþ.   1407. mes soþ.   1415. tellen, stroke through top
of the first l.   1416. i with contraction for n omitted.   1417. Þet.
1428. þurþ.

1403. *ʒeoneþ* (J. *wunneþ*) = "gapes." The C. reading (< O.E. *geonian*, to
gape, yawn) gives good sense. The word occurs as *ʒonie* in l. 292, and is a
strong picturesque term characteristic of the poet, cf. Ps. xxii. 13. It is therefore unnecessary to emend it to *ʒeorneþ* (yearns) as is done by Str. and W.
The J. reading (*wunneþ* = strives) evidently represents a scribal attempt to
emend what was possibly in this connection an unfamiliar expression (see
Intro. § 3 (*b*) (ii) (β)). The more normal form would be *winneþ* (< O.E. *winnan*):
but *wunnan* (inf.), *Anc. Riw.* 238, is quoted by Str.-Br.
1405–6. *-nesse* : *lasse*, for the rhyme see note l. 370.
1412. *deouel-imene* = "devil-companion," cf. *deoulene fere* (l. 932). Str.-Br.
quotes O.E. *Hom.* II. 31, *imene* (companion). W. (*Gloss.*) takes *imene* as adv.
and translates "a devil commonly."

ꞇ wunneþ after more and more,

ꞇ lutel rekþ of [m]ilce and ore;

1405 ꞇ styhþ on heyh þur[h] modynesse,

ꞇ ouerhoweþ þane lasse.

Sey me soþ, if þu hit wost,

Hweþer doþ wurse, fleys þe gost?

Þu myht segge, if þu wult,

1410 Þat lasse is þes fley[s]es gult:

Mony mon is of his fleysse clene,

Þat is myd mode deouel-imene.

Ne schal no mon wymman bigrede,

ꞇ fleysses lustes hire vpbreyde:

1415 Such heo mahte beo of golnesse,

Þat sunegeþ wurse in modinesse.

Hwet if ic schulde a-luue bringe

Wif oþer mayde, hwanne ic singe?

Ic wolde wiþ þe mayde holde,

1420 If þu const aryht atholde:

Lust nv, ic segge þe hwarvore,

Vp to þe toppe from þe more.   Fol. 239 r. col. 2.

If mayde luueþ derneliche,

Heo stumpeþ ꞇ falþ icundeliche:

1425 Vor þaih heo sum hwile pleye,

Heo nys noht feor vt of þe weye;

Heo may hire guld atwende

A rihte weye þurh chirche-bende,

ꞇ may eft habbe to make

1430 Hire leofmon wiþvte sake,

1404. *Milce.*   1405. *þur.*   1410. *fleyes.*

1415–6. Trans. "He may charge such women with wantonness while he himself sins worse in pride." The supremacy of Pride over the other Deadly Sins was a commonplace from the first. W. preserves the MS. reading *tellen*, but *telen* (O.E. *tǣlan*) is the better reading. The fact that a totally different form occurs in J. suggests that the incorrect *tellen* appeared in the intermediate text.

1417. *ȝet* (C. *Bet*, J. *Hwet*). Str. *Hwat*, W. and G. *Bet*. The C. reading as it stands is awkward: and as a capital ȝ might easily be read as B (see facsimile (a) ll. 625, 630) the form *ȝet* is preferable.

1419. *wiþ* = "with." For this exceptional use of the word see note l. 18.

1422. Trans. "from top to bottom," i.e. all about it.

1430. *sake* (O.E. *sacu*) = "questioning": a legal term generally used with *sōcn* to express a single idea, viz. "inquisition into a disputed matter" (see H. p. 267).

an go to him bi daies lihte,
þat er stal to bi þeostre nihte.
An ȝunling not hwat swuch þing is:
his ȝunge blod hit draȝeþ amis,
1435 an sum sot mon hit tihþ þarto
mid alle þan þat he mai do.
He comeþ ꝛ fareþ ꝛ beod ꝛ bi[t]
an heo bistant ꝛ ouersi[t],
an bisehþ ilome ꝛ longe.
1440 Hwat mai þat chil[d] þah hit misfonge?
Hit nuste neauer hwat hit was,
forþi hit þohte fondi [þ]as,
an wite iwis hwuch beo þe gome
þat of so wilde makeþ tome.
1445 Ne mai ich for reo[w]e lete,
wanne ich iseo þe tohte ilete
þe luue bring[e] on þe ȝunglinge,
þat ich of murȝþe him ne singe.
Ich [t]eache heom bi mine songe
1450 þat swucch luue ne lest noȝt longe:
for mi song lutle hwile ilest,
an luue ne deþ noȝt bute rest

1437. *bid.*   1438. *ouersid.*   1440. *chil.*   1442. *þas, þ* with dot.
1445. *reoþe.*   1447. *bring.*   1449. *dreache* with *d* deleted.

1433. *ȝunling,* cf. *wraslinge,* l. 795 note.
1434. *his* = "its" = "her": the reference is to *ȝunling* (l. 1433). Through-out this passage *ȝunling* and *child* (l. 1440) = "young girl," see note l. 1115: and the use of the neuter points to the preservation of O.E. grammatical gender, cf. O.E. *cild* (neu.).
1437 f. *beod* = "commands": for the *d*-ending see Appendix I (*d*) (iv) (β). *bit* (C. ꝛ *bid,* J. *abid*) < O.E. *bitt* (*biddeþ*). The scribe of the intermediate text probably wrote *bid* (for *bit,* cf. l. 445) under the influence of the preceding *beod,* and *sid* (for *sit*) in the next line on account of the rhyme. Trans. "He comes and goes, he commands and entreats: he pays her attention and then neglects her."
ouersit = "neglects." Str. trans. = "supersedet," W. = "takes possession of." The word is derived from O.E. *ofersittan,* which means (1) to win, (2) to abstain from (cf. Lat. *supersedere*): and, as Mr B. Dickins suggests, the latter meaning is preferable here. He points out that by such an interpretation (a) the sequence of events is better kept, (b) *bistant : ouersit* are parallel to *comeþ : fareþ,* and *beod : bit,* and (c) the passage gains in psychological truth, since at certain stages, neglect is more effective than persistent attention.
1439. *bisehþ* (J. *bisekþ*) = "beseeches, courts." For *-hþ* as variant of *-kþ* in verbal forms see note l. 1291.
1442. *þas* = "it" (< O.E. *þæs*) gen. sg. after *fondi* (O.E. *fandian,* to try). For a similar use of article as pronoun cf. *þare* (l. 1526).

ᛏ gon to him bi dayes lyhte,
Þat er bistal on þeoster nyhte.
Þat yongling not hwat such þing is:
His yonge blod hit drahþ amys,

1435   ᛏ sum sot man hit tyhþ þarto
Mid alle þan þat he may do.
He cumeþ ᛏ fareþ and beod abid,
ᛏ he bistarte an oþer sid,
ᛏ bisekþ ilome and longe.

1440   Hwat may þat child þah hit misfonge?
Hit nuste neuer hwat hi[t] was,
Vorþi hit þouhte fondi þas,
ᛏ wyte iwis hwich beo þe gome
Þat of þe wilde makeþ tome.

1445   Ne may ic vor reuþe lete,
Hwanne ic iseo þe tohte ilete
Þe luue bring on [þ]e [y]unglinge,
Þat ic of murehþe him ne singe.
Ic theche heom bi myne songe

1450   Þat suych luue ne last noht longe:
For my song lu[tl]e wile ileste,
ᛏ luue ne doþ noht bute reste

1441. *his.*   1447. *me* (*m* deleted); *wunglinge.*   1451. *lude.*

1444. See note l. 1109 for later echo of this line.
1445. *lete* = "prevent, refrain" < O.E. *lǣtan*: see note l. 1018.
1447. *bringe* (C. and J. *bring*). Str. and J. read *bringþ*, W. *bring*. The opt. form with *-e* would be expected here, since the verb occurs in a dependent adj. clause introduced by a rel. pro. The final *-e* was omitted by the scribe of the intermediate text, either through carelessness, or because it would not be pronounced in view of the vowel immediately following.
1448. *him* = "to it," here equivalent to "to her": see note l. 1434.
1449. *teache* (C. *dreache* with *d* deleted, J. *theche*) = "teach." The *r* in the C. form is obviously a scribal error for *t* (see Intro. § 3 (*d*) (v) (δ)). W. and G. retain *reache* which they translate as "relate" < O.E. *reccean*: but *ea* < O.E. *ĕ* would be quite irregular in this poem.
1451–2. *ilest...rest* (J. *ileste...reste*). W. retains the C. reading: Str. and G. adopt that of J. Both versions however present difficulty. For if (1) the C. forms be retained, *ilest* = pres. 3 sg., but *rest* (infin.) would require a final *-e*: whereas if (2) the J. forms be retained, *reste* = infin. form, but *ileste* as pres. 3 sg. would be abnormal. In order to get over the difficulty, Kenyon (*J.E.G.P.* xii. 590), while suggesting the adoption of the C. reading, takes *bute* as a conjunction, *ilest* and *rest* as contracted forms (pres. 3 sg.). He would therefore translate "For my song lasteth but a short while, and love doth nought but alighteth on such children (i.e. maids)." He further notes parallel constructions (of *noght bute* followed by the indic.) in Chaucer, ex. *C.T.* B 2121: "Thou doost noght elles but despendest tyme"; *C.T.* A 2664:

on swuch childre, ꜩ sone ageþ,
an falþ adun þe hote breþ.
1455 Ich singe mid heom one þroȝe,
biginne on heh ꜩ endi laȝe,
an lete [mine] songes falle
an lutle wile adun mid alle.
Þat maide wot, hwanne ich swike,
1460 þat luue is mine songes ili[k]e,
for hit nis bute a lutel breþ,
þat sone kumeþ, ꜩ sone geþ.
Þat child bi me hit understond,
an his unred to red[e] wend,   Fol. 243 v. col. 2.
1465 an iseȝþ wel, bi mine songe,
þat dusi luue ne last noȝt longe.
Ah wel ich wule þat þu hit wite,
loþ me beoþ wiues utschute:
ah [w]if mai [of] me nime ȝeme,
1470 ich ne singe nawt hwan ich teme.
An wif ah lete so[t]tes lore,
þah spusing-bendes þuncheþ sore.
Wundere me þungþ wel starc ꜩ stor,
hu eni mon so eauar for,
1475 þat [h]e his heorte miȝte driue
[to] do hit to oþers mannes wiue:
for oþer hit is of twam þinge,
ne mai þat þridde no man bringe;
o[þ]ar þe lauerd is wel aht,
1480 oþer aswunde, ꜩ nis naht.
Ȝef he is wurþful ꜩ aht man,
nele no man, þat wisdo[m] can,

1457. *mines.*   **1460.** *iliche.*   **1464.** *red.*   **1469.** *ȝif, of of.*
1471. *sortes.*   **1475.** *e.*   **1476.** *an o.*   **1479.** *oþar* with *þ* dotted.
1482. *wisdon.*

"What dooth this queene of love but wepeth so"; and *House of Fame*, iii. 546:
"What did this Eolus but he | Toke out hys blake trumpe" (see *Chau. Soc.
Pub.* 2nd S. 44 (1909), pp. 146 ff.).
    1460. *ilike* (C. and J. *iliche*). The rhyme requires *ilike* (cf. ll. 157, 806):
the common error is due to the intermediate text.
    1463–4. The forms *-stond : wend* are probably due to scribal alteration, the

On such childre, ⁊ sone ageþ,
⁊ falþ adun þe [hote] breþ.

1455　I singe myd heom one þrowe,
Biginne an heyh ⁊ endi lowe,
⁊ lete mine songes falle
A lu[tl]e wi[l]e adun myd alle.
Þat mayde wot, hwenne I s[w]ike,　　Fol. 239 v. col. 1.

1460　[Þat] luue is myne songes ili[k]e,
Vor hit nys bute a lutel breþ,
Þat sone cumeþ, and sone geþ.
Þat child bi me hit vnderstond,
⁊ his vnred to rede iwend,

1465　⁊ syhþ wel, bi myne songe,
Þat dusy luue ne last noht longe.
Ac wel ic wile þat þu hit wite,
Loþ me beoþ wifes vtschute:
Ac wif may of me nyme yeme,

1470　Ic ne singe noht hwen ic teme.
⁊ wif auh lete sottes lore,
Þauh spusyng-bendes byndeþ sore.
Wunder me þinkþ stark ⁊ sor,
Hw eny mon so haueþ for

1475　Þat his heorte myhte dryue
To do hit to oþres mannes wyue:
Vor oþer hit is of twam þinge,
Ne may þe þridde no mon bringe;
Oþer þe louerd is wel auht,

1480　Oþer aswunde, ⁊ nys nouht.
If he is w[u]rþful ⁊ auht mon,
Nele no mon, þat wisdom can,

1454. *heorte.*　　1458. *lude wise.*　　1459. *sike.*　　1460. ⁊; *iliche.*
1464. *iwent, t* altered to *d.*　　1481. *wrþful.*

original spellings being -*stent : went* (syncopated 3rd sg. pr. ind.), see Appendix I (*d*) (iv) (*β*).
　1471. *sottes* (C. *sortes*, J. *sottes*) = "fool's." For scribal error in C. form (*r* written for *t*) see Intro. § 3 (*d*) (v) (*δ*).
　1476. *to* (C. *an o*, J. *to*). The C. scribe has clearly read *t* in the intermediate text as ⁊ (cf. l. 1489).
　1477. Trans. "For it is one (either) of two things."

hure of is wiue do him schame:

for he mai him adrede grame,

1485   an þat he forleose þat þer hongeþ,

þat him eft þarto noȝt ne longeþ.

An þah he þat noȝt ne adrede,

hit is unriȝt ꝺ gret sothede

[to] misdon one gode manne,

1490   an his ibedde from him spanne.

ȝef hire lauerd is forwurde

an unorne at bedde ꝺ at borde,

hu miȝte þar beo eni luue

wanne [a] cheorles buc hire ley buue?

1495   Hu mai þar eni luue beo,

war swuch man gropeþ hire þeo?

Herbi þu miȝt wel understonde

þat on [is a reu], þat oþer schonde,   Fol. 244 r. col. 1.

to stele to oþres mannes bedde.

1500   For ȝif aht man is hire bedde,

þu miȝt wene þat þe mistide,

wanne þu list bi hire side.

An ȝef þe lauerd is a w[re]cche,

hwuch este miȝtistu þar uecche?

1489. *an o.*   1494. *aswuch. leþ* or *ley.*   1498. *his areu.*
1503. *wercche.*

1483. *hure.* Str.-Br. trans. = "hear" (<O.E. *hȳran, hieran*): but the usual form of that verb in the poem is *ihere* (see Gloss.). Hence a better interpretation and one more in keeping with the context would be *hure* = "hire" (<O.E. *hȳran*)—an explanation supported by the expression *bugge* = "buy" (l. 1506), and adopted by W. The explanation of G. is however still better as being free from all difficulties, viz. *hure* = "especially" (O.E. *hūru*).

Trans. "No man who is wise will shame him (i.e. the brave husband) especially through his wife."

1485. A reference to the mutilation which was the punishment of the man who committed adultery with another man's wife (see Pollock and Maitland, *Hist. of Eng. Law*, II. 483, 542).

1489. *to* (C. *an o*, J. *to*), see note l. 1476.

1490. *spanne* = "entice." In form the word = O.E. *spannan* (fasten, clasp): in meaning it is equivalent to O.E. *spanan* (entice). The two words may possibly have been confused at this date, especially as in the pret. they had identical forms (i.e. *spēon*), cf. M.E. *hyȝt* = "is called," a confusion of O.E. *heht* and *hatte*: see also *leten* (l. 1018 note).

1492. *at bedde ꝺ at borde,* a legal formula = "full marital relations" (cf.

Hure of his wive do him schome:
Vor he may him adrede grame,
1485 ꝼt þat he forleose þat þer hongeþ,
Þat him eft þarto noht ne longeþ.
ꝼt þah he þat nouht ne adredeþ,
Hit is vnriht ꝼt gret sothede
To mysdo one gode manne,
1490 ꝼt his ibedde from him spanne.
If hire louerd is forwurþe
ꝼt vnorne at bedde ꝼt at borde,
Hw myhte þar beo eny luue
Hwenne a cherles buk hire lay buue?
1495 Hw may þer eny luue beo,
Hwar such mon gropeþ hire þeo?   Fol. 239 v. col. 2.
Herbi þu miht wel vnderstonde
Þat on is at þen oþres schonde
To stele to oþres mannes bedde.
1500 Vor if auht man is hire ibedde,
Þu myht wene þat þe mystide,
Hwanne þu lyst bi hire side.
ꝼt if þe louerd is a wrecche,
Hwych este myhtestu þar vecche?

---

a mensa et thoro). Here we have an early use of this alliterative phrase, see
N.E.D. *bed.*

1494. A metrically faulty line. C. reads *aswuch cheorles,* J. *a cherles.*
The C. form *swuch* is probably an insertion due to scribal error, the eye of
the scribe having been caught by the word in l. 1496.

ley (C. *leþ* or *ley,* J. *lay)* = O.E. *læg* (lay): for similar forms see l. 1091 note.
The C. reading is doubtful (*leþ* or *ley*): Str. reads *ley,* W. *leþ.* But *ley* is
preferable, because, apart from the J. reading (*lay*), the pret. form is required
after *miȝte* (l. 1493) as opposed to the pres. form *gropeþ* (l. 1496), which follows
mai (l. 1495) in the parallel couplet which repeats the idea of ll. 1493-4.

1498. *a reu* (C. *areu*). The J. scribe alters the line altogether and writes
at þen oþres. But in so doing he omits the alternatives which C. presents, and
which are required by the context. In the following lines, it will be noticed,
the two alternatives are explained: viz. (a) *ȝif aht man* (l. 1500), (b) *ȝef
lauerd is a wrecche* (l. 1503). W. retains *areu* which he translates as "base"
< O.E. *earg*: but this cannot be regarded as a suitable alternative to "shame"
(*schonde*). Moreover the parallel abstract sb. would be "cowardice, baseness":
but *areu* does not admit of this interpretation. Str. and G. are probably right
in reading *a reu* = "in sorrow, regret" (< O.E. *hrēow*) which gives good
sense and supplies a suitable alternative to *schonde.* Trans. "From this thou
mayst easily understand that in one case there is sorrow, in the other,
disgrace (as the result) of stealing...."

1505   Ȝif þu biþenchest hwo hire ofligge,
       þu miȝt mid wlate þe este bugge.
       Ich not hu mai eni freo-man
       for hire sechen after þan.
       Ȝef he biþencþ bi hwan he lai,
1510   al mai þe luue gan awai."
       Þe hule was glad of swuche tale:
       heo þoȝte þat te nihtegale,
       þah heo wel speke atte frume,
       hadde at þen ende misnume:
1515   an seide: "Nu ich habbe ifunde
       þat maidenes beoþ of þine imunde:
       mid heom þu holdest, ꝺ heom biwerest,
       an ouerswiþe þu hi herest.
       Þe lauedies beoþ to me iwend,
1520   to me heo hire mo[n]e send.
       For hit itit ofte ꝺ ilome,
       þat wif ꝺ were beoþ unisome:
       ꝺ þerfore þe were gulte,
       þat leof is over wummon to pulte,
1525   an speneþ on þare al þat he haueþ,
       an siueþ þare þat no riht naueþ,

1520. *mode*.

1506. *bugge* (C. and J.).   Str., W. and G. retain *bugge*: but Morsbach
(§ 133, a 3) unnecessarily suggests *bigge* on account of the rhyme: see note
l. 116.
    1507. *freo-man*. Mention is made in the poem of the following ranks of
society: *kniȝt* (ll. 768, 1087), *freoman* (l. 1507), *bondeman* (l. 1577), and *chorles*
(ll. 509, 632, 1494): and although the words are, for the most part, loosely
used, they still afford some evidence as to the current usage of such terms.
Before the Conquest, the *freoman*, *bonda*, and *ceorl* were freemen who tilled
their own soil: but by 1200 all three stood for tenants who rendered certain
dues to their feudal lords. At the same time, certain differences are per-
ceptible between them: whereas some amount of respect and dignity is
associated with *freoman* and *bondeman*, the term *chorl* has become one of
contempt (= a boorish peasant). Possibly the *freoman* was a tenant who was
free from feudal services, the *bondeman* a tenant (*villein*) who rendered full
services to his lord, while the *chorl* had already degenerated into the serf
class.
    1509. *biþencþ* = "bethinks himself." The C. reading is instructive here:
it might be read in the MS. as *biþeneþ*, *biweneþ* or *biþencþ*: but J. *biþenkþ*
confirms *biþencþ*: see Intro. § 3 (d) (v).
    1520. *mone* (C. *mode*, J. *mone*) = "moans, complaints." The J. reading
suits the context better than *mode* (= "moods"): for the reference is to
complaints concerning quarrels between husband and wife (cf. l. 1522: also

1505 If þu biþenchest hwo hire ofligge,
Þu myht myd wlate þe este bugge.
Ich not hw may eny freomon
Vor hire sechen after þan.
If he biþenkþ bi hwam he lay,
1510 Al may þe luue gon away."
     Þe vle wes glad of suche tale:
Heo þouhte þat þe nyhtegale,
Þah heo wel speke at þe frume,
Hadde at þan ende mysnume:
1515 ᛫t seyde "Nv ich habbe ifunde
Þat maydenes beoþ of þin imunde:
Mid heom þu holdest, ᛫t heom biwerest
᛫t ouerswiþe þu hi herest.
Þe lauedies beoþ to me iwend,
1520 To me hire mone heo send.
For hit ityd ofte and ilome,
Þat wif ᛫t were beoþ vnisome:
᛫t þerfore þat were gulte,
Þat leof is oþer wymmon to pulte,
1525 ᛫t speneþ on þare al þat he haueþ,
᛫t syweþ þare þat noht naueþ,

---

herof þe lauedies to me meneþ, l. 1563). W. and G. retain *mode*. In any case the J. reading is notable as one of the earliest instances of *mone* < O.E. *mān* (moan).

send (C. and J.) for *sendeþ* (O.E. *sendaþ* pres. pl.). The verbal endings in this section are somewhat loosely used, and this uninflected form may be due (apart from rhyming exigencies) to analogy with pres. sg. forms ending in *d*, see Appendix I (*d*) (iv) (β). G. unnecessarily reads *iwend(ed)* : *send(eþ)* ; cf. *chid* and *gred* (l. 1533).

1522. *were* (C. and J.) < O.E. *wer* (man). Since the beginning of the 11th century the form *were* (for *wer* (nom.)) frequently occurs, and after 1200 no safe case of *wer* is found (cf. *werewulf, weremod*). The inorganic -*e* was probably due to the influence of (1) commonly-used words like *spere, here, bere, mere*, (2) the agent suffix -*ere* (see Napier, *P.B.B.* xxiii. 571).

1523. *gulte* (C. and J.) = *gulteþ* (is guilty, does wrong). Str.-Br. and G. describe the form as opt., but W. more correctly describes it as indic. For a similar loose treatment of verbal endings in the rhyming position, see note l. 1520.

1524. *þat leof is.* Either (1) an impersonal construction with *þat* = indecl. rel. i.e. "to whom it is dear (= who likes)," or (2) a transitional form between the old impersonal and the modern personal constructions, i.e. "who (*þat*) is apt (*leof*)."

over (J. *oþer*) = "over." G. adopts *oþer*.

1525. *speneþ*, see note l. 165.

þare, see note l. 1442.

A.   9

an haueþ attom his riȝte spuse,
wowes weste, ꝛ lere huse,
wel þunne isch[r]ud ꝛ iued wroþe,

1530 an let heo bute mete ꝛ cloþe.
Wan he comeþ ham eft to his wiue,
ne dar heo noȝt a word ischire: Fol. 244 r. col. 2.
he chid ꝛ gred swuch he beo wod,
an ne bringþ [hom] non oþer god.

1535 Al þat heo deþ him is unwille,
al þat heo spekeþ hit is him ille:
an oft hwan heo noȝt ne misdeþ,
heo haueþ þe fust in hire teþ.
Þ[er] is nan mon þat ne mai ibringe

1540 his wif amis mid swucche þinge:
me hire mai so ofte misbeode,
þat heo do wule hire ahene neode.
La, Godd hit wot! heo nah iweld,
þa[h] heo hine makie kukeweld.

1545 For hit itit lome ꝛ ofte,
þat his wif is wel nesche ꝛ softe,
of faire bleo ꝛ wel idiht:
[For]þi hit is þe more unriht
þat he his luue spene on þare,

1550 þat nis wurþ one of hire heare.
An swucche men beoþ wel manifolde,
þat wif ne kunne noȝt ariȝt holde.
Ne mot non mon wiþ hire speke:
he ueneð heo wule anon tobreke

1555 hire spusing, ȝef heo lokeþ
oþer wiþ manne faire spekeþ.

1529. *ischud*.   1534. *heom*.   1539. *þ*, contraction mark omitted.
          1544. *þa*.   1548. *þi*.

1527 ff. For reference to the *mal mariée* motive see Intro. § 8, p. lxx.
    1532. *ischire* (C. and J.)="declare, speak." The irregular rhyme here
(*wiue* : *ischire*) suggests a departure from the original form, which may have
been *ne dar he noȝt a word ischriue* ("He dare not confess a single word").
Apart from the improved rhyme thus obtained, it may be noted that J. reads
he (C. *heo*), as if the subject of ll. 1531, 1532, and 1533 is one and the same.
But the evidence is not conclusive. Occasional assonances are found in the
poem: and the reading of the MSS. is a tolerably good one.
    1533. *chid...gred*, see Appendix I (*d*) (iv) (β).

⁊ haueþ atom his riche spuse,
Wowes west, and lere huse,
Wel þunne isrud ⁊ ived wroþe,
1530 ⁊ let heo bute mete ⁊ cloþe.
Hwenne he cumeþ hom eft to his wyue,
Ne dar he noht a word ischire:
He chid ⁊ gred such he beo wod,   Fol. 240 r. col. 1.
⁊ ne bringþ hom non oþer god.
1535 Al þat heo doþ him is vnwille,
Al þat heo spekeþ hit is him ille:
⁊ ofte hwenne heo noht ne mysdeþ,
Heo haueþ þe fust in þe theþ.
Nis nomon þat ne may ibrynge
1540 His wif amys myd suche þinge:
Me hire may so ofte mysbeode,
Þat heo do wile hire owe neode.
La, God hit wot! heo nah iwelde,
Þah heo hine make cukeweld.
1545 For hit ityt ilome and ofte,
Þat his wif is neysse ⁊ softe,
Of fayre bleo ⁊ wel idiht:
[For]þi hit is þe more vnryht
Þat he is [luue] spene on þare,
1550 Þat nis wurþ on of hire heare.
⁊ suche men beoþ wel manyfolde,
Þat wif ne cunne ariht holde.
Ne mot no mon wiþ hire speke:
He weneþ heo wile anon tobreke
1555 Hire spusyng, if heo lokeþ
Oþer wiþ manne veyre spekeþ.

1548. *þi.*   1549. *luue* omitted.

1543. *iweld* (J. *iwelde*) = "power." Str. suggests the forms *iweald* (and *kukeweald*, l. 1544). But both C. and J. agree in reading *e* (not *ea*): and more-over the *e*-form is etymologically correct for it represents *ẹ̄* (long, open) < L.O.E. *ēa* lengthened before *ld*. The form *kukeweld* (< O.Fr. *cucuault*) represents a popular spelling of a borrowing from the French. G. reads J. as *aikeweld*, which he glosses as = "cuckold": but his reading is merely a ghost-word, a misreading of the actual J. text.
1548. *Forþi* (C. and J. *þi*). W. and G. retain the MS. reading. But *þi* as it stands is an abnormal form: cf. *forþi* (l. 409). The metre suggests that

He hire bilu[k]þ mid keie ⁊ loke:
þar-þurh is spusing ofte tobroke.
For ȝef heo is þarto ibroht,
1560   he deþ þat heo nadde ear iþoht.
Dahet þat to swuþe hit bispeke,
þah swucche wiues [heom] awreke!
Herof þe lauedies to me meneþ,
an wel sore me ahweneþ:
1565   wel neh min heorte wule tochine,
hwon ich biholde hire pine.   Fol. 244 v. col. 1.
Mid heom ich wepe swi[þ]e sore,
an for heom bidde Cristis ore,
þat þe lauedi sone aredde
1570   an hire sende betere ibedde.
An oþer þing ich mai þe telle,
þat þu ne schal[t], for þine felle,
ondswere none þarto finde:
al þi sputing schal aswinde.
1575   Moni chapmon ⁊ moni cniht
luueþ ⁊ [hald] his wif ariht,
an swa deþ moni bondeman:
þat gode wif deþ after þan,
an serueþ him to bedde ⁊ to borde
1580   mid faire dede ⁊ faire worde,
an ȝeorne fondeþ hu heo muhe
do þing þat him beo iduȝe.
Þe lauerd into þare [þ]eode
fareþ ut on þare beire nede,
1585   an is þat gode wif unbliþe
for hire lauerdes hou[h]siþe,

1557. *biluþ.*   1562. *hire.*   1567. *swise.*   1572. *schald.*
       1576. *hlad.*   1583. *þeode,* þ dotted.   1586. *houdsiþe.*

---

a syllable at the beginning of the line is wanting, and in all probability *for*
was omitted by the scribe of the intermediate text.
   1560. *he*=*heo* (she).
   1561. *dahet* (J. *dehaet*), see note l. 99.
   1572. *for þine felle*="to save thy skin."
   1576. *hald*, see Appendix I (*d*) (iv) (β).
   1577. *bondeman*, see note l. 1507.

He hire bilukþ myd keye ⁊ loke:
Þar-þurh is spusing ofte ibroke.
Vor if heo is þarto ibrouht,
1560　He deþ þat heo nedde ear iþouht.
Dehaet þat to swiþe hit bispeke,
Þah suche wiues heom awreke!
Herof to me þe leuedies heom meneþ,
And wel sore me ahweneþ:
1565　Wel neyh myn heorte wile tochine,
Hwenne ic biholde heore [pine].
Mid heom ic wepe swiþe sore,
⁊ for heom bidde Cristes ore,
Þat þe leuedi sone aredde
1570　⁊ hire sende betere ibedde.　　　Fol.°240 r. col. 2.
An oþer þing ic may þe telle,
⁊ þu ne schalt, for þine felle,
Onswere non þarto fynde:
Al þis sputing schal aswinde.
1575　Mony chapmon ⁊ mony knyht
Luueþ ⁊ halt his wif ariht,
⁊ so doþ mony bondeman:
Þat gode wif doþ after þan,
⁊ sarueþ him to bedde ⁊ to borde
1580　Mid fayre dede ⁊ fayre worde,
⁊ yorne vondeþ hw heo mowe
Do þing þat him beo iduwe.
Þe louerd into þare þeode
Vareþ vt on þare beyre neode,
1585　⁊ is þat gode wif vnbliþe
Vor hire louerdes hou[h]syþe,

1566. *wiue*.　　　1586. *houþsyþe*.

1586. *houhsiþe* (C. *houdsiþe*, J. *houþsyþe*). A difficult form. W. reads *houdsiþe*, G. *oudsiþe*, both editors taking the form to be a scribal variant of *utsiþe* (departure), the form adopted by Str. This would give the sense required: but we have to presuppose (a) the addition of initial *h* (cf. *hule*, l. 41), (b) the use of *ou* for O.E. *ū* (very rare at this date, but cf. *houle* (l. 1662)), (c) the use of *d* (*þ*) for *t* (unusual except in verbal forms in this section of the poem, cf. *schald* (l. 1572)). On the whole, this accumulation of scribal peculiarities in one word seems to be unlikely: and more probably

an sit ꝛ sihð wel sore oflonged,
an hire sore an horte ongred:
al for hire louerdes sake
1590 haueþ daies kare ꝛ niȝtes wake:
an swuþe longe hire is þe hwile,
an [ech] steape hire þunþ a mile.
Hwanne oþre slepeþ hire abute,
ich one lust þar wiðþute,
1595 an wot of hire sore mode,
an singe aniȝt for hire gode:
an mine gode song, for hire þinge,
ich turne su[m]del to murni[n]ge.
Of hure seorhe ich bere sume,
1600 forþan ich am hire wel welcume: Fol. 244 v. col. 2.
ich hire helpe hwat [I] mai,
for [ho geþ] þane rehte wai.
Ah þu me hauest sore igramed,
þat min heorte is wel neh alamed,
1605 þat ich mai unneaþe speke:
ah ȝet ich wule forþure reke.
Þu seist þat ich am manne [loð],
an euereuch man is wið me wroð,
an me mid stone ꝛ lugge þreteþ,
1610 an me tobu[r]steþ ꝛ tobeteþ,

1592. *ek.*   1598. *sun-, murnige.*   1601. *i.*   1602. *hoȝeþ.*
1607. *wloð, o* written over *a, l* over *r.*   1610. *tobusteþ.*

---

we have here an error in copying, an error due (as elsewhere) to an obscurity
in the common original. Thus it would seem that both scribes intended to
write *houþsiþe.* This is practically the J. form; while in C. the symbol *d*
may very well stand for an incomplete ð (=þ occasionally in this part of the
MS., cf. ll. 938, 943, 944). Working therefore on the hypothesis of this
common reading *houþsiþe* (which, as it stands, gives no sense), it becomes
clear that we have here yet another instance of scribal confusion between þ
and *h* (see Intro. § 3 (*d*) (v) (*a*)) and that the intermediate text read *houþsiþe*
in place of original *houhsiþe* (< O.E. *hoh, hog-* + *siþ*) = " sorrowful, anxious
journeyings "—the form therefore adopted in the present text.
  1588. *ongred* (J. *ongreþ*). Str. reads *ongreþ,* W. and G. *ongred.* The
C. reading (= " vexed," p.p.) is preferable on the whole, since it supplies (1) a
participial clause parallel to the clause in l. 1587, (2) a more regular rhyme
with *oflonged.* Trans. " distressed at heart by her pain " (*sore*=sb.). In that
case J. *ongreþ* represents a scribal emendation. On the other hand, it is
possible that C. *ongred* is intended for *ongreþ* (cf. l. 1586) and that the
original rhyme was *-longed : ongreð* (cf. ll. 501–2). In that case the passage
would read : " she is vexed (vexes herself) sorely at heart."

ꝺ sit ꝺ sykþ wel sore oflonged,
ꝺ hire sore an heorte ongreþ:
Al vor hire louerdes sake
1590 Haueþ dayes kare ꝺ nihtes wake:
ꝺ swiþe longe hire is þe hwile,
ꝺ vych stape hire þinkþ a [m]ile.
Hwenne oþre slepeþ hire abute,
Ich one lust þar wyþþute,
1595 ꝺ wot of hire sore mode,
ꝺ singe anyht for hire gode:
ꝺ myn gode song, for hire þinge,
Ic turne sumdel to [m]urnynge.
Of hure seorwe ic bere sume,
1600 Vorþan ic am hire wel welcume:
Ic hire helpe hwat ich may,
For [ho geþ] þane rihte way.
ꝺ þu me hauest sore igremed,
Þat myn heorte is neyh alemed,
1605 Þat ic may vnneþe speke:
Ac yet ic wile forþurre reke.
Þu seyst þat ic am monne loþ,   Fol. 240 v. col. 1.
ꝺ vich mon is wiþ me wroþ,
ꝺ me myd stone ꝺ lugge þreteþ,
1610 ꝺ me toburste[þ] ꝺ tobete[þ],

1592. *Mile.*   1598. *Murnynge.*   1602. *howeþ.*   1610. *-burste, -betc.*

1592. *þunþ = þun(k)þ*, "seems": cf. note l. 795.
1602. *ho geþ* (C. *ho ȝeþ*, J. *howeþ*) = "she goeth." The false readings of both MSS. are due to an error of spacing which existed in the intermediate text. The C. and J. scribes have altered what they took to be medial *g* to *ȝ* and *w* respectively.
1604. *alamed* (J. *alemed*), cf. O.E. *-lemian*. The C. form points to the existence of a new verb in M.E. formed from the adj. *lam*: whereas in J. the normal O.E. mutated root is preserved; see note l. 1291 for other new formations.
1606. *reke* = "go." W. and G. incorrectly translate the word = "relate" < O.E. *reccean* (cf. l. 1449). Str. derives the word from an O.E. *recan* which he queries: but the O.E. form is recorded by Sweet (*Stud.-Dict.*) under *recan* (go), where *inrǣcan* = "ingesserunt" (Gloss.) is quoted.
1607. *loð* (C. *wloð*, J. *loþ*) = "hateful." The C. scribe evidently copied *wrað* or *wroð* from the following line and afterwards altered it to *loð* (see footnote, cf. *manne loþ* (l. 1641).
1609. *lugge* = "sticks, poles." The meaning of this word is clearly shown by the Mod. dial. forms. In Glouc. and Heref. it stands for a long pole for

an hwanne heo hab[b]eþ me ofslahe,
heo hongeþ me on heore hahe,
þar ich aschewele pie an crowe
fro[m] þan þe þar is isowe.
1615 Þah hit beo soþ, ich do heom god,
an for heom ich [s]chadde mi blod:
ich do heom god mid mine deaþe,
waruore þe is wel unneaþe.
For þah þu ligge dead ⁊ clinge,
1620 þi deþ nis nawt to none þinge:
ich not neauer to hwan þu miȝt,
for þu nart bute a wrecche wiȝt.
Ah þah mi lif me beo atschote,
þe ȝet ich mai do gode note:
1625 me mai up one smale sticke
me sette a-wude ine þe þicke,
an swa mai mon tolli him to
lutle briddes ⁊ iuo,
an swa me mai mid me biȝete
1630 wel gode brede to his mete.
Ah þu neure mon to gode
liues ne deaþes stal ne stode:

1611. *habeþ.*   1614. *fron.*   1616. *chadde.*

---

knocking apples from trees: in Berks, it represents the pole placed across a barn-door: in Hants it is a stick used for a clothes-line or hen-roost. From this primary meaning (stick), the word came to mean "a measure of land": cf. Spenser, *F.Q.* Bk ii. x. 11, "eight lugs of grownd." And in Dorsets at the present day "land is measured by the goad or lug of 15 ft. and an inch" (*E.D.D.*), cf. also Barnes, *Poems*, 198:
    An' yeet this rotten groun' don't reach a lug.
1614. Trans. "From that which is sown there."
1616. *schadde* (C. *chadde*, J. *schedde*) = "shed" pt. 1 sg. < O.E. *scēadan*: instance of an O.E. str. verb which had already become weak.
1618. *unneaþe* (C. *inmeaþe* or *unneaþe*, J. *unmeþe*) = "difficult" < O.E. *unēaþe*. Str. reads *uneaþe*, W. *inmeaþe*, G. *unneaþe*. W. interprets *inmeaþe* (which is supported by J.) as "error, blame, transgression" < O.E. *unmǣþ* and translates the line as "wherefore is indeed blame for thee." The form *inmeaþe* however is unusual: *unmeaþe* (which would involve an additional stroke) would be the form naturally expected. In all probability however the root-form is not -*meaþe* (O.E. -*mǣþ*) but *eaþe* (O.E. -*ēaþe*) since O.E. *ēa* : *ǣ* rhymes are avoided throughout the poem (see Appendix I (c) (iv)). Moreover the adv. form *wel* normally requires an adj. instead of a sb., though W.'s reading of *wel* = "indeed" is possible. So that, on the whole, *unneaþe* (which occurs in l. 1605) is the safer form: and it is a form which, carelessly written in the intermediate text, might be copied as *inmeaþe* (J. *unmeþe*).

ꝥ hwanne hi habbeþ me ofslawe,
Heo anhoþ me in heore hawe,
Þar ich aschevle pie ꝥ crowe
From þan þat þer is isowe.

1615 Þah hit beo soþ, ic do heom god,
ꝥ for heom ic schedde my blod:
Ic do heom god myd myne deþe,
Þarfore þe is wel unmeþe.

For [þah] þu ligge ded ꝥ clinge,
1620 Þi deþ nys nouht to none þinge:
Ic not neuer to hwan þu myht,
For þu nart bute a wreche wiht.

Ah þah my lif me beo atschote,
Þe yet ic may do gode note:
1625 Me may vppe smale sticke
Me sette a-wude ine þe þikke,
ꝥ so may mon tolli him to
Lutle briddes and ivo,
ꝥ so me may myd me byete
1630 Wel gode brede to his mete.
Ah þu neuer mon to gode
Lyues ne deþes stal ne stode:

1619. *þhah.*

1620–1. Trans. "In death thou art useless in every respect (lit. thy death is useless…): I know not what good thou art (lit. …for what thou art able)."

1624. *þe ȝet* (< O.E. *þā giet*) = "yet, still," cf. *A.S. Chron.* 1106, *oðre… þe mid þam eorle…þe gyt heoldan.*

1627. *tolli* = "entice" (see Str.-Br. for this word in M.E.). A parallel *u*-form appears in O.E. *fortyllan* ("seduce") and for similar variants in *o* and *u* see note l. 379.

1628. *iuo* = "capture" (< O.E. *gefōn*). The verbal form (not *iuo* < O.E. *gefā*, foes) is required here on account of the rhyme with *to* (O.E. *tō*) which gives a rhyme on *ǭ* (< O.E. *ō*).

The meaning of the passage is that the Owl, as scarecrow in the corn-fields (cf. l. 1611), preserves the wheat from crows and other birds, while in the wood its corpse attracts inquisitive small birds and brings about their capture.

1629–30. Trans. "And so with my help a good supply of roast meat (*brede*) is obtained for food."

1631–2. Trans. "Neither alive nor dead hast thou been (lit. occupied a place, viz. *stode stal*) of service (*to gode*) to man." The oblique case of *mon* (i.e. *monne*) would however be more regular. The form *stode* = pt. 2 sg. with O.E. final *e* preserved, cf. *stele* (l. 103).

ich not to hwan þu bre[d]ist þi brod,

liues ne deaþes ne deþ hit god."　　Fol. 245 r. ool. 1.

1635　Þe nihtegale ih[e]rde þis,

an hupte uppon on blowe ris,

an herre sat þan heo dude ear:

"Hule," he seide, "beo nu wear,

nulle ich wiþ þe plaidi namore,

1640　for her þe mist þi rihte lore:

þu ȝeilpest þat þu art manne loþ,

an euereuch wiht is wið þe w[ro]þ;

an mid ȝulinge ⁊ mid igrede

þu wanst wel þat þu art unlede.

1645　Þu seist þat gromes þe ifoð,

an heie on rodde þe anhoð,

an þe totwichet ⁊ toschakeð,

an summe of þe schawles makeð.

Me þunc[þ] þat þu forleost þat game,

1650　þu ȝulpest of þire oȝe schame:

me þunc[þ] þat þu me gest an honde,

þu ȝulpest of þire oȝene scho[nd]e."

Þo heo hadde þeos word icwede,

heo sat in ore faire stude,

1655　an þarafter hire steuene dihte,

an song so schille ⁊ so brihte,

1633. *breist.*　　1635. *hrde.*　　1642. *worþ.*　　1649, 1651. *þunch.*
1652. *schomme.*

1633. *bredist* (C. and J. *breist*). Str. emends to *bredst* (< O.E. *brēdan*, breed); W. retains *breist* (< O.E. *bregdan*, to draw forth, produce): G. retains *breist* which he glosses (without further comment) as pres. 2 sg. of *breden* (to breed). In no case however is the *i*-form satisfactorily explained, though W. would connect *breist* (J. text) with O.Fr. *braire* (bray) and trans. "brayest thy speech." But this rendering will not do for C., and the emendation of the J. scribe, which incidentally spoils the rhyme, suggests that he was puzzled by the reading of the intermediate text and so changed the meaning of the whole passage. It would therefore seem certain that the common reading *breist* is due to an error of copying in the intermediate text, viz. to the omission of *d* which had appeared in the original.

Trans. "I know not why thou rearest thy brood."

1635-6. With this rhyme *þis* (O.E. *þis*) : *ris* (O.E. *hrīs*) cf. ll. 569-70.

1640. *þe* (J. *þu*). Str. and Sk. read *þu*, W. retains *þe*. The C. reading gives good sense, though it involves an unusual inversion in the sentence-order: trans. "thy usual skill fails thee."

Ic not to hwan þu breist þi word,
Lyues ne deþes ne doþ hit god."

1635 Þe Nihtegale iherde þis,
⁊ hupte vppe on blowe ris,
⁊ herre sat þane heo dude er:
"Vle," he seyde, "beo nv wer,
Nule ic wiþ þe playdi namore,   Fol. 240 v. col. 2.

1640 Vor her þu myst þi ryhte lore:
Þ[u] yelpest þat þu art monne loþ,
⁊ euervich wiht is wiþ þe wroþ:
⁊ myd yollinge ⁊ myd igrede
Þu þinchst wel þat þu art vnlede.

1645 Þu seyst þat gromes þe ivoþ,
⁊ heye on rode þe anhoþ,
⁊ þe totwiccheþ ⁊ toschakeþ,
⁊ summe of þe scheules makeþ.
Me þinkþ þat þu forlest þat game,

1650 Þu yelpest of þire owe schome:
Me þinkþ þat þu me gest an honde,
Þu yelpest of þine owe schonde."
Þo heo hadde þeos word [icwede],
Heo sat in one fayre stude,

1655 ⁊ þarafter hire stefne dihte,
⁊ song so schille ⁊ so brihte,

1641. þ.   1653. *icwede* omitted.

1644. *wanst* (J. *þinchst*). The C. form (unfamiliar apparently to the J. scribe) is undoubtedly correct, since it gives the sense required, whereas the J. reading is ambiguous at least. W. and G. incorrectly describe *wanst* as pr. 2 sg. of *wene* (O.E. *wēnan*, suppose): but the form is really = pr. 2 sg. of *wane* (O.E. *wānian*, to complain or lament).

1648. *schawles* (J. *scheules*) = "scarecrow," probably a variant form of *scheueles* (see note l. 1128), due to analogy with M.E. *scheawen*, *schawen* (< O.E. *scēawian*, to show)—the idea of "a show, a spectacle" being associated with the word.

1649. *þuncþ* (C. *þunch*, J. *þinkþ*). For scribal confusion between þ and h see Intro. § 3 (*d*) (v) (*a*).

þat game. Fines for slight offences made in the course of pleading were so common that it was like "playing a game of forfeits. Already in the 12th century a Norman baron compared the procedure of the duke's court to a boys' game" (see Pollock and Maitland, *Hist. of Eng. Law*, II. 519).

1651. *me gest an honde* = "dost surrender to me," cf. *A.S. Chron.* 882, *And twa him on hand eoden.*

þat feor ꝛ ner me hit iherde.

Þaruore anan to hire cherde

þrusche ꝛ þrostle ꝛ wudewale,

1660   an fuheles boþe grete ꝛ smale:

forþan heom þuhte þat heo hadde

þe houle ouercome, uorþan heo gradde

an sungen alswa uale wise,

an blisse was among þe rise.

1665   Riȝt swa me gred þe manne a schame,

þat taueleþ ꝛ forleost þat gome.

    Þeos hule, þo heo þis iherde,

"Hauestu," heo seide, "ibanned ferde?   Fol. 245 r. col. 2.

an wultu, wreche, wiðð me fiȝte?

1670   Nai! nai! nauestu none miȝte!

Hwat gredeþ þeo þat hider come?

Me þuncþ þu ledest ferde to me.

Ȝe schule wite, ar ȝe fleo heonne,

hwuch is þe strenþe of mine kunne:

1675   for þeo þe haueþ bile ihoked,

an cliures [s]charpe ꝛ wel icroked,

alle heo beoþ of mine kunrede,

an walde come ȝif ich bede.

1670. *Na nai* with *i* written over the *a* of the first word.   1676. *charpe*.

1658 ff. This gathering of the birds is of considerable literary interest. A scene embodying such an assembly is somewhat common in medieval poetry. The convention dates back at least to Marie de France's fable, *Li parlemens des Oiseaux por faire Roi*, while in *De Planctu Naturae* of Alanus de Insulis, a host of birds is depicted on the robe worn by the goddess Natura; and to both of these works Chaucer's *Parlement of Foules* was possibly indebted. In many other places, the birds are introduced to grace the scene of Paradise, the Court of Love, or the spring season: and then they are represented as singing their "matins" or "hours" (see notes ll. 26, 323–8). Thus St Brendan in his wandering (see *H.* II. 574) came to the birds' paradise where "*þe foweles sunge ek ·here matyns*" (*Legendary*, ed. Horstman, 225/223); and in Dunbar's *Thrissil and the Rois* (ll. 4–5) the birds in May are said *to begyn thair houris* (cf. also Clanvowe, *Cuckoo and Nightingale*, l. 70). In Lydgate's *Devotions of the Fowls* (*Minor Poems*, ed. Halliwell, p. 78), again, chants are sung by the popinjay, pelican, nightingale, lark and dove (cf. also *Court of Love*), while in Dunbar's *Thrissil and the Rois*, the chorus includes the mavis, merle, lark and nightingale. From the first, however, the birds play a special part in the "debates." Sometimes (as in *O. and N.*), they acclaim the victor: this is their function in *Goliae dialogus inter Aquam et Vinum* (cf. l. 159). Elsewhere, as in *Florence and Blancheflor*, they figure as champions, the dispute being decided at the Court of Love by a duel fought before a council of birds by a nightingale and a parrot; while in Clanvowe's *Cuckoo*

Þat fur ⁊ neor me hit iherde.

Þarvore anon to hire cherde

Þruysse ⁊ þrostle ⁊ wodewale,

1660 ⁊ foweles boþe grete ⁊ smale:

Vorþan þat heom þuhte þat heo hadde

Þe vle ouercome, forþan heo gradde

⁊ sungen also uale wise,

Þat blisse wes among þe ryse.

1665 Riht so me gred þe monne a schame,

Þat taueleþ ⁊ forleost þat gome.

   Þeos vle, þo heo þis iherde,

"Hauestu," heo seyde, "ibanned ferde?

⁊ wiltu, wrecche, wiþ me vyhte?

1670 Na, nay! nauestu none [m]ihte!

Hwat gredeþ heo þat hider come?   Fol. 241 r. col. 1.

Me þinkþ þu ledest ferde to me.

Ye schulle wite, ar ye fleo heonne,

Hwuch is þe strengþe of myne kunne:

1675 Vor þeo þat haueþ bile ihoked,

⁊ clyures scharpe ⁊ wel icroked,

Alle heo beoþ of myne kunrede,

⁊ wolde cumen if ich bede.

          1670. *Mihte.*

---

and Nightingale they appear as judges, the nightingale in the end flying to the assembly of birds to submit her case. In the *O. and N.*, therefore, the gathering of the birds is reminiscent of more than one medieval convention: but it also has features of its own and illustrates the originality of the poet's treatment.

1659. *wudewale* = "woodwale," a term formerly applied to the greenfinch and latterly to the green woodpecker (cf. *Pr.P.* 531). Florio (ed. 1598) gives *witwal* or *wittal* as the later form of the word; hence *wittol* ("cuckold"), on account of the liability of the nest of the green woodpecker to be used by the cuckoo (see Skeat, *Etym. Dict.* s.v. *wittol*).

1665. Trans. "one cries in shame (at) the man."

1666. *taueleþ* = "gambles (at dice)." T. Wright in his Preface to Neckam's *De Naturis Rerum* (Rolls Series), pp. lxx–lxxi, states that "gambling was a vice which prevailed to a great extent in the feudal ages and among all classes of society, and we meet with frequent allusions to its pernicious effects": cf. *ibid.* ch. 183 *De Aleatoribus*, also M.E. *Apoph. of Cato* (ll. 89–90):

> Tak a toppe, ȝif þou wolt pleye,
> And not at þe hasardrye.

1668. *ibanned* = "summoned" (< O.E. *bannan*). An instance of O.E. str. vb. > weak, cf. notes ll. 952, 1616.

1671–2. *come*: *to me*, see note ll. 545–6.

Þe seolfe coc, þat wel can fiȝte,

1680 he mot mid me holde mid riȝte,

for [boþe] we habbeþ steuene briȝte,

an sitteþ under weolcne bi niȝte.

Schille ich an utest uppen ow grede,

ich shal swo stronge ferde lede,

1685 þat ower pr[u]de schal aualle:

a tort ne ȝiue ich for ow alle!

ne schal, ar hit beo fulliche eue,

a wreche feþer on ow bileaue.

Ah hit was unker uoreward,

1690 þo we come hiderward,

þat we þarto holde scholde,

þar riht dom us ȝiue wolde.

Wultu nu breke foreward?

Ich wene dom þe þing[þ] to hard:

1695 for þu ne darst domes abide,

þu wult nu, wreche, fiȝte ꞇ chide.

Ȝ[u]t ich ow alle wolde rede,

ar [ich] utheste uppon ow grede,

1681. *bo þe.*   1685. *proude.*   1694. *þing.*   1697. *ȝot.*   1698. *ihc.*

1679. This is probably one of the earliest references to the fighting qualities of the cock. Cock-fighting first became a popular sport in the reign of Edward III: but Fitzstephen (1174) describes it as the sport of schoolboys on Shrove Tuesday. He states how "the boys of the respective schools bring to their masters each one his fighting-cock and they are indulged all the morning with seeing their cocks fight in the school-room" (W. Fitzstephen, *Descriptio nobilissimae Civitatis Londiniae*, 13), (*Materials for History of Thomas Becket*, p. 9, Rolls Series, 1877). For the subsequent history of the sport, see *Shakespeare's England* (Oxford, 1917), vol. II. pp. 434 ff. In Neckam's *De Laudibus Divinae Sapientiae*, II. ll. 809 ff. (Rolls Series, 1863) occurs a vivid description of a cock-fight which illustrates the reference above. "The combatants, having excited themselves into a state of fury:

Pectora collidunt, superaddunt ictibus ictus,
    Crescit amor belli, concrepat ala, ruunt.

. . . .

Tempore sed modico respirant, inde resumunt
    Vires, virtutem colligit ira novam.
Tunc motu capitis galeati provocat iram,
    Et gestu tumido saevit uterque minans.

. . . .

Insurgunt, saltuque levi concurritur, ictus
    Ingeminant, vires saepius arte juvant."

1681. *boþe* (C. *bo þe*, J *beo þat* or *þer*). The common error is due to an error in spacing in the intermediate text, cf. l. 1602.

1682. *weolcne* (J. *welkne*) < O.E. *wolcen, welcn* ("sky, clouds"). The *eo* in *weolcne* is probably a scribal variant for *o*, cf. *neoþeles* (l. 1297), *seorhe* (l. 1599), though it may possibly stand for an *e*, cf. *seolliche* (l. 1299).

Þe seolue cok, þat wel can vihte,
1680 He mot myd me holde wiþ rihte,
Vor [boþe] we habbe stefne brihte,
℩ sitteþ vnder welkne bi nyhte.
Schulle ic up eu on vtest grede,
Ich schal swo stronge verde lede,
1685 Þat oure prude schal aualle;
A tord ne yeue ic for eu alle!
Ne schal, ar hit beo fullich eue,
A wrecche veþere on eu bileue.
Ah hit wes vnker uoreward,
1690 Þo we comen hyderward,
Þat we þarto holden scholde,
Þar riht dom vs yeue wolde.
Wultu nv breke foreward?
Ic wene dom þe þinkþ to hard.
1695 Vor þu ne darst domes abyde,
Þu wilt nv, wreche, fihte ℩ chide.
Yet ich eu wolde alle rede,
Ar ich uthest vp eu grede,

1681. *beo þat.*

1683. *schille=schulle* (cf. l. 442) pres. opt. 1 sg. of *schal.* J. reads *schulle* the form adopted by G.

uthest < O.E. *uthǣs* = "outcry" (cf. O.E. *hātan*): the final *t* is excrescent, as in O.E. *cēast* alongside O.E. *cēas* (dispute), cf. Chau. *C.T.* A. 2012, *outhees.* The technical term for *uthest* was "*hutesium et clamor*": and the outcry was raised on discovering that a crime had been committed. The neighbours were required "to turn out with the bows, arrows, and knives that they were bound to keep: and besides much shouting there would be horn-blowing." In fact the hue-and-cry would be "horned" from "vill to vill"; possibly the proper cry would be "Out! out!" (see Pollock and Maitland, *Hist. of Eng. Law,* II. 578–9).

1685. *prude* (C. *proude,* J. *prude*) < O.E. *prȳt, prȳd* (pride). The C. reading is probably due to a scribal error as the *ou* (very rare at this date, but cf. *houle,* l. 1662) would point to an adj. form (i.e. O.E. *prūd*) whereas a sb. (viz. "pride") is clearly required by the sense.

1687. *fulliche eue.* Kenyon (*J.E.G.P.* XII. 591) points out that the dramatic action corresponds closely with the natural facts. He states that "the approach of morning with the end of the debate is delicately indicated by ll. 1635–6 and 1655 ff., where the other birds (of the day) gather about at the first sign of the dawn and begin to sing. The Owl's remark (ll. 1687–8) is addressed to these day-birds at the very beginning of the day."

eue, "refers to the evening of the approaching day. Then the poet imagines the house-wren as attracted by the chorus of wood-birds and as going (l. 1717) to the scene of the contest when morning is more fully come" (*ibid.*).

1697. *ȝut* (C. *ȝot,* J. *yet*) = "yet." The C. reading is probably a scribal error for *u* or *e,* though *o* does occasionally occur for *u.* See Appendix I (c) (iii).

þat ower fihtlac leteþ beo,

1700   an ginneþ raþe awei fleo.

For, bi þe cliures þat ich bere,

ȝef ȝe abideþ mine here,   Fol. 245 v. col. 1.

ȝe schule on oþer wise singe,

an acursi alle fiȝtinge:

1705   vor nis of ow non so kene,

þat durre abide mine onsene."

Þeos hule spac wel baldeliche,

for þah heo nadde swo hwatliche

ifare after hire here,

1710   heo walde neoþeles ȝefe answere

þe niȝtegale mid swucche worde.

For moni man mid speres orde

haueþ lutle strencþe, ⁊ mid his [s]chelde,

ah neoþeles in one felde,

1715   þurh belde worde an mid ilete,

deþ his iuo for arehþe swete.

Þe wranne, for heo cuþe singe,

þar com in þare moreȝen[i]nge

to helpe þare niȝtegale:

1720   for þah heo hadde steuene smale,

heo hadde gode þ[ro]te ⁊ schille,

an fale manne song a wille.

Þe wranne was wel wis iholde,

vor þeȝ heo nere ibred a-wolde,

1725   ho was itoȝen among man[k]enne,

an hire wisdom brohte þenne:

heo miȝte speke hwar heo walde,

touore þe king þah heo scholde.

1711. New paragraph in MS. 1713. *chelde.* 1718. *more ȝennge.* 1721. *þorte.*
1724. This line is inserted at the foot of the column (after 1735).
1725. *mann enne.*

1703. *schule* (J. *schulleþ*) = "shall"; see note l. 1133.
1711. "New paragraph in both MSS. contrary to sense, points to a common original, which, from the error, must have been a copy" (W.).
1715. *belde* < O.E. *bēald* with lengthened *ea* before *ld* in L.O.E.
1721–2. Neckam (*De Nat. Rerum,* II. ch. 78) after explaining that the *regulus* was also called *parra* on account of its diminutive (*parva*) size, mentions also the singing qualities it possesses.
1724. *a-wolde* = "in the woodland." The meaning of the passage is:

Þat eur fihtlac leteþ beo,
1700   Ꞇ gynneþ raþe ayeyn fleo.
Vor, bi þe clyures þat ic bere,
If ye abideþ myne here,
Ye schulleþ an oþer wise singe,
Ꞇ cursy alle fihtinge:
1705   Vor nys of ou non so kene,
Þat durre abide myn onsene."
Þeos vle spak wel baldelyche,
Vor þah heo nadde so hwatliche
Iuare after hire here,
1710   Heo wolde naþeles yeue answere   Fol. 241 r. col. 2.
Þe [n]ihtegale myd sweche worde.
For mony mon myd speres orde
Haueþ lutle strengþe, Ꞇ mid his schelde,
Ah naþeles in one felde,
1715   Þurh belde worde Ꞇ myd ilete,
Deþ is iuo for arehþe swete.
Þe wrenne, for heo cuþe singe,
Þar com in þare moreweninge
To helpe þare nyhtegale:
1720   Vor [þeih] heo hadde stefne smale,
Heo hadde gode þrote Ꞇ schille,
Ꞇ fale monne song a wille.
Þe wrenne wes wel wis iholde,
Vor þeih heo nere ibred a-wolde,
1725   Heo wes itowen among mankunne,
Ꞇ hire wisdom brouhte þenne:
Heo myhte speke hwar heo wolde,
Tofore þe kinge þah heo scholde.

1711. *Nihtegale*, new paragraph with rubric.   1720. *Vor heo.*

"for though by her place of birth she was weak in woodcraft, she had learnt wisdom from the men by whom she had been brought up" (H.).
1725. *mankenne* (C. *mann enne*, J. *mankunne*)="mankind." Str. and Sk. read *monne* (Str. refers to a similar form l. 563): W. has *mannenne* (d. pl.): H. *menne*. The difficulty probably arose from a badly-made *k* in the intermediate text, which (with a short upper stroke) might be read as *n*. The C. scribe, puzzled by the resulting form, read it as two words *mann enne*, while the J. scribe wrote *k* and restored the Southern *u* form.
The form *mankenne* is a Kentish variant, see Appendix I (*a*) (i).
1727 ff. The respect accorded to the wren and the dignified part she plays

"Lusteþ," heo cwaþ, "lateþ me speke.
1730 Hwat! wulle ȝe þis pes tobreke,
an do þanne [kinge] swuch schame?
ȝe[t] nis he nouþer ded ne lame.
Hunke schal itide harm ꝧ schonde,
ȝef ȝe doþ griþbruche on his londe.
1735 Lateþ beo, ꝧ beoþ isome,
an fareþ riht to o[w]er dome,   Fol. 245 v. col. 2.
an lateþ dom þis plaid tobreke,
al swo hit was erur bispeke."

"Ich an wel," cwað þe niȝtegale,
1740 "ah, wranne, nawt for þire tale,
ah do for mire lahfulnesse.
Ich nolde þat unrihtfulnesse
me at þen ende ouerkome:
ich nam ofdrad of none dome.
1745 Bihote ich habbe, soþ hit is,
þat Maister Nichole, þat is wis,
bituxen vs deme schul[l]e,
an ȝe[t] ich wene þat he wule.
Ah, [w]ar mihte we hine finde?"
1750 Þe wranne sat in ore linde;

1731. *þanne swuch.*   1732. *ȝe.*   1736. *oþer.*   1747. *schulde.*
    1748. *ȝef.*   1749. *þar.*

---

in the debate at this stage, are quite in keeping with medieval notions, according to which the wren, though the smallest of birds, had been elected king by the rest of its kind. The tradition was widely spread: it is common to Scotland, Ireland, France, Germany and Norway: and a story almost identical (with the linnet in the place of honour) was current among the tribes of North America. The very name of the wren in the various languages bears witness to this tradition: cf. βασιλίσκος, *Roitelet*, *Zaunkönig*. The tradition runs that on one occasion the birds met to choose a king. The title was to be given to the bird that flew the highest: whereupon the wren concealed itself under the wing of the eagle and thus shared in her flight. When the eagle had mounted above all the other birds she proceeded to claim her promised reward: but the wren, starting from its place of conceal- ment, impudently flew on to the head of the eagle and boldly claimed that she had won. Her claim was allowed: and the eagle in revenge snatched up the little bird, flew with it to a dizzy height and let it fall. As a result, so it was said, the wren lost part of its tail; while, according to another story, its wing was said to be so badly damaged that it has never since been able to fly higher than a hawthorn bush (cf. l. 278). The tradition is alluded to by Aristotle when he describes the wren as ἀετῷ πολέμιος: and by Pliny in the passage *Dissident aquila et trochilus, si*

"Lusteþ," heo queþ, "leteþ me speke.
1730 Hwat! wille ye þis pays tobreke,
˥ do þanne [kinge] such schome?
Yet nys heo nouþer ded ne lome.
Hunke schal ityde harm ˥ schonde,
If we doþ gryþbruche on his londe.
1735 Leteþ beo, ˥ beoþ isome,
˥ fareþ riht to eure dome,
˥ leteþ dom þis playd tobreke,
Al so hit wes erure bispeke."
"Ich vnne wel," queþ þe Nihtegale,
1740 "Ah, wrenne, nouht for þine tale,
Ac do myre lauhfulnesse.
Ic nolde þat vnrihtfulnesse
Me at þen ende [ouercome]:
Ic nam ofdred of none dome.
1745 Bihote ic habbe, soþ hit is,
Þat Mayster Nichole, þat is wis,
Bitwihen [us] deme schulle,
˥ yet ic wene þat he wulle.
Ah [w]ar myhte we hine fynde?" Fol. 241 v. col. 1.
1750 Þe wrenne sat in hore lynde:

1731. *þanne such.* 1743. *me ouercome.* 1747. *eu deme.* 1749. *þar.*

---

credimus, quoniam rex appellatur avium (*Hist. Nat.* x. 74). There is a further allusion in Plutarch's *Rei publicae gerendae praecepta* (πολιτικὰ παραγγέλματα), p. 806 e, where the story is ascribed to Aesop, though, as Professor E. Bensly (to whom I am indebted for this reference) points out, the fable is not in the collection by Halm (ed. 1901).

1731. *kinge.* Neither of the MSS. has this reading: but Str., Sk., W. and G. all agree in inserting it. It is required (1) to provide an antecedent for *he* (1. 1732), (2) to improve the metre: and was probably omitted from the intermediate MS.

1732. For possible allusion here, see Intro. § 4, p. xxxviii, note 2.

1733. *hunke* (C. and J.) = *unke* < O.E. *unc* (to us two). The dual form is here used in a loose sense to stand for the speaker and those addressed. G. takes *hunke* < O.E. *ync* (*inc*) = "to you two" which gives a good reading: but the form *ync* seems doubtful.

1734. *gryþbruche* = the legal term for "breach of the king's peace." At one time the king's peace or protection was not universal but particular: it was not for all men or for all places. And in the L.O.E. period the king's particular protection was called *griþ* as distinct from the more general word *friþ.* After the Norman Conquest, however, "the king's peace" becomes the normal and general safeguard of public order, and it is used in that general sense in the present instance (see Pollock and Maitland, *Hist. of Eng. Law,* I. 45).

"Hwat! nu[s]te ȝe," cwaþ heo, "his hom?
He wuneþ at Porteshom,
at one tune ine Dorsete,
bi þare see in ore utlete:
1755 þar he demeþ manie riȝte dom,
an diht ꝉ writ mani wisdom,
an þurh his muþe ꝉ þurh his honde
hit is þe betere into Scotlonde.
To seche hine is lihtlich þing;
1760 he naueþ bute one woning.
Þat [is] bischopen muchel schame,
an alle [þ]an þat of his nome
habbeþ ihert, ꝉ of his dede.
Hwi nulleþ hi nimen heom to rede,
1765 þat he were mid heom ilome
for teche heom of his wisdome,
an ȝiue him rente auale stude,
þat he miȝte heom ilome be mide?"

1751. *nuȝte.* 1761. *his.* 1762. *þan, þ* dotted. 1766. *theche,* first *h* deleted.

1751. *nuste* (C. *nuȝte,* J. *mihte*). Both MS. 'readings present difficulty: the C. form corresponds to nothing in O.E., the J. reading gives no sense. W. retains *nuȝte* and derives it from O.E. *nyton* without any explanation. Str. alters it to *nute* (<O.E. *nyton*). But both MSS. agree in reading a form consisting of four short strokes and one longer stroke before -*te*: and this gives a clue to the reading of the intermediate text. That reading cannot have been *nute* (which has only four short strokes before -*te*), but may well have been *nuste*: in which case, the intermediate scribe, or the C. scribe (as suggested by H.), "being acquainted with the graph *st* for *ȝt*, mechanically substituted the latter here," cf. ll. 78, 642, 1300.
nuste < O.E. *nyston* = "did ye not know?"
1752–4. *Porteshom* = "Portisham," a Dorsetshire village lying under furze-covered hills from which a little rivulet runs down to the sea. It stands about 2 or 3 miles N.E. of the head of the inlet called the Fleet, and in a S.W. direction from Dorchester. It has an interesting old church with Norman details and Early English windows: and formerly it belonged to the neighbouring monastery at Abbotsbury.
It is however somewhat difficult at first sight to reconcile the position of the village—some distance inland—with the description given in l. 1754, viz. that it is *bi þare see in ore utlete*: though a closer examination of the local geography goes some way towards explaining things. Between Frome Vale and the sea there extends a coast-ridge running from Lulworth to Swyre (near Bridport), the average height of which is about 500 ft. The ancient Dorchester is completely cut off from the sea by this ridge. But Portisham lies on the sea side of it: and by a Dorsetshire man it might reasonably be described as *bi þare see*, as opposed to the sequestered places in Frome Vale. Moreover the ridge behind Portisham commands a view of the English Channel, and the monument (3 miles N.E. of Portisham) erected in memory of Hardy, Nelson's captain (who was born at Portisham 1769) is a landmark

"Hwat! [nute ye]," quaþ heo, "his hom?
Heo wuneþ at Porteshom,
At one tune in Dorsete,
Bi þare see in ore vtlete:
1755 Þar he demeþ mony riht dom,
ꝥ diht ꝥ wryt mony wisdom,
ꝥ þurh his muþe ꝥ þurh his honde
Hit is þe betere into Scotlonde.
To seche hyne is lyhtlych þing;
1760 He naueþ buten o wunyng.
Þat is biscopen muchel schame,
ꝥ alle þan þat of his nome
Habbeþ iherd, and of his dede.
Hwi nulleþ hi nymen heom to rede,
1765 Þat he were myd heom ilome
Vor teche heom of his wisdome,
ꝥ yeue him rente on vale stude,
Þat he myhte ilome heom beo myde?"

1751. *Mihte yet.*

---

well-known to sailors. The village (referred to as Pos'ham) is mentioned in *The Trumpet Major*, ch. xxxiii. of Thomas Hardy, as the place where Bob Loveday interviewed Captain Hardy with a view to serving under his command.

But the further detail of the description, viz. *in ore utlete* ("in an outlet") also presents difficulty. The term *utlete* can scarcely refer to the sea, for in that case, "inlet" would have been used: and moreover the West Fleet, the nearest arm of the sea, is some distance away. The explanation seems to be that *utlete* is here used with reference to the coast-ridge, which has openings or outlets to the coast at Upway, Swyre and Portisham. The position of the present roads marks these outlets, which in former times were features of great importance. Hence the description of Portisham as being situated "in an outlet" from Frome Vale to the sea, is perfectly natural: it would appear obvious to a man familiar with the district.

1757–8. H. regards the statement that the judgments and writings of Nicholas improved matters in Scotland as "a playful exaggeration," and it may well have been so. Indeed, here is perhaps the beginning of the development of certain "imperfect sympathies," found later in Dr Johnson and Lamb! Yet a claim of this kind made on Nicholas' behalf would have been of little use for the object in view, unless it rested on some basis of fact: and one is therefore tempted to inquire whether Master Nicholas may not have been responsible for that version of Glanvil's popular *Tractatus de Legibus* (1187), which seems to have been put together in the early years of the 13th century, and which became current in Scotland under the title of *Regiam Maiestatem* (see Pollock and Maitland, *History of English Law*, i. 145).

1764. Trans. "Why will they not take as a counsel to themselves," i.e. arrange in their own interests, or adopt as their plan, that etc. H. incorrectly translates: "Why will they not betake themselves to counsel," though in a parallel idiom *nam him to rede* (H. p. 277), he rightly translates "took to himself for counsel, adopted the plan": cf. 1. 680 for a similar expression.

"Certes," cwaþ þe hule, "þat is soð:
1770　þeos riche men wel muche misdoð,　Fol. 246 r. col. 1.
þat leteþ þane gode mon,
þat of so feole þinge con,
an ȝiueþ rente wel misliche,
an of him leteþ wel lihtliche.
1775　Wið heore cunne heo beoþ mildre,
an ȝeueþ rente litle childre:
swo heore wit hi demþ adwole,
þat euer abid Maistre Nichole.
Ah ute we þah to him fare,
1780　for þar is unker dom al ȝare."
　　"Do we" þe niȝtegale seide:
"ah [w]a schal unker speche rede,
an telle touore unker deme?"
　　"Þarof ich schal þe wel icweme,"
1785　cwaþ þe houle; "for al, ende of orde,
telle ich con, word after worde:
an ȝef þe þincþ þat ich misrempe,
þu stond aȝein ꞇ do me crempe."
Mid þisse worde forþ hi ferden,
1790　al bute here ꞇ bute uerde,
to Portesham þat heo bicome.
Ah hu heo spedde of heore dome,
ne [c]an ich eu namore telle:
her nis namore of þis spelle.

1782. *þa, þ* dotted.　1791. *þ*, with abbreviation for *at* or *ar*.　1793. *chan*.

1775 ff. There is abundant evidence as to the contemporary practice of inducting into livings persons of influence whom either ignorance or youth disqualified for such charges. Bishop Grosseteste in the first half of the 13th century tried to put an end to these abuses (see *Letters, passim*). In 1235, for instance, he refused to admit one William de Grama to a cure of souls, though presented by W. Raleigh, Treasurer of Exeter, on the ground that the said William de Grama was *minoris aetatis*. Three years later, Grosseteste objected to the appointment of Thomas, son of Earl Ferrors, to a benefice, not only because of the candidate's youth, but also because he was not in orders: and at the same time, other candidates were refused, one, because he was "a boy still in his Ovid," another, because he had been presented "wearing clothes of scarlet and with rings on his fingers." In fact, such was the extent to which these practices prevailed, that Grosseteste in 1253 described such abuses as amongst the chief evils of the time. H. further quotes from Odo of Cheriton (p. 262) by way of illustration. See also G. G. Coulton, *A Medieval Garner*, pp. 193, 308.

1777-8. A difficult passage, which W. divides into two sentences with a full-stop after *adwole*. Line 1777 he translates: "So they condemn their intelligence [as] in error (foolish)": and the following line apparently he

"Certes," quaþ þe vle, "þat is soþ:
1770 Þeos riche men [m]uchel mysdoþ,
Þat leteþ þane gode man,
Þat of so fele þinge can,
ꞇ yeueþrente wel [m]islyche,
ꞇ of him leteþ wel lyhtliche.
1775 Wiþ heore kunne heo beoþ [m]ildre,
ꞇ yeueþ rente lutle childre:
So heore wit hi demeþ a-dwole,
Þat euer abit Mayster Nichole.
Ah vte we þah to hym fare,
1780 Vor þa[r] is vnker dom al yare."
"Do we," þe Nihtegale seyde:
"Ah hwo schal vnker speche rede,
ꞇ telle tovore vnker d[e]me?"
"Þarof ic schal þe wel iqueme,"
1785 Queþ þe vle; "for al, ende of orde,
Telle ic con, word after worde: Fol. 241 v. col. 2.
ꞇ if þe þinkþ þat ic misrempe,
Þu stond ayeyn and do me crempe."
Mid þisse worde forþ hi ferden,
1790 Al bute here and bute verde,
To Portesham þer heo bicome.
Ah hw heo spedde of heore dome,
Ne can ic eu namore telle;
Her nys namore of þisse spelle.
Explicit.

1770. *Muchel.*   1773. *Mislyche.*   1775. *Mildre.*   1780. *þat.*   1783. *dome.*

takes to mean "and this M. Nicholas ever endures." But as H. points out, this "is against the order of the words, and syncopated pres. plurals are rare." Better sense is obtained by taking the lines as one complex sentence, viz. "Thus their good sense will convict them of error, in that M. Nicholas still suffers neglect." For *abid* see Appendix I (d) (iv) (β).

adwole is described by Str.-Br. as p.p. of *adwelen* (cf. O.H.G. *artwelan* = torpere), "to grow stupid": but more probably it is an adverbial form = *on dwole* ("in error") < O.E. *dwola.*

1785. *al, ende of orde* = "all, the end from the beginning," i.e. from beginning to end.

1790 Trans.: "without supporters of any kind." It is worth noting that *here* = "the army" of the Owl (cf. ll. 1702, 1709), and *uerde* = "the army" of the Nightingale (cf. ll. 1668, 1672). And this fact is not without its significance: for while the O.E. distinction between *here* (Danish army) and *fierd* (English levies) is here maintained, the side on which the poet's sympathies lay is also implied. The Owl and her forces were clearly to him the enemies of national culture.

1791. *þat* (J. *þer*) = "until," cf. O.E. *æuere heo uerden alle niht þat hit wes dæi-liht,* Laȝ, 19200 (H.).

TRANSLATION

In a haunt remote of a certain valley I heard an Owl and a Nightingale hold great debate. Their dispute was stern and strenuous and stubborn: quiet at times, then loud again. Each bird raged against the other, uttering many a malicious thought: each one spake of the other's character the worst things that she could devise. But above all, they made their plaints of each other's singing: and this they did in downright terms.

The Nightingale began the pleading, in the corner of a spinney, seated on a twig that was rich with blossom, in a close thick hedge with reeds and sedge entangled. Rejoicing she sang with many a trill and quaver, so that her notes seemed to come from harp or pipe—from harp or pipe, not from living throat.

Near by there stood an old tree-stump, where the Owl was wont to sing her "hours." It was all overgrown with ivy, and was the dwelling-place of the Owl.

The Nightingale beheld the Owl, and looked her up and down in scorn: for she thought but ill of her opponent, and, indeed, all men reckon her loathsome and foul. "Monster," said she, "away with thee! I am the worse for seeing thee. And, truly, the sight of thine ugliness often brings my song to untimely end. My heart doth sink, my tongue fails me, when thou dost thrust thyself upon me. I had rather spit than sing on hearing that gurgling noise of thine."

The Owl waited till evening fell, and then she could contain herself no longer: for her heart had become so swollen, that she was almost breathless with rage. And after a while she spake these words: "What dost thou think now of my singing? Dost thou suppose that I cannot sing, though I know naught of all thy trilling? Time and again thou doest me wrong, saying things both annoying and shameful. If I but held thee on my foot, (would that such a thing might happen!) and thou wert away from that twig of thine, thou shouldst sing another tune!"

To this the Nightingale gave answer: "If I can avoid coming into the open, and find protection against hard weather, I care nothing for all thy threats. If I keep quiet in my hedge, I reck naught of what thou sayest. Well do I know that thou art merciless to those who cannot protect themselves against thee: and that, wherever thou canst, thou dost attack little birds in cruel and wanton fashion. Therefore art thou hated by all manner of birds, who are wont to chase thee out of their midst, crying and screeching in hot pursuit of thee. Even the very titmouse would gladly tear thee to pieces! Then thou art loathsome to behold: and loathsome art thou in many ways. Thy body is short: thy neck is thin: thy head is bigger than all thy body. Thine eyes also are coal-black and broad, just as if they were painted with woad: and with them thou glarest, as if thou wouldst devour all that thou mayst clutch by means of thy claws. Thy bill is strong and sharp and hooked, like to an awl crooked in shape: and with this bill thou clackest continually—which, indeed, is one of thy songs. But thou dost also threaten this body of mine: with thy claws thou wouldst like to crush me. More fitting would it be for thee to feed on the frog [that sits underneath the cogwheel of the mill]: snails and mice and other foul creatures are thy natural and proper food. Thou lurkest by day and fliest at night, showing by this thou art unnatural. And thou art horrible and dirty as well,—I refer to thy nest and to thy foul brood, in which thou dost rear a most filthy family. Well knowest thou what they do therein: they defile their nest up to their chins, sitting meanwhile as if they were blind. And of this matter men make a proverb: 'Cursed be the creature that defiles its own nest.' Once upon a time a falcon bred: his nest he did not well protect: and one day thither thou didst steal, laying therein thy filthy egg. In course of time the eggs were hatched, and from them came little nestlings, to which the falcon brought some food. He watched his nest: he saw them eat: and the outside of the nest he saw had been defiled. Then was he angry with his brood: he screamed aloud as he sternly scolded them. 'Tell me,' quoth he, 'who have done this thing? for it is quite against your nature. A hateful trick has been played on you. Tell me if ye knew aught about it.' Then spake one and spake another: 'Truly it was a brother of ours, yonder fellow with the big head. Bad luck to that head of his! Cast him out forthwith, and break his neck!' Whereupon the falcon, believing his brood, took the ugly bird by the middle, and threw it down from the wild-wood bough to where magpie and crow plucked it to pieces. And of this fable men make a parable, though the story be not complete. For thus it is with the worthless man, who has come from vicious stock. Although he live among noble folk, he will always betray from whence he sprang: he shows that he came from an addle egg, though he dwell in a splendid nest. An apple may roll from the parent tree, on which it once grew along with others: yet, though it roll far, it will always show from whence it came."

Such was the speech of the Nightingale, and after making this long indictment, she sang in tones that were loud and piercing, just as though one had plucked the resonant strings of a harp. Meanwhile the Owl had been listening, keeping her eyes fixed to the ground: and as she sat, puffed out and swollen, it was as if she had swallowed a frog. For she knew and was well aware, that the Nightingale sang in mockery of her: and yet she had her answer ready. "Why then wilt thou not fly into the open, and show which of us two has the brighter colouring, the fairer hue?" "No!" [replied the Night-ingale] "for thou hast claws that are very sharp, and I am not anxious that thou shouldst claw me. Thou hast talons mighty and strong, with which thou dost squeeze like a pair of tongs. Thou didst think, as do birds of thy feather, to lead me astray with plausible words. But I would not follow thine advice: I knew well thou wouldst advise me badly. Shame on thee for thy false counsel, for now thy deceit is made plain to all. Cover thy treachery from the light, and hide what is wrong behind the right. When thou dost wish to practise evil, take good heed it is not seen; for treachery brings but shame and hatred, if it is obvious and plain to all. With thy wicked tricks thou hast not succeeded, for I am wary and can dodge them: nor is thy daring of any avail, for my skill in fighting is greater than thy brute strength. I have, besides, on this branch of mine, a splendid stronghold broad and long; and, as the wise man says, 'He fights well who flies well.' But let us now stop this squabbling, for such talking serves no purpose: and let us get on with a proper trial, using fair and friendly words. For though we may not be agreed, we can conduct this case in better fashion, by observing decency and law, and with friendly argument, free from strife and violence: so that each may say whatever he will, with due regard to law and reason."

"But," said the Owl: "Who is there to settle our difference? Who can and will give lawful judgment?" "I know well," the Nightingale answered, "of that there need be no discussion. Master Nicholas of Guildford is the man: for he is wise and cautious of speech, prudent as well in giving judgment, and an enemy to vice of every kind. Then, too, he has taste in matters of song: he knows who sings well, and who sings badly. He can distinguish the wrong from the right, the things of darkness from things of the light."

The Owl for a time pondered on this, and at length she replied as follows: "I am willing that he should judge: for although somewhat wild in days gone by—fond of the night-ingales, and other creatures, too, gentle and neat—I know that now his ardour is cooled. He will not be befooled by thee, so that, for old time's sake, he may prefer thy cause to mine. Thou art unable so to please him, that he for thy sake will utter false judgment. Now he is settled and steady of mind: follies for him have no attraction. He delights no longer in flighty ways: he will adopt the course that is straight."

The Nightingale, meanwhile, was ready for action: her wit was drawn from many sources. "Owl!" she said, "tell me truly: why behavest thou in unnatural fashion? Thou singest at night and not by day: and thy whole song is a lament, with which thou dost terrify all who hear thy noise. Thou shriekest and hootest to thy mate in a way that is awful to hear: so that to men, both wise and foolish, it seems not that thou singest but that thou dost weep. Then, too, thou fliest at night and not by day: at this I wonder, and well I may. For everything that shuns what is right loves the darkness and hates the light. And everything that inclines to evil likes the darkness for its deed. A wise saying there is, which, though unpolished, is often heard on the lips of men, for King Alfred said and wrote it: 'A man shuns that which knows him to be foul.' And so it is, I suppose, with thee: for ever dost thou fly at night. And another thing I have in mind: thou hast at night the clearest vision, whereas by day thou art stone-blind, seeing neither tree nor stream. In the day-time thou art blind and sightless: and of this, men make a parable. 'So it is with the wicked man who sees naught to any good purpose, and is so full of evil tricks that no man is able to deceive him. He knows well the way of darkness and avoids the way of light.' Thus do all of thy kindred: of the light they have no care."

The Owl listened for a while in a state of great vexation. At length she spake: "Thou art called the Nightingale: but 'Chatterbox' would describe thee better, for thou hast too much to say. Let thy tongue now have a rest! Thou dost suppose that the whole day is thine: but let me now have a chance. Keep quiet and let me speak: and I shall be revenged on thee. And listen how I can clear myself with truthful words without ado. Thou sayest that I hide by day: and this I in no way deny. But listen and I'll tell thee why—the whole reason for the same. I have a strong and sturdy beak, good claws as well both sharp and long, as befits one of the hawk-tribe. It is my joy, my delight as well, that I live in accord with Nature: and for this no man can blame me. In me it is plainly seen that by Nature's laws I am so fierce: and that is why I am hated by the little birds, that fly near the ground and in the thickets, as they twitter around me, uttering their cries and bringing their flocks in force against me. But I prefer to take a rest, sitting quietly in my nest: for I should be no better off if I put them to rout with scolding or with chattering, or by using bad language as the shepherds do. Nor do I care to bandy words with such spit-fires: and therefore I keep them at a distance. There is a wise proverb in common use among men, that 'one should not rail against a fool nor vie in yawning with an oven': while once I heard that Alfred had said 'Be not present where railing and ruffling are rife: let fools quarrel and go thy way.' And I am wise and follow this counsel. Moreover Alfred said in another place a proverb that is also familiar: 'He that has to do with what is foul, never comes off entirely clean.' Dost thou then think the hawk is any the worse, though crows cry out against him in the marshes, and though they draw near with their cawing as if they were about to attack him? He, for his part, takes the wise course: he flies away, and lets them caw."

"But thou dost charge me with other things: thou sayest that I cannot sing, that my one theme is lamentation and that it is awful to hear. This is not true: I sing smoothly, with full melody and in loud tones. Thou dost regard every song as dreadful that is different from thy piping tones. As for my note, it is bold and masterful—much like the sound of a great horn; while thine is like that of a tiny pipe fashioned out of a reed unripe. My singing indeed is better than thine. Thou dost chatter like an Irish priest: but I sing in the evening at the proper time, afterwards at bed-time, and again at midnight: and once more I begin my song when I behold the dawn, the morning-star rising from afar. Thus I do good with my song, warning men to their advantage. But thou dost sing all the night long, from evening until dawn: and thy song is ever the same while darkness lasts. Thy wretched throat keeps up its noise, never ceasing night nor day: and with this din thou assailest the ears of all who dwell around, making thy song so cheap withal, that men reckon nothing of it. For every pleasure may last so long that in the end it ceases to please: whether it be note of harp or pipe or bird, each shall displease if kept up too long. Be the song ever so merry, it shall become quite distasteful if it lasts beyond the proper time. For it is true—Alfred said it, and it may also be read in books—'Every thing may lose its virtue by excess and superfluity.' With pleasure thou mayst glut thyself, and a surfeit brings on loathing: so every joy may cease to be if ever maintained the same. And this is true, with one exception—that is the kingdom of God, which alone remains dear and ever the same. Though continually thou take from its fulness as from a basket, yet it remains full to overflowing. This is the marvel of the kingdom of God, that for ever it gives, and for ever it remains the same."

"But thou dost bring forward another shameful charge— that I am defective in my eyes. Thou sayest that because I fly at night, I am unable to see by day. But there thou liest! for it is clear that I have good eyesight, since no darkness is so dim as to prevent my seeing. Thou dost suppose that I cannot see, because I do not fly by day. But the hare lies low throughout the day, and nevertheless he sees quite well. If the hounds perchance come out against him, he darts away quickly, winding his way along narrow tracks, turning to account his ready tricks, hopping and leaping in swiftest fashion as he makes his way to a place of covert. This he could not do, despite his eyes, unless with them he saw things clearly. And I can see as well as the hare, though by day I sit and lurk. When bold men go to war and make their expeditions far and near, when they overrun many peoples, performing at night their good pleasure, then I follow in their train and fly by night in their company."

All this the Nightingale took to heart, and pondered long as to what she should answer. She could not refute what had just been said, for the Owl had spoken wisely and well: and, annoyed that she had carried the argument so far, she feared lest her reply should somehow miscarry. In spite of this she spake out boldly; for he is wise who, undismayed, presents a brave front to his foe, so that he through cowardice be not found wanting. For the foe who will yield if thou turnest not away, will yet become bold if thou shouldst flee. If he sees thou art no craven, he from a boar will become a tame pig. And therefore, though the Nightingale was shaken, yet she spake up bravely.

"Owl!" said she, "why behavest thou so, ever chanting in winter thy song of woe? Thy song is like that of a hen in the snow, clucking out of her sheer misery. In winter thou singest angrily and mournfully: whereas in summer thou remainest dumb. It is all because of thy malicious spite that thou art unable to rejoice with us: for thou art almost consumed with envy, when happiness chances to come our way. Thy conduct is like that of the churlish man to whom all gladness is displeasing: grumbling and frowning come readily to him, if ever he sees that men are happy. He would like to see tears in the eyes of all: nor would he care though the wool-tufts were mere tangles of threads and hairs. And so, for thy part, dost thou behave: when snow lies deep both far and wide, and hardships are the lot of all, then dost thou sing from evening to dawn. But I all happiness with me bring: every creature is glad because of me, making merry at my coming, rejoicing even before I come. Blossoms burst forth and unfold themselves on the trees and in the meadows. The lily with her lovely hue welcomes me, as thou dost know: clad in beauty she doth bid me that I forthwith should fly to her. The rose, also, with tint of red, that peeps out of the briar-bush, bids me to sing for her sake one pleasing ditty. And this I do, both night and day: the more I sing, the more I may, giving delight with my songs. Yet never is my song too long: for when I see that men are pleased, I do not wish to tire them out. When that for which I came is done, I go away, and wisely go. When the thoughts of men are on har-vest sheaves, and autumn brown doth stain the leaves, then I go home and take my leave: for I care not for winter's spoil. When I see hard weather coming I go home to my own land, taking with me love and thanks for my presence and my pains. Should I remain when my task is over? Nay! why should I? For he has neither wit nor wisdom that lingers where he is not needed."

The Owl listened to this speech, storing up carefully every word: and afterwards she thought how best she might con-trive a fitting answer. For he who fears the tricks of pleading must ever take counsel with himself.

"Thou dost ask me," said the Owl, "why I sing and cry out in winter. It is usual among good people—and has been so from the beginning of things—that every man should cherish his friends, rejoicing with them on certain occasions, with merry talk and kindly words at his own domestic board. Especially is this so at Christmas time: and then, when rich and poor, folk great and simple, sing their dance-songs by night and day, I do all I can to help them. But I think also of other things than of merry-making or mere singing : and here I have a fitting answer prompt and ready. For summer-time is all too rank : it is apt to lead a man's thoughts astray, so that he recks not of purity but gives himself up to wanton thoughts. No beast is there that restrains itself, but each doth ride upon the other : even the horses in the stud are filled with a wild longing for the mares. And thou thyself art much the same: for of wantonness is all thy song : and just before the breeding season thou art most passionate and excited. When thou hast thy will performed, then canst thou utter not a word : thou dost twitter like the titmouse, chucking with a husky voice. Thy note becomes worse than that of the hedge-sparrow that flies near the ground amongst the trees : for when thy love-longing is over, then is thy singing over as well. In the summer season peasants rage and ramp and corrupt themselves,—but all the same, not for love. It is rather a mad impulse with the peasant : for when he has achieved his object, then his rashness soon departs,......nor does his love any longer last. And thy mood is just the same: as soon as thou dost sit a-brooding, thou dost lose all thy tune. On thy twig the same things happen: when thou hast performed thy pleasure, thy note at once becomes discordant. But when the long nights come, bringing frosts severe and hard, then for the first time it is seen where are those who are active and brave. In bad times one discovers who does things and who holds back : one can see in times of need to whom one may assign hard duties. Then am I active : I frolic and sing, amusing myself with my chanting. I care nothing for any winter: I am no wretched flabby creature. Rather do I bring comfort to many beings who in themselves are without any strength, such as are anxious and very miserable, in eager longing for some warmth. For them I often sing the more, to lessen something of their pain. How now? Art thou cornered? Hast thou not been fairly beaten?"

"Nay! nay!" retorted the Nightingale, "Thou shalt hear yet another charge: this case of ours is not yet ripe for judgment. Be silent now and listen to me: for by making a mere allegation I shall break down thy whole defence."

"But that would be illegal," said the Owl. "In accordance with thy request thou now hast made thy formal charge: and to that I have replied. But before we proceed to judgment I wish first to state a case against thee, as thou already hast dealt with me: and do thou answer if thou canst! Tell me now, thou miserable thing! art thou really of any use, apart from that shrill throat of thine? Thou dost serve no other purpose, though thou art a clever babbler: for thou art tiny as well as frail, and thy defence is nothing great. What good art thou to the race of men? no more indeed than a poor wren. From thee men get no good whatever, except that thou criest like a mad thing: and when this piping of thine is over, then art thou good for nothing else. Alfred in his wisdom said (and well he might, for true it is), 'No man is esteemed long for a mere song: for he is worthless who can do naught but sing.' Thou art therefore but a futile thing: in thee is nothing but empty talk. Then, too, thou art dark and filthy in colour: a little dirty ball is what thou art like. Thou hast no beauty, thou art not strong, thou art lacking in breadth and size as well. All qualities of beauty thou hast missed, and there is little that is good about thee. And another thing I lay to thy charge: thou art not attractive, not even clean. When thou comest near the dwellings of men, where thorns and twigs are closely drawn, near to a hedge or a dense wood......,thither thou goest, there thou dwellest, avoiding other and cleaner places. And when I chase mice in the night-time, there do I find thee,......sitting amidst the thicket, among the nettles....... Yet thou dost reproach me with what I eat, saying that foul creatures are my food. But what dost thou eat, if the truth were known, apart from spiders and filthy flies—and worms as well, if thou mightest find them amidst the crevices of the bark of the trees? But I can render services of a useful kind: for I can protect the dwellings of men. And my services are very valuable, for I help with the food of men. I can catch mice in the barns: and also in church

A.

during the hours of darkness. For the house of God is dear
to me : I love to cleanse it of loathsome mice. Nor shall any
vile creature enter there if I can get hold of it. And if it
is my pleasure when I sing to refuse all other dwellings, I
have still in the woods some mighty trees, with thick boughs
that are never bare, covered over with ivy that is ever in leaf,
and evergreen whether it snows or freezes. And there I have
a splendid stronghold, warm in winter, in summer, cool : and
when that dwelling stands bright and green, then of thine
is nothing seen. Yet thou dost mention other matters : of my
little ones thou pratest foolishly, saying that their nest is not
clean. But the fault is common to many creatures : for the
horse in its stable, the ox in its stall, both do follow their own
inclinations. And little children in their cradles, whether of
lowly or gentle birth, also do things in their early days which
they avoid in later years. Well ! can the infant really prevent
it ? If it does wrong it cannot be helped. And there is as
well an old-fashioned saying, that 'need doth make the old
wife trot.' But I have yet a further point to make, if thou wilt
first come to this nest of mine to examine its structure ; for if
thou art wise thou art able to learn. My nest in the middle
is hollow and roomy, as is most cosy for my birds : but all
around on the outside it is plaited, away from the inside of
the nest. And thither they go in their need : and what thou
complainest of, that I forbid. We take note of the dwellings
of men, and ours are made after their fashion...... Now keep
quiet, Dame Chatterbox ! thou hast never been in tighter
corner. To what I have said thou canst never answer. Hang
up thine axe ! it is time to end."

The Nightingale, on hearing this speech, was almost at her
wits' end : and eagerly she wondered to herself whether she
knew anything else—whether she could do aught but sing—
that might be useful in other affairs. To that question an
answer was needed, or else she would be hopelessly out of the
running : and hard indeed it is to strive against truth as well
as right. The man whose heart is in great straits must ever go
to work with cunning. Such a man must speak with dissimulation : he must trim his words and explain them away, if

the mouth perchance can keep its secrets, so that the heart within is not revealed. For quickly can a word go astray, when what a man says is not what he feels : and quickly can a speech go wrong, when tongue and heart do not agree. Yet nevertheless, in spite of this, here is encouragement for him who knows it : for never is a man's mind so keen as when in doubt what to do. Then first its cunning doth appear when the mind is in the greatest fear. For Alfred, long ago, uttered a saying, which even now is not forgotten : "When trouble is at its highest, then is the remedy nearest at hand." For the understanding grows in time of trouble, and because of the trouble doth it grow. Therefore never is a man devoid of counsel, unless his heart lacks understanding : but if he should lose that understanding then his pocket is picked of all its wisdom. If good sense he cannot retain, nowhere in his purse shall he find counsel. For Alfred in his wisdom said, ever speaking with truthful lips : "When trouble is at its highest, then is the remedy nearest at hand."

Meanwhile the Nightingale, with all care and wisdom, had gone to work in circumstances both difficult and strained ; well and wisely had she pondered, and had found a fitting answer in the midst of her perplexity.

"Owl!" she said, "thou askest me if I can do aught but sing at certain seasons, diffusing happiness far and wide. Why dost thou ask about my accomplishments ? The one I possess is better than all thine : better the one song that I sing than all that thy tribe ever knew. And listen, and I'll tell thee why. Dost thou know why man was born ? He was born for the joy of heaven, where there is song and mirth eternal. And thither hastens every man who has skill in any good thing. Therefore men sing in holy church, and clerks as well their songs compose, so that one may remember through the songs, whither he is destined, there to be for ever : that he moreover may not forget heaven's joy, but, thinking thereon, he may attain it, thus taking heed of the Church's teaching how glorious is the bliss of heaven. Clerks and monks and canons as well, in places where there are religious houses, are wont to rise up at the hour of midnight in order to sing of the light of heaven: and secular priests in their parishes take up the singing when daylight comes. And I help them as far as I can: with them I sing both night and day. They are the happier on my account, readier far to sing their chants. Thus do I caution men for their good that they should ever be glad at heart: I pray also that they might attain that self-same song that is eternal. Now, thou Owl, mayst thou sit and shrivel! on this matter there can be no babbling. I am willing that we should go to judgment—before the very Pope of Rome. Yet, nevertheless, wait a bit! thou shalt hear pronounced another sentence, which thou, for all England, shalt not refute. Why dost thou reproach me with my weakness, my lack of size as well as length, saying that I possess no strength because I am neither large nor long. Thou dost not know what thou sayest: mere lying words thou dost utter. For I am accomplished, I have much skill: and that is why I am so bold. I can provide good sense and song-craft: I rely on no other power. For true it is, as Alfred said: 'Mere strength can do nothing against skill.' Often a little skill brings success, where great strength would have missed the mark. With little force, but by strategy, castle and city may be won. Ramparts by artifice are overthrown, and brave knights hurled from the saddle. Mischievous strength is of little worth, [but wisdom never loses its value: and thou canst see in everything] that such wisdom is without rival. A horse, for instance, is stronger than a man. But, because it is without understanding, it bears great burdens on its back, leading withal great teams of horses; it suffers the smart of stick and spur: it stands fastened to the mill-doors: it does whatsoever it is commanded: and because it is devoid of reason, it has, in despite of all its strength, to give obedience to little children. Man, in short, contrives, through his strength and sense, that nothing else is a match for him. Though the strength of all things were united in one, yet human skill would be still the more powerful: for man with his cunning remains master of all the creatures of earth. And so I do better with my one song than thou canst do throughout the year. I am beloved by men for my skill: on account of thy violence thou art shunned. Dost thou reckon the worse of me because I have but a single craft? If two men enter a wrestling match, and each of them plies the other hard: and while one of them knows a host of tricks which he is able to keep to himself, whereas the other has but one device, which however comes off against every man, so that one after another is quickly thrown—why need he trouble about further tricks, when the one he has succeeds so well? Thou sayest that thou canst perform many services, and that I am ever unlike thee in this. Put thy crafts all together, yet is my wit alone the better. Often when hounds hunt down the foxes, the cat is left quite alone by himself, though he has but a single trick. Though the fox may know many devices, he has none so good as to lead him to hope he shall cheat every hound. Thus the fox knows of paths that are straight and devious: he also knows how to hang from a bough, thus making the hound lose the trail and return again back to the moorland. The fox, besides, can creep by the hedges, turn aside from his first line of flight, and double back quickly on his tracks again. Then is the scent of the hound quite done for: he knows not whether to go on or back, owing to the confusion of scents. And if the fox fails after all this manœuvring, in the end he goes to earth. Yet nevertheless, with all his trickery, though, too, he is cunning and very nimble, he cannot avoid losing his coat of red fur, however much he plans and plots. The cat, on the other hand, has but one trick, whether on the hills or in the fenland: but then he is an excellent climber, and by means of climbing he saves his grey fur. And the same thing may be said of me: better is my one craft than the dozen thou hast."

"Stop! stop!" exclaimed the Owl, "thou proceedest in far too wily a fashion. All thy words thou dost colour, so that everything thou sayest seems to be true: thy whole utterance is unctuous, so plausible and specious that all who hear it suppose it to be true. But stay! stay! thou shalt yet be answered: and when thy lies are laid bare, the extent of thy falsehood shall plainly be seen. Thou sayest, for instance, that thou dost sing to mankind, teaching them of their journey hence, up to the chanting that lasts for ever. But most strange it is that thou shouldst venture on such barefaced lies. Dost thou think to bring them so easily to God's kingdom—by mere singing? Nay! nay! they shall indeed find that before ever they come there, they must with many tears ask forgiveness for their sins. My advice is therefore that those who yearn for the king of heaven should get ready to weep rather than sing, since there is no man who is free from sin. Therefore, a man, before he goes hence, must make due atonement with tears and with weeping, so that what before was sweet may henceforth be bitter. And, God knows, I help mankind in this matter. I sing to men no foolishness. My song is of yearning and partly of lament, so that man in consequence may take heed to himself and bewail his transgressions: with my singing I urge him to groan for his misdeeds. And if thou art inclined to dispute this point, then I claim to weep better than thou dost sing: if what is right takes precedence over what is wrong, then better is my weeping than thy song. Some men there are who are good throughout, quite pure in heart; yet nevertheless they, too, long to depart this life. That they are here is but grief to them: for though they themselves are saved, around them do they see naught but sorrow. Bitter tears they shed for other men, and for them they entreat the mercy of Christ. Thus do I help men in either case: my mouth has healing power of a twofold kind. The good I encourage in their yearning: for when they are filled with longing, to them do I sing. And sinful men I help as well, for I teach them where true misery lies. But I confute thee also on other grounds: for when thou art perched upon thy twig, thou enticest to carnal lusts all who hear thee. The joys of heaven thou dost wholly neglect: thou hast no voice to utter such things. All thy song is of wantonness: in thee there is found no holiness: nor could any one take thy piping note for the singing of a priest within the church. But I will speak to thee on another matter, to see if thou canst reasonably explain it away. Why wilt thou not sing to other peoples by whom thy song is much more needed? In Ireland thou dost never sing: nor dost thou ever visit Scotland. Why wilt thou not go across to Norway,

and sing to the men of Galloway? For there live men who
have but little skill in songs of any sort. Why wilt thou not
sing there to the priests, and in teaching them something of
thy trills, show them by thy notes how the angels in heaven
are wont to sing? Thou dost behave like a useless spring, that
breaks forth near some rapid stream and lets the hill-side get
quite parched, while running fruitlessly to the plain. But I go
north as well as south: I am well-known in every land. East
and west, far and near, I do my duty passing well, warning
men in clamorous tones that they be not enticed by thy
mischievous song. I urge men by my singing not to continue
long in sin: I bid them cease from deceiving themselves: for
better it is, that in this life they should weep, than be here-
after companions of devils."

The Nightingale by now was angry, and a little ashamed
as well, for the Owl had reproached her for the place wherein
she sat, uttering her cries—behind the dwelling, amongst the
weeds....... She therefore remained deep in thought for a
time: for well she knew in her heart of hearts, that anger doth
rob a man of wisdom. Alfred the king had already also said
it: "Seldom ends well the man disliked, seldom pleads well
the angry man." For wrath stirs up the blood of the mind,
so that it flows like a wild flood, overpowering all the mind
and leaving to it naught but passion. The mind thus loses
all its light, and can discern neither truth nor right. The
Nightingale was aware of this, and she let her mood of anger
pass. She could speak better in a good humour than by
bandying words in a temper.

"Owl!" said she, "now listen to me. Thou shalt trip: thy
course is treacherous. Thou sayest that I flee behind the
dwelling: that is true, the dwelling is ours. Where lord and
lady lie together, there, near by, shall I sit and sing. Dost
thou suppose that wise men leave the high road for the muddy
track? Or that the sun no longer shines, though it be filthy
within thy nest? Ought I then for a hollow log to forsake my
proper place, and sing no longer near the bed where the lord
and his beloved lie? It is my duty, it is my law, ever to
follow the highest things. But thou dost also boast of thy

singing, that thou canst scream in fierce and mighty fashion:
thou dost claim to direct mankind that they should bewail their
transgressions. Yet were all men to make lament, crying out
as if in torment, should they scream as thou art wont, they
could but bring terror to their souls. A man must be calm, not
given to wild words, even though he must bewail his sins.
But when Christ is praised, then shall he cry aloud, singing
with all his might. Hymn-singing in season can be neither
too loud nor too long. Thou dost scream and lament, whereas
I sing: thy note is tearful, mine gives delight. Ever may
thou scream and weep to depart this life! and may thou
also scream so high as to burst both thine eyes! For which
is the better of the two things, that a man be happy or
else perturbed? So be it ever the lot of us two, that thou be
sad and I be merry. But thou again dost ask why I go not
hence, and sing my song in another land. No! what should
I do amongst such people, to whom all happiness is unknown?
That country is poor, it is not gracious, but mere wilderness,
a barren land. Crags and rocks reaching up to heaven, snow
and hail are common there. It is a horrible, an uncanny
land: the inhabitants thereof are wild and wicked: they keep
neither truce nor peace: nor do they care how they live.
They eat raw fish, raw meat as well, tearing it to pieces like
wolves. Milk they drink and also whey: they know not
otherwise what to drink, having neither wine nor beer.
They live, in truth, like wild beasts: and they go clad in
shaggy hides just as if they hailed from hell. If some good
man to them came—as once upon a time one came from Rome,
in order to teach them better manners and to leave their evil
ways—he would do better to remain at home, for he would but
waste his time. He could sooner teach a bear how to carry
shield and spear, than he could bring a people so disorderly
to listen to the song I sing. What should I do there with my
singing? However long to them I sang, my song would be
completely wasted: for neither halter nor bridle, instrument
of steel nor of iron, can check them in their mad behaviour.
But in a land which is pleasant and good, and where the
people have gentle ways, there I turn my throat to account,

for there I can render useful service: and glad tidings to them I bring, for I sing of the hymns of the Church. It was stated in the law of old time—and the wise saying still remains —that 'a man must plough and also sow where he expects to reap a harvest': for he is mad who sows his seed where no grass or blossom doth ever appear."

The Owl was now angry, ready for strife: and after this speech she rolled her eyes. "Thou sayest that thou dost guard the dwellings of men where there are leaves and flowers that are fair: and where two lovers lie abed, well protected in each other's arms. Once didst thou sing—I know well where —near to a dwelling. The lady thou wouldst tell of unlawful love: and, with song high and low, thou didst teach her to indulge a shameful and evil passion. Her lord, soon seeing how things were, set bird-lime and snares, and many other things in order to capture thee: and quickly didst thou come to the casement. Thou wert caught in a gin: thy shins paid thee out: and the doom decreed was none other than that thou shouldst be torn asunder by wild horses. Try, then, if thou canst again seduce either wife or maid: thy singing, forsooth, may prove so successful, that thou shalt flutter helplessly in a snare!"

The Nightingale, on hearing this, would have attacked with sword and spear, had she but been a man: but since she could do nothing better, she took as her weapon her prudent tongue. "He fights well who talks well," so the song runs: and to her tongue she looked for help. "He fights well who talks well," as Alfred said.

"What!" exclaimed the Nightingale, "sayest thou so, to put me to shame? But the husband in the end had the worst of it. He was so jealous of his wife, that, to save his life, he could not bear to see a man speak with her, but his heart would break. He therefore locked her up in a certain dwelling—to her, a harsh and bitter treatment. And I had pity and compassion on her: I felt sorry for her trouble, and amused her with my singing as much as I could, both early and long. And that was why the knight was wroth with me: he hated me out of sheer spite. He thrust on me his own disgrace, but it all turned to his own injury. King Henry got to know of this—may Christ have mercy on his soul! Then did he outlaw the knight, who, through sheer spite and envy foul, had behaved so badly in that good king's land, as to have the little bird taken and condemned to death. That was an honour to all my kind: for the knight forthwith forfeited his happiness, and paid for me a hundred pounds. And, ever since, my birds have lived unharmed: they have lived in happiness and in joy, and have been of good cheer— as well they might. Thus was I so well avenged, that, ever since then, I speak more boldly; for since it happened so on one occasion, I am the blither ever more. And now I can sing wherever I will: nor durst any man annoy me. But as for thee, thou miserable thing! thou ghastly object! thou canst not find, thou knowest not of, a single hollow tree wherein to hide thee and so save thy skin. For girls and boys, masters and men all are keen on hurting thee. If they but see thee sitting quiet, they put stones in their pockets, and they pelt thee, and ill-treat thee, and break thine ugly bones to pieces. If thou art knocked over, or perchance, shot, then for the first time art thou useful. For then thou art hung upon a stick: and with thy grim and baggy body, and that hideous neck of thine, thou dost protect the cornfields from all animals. Alive and full-blooded, thou art useless: but as a scarecrow, thou art excellent. For where new seeds have been sown, there neither hedge-sparrow nor goldfinch, rook nor crow will ever venture, if thy carcase but hang near by. And where trees shall bloom in the spring-time, and young seeds burst forth and grow, there durst no bird venture to pluck them, if thou art hanging overhead. All thy life thou art sordid and vile: thou art useless except when dead. Now, indeed, canst thou know of a truth, that in life thine appearance is awesome: for even when thou art hanging dead, the birds that before cried out against thee, still remain in terror of thee. And rightly, too, are men hostile to thee: for thou dost sing ever of their troubles. All that thou singest, early or late, has to do with the misfortunes of men: and after thou hast cried out at night, men are mortally afraid of thee. Thou singest where someone

is going to die: ever dost thou foretell some mischief or other.
Thou singest before the loss of property, or of the ruin of a
friend. Or else thou foretellest a house a-burning, an invasion
of men, or the pursuit of a thief. Thou dost also predict a
cattle-plague, that neighbours will suffer much distress, that
a wife, again, shall lose her husband: or thou dost prophesy
strife and disputes. Ever dost thou sing of the troubles of
men: through thee they become both sad and miserable. Never
at any time dost thou sing except of some disaster or other. And
this is the reason why thou art shunned, why thou art pelted
and beaten with sticks and with stones, with turf and clods, so
that no way of escape is left open for thee. Bad luck to such
a herald amongst men, who is ever proclaiming futile secrets,
bringing continually unwelcome tidings, and telling ever of
unlucky things! May the wrath of God Almighty and of all
decent folk descend upon him!"

The Owl lost no time in making a rejoinder, stern and
vigorous. "What!" she exclaimed, "art thou of priestly rank?
or dost thou excommunicate, not being ordained? For the
priestly office thou art surely performing. I am not aware
that thou wert ever a priest: I doubt if thou canst really sing
mass, though thou knowest much of the Church's curse. It is
because of thine ancient malice that thou hast cursed me this
second time: and to this curse I can easily reply. 'Go to!' as the
carter said. Why dost thou twit me with my foreknowledge,
mine understanding and my power? For most certainly I
have much wisdom and am acquainted with all that the future
holds. I have foreknowledge of famine and invasion: and I
know if men are to have long life. I know, too, whether a
wife shall lose her husband: also where malice and vengeance
shall be rife. I can tell who is fated to be hanged or to come
to some other vile end: and if men come together in battle,
I am aware which side will be beaten. I know, also, if a pestilence is to fall on the cattle and whether the wild beasts shall
lie still in death. I know if trees shall bear their blossom, if the
cornfields also shall yield their increase. I can predict the burning of houses: whether men shall run afoot or proudly ride.
I know if ships will founder at sea, and if snow shall bind the

earth with harsh fetters. And I know much more as well. I
am well skilled in bookish lore: I know more of Holy Writ
than I will tell thee, for I go often to church and learn
much wisdom. I know all the symbolical meanings, and many
other things as well. If a man is to undergo the hue-and-cry,
I know all about it before it happens. And so, because of my
great knowledge, oft-times I sit, sad at heart and perturbed:
for when I see trouble approaching to men, I cry aloud lustily,
bidding them to be wary and to look to themselves. For
Alfred said a wise thing which all men should treasure
up: 'If thou seest [trouble] before it comes, it is robbed of
wellnigh all its force.' And violent blows become the weaker,
if one but cautiously takes heed of them; just as an arrow
shall miscarry if thou seest it fly from the string. For then
mayst thou well flinch and start aside, if thou seest it making
for thee. If any man have fallen into disgrace, why shall he
blame me for his trouble? For although I see his trouble
coming, it is not my fault that it comes. Or again, if thou
shouldst see some blind man or other, who, unable to walk
straight, pursues his erratic course to a ditch, and falling therein, becomes covered with mud, dost thou suppose, although I
see it all, that it happens any sooner because of me? And so
it is with my foreknowledge: for when I am perched upon my
bough, I know and discern very clearly, that on someone
trouble is straightway coming. Shall he therefore, who knows
nothing of it, put the blame on me because I know? Shall
he upbraid me for his misfortune, simply because I am wiser
than he? When I see that some trouble is coming, I call
out lustily, bidding men earnestly to be on their guard, because a cruel disaster approaches. But though I exclaim
both loudly and quietly, it all comes about by the will of
God. Why will men therefore complain of me, even though
I annoy them with the truths I tell? For though I warn
them all the year round, the trouble is no nearer on that
account. But to them I sing because I wish them to know,
that when my hooting reaches their ears, some misfortune is
hard at hand. For no man can be sure that he is exempt
from the prospect and the fear of approaching trouble, even

though he cannot see it. Alfred therefore said very wisely, and his words were gospel truth, that 'every man, the better off he is, the better he must look after himself.' And again: 'Let no man trust too much to his wealth, though he be rich: for there is nothing so hot that it does not grow cool, nothing so white that it does not soil, nothing so beloved that it does not become hateful, nothing so merry that it does not become angry. But every thing that is not eternal, and all worldly happiness, must pass away.' Now thou mayst clearly see that thy talk is foolish; for all that thou sayest to my shame, the same turns ever to thine undoing. However things go, in every bout, thou dost trip thyself up by thine own tricks. All that thou sayest to put me to shame, adds to mine honour in the end. Unless thou make a better beginning, thou shalt win naught but disgrace for thyself."

The Nightingale, meanwhile, sat still and sighed: anxious was she—and with good reason—seeing in what way the Owl had spoken and managed her case. She was anxious and much puzzled as to what her reply should be: but nevertheless she bethought herself. "What!" she exclaimed, "Owl! art thou mad? Thou art boasting of a strange wisdom, and thou wert ignorant from whence it came, unless by witchcraft it came to thee. And of witchcraft, thou wretch, thou must cleanse thyself, if thou art anxious to remain amongst men: otherwise must thou flee the country. For all those, who were skilled in witchcraft, were cursed of old by the mouth of the priest: as thou art still, since thou hast never forsaken witchcraft. I told thee this a short while ago: and thou didst ask in scornful tone, if I were ordained priest. But the cursing of thee is so common a thing, that were no priest to be found in the land, thou wouldst still be an outlaw. For every child calls thee vile, and every man, a despicable owl. I have heard—and true it is—that he who knows rightly what things are coming, as thou sayest is true of thee, must be well versed in star-lore. But what dost thou know of the stars, thou miserable object! except that thou beholdest them from afar?—as doth many a beast and man, who knows naught about such matters. An ape, for instance, may gaze on a book, turn its leaves, and close it again: but it is unable, all the same, to make head or tail of what is written. And though in like fashion thou gaze at the stars, still art thou none the wiser for it. And yet, thou vile thing! thou dost chide and reproach me viciously for singing near to the dwellings of men and for teaching their wives to break their vows. Thou liest for certain, thou loathsome object! Wedlock through me was never impaired. Yet true it is that I sing and declaim, where ladies and fair maidens be: and true is it also that of love I sing. For a virtuous wife may, in her married state, love her own husband better far than any philanderer: and a maid may take a lover without loss of honour, with true affection loving him to whom she grants her favour. Such love as this I teach and commend: this is the burden of all my utterance. But if a wife be weak of will—for women are soft-hearted by nature—so that through the wiles of a fool, who doth eagerly entreat with many a sad sigh, she happen to go astray and do wrong on occasion, shall I in that matter be held to blame? If women love foolish courses, am I to be scolded for their misdeeds? Though a woman be bent on a secret love, I cannot nevertheless refrain from singing. A woman may frolic as she will—either honestly or viciously: and as a result of my song, she may do as she will—either well or badly. For there is naught in the wide world so good that it may not do evil if turned to wrong uses. Gold and silver, for instance, are always valuable: yet with them may be bought adultery and other like crimes. Weapons, again, are useful in keeping the peace: yet men with them are unlawfully slain in lands where thieves make use of them. And so it is with my singing: though it be chaste, it may yet be abused and connected with foolish and evil deeds. But must thou, wretched creature, speak evil of love? Of whatever kind it be, all love is pure between man and woman, unless it be stolen: for then it is impure and also corrupt. May the wrath of the Holy Rood descend upon those who thus transgress the laws of nature! Strange is it that they go not mad. Yet, indeed, they do: for mad are they who go to brood without a nest. Woman is but frail of body: and since carnal lust is hard to crush, no wonder is it that it persists. But though fleshly lusts make women err, they are not all completely lost, who trip at the stumbling-block of the flesh. For many a woman, who has gone wrong, rises again out of the slough. Nor are all sins quite the same: they are, indeed, of two different kinds. One is the fruit of carnal lust: the other, of the spiritual nature. For whereas the flesh doth lead men to drunkenness, to sloth and also to wantonness, the spirit goes wrong through malice and anger, and through the joy felt at another's shame. It also gapes after more and more, recking but little of mercy and grace: and, ascending on high through haughtiness, it proudly disdains what is below. Tell me truly, if thou canst, which is the worse, the flesh or the spirit? Thou mayst answer, if thou wilt, that the flesh is the less evil: for many a man is pure of body, who in his heart is of devilish nature. No man must therefore cry out on a woman, upbraiding her for the lusts of the flesh: but such may he blame for wantonness as indulge in the greater sin of pride. Yet if through my singing I cause wife or maid to fall in love, I would defend the cause of the maid—if thou canst grasp my meaning aright. Listen now and I'll tell thee why—the reason complete from beginning to end. If a maid doth love privily, she stumbles and falls according to nature: for though she frolic for a time, she has not gone very far astray. From her sin she may escape lawfully through the rites of the Church, and afterwards have her lover as husband, free from all questioning: and to him she may go in the full light of day, whom before she had received under cover of darkness. A young maid knows nothing about such things: her young blood doth lead her astray, and some foolish fellow entices her to evil with all the tricks at his command. He comes and goes, he commands and entreats: he pays her attention, then neglects her, and thus does he woo her oft and persistently. How can the girl help but go wrong? She never knew what things were: and so she thought to make experiment, and learn for certain of the sport that tames high spirits. And when I see the drawn expression which love gives to the young maid, I cannot refrain, out of sheer pity, from singing to her some song of cheer. Thus do

I teach them by my singing, that love of this kind doth not
last long. For my song is but short-lived: and love merely
alights upon such girls: it soon passes, and the hot passion
quickly subsides. With them I sing for a while: I begin
high and end low: and after a time, I cease completely.
The maid doth know, when I have finished, that love is
just like my singing: for it is but a brief excitement that soon
comes and soon goes. The girl through me doth understand
things: and her unwisdom is to wisdom turned. She sees
clearly from my song, that unbridled love doth not last long.
But this I would that thou shouldst know; hateful to me are
the lapses of wives. And if a married woman will take heed
of me, she will see that I do not sing in the breeding season.
Though marriage bonds may seem to be harsh, yet a wife
should ignore the teaching of fools. And to me it appears
a most astounding thing, how a man could find it in his
heart to wrong another's wife. For it means one of two alternatives; there can be no other possibility. Either, on the
one hand, the husband is doughty; or else he is feeble and of
no account. If he is honoured and courageous, no man, who
is wise, will wish to shame him, especially through his wife:
for he will stand in awe of the good man's anger, and the
payment of that penalty which shall deprive him of future
longings. And even if that terror is not present with him, yet
it is wicked and senseless in a high degree, to injure in this way
a worthy man by alluring his partner away from him. If, on
the other hand, the husband is futile, and feeble as well, in all
his relations, how could there exist any affection whatsoever,
when such a boor makes love to her? How can there be any sort
of love, when he doth lie abed with her? From this thou art
able clearly to see, that in one case there is sorrow, in the other,
disgrace, as a result of stealing another man's wife. For if
the man of courage be her husband, thou canst look out
for trouble when lying by her side. And if the husband be
good for nothing, what pleasure can be derived from the
deed? If thou dost remember who is her bed-fellow, thou
mayst with loathing pay for her favour. I know not how any
man with self-respect may after that make advances to her.

If he but thinks by whom he lay, all his love will forthwith vanish."

The Owl was glad to hear this charge: for she thought that the Nightingale, though arguing well to begin with, had in the end now come to grief. And so she exclaimed, "Now do I see that maidens are thy peculiar care: with them thou dost side, defending them and praising them beyond all reason. The married women to me do turn: to me they make their complaints: for it happens, oft and frequently, that man and wife are at variance. Therefore that man is guilty of sin, who takes delight in loose living: who spends on a woman all that he has, making love to one without claim on him, and leaving at home his lawful wife, with bare walls and an empty house, leaving her, too, but thinly clad and poorly fed, without food and without clothing. And when he comes home to his wife again, she dare not utter a single word: he storms and shouts like a madman—and this is all the kindness he brings. All that she does merely annoys him: all that she says is utterly wrong. And often when she does nothing amiss, her reward is a blow from his fist in her teeth. There is no man living who cannot send wrong his wife by such treatment. Such a one may be so often maltreated, that on occasion she may consult her own pleasure. Lo! God knows! she cannot help it even if she makes a cuckold of him. For it happens, time and again, that the wife is tender and gentle, fair of face and of good figure: and this but makes it the more unjust that he should shower his love on one who is not worth a hair of her head. And men of this sort are very plentiful, so that a wife is unable to behave properly. Nor may any man speak to her: for he thinks that she is about forthwith to betray him, if she but looks at a man or speaks him fair. And so he puts her under lock and key, as a result of which, marriage ties are oft-times broken. For if she is brought to such a pass, she does what before she had not thought of. Accursed be he who talks too much, if such wives proceed to avenge themselves. Concerning this matter, wives to me make their complaint: and sadly enough do they grieve me. My heart, indeed, is wellnigh breaking when I behold their great distress. With them I weep bitter tears, and pray

A.   12

that Christ shall have mercy on them, so that he may quickly succour the wife, and send to her a better husband. And, moreover, I can tell thee this, that to what I have said, thou shalt find no answer, even to save thy skin: for all thy talking shall now be futile. Full many a merchant and many a knight loves and cherishes his wife aright; as does many a husbandman too. And then the goodwife behaves accordingly, rendering him service at bed and at board, with gentle deeds and kindly words, anxiously striving how to please him. The husband goes away amongst other people, bent on supplying the needs of them both: and then is the goodwife sad at heart, because of her husband's anxious journeyings. She sits a-sighing, full of sad longings, and with sore vexation at her heart. Because of her husband she spends days that are troublous and watchful nights: and long to her the time doth appear, for every step seems a mile. While others around her lie wrapt in sleep, I alone am listening outside the house: for well do I know her sad heart, and I sing at night for her benefit. And my song for her sake I turn partly into mourning. Thus of her sorrow I take a share, and that is why she welcomes me. I give to her what help I can, because she tries to do what is right. But thou hast sorely angered me, so that my heart is almost crushed, and with difficulty may I speak. And yet I will continue my charge. Thou sayest that I am hateful to men, that every man is angry with me, and, attacking me with stones and sticks, they beat me and break me all to pieces: and, moreover, when they have me slain, that they hang me high upon their hedges to scare away magpies and also crows, from the seeds that are sown near by. Though this be true, it is also true that I render them service; for them indeed did I shed my blood. I do them good by my death—which for thee is very difficult. For although thou liest dead and shrivelling up, thy death nevertheless serves no purpose. I know not in the least what use thou art: for thou art only a miserable thing. But if the life is shot out of me, yet even so may I do some good. I can be fastened to a small stick in the thick-set of a wood, so that man can attract and capture little birds, and thus obtain through my help roast meat for his food.

But neither alive nor dead hast thou been useful to man. I know not why thou dost rear thy young: neither living nor dead are they any good."

The Nightingale heard what had been said; and hopping on to a twig in blossom, she perched herself higher than before. "Owl!" she said, "now take good heed. I will plead with thee no further, since here thy usual lore doth fail thee. Thou boastest that thou art hated by men, that every creature is angry with thee, and with yells and shouts thou dost bewail that thou art accursed. Thou sayest that boys catch thee and hang thee aloft upon a stick: that they also pluck thee and shake thee to pieces: while some of them make a scarecrow of thee. To me it seems that thou dost forfeit the game: for thou art boasting of thine own shame. Thou dost appear to be making a surrender, for thou boastest of thine own disgrace." When she had thus spoken, the Nightingale alighted in a lovely spot: and after having tuned her voice, she sang so shrilly and so clearly, that both far and near her notes were heard. And therefore presently to her came thrush and throstle and woodpecker, and other birds as well, both great and small. And since they assumed that she had beaten the Owl, they also cried aloud and sang many a tune. In just the same way does one cry shame on the gambler who plays at dice and loses the game.

The Owl, on hearing this, forthwith exclaimed: "Hast thou indeed summoned an army? And dost thou, wretched creature, wish to fight with me? Nay! nay! thou art not strong enough for that. What are they crying who have thus come hither? Methinks thou art bringing an army against me. But ye shall all learn, before ye fly hence, what is the strength of my particular tribe. For all with hooked bills and claws sharp and crooked, all belong to my own race, and would come if I but asked them. The cock himself, that valiant warrior, he must naturally side with me; for we both have voices clear, and both sit under the clouds at night. If I but raise the hue-and-cry against you, I shall bring up so mighty a host that your pride shall have a fall. I care not a straw for you all! Nor shall there be left by evening time one wretched feather amongst you all. But it was agreed by us both when we came hither, that we should abide by that decision, which lawful judgment would give to us. Dost thou then wish to break this agreement? Judgment, I presume, seems too hard for thee: ánd since thou durst not await the verdict, thou dost wish, wretched creature, now to fight and quarrel! Yet I would give you all this piece of advice, before raising the hue-and-cry against you, that you should have done with your fighting, and fly away quickly and at once. For by these very talons of mine, if ye wait here for my ruthless horde, ye shall sing another tune and curse all fighting. For there is no one amongst you so brave as to endure the sight of my face." Thus with all boldness spake the Owl: for although she would not have gone so quickly after her host, yet she wished to reply in such terms as these. For many a man, feeble enough with spear and shield, yet causes his foe in the field to sweat out of sheer cowardice; so brave are his words, his countenance so dread. The Wren, however, because of her skill in singing, came in the morning to the help of the Nightingale: for though her voice was but small, she had a throat that was good and shrill, and her songs were a source of pleasure to many. Moreover she was reckoned a bird most wise, for although she had not been bred in the woodland, she was brought up among the race of men, and from them she derived her wisdom. She could speak wherever she pleased—before the king if she wished. "Listen!" she said, "and let me speak! What! do you wish to break the peace, and to put the king to this disgrace? But he is neither dead nor infirm; and to both of you shall come trouble and shame, if in his land ye commit a breach of the peace. Therefore, have done and come to an agreement! Proceed at once to hear judgment; and let the verdict end this plea, as was arranged at an earlier stage."

"I am quite willing," said the Nightingale, "but not, Mistress Wren, because of thine argument, but on account of my own law-abiding nature. I do not want lawlessness to win in the end: nor am I afraid of any judgment. I have promised—true it is—that Master Nicholas, with his wisdom, should be our judge: and I still hope that he will act. But where should we be able to find him?" The Wren replied, as she sat in her lime-tree, "What! did ye not know of his abode? He dwells at Portisham, a place in Dorset, in an outlet near the sea: and there he delivers many lawful judgments, he composes and writes many wise sayings, and indeed through his sayings and also his writings things are the better even in Scotland! To seek him out is an easy task, for he has but one dwelling—much to the shame of the bishops, and of all who have heard of him and his work. Why will they not arrange in their own interests, that he should frequently be with them, teaching them out of his store of wisdom? Why not give him livings in several places, so that he might often be at their service?"

"Certainly," quoth the Owl, "that is quite true. These great men are much to blame, in passing over this excellent man—so well instructed in many things—and in bestowing livings indiscriminately, while him they hold in but light esteem. Towards their own kin they are more generous: they grant livings to little children. Thus their good sense shall convict them of error, in that Master Nicholas still suffers neglect. But let us however go now to him, for with him our judgment is ready."

"Yes, let us do so," said the Nightingale, "but who is there to present our statement, and to speak before this judge of ours?"

"On that point," replied the Owl, "I can set your mind at ease: for I can repeat every word from beginning to end: and if perchance I seem to go wrong, do thou protest and pull me up." And having thus spoken, they went on their way without any supporters, until they arrived at Portisham. But as to how they fared in the matter of judgment, I can tell you nothing: this is the end of this particular story.

BIBLIOGRAPHY

I. EDITIONS AND SELECTIONS

(1) Stevenson, J. *The Owl and the Nightingale* with Intro. and Glossary: for the Roxburghe Club. London, 1838. (Text based on C. with some J. readings.)

(2) Wright, T. *The Owl and the Nightingale*: for the Percy Soc. London, 1843. (The C. text with short Intro.)

(3) Mätzner, E. *Altenglische Sprachproben*, I. 40 ff. Berlin, 1867. (ll. 701—1040 with notes.)

(4) Stratmann, F. H. *The Owl and the Nightingale*: privately printed. Krefeld, 1868. (Critical text. MSS. readings in footnotes: normalised spelling: brief but useful notes.)

(5) Morris and Skeat, *Specimens of Early English*, I. 171 ff. Oxford, 1882. (The selection includes ll. 1—94, 139—232, 253—282, 303—352, 391—446, 549—555, 597—624, 659—668, 707—750, 837—855, 905—920, 1635—1682, 1689—1794.)

(6) Wells, J. E. *The Owl and the Nightingale* (Belles Lettres Series). Boston and London, 1907, revised 1909. (Texts of both MSS. printed: with full critical apparatus: Intro. 62 pp. Notes and Glossary. An edition specially valuable for its accurate reproduction of MSS.)

(7) Gadow, W. *Das Mittelenglische Streitgedicht Eule u. Nachtigall*, Berlin dissertation, 1907: full treatment *Palaestra*, LXV. 1909. (Critical text with suggestive Intro., useful Notes and Glossary.)

(8) Manly, *English Poetry*. Boston, 1907.

(9) Cook, A. S. *Literary Middle English Reader*, pp. 321 ff. Boston and London, 1915. (The selection includes ll. 1—94, 101—285, 287—348.)

(10) Brandl u. Zippel, *Mittelenglische Sprach- und Literaturproben*, pp. 124—7. Berlin, 1917. (ll. 1043—1290 based on C. with variant readings from J.).

(11) Hall, Joseph. *Selections from Early Middle English* 1130—1250. Oxford, 1920. Vol. I. Text (2 MSS.), ll. 1—94, 139—232, 253—282, 303—353, 391—446, 707—735, 1710—1795. Vol. II. Intro., Phonology, Notes, pp. 553—579.

II. LITERARY CRITICISM

(a) HISTORICAL BACKGROUND.

(1) Adams, G. B. *Civilisation during the Middle Ages*. Revised ed. London, 1915.

(2) Anglade, J. *Les Troubadours*. Paris, 1908. New ed. 1919.

(3) Bateson, M. *Mediæval England*. London, 1903.

(4) *Cambridge History of English Literature*, vol. I. Cambridge, 1907.

(5) Chambers and Sidgwick. *Early English Lyrics*. London, 1921.

(6) Coulton, G. G. *A Medieval Garner*. London, 1910.

(7) Coulton, G. G. *Social Life in Britain from the Conquest to the Reformation*. Cambridge, 1918. Revised ed. 1921.

(8) Emerton, E. *Introduction to the Study of the Middle Ages*. Boston, 1888.

(9) Faral, E. *Les Jongleurs en France au moyen âge*. Paris, 1910.

(10) Gasquet, F. A. *Parish Life in Mediæval England*. London, 1907.

(11) Jeanroy, A. *Les origines de la poésie lyrique en France au moyen âge*. Paris, 1904.

(12) Lavisse et Rambaud. *Histoire Générale*, II. (L'Europe féodale. Les Croisades 1095—1270). Paris, 1893. 6th ed. 1912.

(13) Luchaire, A. *Histoire de France*, II. 2 (987—1137), III. 1 (1137—1226). Paris, 1901.

(14) *Mediæval Contributions to Modern Civilisation*. Ed. by Hearnshaw, J. C. London, 1921.

(15) Moore, George. *Héloïse and Abelard*. 2 vols. London, 1921.

(16) Paris, Gaston. *L'Esquisse historique de la litt. franç. au moyen âge*. Paris, 1907.

(17) Patterson, F. A. *The Middle English Penitential Lyric*. New York, 1911.

(18) Pollock and Maitland. *History of English Law*. 2 vols. Cambridge, 1895.

(19) Schofield, W. H. *English Literature from the Norman Conquest to Chaucer*. London, 1906.

(20) Stubbs, W. *Seventeen Lectures on the study of Med. and Mod. History*. (Ch. VI deals with learning and literature at the Court of Henry II.) Oxford, 1878.

(21) Taylor, H. O. *The Classical Heritage of the Middle Ages*. New York, 1901.

(22) Taylor, H. O. *The Medieval Mind*. 2 vols. London, 1911.

(*b*) Sources. (Fable Literature, etc.)

(1) Du Méril, E. *Poésies inédites du moyen âge, précédées d'une histoire de la fable ésopique*. Paris, 1854.

(2) Harry, P. *Comparative Study of Aesopic fable in Bozon* (Univ. Press, Cincinnati). Diss. 1903.

(3) Hensel, W. *Die Vögel in der prov. u. nordfranz. Lyrik in des Mittelalters*. (*Romanischen Forschungen*, Bd. XXVI.) Diss. Königsberg, 1908.

(4) Hervieux, L. *Les Fabulistes latins depuis le siècle d'Auguste jusqu'à la fin du moyen âge*. 5 vols. 1st ed. I—II Paris, 1884. 2nd ed. I—V Paris, 1893—8. (Contains the fable literature of Anglo-Latin *Romulus*, Odo of Cheriton, John of Sheppey, etc.)

(5) Jacobs, J. *Fables of Aesop*. 2 vols. London, 1889.

(6) Little, A. G. *Liber Exemplorum ad Usum Praedicantium*. (Soc. for Franciscan Studies.) Aberdeen, 1908.

(7) Mosher, J. A. *The Exemplum in the Early Religious and Didactic Literature of England.* New York, 1911.

(8) Neckam, A. *De Naturis Rerum,* ed. T. Wright (Rolls Series). London, 1863.

(9) Oesterley, H. *Romulus.* Berlin, 1870.

(10) Toulmin Smith, L. et Meyer, P. *Les Contes moralisés de Nicole Bozon* (Soc. des Anc. Textes françaises). Paris, 1889.

(11) Warnke, K. *Die Lais der Marie de France.* Halle, 1885. 2nd ed. 1900.

(12) Warnke, K. *Die Fabeln der Marie de France* (*Bibliotheca Normannica* herausg. Suchier). Halle, 1898.

(13) Warnke, K. *Die Quellen des Esope der Marie de France* (*Forschungen zur Rom. Philol.* Festgabe für H. Suchier). Halle, 1900.

(14) Wells, J. E. *Manual of the Writings in Middle English* (Yale Univ. Press). New Haven, 1916. 1st Supp. 1919. (Fables etc. pp. 180 ff. Bibliog. p. 790.)

(15) Wright, T. *Selection of Latin Stories* (Percy Soc. VIII.). London, 1842.

(c) FORM. (Debate, etc.)

(1) Alcuin. *Conflictus ueris et hiemis* (A. Riese, *Anthologia latina,* II. 687).

(2) *Altercatio Ganymedis et Helenae* (Hauréau, *Notices et Extraits,* t. 29 (2) 274).

(3) Calpurnius. *Eclogues* (Baehrens, *Poetae lat. minores,* XX. t. III. 65 ff.).

(4) Chardry. *Le Petit Plet,* ed. J. Koch. Heilbronn, 1879.

(5) Cousin, V. *Oeuvres inédits d'Abélard.* Paris, 1836. (Containing Abelard's *Sic et Non* with Intro.)

(6) *De Phillide et Flora* (Hauréau, *Notices et Extraits,* 32 (1) 259 ff.).

(7) *Dispute between the Violet and the Rose* (Herrig, *Archiv,* XC. 152 ff.).

(8) Faral, E. *Les débats du clerc et du chevalier* (*Romania,* XLI. 472 ff.: of great bibliographical value).

(9) Greif. *Zeitsch. für vergleichende Literaturgeschichte.* N.F. I. 289—95. (An account of the diffusion of the *Conflictus* in various literatures.)

(10) Gröber. *Grundriss der Romanischen Philologie.* Strassburg, 1888—1902, new issue 1897—1906. 2nd ed. 1904— (see *Conflictus* etc.).

(11) Hanford, J. H. *Classical eglogue and the mediaeval debate* (*Romanic Review,* II. 1911, pp. 1 and 229). (Articles 2, 3 and 4 find the origin of the medieval debate in the eclogue of classical poetry.)

(12) Jeanroy, A. *La Tenson provençale* (*Annales du Midi,* II. 281 ff., 444 ff.).

(13) Knobloch, H. *Die Streitgedichte im Provenz. u. Altfranz.* Diss. Breslau, 1886.

(14) Manitius, M. *Geschichte der lat. Lit. des Mittelalters,* I. 574 ff. (for the influence of Theodulus). München, 1911.

(15) Manitius, M. Article in *Philologus*, t. LVI. (1897), 540 ff. (dealing with the influence of Calpurnius and Nemesianus in the Middle Ages).

(16) Nemesianus. *Eclogues* (Baehrens, *Poetae lat. minores*, XXXIII. t. III. 176).

(17) Sedulius Scotus. *De rosae liliique certamine* (*Monumenta Germaniae historica. Poetae lat. aevi Carolingi*, t. III. 230).

(18) Selbach, L. *Das Streitgedicht in der altprovenz. Lyrik, und sein Verhältniss zu ähnlichen Dichtungen anderer Litteraturen.* Marburg, 1886.

(19) Theodulus. *Eclogues*, ed. Osternacher. 1902.

(20) Vespa. *Judicium coci et pistoris judice Vulcano* (A. Riese, *Anthol. lat.* 199 (I. pp. 140—3)).

(21) Wattenbach, W. *Ganymed und Helena* (*Zeitsch. für das deutsches Alterthum* (N.F. VI.) XVIII. 127).

(22) Wright, T. *Latin Poems attributed to W. Mapes.* Camden Soc. 1841. (Containing *Goliae Dialogus inter Aquam et Vinum, Disputatio inter Cor et Oculum, Dialogus inter Corpus et Animam, De Clarevallensibus et Cluniacensibus, De Mauro et Zoilo, De Presbytero et Logico*, etc.)

(*d*) GENERAL. (Author, Date, Literary Appreciation.)

(1) *Cambridge History of English Literature*, I. 238—42. Cambridge, 1907.

(2) Courthope, W. J. *History of English Poetry*, I. 131—6. London, 1895.

(3) Hinckley, H. B. *The Date of the Owl and the Nightingale* (*Mod. Phil.* XVII. No. 5), 63 ff. 1919. (An attempt to date the poem 1177 or 1178 or not later than 1189.)

(4) Ker, W. P. *English Literature Medieval* (Home Univ. Library), pp. 180—3. London, 1912.

(5) Morris, R. *An O.E. Miscellany* (E.E.T.S. 49), Intro. x—xi. 1872.

(6) Schofield, W. H. *English Literature from the Norman Conquest to Chaucer*, pp. 427—30. London, 1906.

(7) Ten Brink. *Early English Literature*, trans. by H. M. Kennedy (pp. 214—8). London, 1883.

(8) Warton, T. *History of English Poetry*, ed. W. C. Hazlitt. 3 vols. London, 1871.

(9) Wells, J. E. *The Owl and the Nightingale* (Belles Lettres Series), Intro. xxix—lii. London, 1907. Revised ed. 1909.

(10) Wells, J. E. *Manual of Writings in M. E.* pp. 418—21. (Yale Univ. Press.) 1916.

(11) Weston, J. *The Chief Middle English Poets.* Boston, 1914. (A modern rendering of the poem, pp. 310 ff.)

III. LANGUAGE AND METRE

(1) Atkins, J. W. H. *Notes on the Owl and the Nightingale* (*Athenæum*, 20 Jan. 1906, p. 83).

(2) Börsch, J. *Ueber Metrik und Poetik der ...... O. and N.* Münster Diss. 1883.

(3) Breier, W. *Review of Gadow's edition* (*E. St.* XLII. 408—21).

(4) Breier, W. *Eule und Nachtigall*, Hannover Diss. Halle, 1910 (full print in *Studien zur Englischen Philologie*, 39).

(5) Breier, W. *Syn. und Anal. des Konjunktivs in Ule und Nachtigall* (*Studien zur Eng. Phil.* 50, 251).

(6) Brett, C. *Notes on Passages of Old and Middle English* (*M.L.R.* XIV. pp. 8—9).

(7) Diehn, O. *Die Pronomina in Frühme* (*Kieler St.* I. 26). (Attempt to explain variation of spelling between *e, o, eo.*)

(8) Ebich. *Zur Syntax des Verbums etc.* Leipzig Diss. 1905.

(9) Egge, A. E. *Notes on Specimens of Early English* (*M. L. Notes*, 1887, I. 12—14).

(10) Hall, Joseph. *Selections from Early Middle English* 1130—1250. Oxford, 1920. (Vol. II. pp. 554—66.)

(11) Kenyon, J. S. *Notes on the Owl and the Nightingale* (*J.E.G.P.* XII. 572: a valuable and suggestive contribution to the subject).

(12) Koch, J. *Review of Wells' and Gadow's editions* (*Ang. Beib.* XXI. 227—40).

(13) Kock, E. A. *Interpretations and Emendations of Early English Texts* (*Ang.* XXV. 323—5), consisting of notes on Morris and Skeat's *Specimens of E.E.*

(14) Napier, A. S. *Old English Glosses*, Intro. Oxford, 1900. (For common scribal errors, etc.)

(15) Noelle, H. *Ueber die Sprache des ...... Ule und Nachtigall* (Diss.). Göttingen, 1870.

(16) Saintsbury, G. *History of English Prosody*, I. 56. London, 1906.

(17) Sherman, L. A. *Grammatical Analysis of the Owl and the Nightingale* (*Trans. of Amer. Phil. Assoc.* 1875, pp. 69—88).

(18) Schipper, J. *Englische Metrik*, § 121. Bonn, 1881—.

(19) Schipper, J. *A History of English Versification.* Oxford, 1910.

(20) Stratmann, F. H. *Emendations and Additions to the Owl and the Nightingale* (*E. St.* I. 212—4). (Corrections of the text of 1868.) 1877.

(21) Wells, J. E. *Accidence in the Owl and the Nightingale* (*Ang.* XXXIII. 252 ff.).

(22) Wells, J. E. *Accent-Markings in MS. Jesus* (*M. L. Notes*, XXV. 108 ff.).

(23) Wells, J. E. *Spelling in the Owl and the Nightingale* (*M. L. Notes*, XXVI. 139 ff.).

APPENDIX I

NOTES ON THE LANGUAGE OF THE C. TEXT [1]

(a) DIALECT. ORTHOGRAPHY.

(i) Both texts have come down in the South-Western dialect (see Morsbach § 9, 2 a), though, as Professor Craigie points out, traces of Kentish forms are found, notably in rhymes which imply the original existence of e (= O.E. y) (cf. l. 1725 where e is found); also in ll. 65, 121, 273, 849, 863, where a S.W. u would seem to have been substituted for an original Kentish e [2]: and in ll. 370, 1227, 1406, where a S.W. a has apparently been written for an original Kentish e: cf. also note l. 1030.

(ii) In many places scribal errors have crept into the text [3], and the spelling has frequently been modified by Anglo-French scribes [4], as for instance in the following cases:

    (a) Misuse of initial h. Ex. hule 4, hartu 1177, hunke 1733.

    (β) Use of t for þ. Ex. bigredet 67, wit 131, hatiet 230.

    (γ) Use of s for sch. Ex. sewi 151, fleses 895.

    (δ) Use of w for hw. Ex. wile 199, aiware 216, wei 1009.

    (ε) Use of o for eo. See Intro. § 3, p. xxx.

    (ζ) Omission of the medial of three consonants [5]. Ex. sprinþ 1042, wrechede 1251, wurschipe 1288, ȝunling 1433, þunþ 1592.

More regular is the use of qu (for O.E. cw), ex. quaþ 117, queme 209, quide 685, and the use of ch for O.E. c (pal.), ex. child 1315, cheose 1343. The O.Fr. c [s] moreover appears in merci 1092, milce 1404, certes 1769.

(b) VOCABULARY.

There are comparatively few foreign elements in the language of the poem. They include some 36 or so words of French origin, many of which are legal terms, and while they all represent O.Fr. forms prior to 1250, many of them embody Norman or Picardian characteristics: ex. acorde, afoled, bataile, beste, certes, castel, cundut, cwesse, dahet, disputinge, fals, faucun, flores, foliot, gelus, granti, graunti, grucching, ipeint, kanunes, maister, meoster, merci, pes, pie, plaid, poure, purs, rente, siueþ, sot, spuse, spusbruche, stable, schirme, worre. There are also a certain number of Scandinavian forms, ex. skenten, skil, skere, trusten, grom, ille, loȝe, mishap, some of which like euening and tiþinge may have originally been native words modified by analogy with their Scand.

---

[1] For a systematic treatment of the language, see Bibliography III under Breier, Wells, Hall, etc.

[2] For the bearing of this fact upon the original dialect of the poem and upon the question of authorship see Intro. § 5, p. xli.

[3] See Intro. § 5, p. xxxix.

[4] See Skeat, Trans. of London Phil. Soc. 1897, pp. 402 ff.

[5] See Napier, O.E. Glosses, p. xxix; also Brunot, Histoire de la langue française, I. 175 B.

equivalents. For the rest, the vocabulary consists of native words, of a more colloquial character, however, than the O.E. poetic diction; and many of them survive only in modern dialect, e.g. Dorsets *moor*=root of tree (cf. *more* 1328), *speal*=spare (cf. *spale* 258), *vang*=receive (cf. *afonge* 1196): Hereford *polting lug* (cf. *pulten* 873, *lugg* 1609): Somerset *quat* (cf. *ouerquatie* 353): Berks *shewell* (cf. *sheueles* 1128). Compounds frequently occur as well as new formations like *bichirmen, towepen, fairehede, galegale, spusbruche,* while of the obsolescent type of compound[1], instances are found in *utschute* and *utlete,* the former of which has since disappeared, while the latter survives.

(c) PHONOLOGY.

(i) The shortening of O.E. long vowels before consonant groups is of frequent occurrence, and is illustrated by the following rhymes:

bridde (O.E. *i*)	: *chidde* (O.E. *ī*)	111—2
þriste (O.E. *ī*)	: *liste* (O.E. *i*)	171—2
cheste (O.E. *ēa*)	: *wreste* (O.E. *ǣ*)	177—8
lest (O.E. *ǣ*)	: *rest* (O.E. *e*)	1451—2
ofte (O.E. *o*)	: *softe* (O.E. *ō*)	1545—6

(ii) Traces of the lengthening of O.E. *ă, ě, ŏ,* in open syllables appear only in the following cases:

ȝ*are* (O.E. *ea*)	: *aiware* (O.E. *ā*)	215—6
fare (O.E. *a*)	: *þare* (O.E. *ā*)	995—6
unsode (O.E. *o*)	: *tobrode* (O.E. *ō*)	1007—8
nacoleþ (O.E. *ō*)	: *soleþ* (O.E. *o*)	1275—6

As a rule, however, such forms in O.E. *ă, ě, ŏ* are self-rhyming: and it would therefore seem that the lengthening process was not as yet complete.

(iii) *Short Vowels.* Isolated instances of O.E. *a* > *ai* before pal. *s*(*c*)*h* occur in *aishest* 473, *aisheist* 995.

O.E. *e* is occasionally diphthongised to *ei* before O.E. *-ngþ, -ngd* with loss of *g*[2], ex. *meind* 131, *meinþ* 945: it also shows a tendency to become *a* before *r* in rhyming positions, ex. *bisemar* 148, *cartare* 1186; cf. also *harde : erde* 459—60.

O.E. *i* > *e* in *welcume* 1600, by analogy with *wel*: cf. however *wolcumeþ* 440.

The usual form for O.E. *u* is *u*, ex. *fuȝeles* 343, *sum* 540, *luue* 1510. Occasionally, however, it appears as *o*, ex. *tonge* 37, *wode* 444, *wone* 475, *come* 611, *bote* 884 (cf. Morsbach § 121, *a* 1).

(iv) *Long Vowels and Diphthongs.* O.E. *ā* appears as *a* or *o* [ǫ], ex. *lauerd* 959, *wat* 1179, *gan* 1510, *ore* 1083, *gost* 1111, *one* 1760. When preceded by cons. and *w* this open *o* [ǫ] has not as yet become closed *o* [ọ], cf. the rhymes *so : mo* 237—8, *go : so* 297—8, *alswo : wo* (see however Hempl, *Journal of Germ. Phil.* 1897, vol. I. pp. 14 ff.).

---

[1] See Bradley, *Making of English,* p. 124.
[2] Cf. Napier, *O.E. Glosses,* p. xxvii, and Brunot, *Histoire de la langue française,* I. 176, 2.

It would seem that O.E. *ǣ* had not as yet become identified with O.E. *ēa* as M.E. *ē* (open), for while both forms are represented by *e*, there seems to have been some difference in their values. In any case, throughout the poem these forms are self-rhyming; *ē* (O.E. *ǣ*) is nowhere found in rhyme with *ē* (O.E. *ēa*).

The same holds true of *e* (O.E. *ēo*) and *e* (O.E. *ē*). The C. text has two instances of *ē* : *ēo* rhymes, viz.:

dest (O.E. *ē*)	: *prost* (O.E. *ēo*)	321—2
dest (O.E. *ē*)	: *brost* (O.E. *ēo*)	977—8

cf. also ll. 1179—80. Less clear are

wede (O.E. *ēo*)	: *neode* (O.E. *ēo*)	937—8
þeode (O.E. *ēo*)	: *nede* (O.E. *ēo* or *īe*)	1583—4

As a rule however O.E. *ēo*, *ē* are self-rhyming in this poem and it would appear that they had not as yet become identified in M.E. *ē* [*ę̄*].

M.E. *ē* (O.E. *ǣ* or *ēa*) is occasionally diphthongised to *ei* before a nasal, ex. *dreim* 21, *cleine* 302.

O.E. *ū* is regularly denoted by *u*, except in *houle* 1682 (see Morsbach § 121, *a* 1).

(v) *Consonants.* O.E. medial *g* in a guttural environment retains its value as a voiced guttural spirant [γ]. It occurs after guttural vowels, after *r* and *l*, and is generally written as ჳ. Ex. *idraჳe* 586, *hoჳe* 701, *iloჳe* 847, *iborჳe* 883, *folჳeþ* 307. This value [γ] is shown by the scribal variants *ahene* 1542, *muhe* 1581, *seorhe* 1599, *fuheles* 1660.

There was however a growing tendency for this spirant to become vocalised to *w*, and this is illustrated by the forms *bowe* 125, *todrowe* 126, *þrowe* 478, *sorwe* 884. At a later date the change had become general, and the scribe of J., for instance, uses *w* throughout.

The pal. and gutt. values of O.E. *h* (medial and final) were also preserved at this date, though except in a single instance (viz. *eiჳte* 1153) no indication of any difference of value is found in the orthography of C. In J., on the other hand, the scribe regularly distinguishes the sound-values, by an insertion of *i* (*y*) before pal. *h*, and of *u* before gutt. *h*. Ex. *ayhte* 1153, *auhte* 385, *houhful* 537, *neyh* 1220.

(d) ACCIDENCE.

(i) *Substantives.*

(a) As in O.E., grammatical gender is still maintained. This is shown, sometimes by the preceding def. adj., ex. *þes dai* (m.) 259, *þeos hule* (f.) 1667, *þat game* (n.) 1649: sometimes by the adj. inflexion, ex. *nanne wei* 1238, *þire side* 429, *anne craft* 794: sometimes by the pronouns used in connection with such words as *dreim* (m.) 21, *stefne* (f.) 317, *murჳþe* (f.) 341, *lilie* (f.) 439, *nest* (n.) 649, *wit* (n.) 689, *wisdome* (m.) 1299. At the same time, traces of a tendency in the direction of natural gender exist, notably in the occasional use of the neu. pro. in connection with words like *murჳþe* (O.E. fem.) 355 (see above), *lepe* (O.E. mas.) 359, *songe* (O.E. mas.) 343, *harm* (O.E. mas.) 1235, and of the fem. pro. with words like *wif* (O.E. neu.), *maide* (O.E. neu.) 1341, 1343.

(β) As a rule, final inorganic -e, such as appears in modern forms like "life" and "sore," is not found in the nom. forms of this poem: cf. *lif* 1127, *sor* 1234, *hom* 457, *mus* 87, *ax* 658, *win* 1011, *liim* 1056. The forms in which it is found admit of more than one explanation. In some cases this final *e* is due to L.O.E. forms, e.g. *holinesse* (L.O.E. *-nysse*) 900, *were* (L.O.E. *were*) 1341: elsewhere it would seem due to analogy with oblique cases in -e, e.g. *hiȝte* 272, *tide* 489, *muþe* 1757, *hwile* 1591, *mile* 1592: while in other places it is added for metrical reasons, either to obtain an extra syllable or a proper rhyming form, e.g. *rorde* 311, *bote* 688, *rode* 1382. On the whole however it may safely be inferred that inorganic final -e in such words had not become established at this date.

(γ) The O.E. sb. inflexions are in general retained, though most of them (O.E. -a, -u, -an, -on, -um) have been levelled to -e. In particular, traces of all the O.E. plurals are found, e.g. (1) unchanged neu. acc. pl. of O.E. *o*-stems, [*þing*] 771, *dor* 1012, *bon* 1120 (in *wepne* (O.E. *wǣpnu*) 1369, a *u*-plural is seen), (2) nom. pl. of O.E. *i*-stems, *sunne* 1395, *wiȝte* 87, (3) mutated pl. *men* 1246, *teþ* 1538, (4) dat. pl. of O.E. *-os*, *-es* stems, *childre* 1453, *eyre* 106, (5) n. pl. of the weak declension, *eȝene* 75, *earen* 338, g. pl. *deoulene* 932.

On the other hand, there is evidence of some confusion of the older declensions and this also may be best illustrated from the pl. forms. In some instances the O.E. long-stemmed neu. pl. (unchanged in O.E.) takes the -s plural, ex. *wordes* 178, *sedes* 1129, *cornes* 1202, *huses* 1203, *wiues* 1562. The form *schipes* 1205 is notable as compared with O.E. *scipu*: while sometimes the -s inflexion is used in the d. pl., e.g. *of craftes mine* 711, *mid teres* 865. Then again, with *unwiȝtis* 218, *niȝtes* 523, should be compared the etymologically correct plu. *wiȝte* 87: while *lauedies* 1338 shows the extension of the *s*-plural to a fem. sb. of the weak declension. In *tron* 615, *children* 1115, however the weak pl. inflexion has been added to forms corresponding to O.E. *trēowe, cildru.*

(ii) *Adjectives.*

The O.E. adj. inflexional system is largely maintained though in a weakened form. Most of the adj. endings are found, e.g. fem. d. sg. *sumere* 1, *þire* 914; m. acc. sg. *anne* 799, *godne* 812, *fulne* 1196; n. pl. *brode* 75, g. pl. *beire* 1584: but some amount of irregularity occurs in the case of adjectives removed from their nouns, such words being not always inflected in agreement with the nouns on which they depend, e.g. *lodlich ꝥ fule* (fem. acc. sg.) 32, *sharp ꝥ longe* (acc. pl.) 270, *stif ꝥ stronge* (mas. acc. sg.) 269.

Then again, the wk. form of the adj. is used as in O.E., cf. *þat grete heued* 119, *þe ille* 421, also ll. 943, 1331, 1434; two endings (-ere, -ure) are employed in comparative forms, ex. *gladdere* 737, *uairur* 152: while *more* and *mo* are distinguished as in O.E. (see Gloss.).

An important development, however, becomes visible in the adoption of new def. and indef. articles (*þe* and *a*). In the first place the indeclinable *þe* is already regularly found for O.E. *se* as n. sg. of def. article:

though in the oblique cases the older inflected forms remain, e.g. *þare* 28, *þane* 250, *þen* 1743, cf. also ll. 1072, 1213, 1329. Moreover a new indef. art. appears in the forms *one, an, a*, the form *one* being used in accented positions, *an* and *a* in unaccented positions (cf. *an, one* 4). This indef. art. is frequently inflected (cf. *ane* 1021, *ore* 1750, *one* 1760) : but already indeclinable *a* is commonly found (cf. ll. 45, 94, 1316, 1325), and together with *þe* it points to the decay of adj. inflexions and to the early loss of grammatical gender.

(iii) *Pronouns.*

(*a*) The personal pronouns correspond throughout very closely to those of O.E. Particularly is this the case with pronouns of the 1st pers. where traces of O.E. dual forms are preserved, e.g. *unker* 151, *hunke* 1733, *unker* (poss. adj.) 1782. On the other hand there are signs that the old distinction between the dual and the plural was being lost, cf. *we* (= we two) 177, *ure eiþer* 185 (where *ure* = of us two), and again *us* 1747, where the dual form might have been expected. In connection with pronouns of the 2nd pers. no traces of the dual are found. The personal pronouns (3rd pers.) represent the O.E. forms almost intact, specially notable being *hine* 236, *ho, heo* (she) 216, 1720, *hi* (fem. acc.) 29, *hi, heo* (they) 10, 1791, *hire, heore* (their) 1520, 1775, *hom, heom* (them) 285, 1764. It is significant however that acc. forms, as compared with those in the dat., occur but seldom, owing to the frequency with which O.E. verbs governed the dat. (cf. *him queme* 209, *lust him* 212, also ll. 397, 648, 735, 850, 915, 1017, 1541). In *hire biþoȝte* 704, the dat. form has already supplanted the acc. (cf. l. 471), and this tendency, which was to become general at a later date, led ultimately to the complete loss of the acc. forms.

(*β*) In connection with the relative pronouns certain changes become visible. In place of O.E. *þe*, the rel. pro. commonly used is *þat* (indecl.), cf. ll. 62, 78, 95, 100: though, as in the case of the older form, it is never used with a prep. (cf. l. 1509). A few traces of the older relative *þe*, it is true, remain (cf. ll. 800, 1383, 1447); but more generally it is found combined as in O.E., with a dem. pro. as *þane þe* (= him who) 1346, *þeo þe* (= those who) 1675. Together with *þeo þe* 1675 is found *þeo þat* 1671, pointing to the tendency of the new rel. to take the place of *þe* even in this compound form.

(*γ*) The O.E. interrogative pronouns still retain their earlier function and occur only in direct and indirect questions, cf. *wo* 196, *hwo* 1195, *wat, hwat*, 563, 1433. The indef. pro. *me* (= one) is frequently found, cf. ll. 32, 340 : but no traces of such forms as O.E. *swa-hwa-swa* (whoever) are found.

(iv) *Verbs.*

The verbal forms preserve, for the most part, the O.E. inflexions in weakened form.

(*a*) The infin. and the gerund end in *-en, -e*, for by this time the O.E. gerund in *-anne* had become identified with the infin.: ex. *speten* 39, *deme* 188, *to habbe* 281, *to ihere* 312. Infinitives of the weak conjugation

(2nd Class) however end in *-i*, ex. *liki* 342, *lorni* 642. No traces exist as yet of the later formations *seie(n)*, *lie(n)*, *leie(n)*, etc., the regular forms being *segge* (O.E. *secgan*), *ligge* (O.E. *licgan*), *legge* (O.E. *lecgan*). Signs of O.Fr. influence are seen where the infin. or ger. is preceded by *for*: ex. *for lutli* 540, *for to leten* 1018 (cf. O.Fr. *por a avoir*).

(β) In the pres. indic., syncopated forms, characteristic of W.S. (see Sievers § 358, 2) are frequently found in the 3rd sg., e.g. *cuþ* 138, *fiȝt* 176, *spet* 763, *bit* 1352, *itit* 1521, *sit* 1587: but forms in *-eþ* also occur, cf. *rideþ* 494.

In verbs with stems ending in *-d* the *dþ* of the pr. 3rd sg. sometimes appears as *d*, e.g. *beod* 1437, *understond* 1463, *wend* 1464, *chid* 1533, *hald* 1576, *gred* 1665. For similar forms in O.E. see Sievers § 359, *a* 2.

As in O.E., the root vowel of the pr. indic. sg. (2nd and 3rd pers.) often bears traces of earlier umlaut, e.g. *dest* 49, *liest* 367, *geþ* 528, *deþ* 564, *tihþ* 1435: but unumlauted forms which had also appeared in L.W.S. (see Sievers § 371, *a* 2, 3) are still more frequently found, e.g. *halt* 32, *falt* 37, *doþ* 490, *forlost* 519, *goþ* 522, *stont* 618, *frost* 620.

The ending of the pr. pl. is invariably *-eþ*, e.g. *singeþ* 483, *wepeþ* 885, except in forms like *lete we* 177, *fo we* 179, *ute we* 1779, *do we* 1781, where the O.E. adhortative construction occurs. Cf. however *send* (1520), see note.

(γ) In the pret. forms of the strong verbs the O.E. gradation series are well preserved:

Class	Infin.	Pr. 3 sg.	Pt. sg.	Pt. pl.	P. Part.
I		writ 1756	wrot 235		
II	forleose 1344	forlost 949	forles 1100		forlore 1391
III	singe 39	singþ 721	song 20	sungen 1663	
IV	cumen 1131	cumeþ 302	com 132	come 1671	icumen 130
V	sitte 282	sit 1587	sat 15	seten 1102	
VI	fare 658	fareþ 1437	for 1474		ifare 400
Red.	halde 1369	halt 356	hold 144	holde 12	iholde 1723

Also notable in this connection are the following forms of the indic. pret. 2 sg. in which the O.E. root vowel is preserved: *stele* 103, *bede* 550, *speke* 554, *sunge* 1049, *come* 1058, *stode* 1632.

In the p.p. forms *forworþe* 548, *iworþe* 660, a levelling of O.E. *d* to *þ* is seen (cf. note l. 548).

Instances of O.E. strong verbs becoming weak are found in *ibanned* 1668, and *sihte* 1291. The weak forms *ofdradde* 1143, and *ofdrad* 1150, are to be found in O.E. (see Sievers § 395, *a* 3): while in *lette* 952, *lete* 1018, 1445, the O.E. verbs *lǣtan* and *lettan* have apparently been confused (see note l. 1018).

(δ) The weak preterites retain their O.E. forms and endings, but O.E. *-ode, -ade* have been weakened to *-ede*, e.g. *iherde* 3, *raddest* 159, *cherde* 1658, *askedest* 1310, *akursedest* 1184. It is not until the 14th century that the pt. ending *-e* fell away, and one of the causes then was analogy with the str. pt. forms which had no final *-e* (see Macaulay, *Gower*, I. cxvii).

That the weak conjugation was already establishing itself as the living conjugation is shown by the forms *ipeint* 76, *granti* 201, *afoled* 206. Cf. also *siueþ, plaiding*.

(ε) The O.E. opt. and imperative forms are practically unchanged; and the conditions under which the opt. is employed are the same as in the earlier period.

(e) DEVELOPMENT OF NEW GRAMMATICAL MACHINERY.

In general, the grammatical structure, as compared with that of O.E., shows a marked advance in a modern direction, both as regards the order of words in the sentence, and the use of auxiliaries and prepositions as means of expression. Traces of the old awkward impersonal construction remain (cf. ll. 231, 281, etc.), and the word-forms are still highly inflected: but, in the main, a marked development has taken place, and a movement has begun away from the O.E. synthetic methods to the analytic methods of Modern English.

(i) The O.E. gen. pl. is frequently displaced by *of* with gen., e.g. *full of vuele wrenche* 247, *hoȝeþ of his sheue* (cf. O.E. *hogian* with gen.) 455, also ll. 458, 472.

(ii) A relic of the O.E. passive form is found in *hattest* 255. Elsewhere however the passive is formed by the auxiliary verbs *beon* and *wurþen* followed by a p.p., e.g. *nis bireued* 120, *wurþ forworþe* 548, also ll. 262, 427, 541, 846, 1158.

(iii) The future tense is occasionally represented, as in O.E., by the present form, ex. *uindestu* 657, *telle* 715. At the same time, the aux. verbs *schal* and *wille* are also used for this purpose with increasing frequency: ex. *he wile gon a riȝte weie* 214, *ho shal liki wel unwreste* 342, *ich schal heom singe* 960. On the other hand these verbs also retain at times their original meanings as notional verbs: ex. *man schal* (= must or ought to) *bo stille* 979, *schal* (= ought) *he his mishap wite me* 1249, *wulle* (= wish) *ȝe þis pes tobreke* 1730.

(iv) The perfect and pluperfect tenses are expressed, as in O.E., by means of the aux. verbs *habben* and *beon—habben* with transitive verbs, *beon* with intransitive verbs, especially verbs of motion. Ex. (a) *hauet þis ido* 113, *hadde one frogge isuolȝe* 146, *hadde ilorned* 216, *hadde andsuere gode ifunde* 705; (β) *is icumen* 130, *is ago* 507, *nis of horte islide* 686.

The above examples illustrate the fact that the practice of putting the object after the past participle as in Mod. English was as yet far from general. It became so in the 14th century: cf. however *þat hadde idon so muchel unriȝt* 1094.

(v) The causal constructions of the poem further illustrate the adoption of analytic methods of expression. In O.E. such constructions had been formed by O.E. *dōn* (with *þæt* and a sb. clause) and *lætan* (with infin.). The latter form is found in *let fordrue* 919, *let forbonne* 1093: the former in *ich shal...do þat þi speche wurþ forworþe* 547—8. But in addition to this, another construction (viz. *don* with inf.) is found, ex. *doþ misreken* 490, *deþ his iuo...swete* 1716, *do me crempe* 1788.

APPENDIX II

THE NIGHTINGALE EPISODE

This episode in the first instance appears to have sprung from Breton soil. It is narrated at full length in the *lai* called *Laustic* (c. 1175) of Marie de France, and is there described as "Une aventure...dunt li Bretun firent un lai." Before the end of the 12th century it would seem to have attained a wide popularity. It is, for instance, briefly alluded to in Alexander Neckam's *De Naturis Rerum*: it is related in different forms by each of the disputants in *The Owl and the Nightingale*: while it subsequently is found in the *Renard le Contrefait* (c. 1320), in the French *chansons* of the 15th century and in the English version of the *Gesta Romanorum*, a compilation which appeared originally in Latin form in England (c. 1300), was enlarged on the Continent, and afterwards translated into English about 1445.

The different versions may be summarised as follows:

(a) *The Laustic Account.*

At St Malo there lived two knights, one of whom was married to a beautiful and virtuous lady, while the other was a bachelor famed alike for his valour and courtesy. Love sprang into being between the lady and her neighbour: but meetings were hard to arrange owing to a high wall which separated their respective castles. It was therefore the lady's custom to take her stand near a window which commanded a view of the neighbouring castle, and as a result, her husband's suspicions were in due course aroused. To his angry inquiries the lady replied that it was the nightingale's song that had drawn her thither: whereupon he resolved to put an end to the songstress. Having captured the bird by means of snares, he broke its neck in the presence of his lady, and then flung it at her feet, staining the robe she wore. The body of the hapless victim was afterwards cherished by the lady, who wrapped it in embroidered velvet and sent it to her lover. And by him it was carefully preserved, enclosed in a precious casket, as a token and memorial of his knightly devotion.

(b) *Neckam's Account.*

This appears in summary form (see *De Nat. Rerum*, I. 51) and is devoid of the many details which characterise the other versions. According to Neckam the story runs: "Miles enim quidam nimis zelotes philomenam quatuor equis distrahi praecepit, eo quod secundum ipsius assertionem animum uxoris suae nimis demulcens, eam ad illiciti amoris compulisset illecebras."

(c) *The Versions of the Owl and the Nightingale.*

The story is made to assume different forms in the mouths of the two disputants, each of whom uses it in support of her own particular argument. According to the Owl, the Nightingale was wont to sing her love-songs outside the bower of a certain lady of rank, thereby threatening to undermine her virtue. The husband's anger was after a time aroused; and when the bird had been captured by means of elaborate gins and snares she was condemned to be torn asunder by wild horses! (ll. 1049—62).

The Nightingale's story is of a different colour. She explains how she had sung to cheer a fair lady who was cruelly treated by a brutal and jealous husband and was finally locked up in a hateful chamber. The vengeance which the husband had taken on the offending bird had, however, been amply atoned for. King Henry, in his justice, had inflicted a heavy fine upon the offending knight to the lasting honour of the nightingale-tribe (ll. 1075—1101).

(d) *The Version of Renard le Contrefait.*

Odoire, King of Britain, though advanced in years, had married a young and beautiful wife, Gentille by name, who fell in love with a neighbouring lord by whom she was passionately loved in turn. This lord dwelt in a castle adjoining the palace: and an orchard stood between their respective dwellings. But by ascending to the highest windows, the lovers were able to catch glimpses of each other, and to indulge in this way their mutual passion. The orchard was tenanted by a sweet-throated nightingale: and to the music of her song the lovers were wont to listen. In due course however the king became suspicious, owing to his wife's practice of rising early to stand gazing from her window. And on asking the reason for this he was told of the nightingale's song: whereupon he resolved to capture the bird, and for that purpose he commanded lime to be spread on the trees in the orchard. As a result of these measures, the nightingale was caught and killed in spite of the queen's entreaties. And her complaint having reached the ears of her lover, he quickly summoned his friends and attacked the king, who was slain in the fight.

(See A. C. M. Robert, *Fables inédites des XIIe, XIIIe et XIVe siècles et Fables de la Fontaine*, t. I. s. cxxxiii—clii.)

(e) *The Version of the Gesta Romanorum.*

When Caclides was Emperor of Rome there lived in his dominions two knights who were neighbours. One of them was elderly, but had married a young wife: the other was young, while his wife was well on in years. The young knight in due course fell in love with his neighbour's wife, who, although she was kept closely guarded, was wont to listen at her window to the songs which the knight, her lover, would sing. In front of her bower there grew a fig-tree, and amidst the foliage of this tree a nightingale chanted her passionate songs. Her husband, having perceived that she often visited the casement of this room at night, became greatly angered: and on being told that the nightingale was the cause, he forthwith shot the bird by means of a bow and arrow. Then wrenching out its heart he flung it at his wife—an insult which the young knight quickly avenged by slaying the offending husband. His own wife died soon after: and then he married the young widow whom he had loved so long.

(See E. A. Baker, *Gesta Romanorum*, ch. CXXI. 1905.)

(*f*) *A Chanson of the Fifteenth Century.*

The following extract seems to refer to the same nightingale episode:

> Le roussignol est sur un houx
> Qui ne pence qu'a ses esbaz;
> Le faulx jaloux sy est dessoubz
> Pour luy tirer ung matteras.
>
> La belle a qui il desplaisoit
> Luy a dit par injure:
> "Hellas! que t'avoit il mesfait,
> Meschante creature?"

(See G. Paris et Gevaert, *Les Chansons du XVe Siècle*, CIX. ll. 13—20 (Soc. Anc. Textes), Paris, 1875.)

(*g*) *A Nineteenth Century Version.*

This appears in A. W. E. O'Shaughnessy's *Lays of France* (London, 1872), where modern renderings of five of Marie's *lais* are given, including *Laustic* (pp. 3—41) and *Yonec* (*Yvenec*).

Cf. the *soi-disant* Breton ballad *Ann Eostik* (the Nightingale) in Villemarque's collection *Barzaz-Breiz* (Chantes populaires de la Bretagne), s. 151 ff., Paris, 1867: see also Kohler's remarks in Warnke, *Die Lais der Marie de France*, CXXVII—CXXXIII, and Caroline Watts, *Marie de France, Seven of her Lais* (modern rendering of *Laustic*, pp. 87—91; Notes pp. 188—91). London, 1901.

APPENDIX III

VERSIONS OF THE OWL AND FALCON FABLE

(*a*) *Anglo-Latin Romulus* (Romulus Treverensis)[1].

Accipiter et noctua in una arbore nidificabant, et talis fuit inter eos concordia, ut, mutua familiaritate, alter in alterius nido ova sua poneret. Unde contigit inter pullos Accipitris pullum noctue prodire, et ab Accipitre foveri et pasci. Factum est autem, ut inmundus ille pullus nidum fedaret Accipitris. Quod cum vidit Accipiter, rem fedam abhominatus, nidum despexit et pullos suos. Illi autem iam fame deficientes, ad patrem

[1] See Hervieux, *Les Fabulistes latins*, II. 122.

in fortitudine clamaverunt: Cur nos, pater, deseris, aut quare deficientibus nobis solito pietatis studio escam non tribuis? Quibus ille respondit: Multis iam annis in hac [arbore] resedi et pullos habui: sed numquam prius fedatum nidum meum inveni. Et responderunt illi: Nobis hoc iniuste imputatur, cum frater noster, ille cum magno capite, solus hoc fecerit. Quo audito, ait pater: Potui quidem eum fovere et de testa producere, sed naturam suam non possum inmutare.

Moralitas. Licet doctrina multum possit operari in homine, forcior (*sic*) tamen est in eo ius nature.

(*b*) *Marie de France*[1].

<blockquote>

D'un ostur vuelt recunter ei,
ki sur un fust aveit sun ni,
e li huans ensemble od lui.
Tant s'entramerent ambedui
5　qu'en un ni ensemble puneient
e lur oisels ensemble aveient.
Ore avint si que en un an
li osturs les ués al huan
aveit cuvez e eschapiz
10　od les suens oiselez petiz.
Puis lur ala querre viande,
si cum nature le demande.
Mes quant a els fu repairiez
esteit sis niz orz e suilliez:
15　li huan l'aveient malmis.
Quant li osturs se fu asis,
ses oisels laidi e blasma:
par maltalent lur repruva
que vint anz ot aire tenue,
20　unkes si grant descuvenue
si oisel ni li firent mes.
Cil li respundirent apres
qu'il nes en deit mie blasmer,
lui meïsmes deit enculper:
25　kar lur deriere unt eü foire,
pur ceo est dreiz qu'en sun ni paire.
Il lur respunt, "Vus dites veir.
Legiere chose est a saveir:
de l'oef les poi jeo bien geter
30　e par chalur e par cover,
mais nïent fors de lur nature.
Maldite seit tels nurreture!"

Pur ceo dit hum en repruvier
de la pume del dulz pumier,
35　s'ele chiet sur un fust amer,
ja ne savra tant ruëler
qu'al mordre ne seit cuneüe,
desur quel arbre ele est creüe.
Sa nature puet hum guenchir
40　mes nuls n'en puet del tut eissir.
</blockquote>

---

[1] See Warnke, *Die Fabeln der Marie de Fr.* LXXIX. (De accipitre et noctua).

(c) *Odo of Cheriton*[1].

Busardus in nido Accipitris proiecit unum ouum, et inde creatus est pullus. Alii pulli nobiles fimum fecerunt extra nidum. Sed pullus Busardi semper maculauit nidum suum. Quod aduertens Accipiter ait: Quis est qui nidum maculat? Tandem dixerunt ei pulli de pullo Busardi. Quod attendens Accipiter cepit filium Busardi et extra nidum proiecit, dicens: Of a ey hi ye brohte, of kynde i ne myche[2]: hoc est. De ouo te eduxi, de natura non potui: et confractus est totus.

(d) *Nicole Bozon*[3].

Le huan pria le ostur de norir son fiz: l'autre lui graunta e lui dist que il le feit venir e mettre entre ses pigeons demeignes. Si tost cum cel oysele vynt en cel compaignie, le ostur le dit que il se confurmast a ses pigeons e aprist lur nature: tan qe le ostur voleit quere lur viaunde, revynt et trova son ny ordement soilli. "Qe est ceo" fest il "que jeo trove encontre norture? qui ad ceo fet?"—"Vostre norry" font ses fitz. —"Veir!" fet il "veirs est dist en engleis: *Stroke oule and schrape oule and evere is oule oule.*" Auxint est de plusours gents que sont nez de bas lignage. Mes ke il soyent en haut mountez, sovent apris e enformés en religion ou en siecle ou en dignetee, touz jours retornent a lur estat et a lur nature dont il sont neez. Pur ceo dit l'em en engleys, "*Trendle the appel nevere so fer he conyes fro what tree he cam.*"

(e) *John of Sheppey*[4].

Busardus proiecit in nidum Accipitris ouum suum. Accipiter autem, credens ouum suum esse, cubauit super illud una cum ouis suis et creatus est inde pullus quem nutriuit Accipiter tanquam suum. Pulli vero Accipitris proiecerunt fimum suum extra nidum: pullus maculauit nidum. Quod aduertens Accipiter ait: Quis uestrum est qui sic maculat nidum suum? Et omnes dixerunt: Non ego, domine. Tandem facta pleniori inquisicione, oportebat eos pro sui liberacione prodere ueritatem et dixerunt: Domine, iste est cum magno capite, ostenso filio Busardi. Quem Accipiter cum magna indignacione per capud arripiens, proiecit extra nidum, dicens: De ouo te produxi: extra naturam non potui. Quia vt dicit Oratius.

$$\text{Naturam expellas furta } (sic)$$
$$\text{tamen vsque recurret.}$$

(f) *Latin Translation of Bozon's Contes*[5].

Bubo rogauit accipitrem ut pullum suum nutriret et in bonis moribus educaret, quod sibi concedens jussit illum adducere et nido suo inter pullos suos ponere. Cui dixit accipiter quod in omnibus pullis suis conformaret et illorum educacionem adisceret diligenter. Qui respondit se

---

[1] See Hervieux, *Les Fabulistes latins*, vol. IV. p. 181 (De Busardo et de nido Accipitris).

[2] Also "of eie hi the brothte, of athele hi ne mythte."

[3] See Nicole Bozon, *Les Contes moralisés* (ed. L. Toulmin Smith et P. Meyer, Soc. des Anc. Textes), p. 23.

[4] See Hervieux, *Les Fabulistes latins*, IV. 437 (Busardus et Accipiter).

[5] See Nicole Bozon, *Les Contes moralisés* (ed. L. Toulmin Smith et P. Meyer, Soc. des Anc. Textes), p. 205.

paratum in omnibus suis parere mandatis. Tandem accipiter pro cibo querendo patriam intravit, et rediens nocte nidum suum turpiter invenit [fedatum]. Querenti sibi quis sic nidum maculavit, responsum est quod pullus bubonis illum fedavit. "A !" dixit accipiter "*hyt ys a fowle brydde that fylyȝth hys owne neste.*" Ita est de pluribus natura ignobilibus: . . . . . Ideo anglice dicitur: *Trendul an appull never so ferre, hyt wyll be know fro wheyne he comyth.*

(*g*) Another version of the buzzard story, with however no very distinctive features, is found in *Latin Stories* ed. Thos. Wright (Percy Society, 1842), p. 52 (*Fabula de pullo busardi*).

APPENDIX IV

VERSIONS OF THE CAT AND FOX FABLE

(*a*) *Marie de France*[1].

Uns gupiz e uns chaz alerent
par mi un champ, si purparlerent
que il sereient cumpaignun.
Dunc s'asemblent suz un buissun
5 Li chaz al gupil demanda
par quel engin se defendra
la u il ierent entrepris.
E il gupiz li dist. "Amis,
dous engins sai, u mult me crei,
10 e pleine puche en ai od mei.
Mes jo ne vueil la puche ovrir
desi que cil deient faillir."
Li chaz respunt par brief raisun:
"Nus n'iermes mie cumpaignun:
15 kar jeo ne sai fors un engin,
ceo sevent bien tuit mi veisin."
La u il vunt issi parlant,
dous chiens virent venir curant.
Li gupiz vers le chat escrie:
20 "Ore ai jeo mestier de t'aïe."
Li chaz respunt: "Aïë tei!
N'ai qu'un engin: cil iert od mei."
Dunc sailli li chaz sur l'espine.
Li chien saisissent par l'eschine
25 le gupil, sil vunt detirant,
e li chaz li escrie tant:
"Cumpain," fet il, "pur quei
que ta puchete ne deslies?
Tu l'espargnes trop lungement!
30 Li chien te hastent durement:
pur quei n'as tun sac deslië?"
"Jeo l'ai" fet il "trop espargnié.

[1] See Warnke, *Die Fabeln der Marie de Fr.* xcviii. (De catto et vulpe).

Or te di bien, mielz amereie
tun sul engin, se jeo l'aveie,
35 que cels dunt ai ma puche pleine :
jeo te vei delivre de peine."
"Bien me deit" fet li chaz "membrer
de ceo que j'ai oï cunter :
suvent est ateinz li gupiz,
40 tut seit il quointes par ses diz."

(b) *Odo of Cheriton*[1].

Vulpes siue Reinardus obuiauit Tebergo id est Cato, et dixit Reinardus : Quot fraudes uel artificia nouisti? Et ait Catus : Certe nescio nisi unum. Et ait Reinardus : Quod est illud? Respondit C.: Quando canes me insequuntur, scio repere super arbores et euadere. Et quesiuit Catus: Et tu, quot scis? Et respondit R.: Scio XVII et ab hoc habeo saccum plenum. Veni mecum et docebo te artificia mea, quod canes te non capient. Annuit Catus: ambo simul iuerunt. Venatores et canes insequebantur eos et ait C.: Audio canes : iam timeo. Et ait R.: Noli timere : bene te instruam qualiter euades. Appropinquauerunt canes et uenatores. Certe, dixit C., amplius non uado tecum : uolo uti artificio meo. Et saltauit super arborem. Canes ipsum dimiserunt et Reinardum insecuti sunt et tandem ceperunt, quidam per tibias, quidam per uentrem, quidam per dorsum, quidam per capud. Et C. in alto sedens clamauit "Reinarde, R., aperi sacculum tuum : certe omnes fraudes tue non ualent tibi."

(c) Similar versions are found in the *Anglo-Latin Romulus*[2] and in John of Sheppey's *Fabulae*[3], but they have no special features.

APPENDIX V

NOTE ON CORNIFICIANI[4]

The only reasonable explanation of this curious word seems to be that it signifies "followers of Cornificius." About a dozen persons of that name were prominent in antiquity at various periods (see Paully-Wissowa, *Realencyclopaedie*, s.v.) : and of these the only one at all likely is 8 Q. Cornificius, orator, poet and politician. For his friendship with Cicero and his political sympathies, see especially Cic. *ad fam.* XII. epistulae 17—30: for his relations to Catullus see the latter's pathetic address to him in the 38th poem of our collection. The article (by Wissowa) already quoted gives good grounds for supposing that Cicero's friend and Catullus' fellow-poet were one and the same. So much for the real man.

[1] See Hervieux, *Les Fabulistes latins*, IV. 212.
[2] See *ibid.* II. 578-9.
[3] See *ibid.* IV. 441.
[4] This note is contributed by Professor H. J. Rose of the University College of Wales, Aberystwyth.

Around his personality a curious legend sprang up, by reason, it would seem, of a misunderstanding of Vergil and of his earlier and better commentators (see Wissowa, *op. cit.* col. 1628). In the seventh *Eclogue* (ll. 21 ff.) occurs a complimentary reference to one Codrus who is said to be second only to Phoebus in poetry. The Veronese scholiast on this passage (in Thilo and Hagen's edition of Servius, vol. III. 399) notes: "Many suppose Codrus to be Vergil, others Cornificius, some Helvius Cinna." Now in l. 26 of the same *Eclogue*, the wish is expressed that Codrus may burst with envy (*inuidia rumpantur ut ilia Codro*). No one who knows the post-classical habit (by no means dead yet) of never looking at the context, needs to be told the conclusion that was drawn from this, viz. that if Codrus was to burst with envy it was because he was an envious rival of Vergil. But if this were so, he clearly could not be Vergil himself, nor Cinna who is elsewhere (*Ecl.* IX. 35) spoken of with the greatest respect. Therefore he must be Cornificius. That the wish is expressed by Thyrsis the shepherd, who in the seventh *Eclogue* is overcome by Corydon in singing, and that therefore his views cannot be those of Vergil himself, are considerations which never occurred to the framers of this theory. Consequently, when we leave the Veronese scholia, which appear to go back to very good ancient commentators, and turn to those of Philargyrius[1] (on II. 39, cf. the Bernese scholia *ibid.* and their argumentum of *Ecl.* VII.) we find this note: "STVLTVS AMYNTAS INVIDIT. By Amyntas is to be understood Cornificius, who tried to write against Vergil." Now these scholia of Philargyrius are preserved in three MSS. of which none is less than two centuries older than John of Salisbury: so that he may easily have seen any or all of them or copies of them. But in view of the long-standing quarrel (dating from Plato and Isokrates) between rhetoricians and philosophers, what could be a more natural assumption for him or for any of his contemporaries than that one who had written against Vergil, the supreme master of rhetoric (see the commentary of Servius *passim* and the long discussion of Vergil's rhetorical skill in Macrobius' *Saturnalia*), must have been a philosopher? Hence the name would seem an appropriate one for the anti-Humanistic philosophers of John of Salisbury's own day[2].

---

[1] Cf. also Donatus, *Vita, Cornificius...illum* (*Vergilium*) *non tulit.*

[2] See Tenney Frank, *Cornificius as Daphnis* (*Classical Rev.* XXXIV. pp. 49–51, 1920): Sandys, *Hist. Class. Schol.* I. pp. 18–19.

ADDITIONAL NOTES

125. *wilde bowe* = "wild-wood bough." Mr B. Dickins quotes *Cymbeline*, IV. ii. 390 (Cambridge text), "With wild-wood leaves and weeds I ha' strew'd his grave." The phrase implies a bough belonging to wild or unfrequented woodlands.

322. Reference is further made by G. (note l. 1018) to specific ecclesiastical abuses in Ireland, e.g. the use of diluted wine and soiled wafers at mass, the baptizing of infants of rank in milk, etc. (see A. Bellesheim, *Gesch. d. Kath. Kirche in Irland*, Mainz, 1890, I. 406).

651. *ihende* (C. and J. *iwende*) = "conveniences." All editors retain *iwende*, which Str.-Br. explains as "contrivances (?)," and connects with M.H.G. *gewende*. The M.H.G. form, however (see Lexer, *Wtb.*) = Germ. *wand*, *abgang*, neither of which suggests "contrivances." Moreover M.E. *iwende* apparently does not occur elsewhere; neither is there any corresponding O.E. word. It would therefore seem probable that both MSS. have here copied an error of the intermediate text, and that *iwende* is an attempt to copy intermediate *iþende*, which itself was an error for original *ihende*. For similar scribal errors ($h > þ (w)$) see ll. 748, 1586, etc. If then *ihende* be read, it would be an adj. (O.E. *gehende*, near, convenient) used as sb. = "convenient things, conveniences."

733. The phrase may however mean "in the country" as opposed to "the town": cf. *L.C.S.* 24, *Sy hit binnan byrig, sy hit upp on lande* (B.T.), also Chau. *Prol.* l. 702, and the title of Henryson's fable "The Uponlondis Mous and the Burges Mous."

736 ff. At a later date it is found surviving in Dunbar's *Merle and the Nightingale*, where the merle (blackbird) sings in praise of Love, while the nightingale's theme is that "All love is lost but upon God alone."

868. *foliot* = "foolishness." Godefroi explains O. Fr. *foliot* to mean a snare made up of fluttering feathers to attract foolish inquisitive birds. Elsewhere it = "watch-spring" < O. Fr. *folier* "to play the fool" (see *N.E.D.*). The root idea in each case appears to be that of "restlessness, instability," hence "foolishness": and in 12th century England the word is used as a surname. Possibly there is a satirical reference here to Foliot, Bishop of London (1163–87), the great opponent of Becket: see *D.N.B.*

961–2. Trans.: "Dost thou suppose that wise men leave the high road for the muddy track?" Professor C. Brett (*M.L.R.* XIV. p. 8) would translate "leave the right way, because (= *for*) it is muddy." But the construction *forlete for* is repeated in ll. 965–6, and there *for* clearly = "for," not "because."

1150 ff. From early times, owls have been objects of superstitious terror, partly on account of their association with twilight and darkness, partly from the weirdness of their screaming as they fly. In classical pages the owl is described as "profanus, funereus, sinister, maestus, luctifer": and in *Aeneid* XII. 862 ff., just before the end of the combat between Aeneas and Turnus, the owl is heard, with its flapping wings and its boding cry (cf. also Ovid, *Metam.* v. 550, "ignavus bubo dirum mortalibus omen"). Elsewhere it is spoken of as the bird that snatches away the soul, "the constable from the dark land," while the screech-owl was said to sing near the windows of dying men or men marked out for an early death (cf. Chau. *P. of F.* III. 43) No witch's charm, again, was potent unless a portion of the owl was one of the ingredients (cf. Shak. *Macb.* IV. i.): and in the time of Sir Thomas Browne, these ancient superstitions were still retained, especially by "the credulous and feminine party." See Swainson, *Prov. Names and Folklore of British Birds*, E. Dial. Soc. XVIII.

1380. *þenne* (J. *þeonne*) = "then." W. notes that *þanne*, *þonne* would make better rhyme than *þenne* (< by-form O.E. *þænne*) or than *þeonne* (by analogical substitution of *eo* for *o*): cf. O. Kent. *þanne*.

GLOSSARY

The word-forms given below are taken wholly from the C-text: no J-forms appear. Nor has any attempt been made to cite all the places where any given form appears: so that the Glossary cannot claim to be a complete grammatical index. At the same time it is hoped that all variants have been noted, and that these, together with the etymological matter supplied, will afford the assistance necessary for the correct reading of the text.

a (O.E. *ān*), an, a, 45, 98, 127.

a- (O.E. *on*), in, at, by, 115, 134, 1428; in compounds, **abisemar**, 148; **auele**, 20; **adai**, 89; **asnowe**, 413; **astable**, 629, etc.; see **an, on**.

abak (O.E. *onbæc*), backwards, 824.

abide (O.E. *ābidan*), await, remain, endure, 1215; **abid**, **(n)abideþ**, pr. 3. sg., 1778, 493; **abideþ**, pr. 2 pl., 1702; **abid**, pr. opt. 3. sg., 466; **abod**, pt. 3. sg., 41, 1175; **abid**, imp. 837.

a-bisemar, see **bisemar**.

abiten (O.E. *ābitan*), bite, devour, 77.

aboȝte (O.E. *ābycgan*), paid for, atoned for, pt. plu., 1060.

abrad (O.E. *ābregdan, ābrǣd*), moved rapidly, pt. 3. sg., 1044.

abrode (O.E. *on + brōd*), a-brooding, 518.

abute (O.E. *onbūtan*), around, about, adv., 16; prep., 1593.

ac, ah (O.E. *ac, ah*), but, 83, 177, 1176.

acoled (O.E. *ācōlian*), grown cool, p. p., 205; **(n)acoleþ**, pr. 3. sg., 1275.

acorde (O.Fr. *acord*), accord, dat. sg., 181.

acursi (O.E. *ā + cursian*), curse, 1704; **akursedest**, pt. 2. sg., 1184.

acwalde (O.E. *ācwellan*), killed, p. p., 1370.

adel-eye (O.E. *adel + ǣg*), addle egg, dat. sg., 133.

adiȝte (O.E. *ādihtan*), arrange, compose, pr. 1. sg., 326.

adrede (O.E. *ondrǣdan*), dread, fear, 1266; opt. pr. 3. sg., 1487.

adune (O.E. *of-dūne*), down, 920; **adun**, 208, 1454.

adunest (O.E. *ā + dynian*), dinnest, 337.

adwole, see note 1777.

afere (O.E. *āfǣran*), terrify, 221; **aferd**, **oferd**, p. p., 410, 399.

afoled (O.Fr. *afoler*), befooled, p. p., 206.

afonge, see note 1196.

after (O.E. *æfter*), after, 140, 1709; **after þan**, accordingly, 650, 1578; **after þan**. afterwards, 1508.

aȝaf (O.E. *āgiefan*), replied, pt. 3. sg. 139.

aȝein (O.E. *ongegn*), against, adv., 1788; **aȝeines**, prep., 1371.

aȝen (O.E. *ongēan*), against, prep., 7, 668; just before, 436, 499, 1153; adv., again, 454, 818.

aginne (O.E. *āginnan*), begin, 1289.

agon (O.E. *āgān*), pass away, 355; **ageþ**, pr. 3. sg., 1453; **ago**, p. p., 507.

agrulle (O.E. *ā + gryllan*), annoy, disturb, 1110.

aȝt, aht (O.E. *āht*), valiant, worthy, 1479, 1500; **aȝte**, nom. pl., 385.

ah (O.E. *āgan*), pr. 3. sg. ought, 1471; **(n)ah**, has (not), 1543.

ahene, see **oȝe**.

ahwene (O.E. *āhwǣnan*), vex, trouble; **ahweneþ**. pr. pl., 1564; **awene**, pr. 1 sg., 1258.

aishest, see **askedest**.

aiþer, eiþer (O.E. *ǣgþer*), either (adj. or pro.), 7, 9, 796, 887.

aiware (O.E. *ǣghwǣr*), everywhere, 216.

al (O.E. *eal(l)*), all, adj., sg. nom. dat. acc., 74, 65, 78; plu. nom., 1174, 1348; adv. = wholly, entirely, 27; **alle**, sg. nom. dat. acc., 785, 1436, 381; plu. nom. dat. acc., 66, 827, 222; mid **alle**, wholly, 666; **alre**, gen. plu., esp. in comp. **alre-hecst**, 687; **alre-worste**, 10.

alamed (see note, l. 1604), crushed, p. p., 1604.

ald, see **old**.

alegge (O.E. *ālecgan*), refute, 394.

Alfred (O.E. *Ælfred*), Alfred, 942; **Alured**, 235; **Aluered**, 685, 697.

almiȝti (O.E. *ælmihtig*), almighty, 1173.

aloþeþ (O.E. *ālāþian*), becomes hateful, 1277.

alswa, alswo, also (O.E. *eal(l)swā*), also, adv. and conj., 1663, 891, 443; as if, 146; just so, 129, 298; as, 503, 977.

amanset (O.E. *āmānsumian*), cursed, p. p., 1307.

amidde (O.E. *on-middan*), in the middle, 643; by the middle, 124.

amis (O.N. *ā-mis*), amiss, astray, 1365, 1434.

among (O.E. *onmang*), among, prep., 164; adv., at intervals, 6; her-among, in this matter, 744.

an (O.E. *an*), in, on, 54, 323, 1246, 1371, 1372.

an (O.E. *ān*), an, a, 4, 80; ane, dat. sg., 1021; anne, mas. sg. = one, 794, 802; see on.

an (O.E. *and*), and, 7, 386, 431.

an (O.E. *ann*), grant, am willing, 1739.

anan, anon (O.E. *on + ān*), at once, anon, 1658, 488.

andsware (O.E. *andswaru*), answer, 639; andswere, 665; andsuare, 149; ondsware, 1185; ansuare, 487; ansvere, 470; answere, 1710.

anhoờ (O.E. *onhōn*), hang; pr. 3. plu., 1646; anhonge, p. p., 1195.

ansuare (O.E. *andswerian*), answer, opt. 2. sg., 555.

ape (O.E. *apa*), ape, 1325.

appel (O.E. *æppel*), apple, 135.

ar (O.E. *ǣr, ār*), ere, conj. with opt., 552, 692; ear, 1216; adv. ear, before, 1560; er, 866.

aredde (O.E. *āhreddan*), deliver, rescue, opt. 3. sg., 1569.

areȝ (O.E. *earg*), cowardly, 407.

areȝþe, arehþe (O.E. *iergþu*), coward-ice, 404, 1716.

ariȝt, ariht (O.E. *onriht*), aright, 400, 904.

arise (O.E. *ārīsan*), arise, 327; arist, pr. 3. sg., 1394; ariseþ, pr. 3. pl., 731.

arme, areme (O.E. *earm*), poor, miserable, plu., 537, 1162.

aschewele (see note, l. 1128), scare away, pr. 1. sg., 1613.

askedest (O.E. *ascian, axian*), didst ask, pt. 2. sg., 1310; aishest, aisheist, pr. 2. sg., 473, 995; axest, 707.

aspille (O.E. *āspillan*), spoil, 348.

astorue (O.E. *āsteorfan*), perished, p. p., 1200.

aswinde (O.E. *āswindan*), cease, languish, 1574; aswunde, asvunde, p. p. = feeble, flabby, 1480, 534.

at (O.E. *æt*), at, in, of, to; at one,

together, 785; ate, atte, at the, 592, 1513; attom, at home, 1527.

atbroide (O.E. *ætbregdan*), stolen, p. p., 1380.

ateliche (O.E. *atelic*), terrible, 1125.

atfliþ (O.E. *ætflēon*), flies away, sinks, 37.

atholde (O.E. *æthealdan*), retain, grasp, 695, 1420; athold, pt. 3. sg., considered, 392.

atprenche (see note, l. 248), deceive, 248, 814.

atrute (O.E. *æt + hrūtan*, see *N.E.D.*), escape, 1168.

atschet (O.E. *æt + scēotan*), vanished, pt. 3. sg., 44; atschote, p. p., expelled, 1623.

atstonde (O.E. *ætstandan*), withstand, 750.

attercoppe (O.E. *ātorcoppe*), spider, dat. pl., 600.

atwende (O.E. *æt + wendan*), escape, 1427.

atwite, atuite (O.E. *ætwitan*), twit, reproach, 1234; atuitest, attwitestu, atwist, pr. 2. sg., 597, 1187, 1332; atwiten, p. p., 935.

aþele (O.E. *æþele*), noble, 632.

aualle (O.E. *āfeallan*), fall, 1685.

auinde (O.E. *afindan*), learn, find, 527, 856.

auorþ (O.E. *on + forþ*), forth, 824.

auoþ (O.E. *onfōn*), receive, pr. pl., 843.

awai, awei (O.E. *on weg*), away, 33, 250; awai-ward, away, 376.

awedeþ (O.E. *āwēdan*), rage, go mad, pr. plu., 509, 1384.

awene, see ahwene.

awene (O.E. *on wēne*), in thought, 239; in doubt (see note), 682.

awer (O.E. *āhwǣr*), anywhere, 1342.

awreke (O.E. *āwrecan*), avenge, opt. 3. plu., 1562; p. p., 262, 1105.

awroþeþ (O.E. *ā + wrāþian*), becomes angry, 1278.

ax (O.E. *æx*), axe, 658.

baldeliche (O.E. *bealdlice*), boldly, 1707.

bale (O.E. *bealu*), trouble, 687.

banne (O.Fr. *ban*), troop, dat. sg., 390.

banne (O.E. *bannan*), summon; ibanned, p. p., 1668.

bare (O.E. *bær*), mere, 547 (see note), 571; sb. = the open, 56, 150.

bareȝ (O.E. *bearh*), barrow-pig, *porcus castratus*, 408.

bataile (O.Fr. *bataille*), battle, 1197.

bedde (O.E. *bedd*), bed, dat., 967, 1492; bed-time, bed-time, 324.

bedde (O.E. *gebedda*), consort, 1500; see **ibedde**.

bede, see **bidde**.

beire (O.E. *bēgen*), both, gen., 1584; bo, neu., 990.

belde, see **bold**.

-bende (O.E. *bend*), bonds, rites, acc. plu., 1428.

beod (O.E. *bēodan*), commands, pr. 3. sg., 1437; bode, inf., 530.

beon, bo (O.E. *bēon*), be, inf., 932; bo, bon, 190, 262; beo, be, 1303, 1151; pr. sg., am, art, is, 170, 38, 34; pr. plu., beoþ, beoð, boþ, 1338, 911, 75; opt. sg., bo, beo, 171, 1443; opt. pl., bo, bon, beon, 97, 452, 1221; pt. sg., was, were, was, 1, 1059, 5; pt. pl., uere, were, 1306, 16; opt. sg., were, 21; opt. pl., were, 203, weren, 76; imp. sg., be, 1638; imp. pl., beoþ, boþ, 1735, 75.

bere (O.E. *gebēru*), cries, 925.

bere (O.E. *beran*), bear, carry, pr. 1. sg., 1599; berþ, pr. 3. sg., 403; bereð, pr. pl., 1372; ibore, p. p., born, 716.

berne (O.E. *bern*), barn, d. sg., 607.

berne (O.E. *biernan*), burn, 1203.

berste (O.E. *berstan*), burst, opt. pl., 990.

beseo (O.E. *besēon*), look after, opt. sg., 1272.

best (O.Fr. *beste*), animal, 99.

best (O.E. *betst*), best, 470.

bet (O.E. *bet*), rather, better, adv., 21, 172.

bete (O.E. *bētan*), make amends, 865.

betere (O.E. *betra*), better, adj., 283, 712.

bi (O.E. *be, bi*), by, through, concerning, 92, 241, etc.

bichermet (O.E. *be + cierman*), scream at, pr. pl., 279.

bicloped (O.E. *becleopian*), made (thy) charge, p. p., 550; see note.

biclopt (O.E. *beclyppan*), clasped, p. p., 1048.

bicume (O.E. *becuman*), happen; bicom, pt. 3. sg., 105; bicumeþ, pr. 3. sg. = is fitting, 271; bicome, pt. pl., arrived, 1791; bicume, p. p., come, 137.

bidde (O.E. *biddan*), ask, bid, pray, inf., 858; pr. 1. sg., 741, 929, 1568; bit (bid), pr. 3. sg., 441, 445, 1437; biddeþ, pr. pl., 886; bede, pt. 2. sg., 550, opt. pt. 1. sg., 1678.

biȝete (O.E. *begietan*), obtain, 1629; opt. pr. sg., 726.

biginne (O.E. *beginnan*), begin, pr. 1. sg., 1456; bigon, pt. sg., 13, 726.

bigrede (O.E. *begrǣdan*), cry out at, 1413; bigredeþ, bigredet, pr. pl., 279, 67; bigradde, pt. pl., 1144.

bigrowe (O.E. *be + grōwan*), grown over, p. p., 27, 617.

bihauest (O.E. *behāwian*), gazest upon, pr. 2. sg., 1322; see note.

bihede (O.E. *be + hēdan*), prevent, 635; bihedde, pt. sg. = guarded, 102; p. p., protected, 1048.

bihemmen (cf. O.E. *hem*), trim, manipulate, 672.

bihinde (O.E. *behindan*), behind, prep., 594; adv., 528, 666.

biholde, bihalde (O.E. *behealdan*), behold, look at, 71, 1325; pr. 1. sg., 1566; bihold, pt. sg., 30, 108.

bihote (O.E. *behātan*), promised, p. p., 1745.

bile (O.E. *bile*), bill, beak, 79, 269.

bileaue, bileue (O.E. *belǣfan*), remain, 1688, 1691; remain (silent), 42.

bileck, see **bilukþ**.

biledet (O.E. *be + lǣdan*), drive, pursue, pr. plu., 68.

bilegge (O.E. *be + lecgan*), disguise, explain away, 672, 904; bileist, dost colour, pr. 2. sg., 839.

biliked (O.E. *be + lician*), made pleasing, p. p., 842.

bilukþ (O.E. *be + lūcan*), locks up, pr. 3. sg., 1557; bileck, pt. sg., 1081.

bineoðe (O.E. *beneoþan*), beneath, 912.

binimeþ (O.E. *beniman*), takes away, pr. 3. sg., 941; binume, p. p., 1226.

bireued (O.E. *berēafian*), bereft, p. p., 120.

bischopen (O.E. *bisceop*), bishops, dat. pl., 1761.

bischricheþ (O.E. *bi + *scrician*), screech at, pr. pl., 67.

bisehþ (O.E. *be + sēcan*), beseeches, woos, 1439; see note.

bisemar (O.E. *bismer*), insult, mockery, acc. sg., 148; a-bisemere = in mockery, 1311.

bisemed (O.E. *be + sēman*), made plausible, p. p., 842.

biside (O.E. *be + sidan*), beside, 25.

bisne (O.E. *bisen*), blind, 97, 243; see note, 243.

bispeke (O.E. *besprecan*), complain about, condemn, opt. pr̄. pl., 1561; p. p., promised, 1738.

bispel (O.E. *bispel*), parable, story, 127.

bistant (O.E. *be + standan*), stands around, pays court to, 1438.

biswike (O.E. *be+swican*), deceive, betray, 158; opt. pl., 930.

bit, see **bidde.**

bitelle (O.E. *betellan*), defend, justify, 263.

bitide (O.E. *be+tidan*), may happen; opt. sg., 52; **bitidde,** pt. sg., 1107.

biti3t (O.E. **betyhtan*), covered, p.p., 1013; see note.

bito3e (O.E. *be + teon*), employed, p. p., 702.

bituxen (O.E. *betweoxn*), between, 1747.

bitweone (O.E. *betweonan*), between, 1379.

biþenche (O.E. *beþencan*), bethink, 471; opt. pr., 871; **biþenchest,** pr. 2. sg. =dost think, 1505; **biþencþ,** pr. 3. sg., 1509; **biþohte, biþo3te,** pt. sg., 939, 199.

biuore (O.E. *beforan*), before, prep., 776; adv., 1235.

biwepe (O.E. *be + wepan*), bewail, 980; **biwepen,** opt. pl., 974.

biwerest (O.E. *bewerian*), protectest, pr. 2. sg., 1126, 1517.

biwro (O.E. *bewreon*), conceal, 673.

bled (O.E. *blæd*), bloom, flower, 1042; see note.

blenche (O.E. *blencan*), escape, slip aside, 170, 1231.

blenches (cf. O.E. *blencan*), tricks, feints, 378.

bleo, blo (O.E. *bleo*), colour, countenance, 1547, 152, 441.

blete (O.E. *bleat*), bare, miserable, 616; sb. =hard weather, 57.

blind (O.E. *blind*), blind, 243, 1237.

blis, blisse (O.E. *bliss*), joy, 1280, 420, 728; acc. sg., 433; dat. sg., 717.

blisse (O.E. *blissian*), rejoice, opt. sg., 478; **blisseþ hit,** reflex. =rejoices, 435.

bliþe (O.E. *bliþe*), joyful, 418; **bliþur,** comp., 1108.

blo, see **bleo.**

blod (O.E. *blod*), blood, 1127; **blode,** d. sg., 1350.

blostme (O.E. *blostma*), blossoms, 437; **blosme,** n. pl., 16.

blowe (O.E. *blowan*), bloom, 1133, 1201; p. p. =adj., in flower, 1636; **iblowe,** p. p. =adj., 618.

bo, see **beon.**

boc (O.E. *boc*), book, 1325; **bokes,** gen. sg., 1208; **boke,** d. pl., 350.

bode, see **beod.**

bodest (O.E. *bodian*), dost announce, 1152, 1155; **bodeþ,** pr. 3. sg., 1170.

bodi (O.E. *bodig*), body, 73.

bo3e (O.E. *bog*), bough, dat. sg., 15; d. plu., 616; **bowe,** d., 125, 1244; **bov=bow,** acc. sg., 242.

bold (O.E. *beald*), bold, strong, 317; **bolde,** 410; **belde,** acc. pl., 1715; see note.

boldeliche (O.E. *bealdlice*), boldly, 401.

boldhede (O.E. *beald + *hædu*), rashness, boldness, 514.

bon (O.E. *ban*), bones, acc. plu., 1120.

bondeman (O.E. *bonda + man*), husbandman, bondman, 1577; see note, l. 1507.

bor (O.E. *beor*), beer, 1011.

borde (O.E. *bord*), table, d. sg., 479, 1492.

bore (O.E. *bar*), wild boar, d. sg., 408.

bore (O.E. *bera*), bear, d. sg., 1021; see note.

bote (O.E. *bot*), remedy, help, n. sg., 688, 700; g. sg., 858.

bote, see **bute.**

boþ, see **beon.**

boþe (O.N. *baþir*), both, 1681, 381; conj., **boþe...and** (an) (=both... and), 50, 225.

bov, bowe, see **bo3e.**

breche (O.E. *bræc, brec*), thicket, copse, 14 (see note).

brede (O.E. *brædu*), breadth, d., 174.

brede (O.E. *bræde*), roast meat, a. sg., 1630.

brede (O.E. *bred*), log, d. sg., 965.

bredist (O.E. *bredan*), breedest, pr. 2. sg., 1633 (see note); **bredde,** pt. sg., 101; **ibred,** p. p., 1724.

breke (O.E. *brecan*), break, 1080, 1334.

breme (O.E. *breme*), spirited, passionate, excited, 202, 500.

breþ (L.O.E. *bræð*), fury, passion, emotion, 1454, 1461; acc., 948; see note.

brid (O.E. *brid*), young bird, nestling, acc., 124; **briddes,** n. pl., acc. pl., 654, 106, d. plu., 107, 626; **bridde,** d. pl., acc. pl., 111, 644, 123.

bridel (O.E. *bridel*), bridle, 1028.

bri3t (O.E. *beorht, bryht*), bright, 623; **bri3te,** a. sg., 250, 1681; **bri3ter,** comp., 152; adv., **brihte,** 1245.

bringe, ibringe (O.E. *bringan*), bring, 710, 1539; pr. 1. sg., 433; **bringeþ, bringþ,** pr. 3. sg., 1171, 1534; **bringe,** opt. 3. sg., 1447; **bro3te, brohte,** pt. 3. sg., 107, 1726; **ibro3t, ibroht,** p. p., 545, 1559.

brod (O.E. *brod*), brood, 1633; **brode,** d. sg., 93, 130.

brode (O.E. *brād*), broad, n. pl., 75.
broiden (O.E. *bregdan*), plaited, woven, p. p., 645.
brost (O.E. *brēost*), breasts, souls, 978.
broþer (O.E. *brōþor*), brother, 118.
brune (O.E. *bryne*), burning, sb., 1155.
buc (O.E. *būc*), stomach, body, 1132, 1494.
budel (O.E. *bydel*), beadle, herald, 1169.
bugge, buggen (O.E. *bycgan*), buy, procure, 1368, 1506.
bur (O.E. *būr*), dwelling, room, 958; bures, g. sg., 652, a. pl., 1045; bure, d. sg., 937, d. pl., 649.
burȝ (O.E. *burh*), city, 766.
burne (O.E. *burne*), stream, brook, 918.
bute (O.E. *būtan, būte*), prep., without, 183; except, 600; but, only, 794, 811; adv., but, only, 756; bote, except, 884.
buue (O.E. *bufan*), prep., above, 1346; adv., 208; high, 1052.

can, con, kan, kon (O.E. *cann*), can, know, know how to, pr. 1. sg., 263, 1208, 170; canst, const, pr. 2. sg., 972, 1420; kunne, pr. pl., 911; cunne, opt. sg., 47, opt. pl., 1552; cuþe, kuþe, pt., 697, 1305, 1717.
cartare (O.N. *kartr* + O.E. *ere*), carter, 1186.
castel (O.E. *castel* < O.N.Fr.), castle, 175, 766.
cat (O.E. *catt*), cat, 831; kat, 810.
certes (O.Fr. *certes*), certainly, 1769.
chapmon (O.E. *cēapmon*), merchant, 1575.
chatere (sound-word), chattering, sb., 284.
chaterest (see above), chatterest, 322.
chaterestre (O.E. *-estre*, female agent), Dame Chatterbox, 655.
chatering, sb., chattering, 576; chateringe, d. sg., 744.
chauling (O.E. *cēafl*), scolding, 296, 284.
cheorles (O.E. *ceorl*), churl's, boor's, g. sg., 1494; chorles, 512, n. pl., 509, 632; see note, 1507.
cheose (O.E. *cēosan*), choose, 1343.
cherde (O.E. *cierran*), turned, pt. pl., 1658.
cheste (O.E. *cēast*), dispute, strife, n. sg., 296, d. sg., 183.
chide (O.E. *cidan*), chide, reprove, storm, 287, opt. sg., 291; chid, pr. 3. sg., 1533; chist, pr. 2. sg., 1331; chidde, pt. sg., 112.
child (O.E. *cild*), (1) child, 1315;

childe, d. sg., 782; children, n. pl., 631; childre, d. pl., 1776; (2) = girl, 1440, 1463; children, n. pl., 1115; childre, d. pl., 1453.
chinne (O.E. *cinn*), chin, d., 96.
chirche (O.E. *cirice*), church, 608; chirche-bende, rites of the church, 1428; chirche-song, hymn-singing, 984.
chirme (O.E. *cierm*), shrieks, clamour, 305.
chist, see chide.
chokeringe (see note), chucking, 504.
clackest (cf. O.N. *klaka*), clack, gabble, 81.
clansi (O.E. *clǣnsian*), cleanse, 610.
clawe (O.E. *clāwu*), claw, a. pl., 153.
clawe (O.E. *clāwian*), claw, scratch, opt. sg., 154.
clenche (O.E. (*be*)*clencean*), fetter, bind, 1206; see *N.E.D.*
clene (O.E. *clǣne*), clean, 584; cleine, 302.
clennesse (O.E. *clǣnnes*), purity, 491.
cleopeþ (O.E. *cleopian*), calls, 1315.
clerk (O.E. *cleric*), cleric, man in religious orders; clerkes, g. sg., 1328, n. plu., 722.
climbe (O.E. *climban*), climb, 833.
clinge (O.E. *clingan*), wither, shrivel up, 743; opt. sg., 1619.
cliure (O.E. *clifer*), claws, d. pl., 78; cliures, d. pl., 84, acc. pl., 1676; cliuers, acc. pl.; 155.
cloþ (O.E. *clāþ*), cloth, garment, 1174; cloþe, d. pl., 1530.
clowe (O.E. *clēowen*), ball, 578; see *N.E.D.*
cludes (O.E. *clūd*), rocks, 1001.
clutes (O.E. **clūta*), clods (of earth), d. pl., 1167.
cniht (O.E. *cniht*), knight, 1575; kniȝt, 1087; kniȝtes, a. pl., 768.
coc (O.E. *cocc*), cock, 1679.
codde (O.E. *codd*), baggy form, 1124.
cogge (see note), d. pl., cogs of a mill-wheel, 86.
col-blake (O.E. *col* + *blæc*), coal-black, 75.
cold (O.E. *ceald*), cold, 622.
com, see cumen.
copenere (O.E. *cōpenere*), lover, 1342.
corn (O.E. *corn*), corn, grain, 1126; cornes, n. pl., 1202.
coue (O.E. *cāfe*), swiftly, 379.
cradele (O.E. *cradol*), cradle, d. sg., 631.
craft (O.E. *cræft*), strength, craft, skill, 757; crafte, d. sg., 787; craftes, n. pl., 568, d. pl., 711.

crei (O.E. **cræg*), neck, throat, 335; see note.

crempe (O.E. **crempan*), restrain, 1788; see note, 510.

Cristes (O.E. *Crist*), of Christ, g. sg., 609; Cristis, 1568.

Cristes-masse (O.E. *Cristes-mæsse*), Christmas, 481.

croked (cf. O.N. *krokr*, see *N.E.D.*), crooked, 80; icroked, 1676.

crope (O.E. *crēopan*), creep, 819; cropþ, pr. 3. sg., 826.

crowe (O.E. *crāwe*), crow, 1130; n. pl., a. pl., 126, 1613.

croweþ (O.E. *crāwan*), croweth, pr. 3. sg., 335.

cumen, comen, kume (O.E. *cuman*), come, 1131, 611, 821; cume, come, pr. 1. sg., 435, 1211; cumest, pr. 2. sg., 908, 585; cumeþ, comeþ, kumeþ, pr. 3. sg., 302, 1437, 683; cumeþ, pr. pl. 523; com, pt. 1. sg., 453; com, pt. 3. sg., 132; come, pt. 2. sg., 1058; come, pt. pl., 1671; come, opt. pt. sg., 1015; comen, opt. pt. pl., 1014; icumen, p. p., 130.

cunde (O.E. *cynd*), kind, nature, d. sg., 88, 273.

cundut (O.Fr. *conduit*, *condut*), part-song, 483; see note.

cunne, see can.

cunne, see kun.

custe (O.E. *cyst*), quality, character, d. pl., 9, d. sg., 1398; fashion, 115.

cuþ (O.E. *cȳþan*), makes known, pr. 3. sg., 132, 138; cuþest, pr. 2. sg., 90.

cuþe, see can.

cuuþ (O.E. *cūþ*), known, 922.

cwalm (O.E. *cwealm*), pestilence, death, 1199; cualm, 1157.

cwaþ, see iqueþe.

cwesse (O.Fr. *quasser*), crush, 1388.

dahet (O.Fr. *dahet*), misfortune, 99; cursed be (he), 1169, 1561; see note, 99.

dai (O.E. *dæg*), day, 259; daies, g. sg., 1431, adv. gen. = by day, 1590; dai, daie, d. sg., 103, 241; adai, by day, 89.

dai-liȝt (O.E. *dægleoht*), day-light, 332.

dai-rim (O.E. *dæg-rima*), day-break, 328.

dai-sterre (O.E. *dæg-steorra*), day-star, 328.

dale (O.E. *dæl*), dale, d. sg., 1.

dar (O.E. *dearr*), dare, pr. 3. sg., 1110; darr, pr. 1. sg., 1106; darst,

pr. 2. sg., 853, 1695; durre, opt. sg., 1706.

dare (O.E. *darian*), lurk, lie hidden, 384; see note.

deale (O.E. *dǣlan*), utter, 954.

deaþe (O.E. *dēaþ*), death, d. sg., 1617; deaþes, adv. gen. = in death, 1632; deþ, 1620.

ded (O.E. *dēad*), dead, 1138; dead, 1619.

dede (O.E. *dǣd*), deed, acc. sg., 513; d. pl., 232, 1376.

del (O.E. *dǣl*), part, 1027; sum-del, somewhat, in some measure, 870, 934; ech del, wholly, 1027.

deme (O.E. *dēma*), judge, 1783.

deme (O.E. *dēman*), judge, pronounce, 188, opt. sg., 201; demeþ, demþ, pr. 3. sg., 1755, 1777.

deouel (O.E. *dēofol*), devil, 1412; deoulene, g. pl., 932; see note.

derne (O.E. *dierne*), dark, d. sg., 608; adv., secretly, 1357.

dernliche (O.E. *diern + lice*), secretly, 1423.

deþ, see deaþe.

diche (O.E. *dic*), ditch, d. sg., 1239.

diȝele (O.E. *diegol*), hidden, secluded, 2.

diht (O.E. *dihtan*), prepares, composes, pr. 3. sg., 1756; dihte, pt. 3. sg., 1655; idiȝt, p. p., 641; idiht, p. p. = formed, 1547.

dim (O.E. *dim*), dim, dark, 369.

disputinge (cf. O.Fr. *disputer*), strife, 875; cf. sputing, 1574.

dom (O.E. *dōm*), judgment, verdict, n. sg., 1694, 1780, acc. sg., 210, 1692; dome, d. sg., 179, 193; domes, g. sg., 1695.

don, do (O.E. *dōn*), do, perform, cause, put, 159, 603; do, pr. 1. sg., opt. sg., 298, 1092; dest, dost, pr. 2. sg., 321, 237; deþ, doþ, pr. 3. sg., 564, 156; doþ, pr. pl., 95, 157; dude, pt. sg., 1016; idon, ido, p. p., 115, 113; do, imp. sg., 1788, 807.

dor (O.E. *dēor*), animal, creature, 493, n. pl. 1012, 1200; dore, d. pl., 1126.

Dorsete (O.E. *Dorsǣte*), Dorset, 1753.

draȝe, drahe (O.E. *dragan*), drag, lead, go, 1375, pr. 1. sg., 970; draȝst, pr. 2. sg., 589; draȝeþ, draheþ, draȝþ, pr. 3. sg., 1434, 1399, 776; idraȝe, p. p., 586.

drede (cf. O.E. *drǣdan*), dread, d. sg., 684.

dreme (O.E. *drēam*), melody, d. sg., 314; dreim, 21.

drenche (O.E. *drencan*), drown, submerge, 1205.

drinkeþ (O.E. *drincan*), drink, pr. pl., 1009.

driue (O.E. *drîfan*), incite, pursue, 1475; **driueþ**, pr. pl., 66, 809.

drunnesse (O.E. *druncenes*), drunkenness, d. sg., 1399; see note.

duȝeþe (O.E. *duguþ*), maturity, d. sg., 634.

dumb (O.E. *dumb*), dumb, 416.

dune (O.E. *dûn*), hill, down, d. sg., 832, acc. sg., 919.

duntes (O.E. *dynt*), blows, n. pl., 1227.

dure (O.E. *duru*), doors, d. pl., 778. **durre**, see **dar**.

dusi (O.E. *dysig*), foolish, unbridled, 1466.

dweole, dwole (O.E. *dweola, dwola*), error, wandering course, d. sg., 825, acc. sg., 1239; **a-dwole** (in error), wrong, 1777; **dweole-song**, song of evil, 926.

ear, see **ar** or **er**.

earding-stowe (O.E. *earding-stow*), dwelling-place, 28.

earen (O.E. *êare*), ears, 338.

east (O.E. *êast*), east, 923.

eauar, eauer, eauereuch, see **euer, euereuch**.

ech (O.E. *ælc*), each, every, 315, 434; *eche*, d. sg., 195, 800.

eche (O.E. *êce*), everlasting, 742, 1279.

eck, see **ek**.

edwite (O.E. *edwit*), disgrace, 1233.

efne (O.E. *efne*), smoothly, 313.

eft (O.E. *eft*), again, afterwards, 818, 1063.

eȝe (O.E. *êage*), eye, d. sg., 426; **eȝe**, **eȝen**, pl., 364, 990; **eȝene**, n. pl., 75.

eiȝte (O.E. *æht*), property, g. sg., 1153.

eiþer, see **aiþer**.

eiwat (O.E. *æghwæt*), everything, 1056.

ek, eke (O.E. *êac*), also, 69, 93, 1209; **eck**, 174.

elles (O.E. *elles*), else, 662, 1010; **elles-hwar**, 932.

ende (O.E. *ende*), end, 652, 1785 (see note); neighbourhood, 1132.

endi (O.E. *endian*), end, pr. 1. sg., 1456; **endeð**, pr. 3. sg., 943.

ene, enes (O.E. *æne*), once, 1107, 1049.

engeles (O.E. *engel*), angels, pl., 916.

Engelonde (O.E. *Englaland*), d., 749.

eni (O.E. *ænig*), any, 557, 720.

eorne, urne (O.E. *eornan, iernan*), run, 1204, 638; **urneþ**, pr. pl., 375.

er, ere (O.E. *ær*), ere, before, 866, 1309; ear, 1560; **erur**, comp., formerly, 1738; **erest**, first, 525; see **ar**.

erde (O.E. *eard*), native country, d., 460.

erede (O.E. *æræde*), at a loss, devoid of counsel, 1295.

ereming (O.E. *ierming*), wretched being, 1111.

erende (O.E. *ærende*), errand, business, 463.

erien (O.E. *erian*), plough, 1039.

erne (O.E. *ærnan*), ride, 1204.

este (O.E. *êst*), pleasure, d. sg., 353; ac. sg., 1504.

este (O.E. *êste*), pleasant, bountiful, 999, 1031.

ete (O.E. *etan*), eat, 108, pr. 1. sg., 598; **etestu**, pr. 2. sg., 599; **eteþ**, pr. pl., 1007.

eu, see **ȝe**.

euch (O.E. *æghwylc*), each, 975, 1224.

eue, eve (O.E. *æfen*), evening, 1687, 41.

euening (cf. O.N. *jafningi*), equal, 772.

euer, evre, eauer, etc. (O.E. *æfre*), ever, always, 132, 333; **eauer, eauere, eauar**, 1272, 1282, 1474; **ȝaure**, see note, 1180; **euer mo**, constantly, 238.

euereuch = **euer** + **euch** (see above), every, 1271, 1316; **eauereuch**, 1279, 1315.

eurich, evrich (O.E. *æfre-ælc*), every, each, 194, 229, 422.

ey (O.E. *æg*), egg, acc. sg., 104; **eye**, d. sg., 133; **eyre**, d. pl., 106.

fair (O.E. *fæger*), fair, 579; **faire, fayre**, 439, 182; **vair, vaire**, 584, 15; **uairur**, comp., 152; **faire**, adv., excellently, 924.

fairhede (O.E. *fæger* + **hædu*), beauty, 581.

fale, see **fele**.

falewi (O.E. *fealu*), reddish brown, 456; see note.

falle (O.E. *feallan*), fall, befall, 956, 630; **fallest**, pr. 2. sg., 1286; **falleþ**, **falþ**, pr. 3. sg., 1240, 1424; **ifallen**, **falle**, p. p., 514, 1233.

fals (O.Fr. *fals*), false, 210.

falt, see **folde**.

fare, vare (O.E. *faran*), go, fare, behave, 658, 909, 640; pr. 1. sg., 454; opt. pl., 552; **farest**, pr. 2. sg., 421; **fareþ, farþ**, pr. 3. sg., 1437, 245, pr. pl., 386; **for**, pt. sg.,

A.

14

1474; **fareþ**, imp. pl., 1736; **ifare**,
p. p., 1709, 400.

faste (O.E. *fæste*), fast, firmly, 796;
uastre, comp., 656.

fastrede (O.E. *fæstrǣd*), steadfast (of
mind), 211.

faucun (O.Fr. *faucun*), falcon, 111;
faukun, 101.

fedest (O.E. *fēdan*), feedest, pr. 2.
sg., 94; **iued**, p. p., fed, 1529.

felde (O.E. *feld*), field, d., 1714.

fele (O.E. *fǣle*), proper, natural, 1378.

fele (O.E. *fela, feola, feala*), many
(with gen.), 234, 797; **fale, uale**,
628, 1663; **feole, ueole**, 1214, 1274;
(a)uele, in many, 20.

felle (O.E. *fiellan*), overthrow, fell,
767.

felle (O.E. *fell*), skin, d. sg., 1572;
uelle, 1013; **uel**, acc. sg., 830.

fenge (O.E. *feng*), grip, bout (of
dialectics), 1285.

feole, see **fele**.

feor, for (O.E. *feorr*), far, 923, 398;
uor, 646; **forre**, comp., 386.

feorre (O.E. *feorran*), from afar,
1322; **vorre**, 327.

ferde (O.E. *fierd*), army, acc. sg.,
1156, 1668, 1672, 1684; **uerde**, d.
sg., 1790; see note.

ferden (O.E. *fēran*), went, pt. pl.,
1789.

fere (O.E. *fēra*), companion, d. sg.,
223, n. pl., 932.

feþer (O.E. *feþer*), feather, 1688.

fiȝte (O.E. *feoht*), strife, d. sg., 183.

fiȝte, viȝte (O.E. *feohtan*), fight, 667,
172; **fiȝt**, pr. 3. sg., 176, 1072;
uaȝt, pt. sg., 1071.

fiȝtinge (see above), d. sg., 1704.

fihs (O.E. *fisc*), fish, acc. sg., 1007.

fihtlac (O.E. *feohtlāc*), fighting, 1699.

finde, uinde (O.E. *findan*), find, 595,
470; **uindestu**, pr. 2. sg., 657; **uint**,
pr. 3. sg., 696; **ifunde**, p. p., 1515.

fitte (see note), equal (sb.), n. sg., 784.

fiehs, see **flesch**.

fleo, flo, flon (O.E. *flēogan, flēon*, see
Sievers, § 384, a 2), flee, fly, 1231,
406, 150; **fleo, flo**, pr. 1. sg., 957;
365; **fliȝst**, pr. 2. sg., 405, 89;
fliȝþ, fliȝt, pr. 3. sg., 506, 176;
floþ, pr. pl., 278; **flo**, imp. sg., 33;
fleo, opt. pl., 1673.

flesch (O.E. *flǣsc*), flesh, 1399; **fiehs**,
acc. sg., 1007; **flesches, fleses**, gen.
sg., 1388, 895; **flesche, fleshe**, d.
sg., 1387, 83.

flockes (O.E. *flocc*), flocks (of birds),
280.

flockes (O.Fr. *floc*), flocks or tufts (of
wool), 427; see note.

flod (O.E. *flōd*), flood, 946.

flores (O.Fr. *flōr, flūr*), flowers, 1046.

floþ, see **floweþ**.

floweþ (O.E. *flōwan*), flows, 946; **floþ**,
pr. 3. sg., 920.

fnast (O.E. *fnæst*), breath, 44.

fo (O.E. *(on)-fōn*), begin, opt. pl.,
179: see **iuo**.

fode, uode (O.E. *fōda*), offspring,
food, d. sg., 94, 606.

foȝe (cf. O.E. *gefōg*), decency, order,
184; see note.

foȝele, see **fuȝel**.

folc (O.E. *folc*), people, 1023.

folde (O.E. *fealdan*), fold, close,
1326; **falt**, pr. 3. sg. =folds up,
stammers, 37; see note.

fole, see **ful**.

folȝi (O.E. *folgian*), follow, pr. 1. sg.,
389; **folȝeþ**, pr. 3. sg., 307; see
fulieþ.

foliot (cf. O.Fr. *folier*), foolishness,
868; see note

fondi (O.E. *fandian*), try (with gen.),
1442; **fondeþ**, pr. 3. sg., 1581;
vonde, imp. sg., 1063.

for (O.E. *for*), because of, for the sake
of, for (prep. and conj.), 35, 32,
962; in order to (with inf.), 540,
1766, 1017; **for-þan, for-þon, forþan þat**, 1396, 1100, 780; **for-þan**,
therefore, 1600; **for-þe, for-þi**,
therefore, 69, 409.

for, see **feor**.

forbernest (O.E. *forbiernan*), art consumed, pr. 2. sg., 419.

forbode (O.E. *forbēodan*), forbid, pr.
1. sg., 648.

forbonne (O.E. *for* + *bannan*), outlaw,
1093.

forbreideþ (O.E. *forbregdan*), pervert,
corrupt, pr. pl., 1383; **uorbredeþ**,
pr. pl., 510; **forbrode**, p. p., 1381.

fordeme (O.E. *fordēman*), condemn,
1098.

fordo (O.E. *fordōn*), p. p., destroyed,
822.

fordrue (O.E. *fordrūgian*), dry up,
919.

fore (O.E. *fōr*), way, acc. sg., 817.

foreward (O.E. *foreweard*), agreement, 1693; **uoreward**, 1689.

forhele (O.E. *forhelan*), conceal, 798.

forleose (O.E. *forlēosan*), lose, opt.
pr. sg., 1344; **forleost, forlost**, pr.
2. sg., 1649, 519, pr. 3. sg., 949,
693; **uorlost**, pr. 3. sg., 619; **forles**,
pt. sg., 1100; **forlore**, p. p., 1391.

forlere (O.E. *forlǣran*), lead astray, 926.

forleten, forlete (O.E. *forlǣtan*), abandon, leave off, lose, 966, 988; forlete, pr. 1. sg., 36, opt. sg., 404, opt. pl., 961; uorleteþ, pr. pl., 634.

forlore, forlost, see forleose.

forme (O.E. *forma*), first, former, 820.

forre, see feor.

forstes (O.E. *forst*), frosts, 524.

fort (O.E. *for + to*), until, 41, 332, 432.

forþ, uorþ (O.E. *forþ*), forth, 528, 297; forþ in on, continuously, 356; forþure, comp., further, 1606.

forþan, forþi, see for.

forworþe (O.E. *forweorþan*), futile, worthless, p. p., 548, 573; forwurde, p. p., 1491.

fox, uox (O.E. *fox*), fox, 812, 819; foxes, acc. pl., 809.

freo, fro (O.E. *frēo*), free, noble, 131, 134.

freoman (O.E. *frēoman*), freeman, man of standing, 1507.

frogge (O.E. *frogga*), frog, 85, 146.

from, urom (O.E. *fram*), from, 62, 135, 1126; vrom, vram, 197, 163.

frome, see frume.

frond (O.E. *frēond*), friends, acc. pl., 477; frondes, g. sg., 1154.

frost (O.E. *frēosan*), freezes, pr. 3. sg., 620.

frouri (O.E. *frōfrian*), comfort, pr. 1. sg., 535.

frume, frome (O.E. *fruma*), beginning, 1513, 476.

fuelkunne (O.E. *fugol-cynn*), birdkind, d. sg., 65.

fuȝel (O.E. *fugol*), bird, 1135; fuȝele, foȝle, d. pl., 64, 277; fuȝeles, g. sg., 343, n. pl., 1144; fuheles, n. pl., 1660.

ful (O.E. *full*), full, 247; fulle, d. sg., 314; ful, adv., full, very, 471, 810, 1292.

ful (O.E. *fûl*), foul, 612; fule, d. sg., 1096; fulne, acc. m., 1196; fole, acc. n., 104; vul, vule, 236, 31, 35; fule, sb., d. sg., 301.

fuleþ (O.E. *fȳlan*), defile, 100, pr. pl., 96; ifuled, p. p., 110.

fulieð (O.E. *fylgan*), follows, pr. 3. sg., 1239; see folȝi.

fulliche, fuliche (O.E. *fullice*), fully, 1687, 128.

fulste (O.E. *fylstan*), help, pr. 1. sg., 889.

fundeþ (O.E. *fundian*), aspire, strive, 719; fundieþ, pr. pl., 850.

fust (O.E. *fȳst*), fist, 1538.

gabbinge (O.N. *gabba*), foolish talk, lies, 626.

ȝaf, see ȝefe.

ȝal, see ȝolle.

galegale (see note), chatterbox, 256.

Galeweie, Galloway, 910.

game (O.E. *gamen*), game, pleasure, acc. sg., 1649; gome, nom. sg., 1443; acc. sg., 521.

gan, gon, go (O.E. *gān*), go, 1510, 214, 1431; gest, pr. 2. sg., 875; geþ, goþ, pr. 3. sg., 528, 522; goþ, goð, pr. pl., 305, 938; go, opt. sg., 1285, opt. pl., 745, imp. sg., 297; gon to, proceed, 669, 838.

ȝare (O.E. *gearu*), ready, n. sg., 215, 1780, n. pl., 296; ȝarre, 1222; ȝarewe, 378.

ȝaure, see euer.

ȝe (O.E. *gē*), ye, 116; eu, ov, ow, dat. and acc., 1793, 114, 1686; see þu.

ȝef, see ȝif.

ȝefe, ȝiue (O.E. *giefan*), give, 1710, 1767; ȝiue, pr. 1. sg., 1686; ȝeueþ, ȝiueþ, pr. pl., 1776, 1773; ȝaf, ȝef, pt. 3. sg., 55, 1176; iȝiue, p. p., 551.

ȝelpst (O.E. *gielpan*), boastest, yelpest, pr. 2. sg., 971; ȝeilpest, ȝeolpest, ȝulpest, 1641, 1299, 1650.

gelus (O.Fr. *gelos*), jealous, 1077.

ȝeme (O.E. *gieme*), care, 649, 727.

ȝene (see note), answer, 845; pr. 1. sg., 893.

genge (O.E. *genge*), effective, 804, 1065; usual, common, 1002.

gengþ (O.E. *gangan*), goes, pr. 3. sg., 376.

gente (O.Fr. *gent*), gentle, n. pl., 204.

ȝeolpest, see ȝelpst.

ȝeoneþ, see ȝonie.

ȝeorne, ȝorne (O.E. *georne*), eagerly, 1352, 538.

ȝep (O.E. *gēap*), cunning, clever, 465.

ȝephede (O.E. *gēap + *hǣdu*), cunning, sb., 683.

ȝer (O.E. *gēar*), year, dat. acc. sg., 101, 790; a-ȝere, in the spring, 1133; see note.

ȝerd (O.E. *gierd*), stick, 777.

ȝet, ȝete (O.E. *giet, gieta*), yet, still, moreover, 545, 747; ȝette, 1307; ȝut, 363, 1697; þe ȝet, see note, 1624.

ȝeueþ, see ȝefe.

gideliche (O.E. *gydig + lice*), foolishly, 1282.

gidie (O.E. *gydig*), foolish, d., 291.

ȝif, ȝef (O.E. *gif, gyf*), if, 56, 347.
ginne (O.Fr. *engin*), skill, cunning, dat. acc. sg., 669, 765.
ginneþ (O.E. *ginnan*), begin, pr. pl., 437, 1700.
glad (O.E. *glæd*), glad, sg., 434; glade, pl., 424, 451; gladur, comp. sg., 19; gladdere, pl., 737.
gleu (O.E. *glēaw*), wise, prudent, 193.
god, gode (O.E. *gōd*), good, sg. and pl., 477, 605; godes, g. sg., 563; godne, acc. m., 812.
God, Godd (O.E. *God*), God, 867, 1543; Godes, g. sg., 357.
Goddspel (O.E. *godspell*), gospel, 1270; Goddspelle, d. sg., 1209.
godhede (O.E. *gōd* + *hǣdu), goodness, merit, 351; godede, 582.
ȝoeþe (O.E. *geogoð*), youth, d. sg., 633.
ȝoȝelinge (see note), outcry, d., 40.
gold (O.E. *gold*), gold, 1366.
golfinc (O.E. *goldfinc*), goldfinch, 1130.
ȝolle, ȝollen (cf. O.E. *giellan*, see note, 223), yell, scream, 972, 977; ȝollest, ȝolst, pr. 2. sg., 223, 985; ȝal, pt. sg., 112.
golnesse (O.E. *gālness*), wantonness, lust, d., 492, 498.
gome, see game.
ȝomere (O.E. *gēomere*), sadly, 415.
ȝond (O.E. *geon*), that, yonder, pro., 119.
ȝong-, see ȝung-.
ȝonie (O.E. *geonian*), yawn, opt. sg., 292; ȝeoneþ, pr. 3. sg., 1403.
gore (O.E. *gāra*), triangular piece set in a garment, gown, 515.
gost (O.E. *gāst*), spirit, ghost, 1401, 1111; gostes, g. sg., 1398.
gradde, see grede.
grame (O.E. *grama*), anger, harm, 49; grome, d. sg., 1090.
granti, graunti (O.Fr. *granter*), grant, pr. 1. sg., 201, 745.
gras (O.E. *græs*), grass, 1042.
grede (O.E. *grǣdan*), cry out, 308, 1683, pr. 1. sg., 474; gredest, pr. 2. sg., 566; gred, pr. 3. sg., 1533; gredeþ, pr. pl., 1671; gradde, pt. sg., 936, pt. pl., 1662; igrad, p. p., 1149.
greie (O.E. *grǣg*), grey, 834.
grene (O.E. *grēne*), green, 18; d. pl., 456.
gret, grete (O.E. *grēat*), great, large, 1488, 318; grettere, comp., 74.
grimliche (O.E. *grimmlice*), cruelly, 1332.

grine (O.E. *grin*), snare, d. sg., 1059; pl., 1056.
grislich (O.E. *grislic*), horrible, 224, 1003.
griþ (O.E. *griþ*), peace, truce, 1005, 1369.
griþ-bruche (O.E. *griþ-bryce*), breach of the peace, 1734.
grom (O.E. *gram*), angry, perturbed, 992.
grome, see grame.
gromes (O.N. *grōmr*), boys, 1115, 1645.
groni (O.E. *grānian*), groan, opt. sg., 872.
gropeþ (O.E. *grāpian*), feel, handle, pr. 3. sg., 1496.
groue (O.E. *grāf*), grove, d. sg., 380.
growe (O.E. *grōwan*), grow, 1134; pt. pl., 136.
grucching (cf. O.Fr. *grouchier*), grumbling, 423.
grulde (O.E. *grillan*), were twanging, opt. 2. sg., 142.
grunde (O.E. *grund*), ground, d., 278.
Guldeforde, Guildford, 191.
ȝulinge (cf. O.E. *giellan*), yelling, sb., 1643.
ȝulpest, see ȝelpst.
gult (O.E. *gylt*), sin, guilt, 1410; guld, 1427; gulte, d. sg., 874.
gulte (O.E. *gyltan*), is guilty, pr. ind. 3. sg., 1523; see note.
ȝunge (O.E. *geong*), young, n. sg., 1434; pl., 1134.
ȝunglinge, ȝunlinge (O.E. *geongling*), young girl, d. sg., 1447, n. sg., 1433; ȝongling, n. sg., infant, 635.
ȝut, see ȝet.

habbe (O.E. *habban*), have, 258, pr. 1. sg., 174, opt. sg., 99; hauest, pr. 2. sg., 153; haueþ, hauet, pr. 3. sg., 301, 113; habbeþ, habbet, habeþ, haueþ, pr. pl., 431, 651, 1611, 1675; hadde, pt. sg., 395, 1083; (n)addest, pt. 2. sg., 1061; hadde, pt. pl., 1008.
hacche (O.E. *hæcc*), casement, d. sg., 1058.
haȝe (O.E. *haga*), homestead, hedge, d. pl., 585; hahe, d. pl., 1612.
haȝel (O.E. *hagol, hægol*), hail, 1002.
haȝte (see *N.E.D.*), hatched, pt. 3. sg., 105.
hahe, see haȝe.
halde, holde (O.E. *healdan*), hold, keep, consider, 1369, 3; holdest, pr. 2. sg., 1517; halt, pr. 3. sg., 356; hold, pt. sg., 144; holde, pt.

pl., 12, pt. opt. sg., 51; **iholde**, p. p., 1723.

hale (O.E. *healh*), corner, secret place, d. sg., 2; see note.

halter (O.E. *hælfter*), halter, 1028.

halue (O.E. *healf*), side, d. sg., 109, 887.

ham, hom (O.E. *hām*), home, adv. acc., 1531, 457, 1534; **attom**, at home, 1527.

hard (O.E. *heard*), hard, severe, 1694; **harde**, 530; as sb. = hard weather, 459; difficult (circumstances), 703.

hardeliche (O.E. *heardlice*), bravely, 402.

hare (O.E. *hara*), hare, n., 373.

harm, harem (O.E. *hearm*), harm, 1254, 1260; **hareme**, d. sg., 1161.

harpe (O.E. *hearpe*), harp, 343, 22.

hatiet (O.E. *hatian*), hates, pr. 3. sg., 230.

hattest, see hot.

hauec, haueck (O.E. *heafoc*), hawk, 307, 303; **hauekes**, g. sg., 271.

he (O.E. *hē*), he, it, etc., 21; **his, is**, g., 100, 403; **him**, d., 122; **hine**, acc., 236, 680, 1374; fem., **ho, heo, he**, n., 19, 934, 141; **hire, hure**, fem. g. and d., 26, 1599; **hi, heo**, acc., 29, 939, 1438; neu., **hit, it**, 28, 1090; **his**, its, 100, 232; plu., **hi, ho, heo**, n., 10, 66, 931; **hore, here, heore, hire**, g., 280, 739, 1612, 1566; **hom, heom**, d., 62, 930; **hi, heo**, a., 108, 926.

heare, here (O.E. *hǣr*), hair, d. pl., 1550, 428.

hecst, see heȝe.

heȝe, heie (O.E. *hēah*), high, adv., 989, 1646; **on heh**, 1405, 1456; **herre**, comp., 1637; (alre-)**hecst**, super., 687; adj., **hexst**, d. sg., 970.

hegge (O.E. *hecg*), hedge, d. sg., 17, 59.

heie (O.E. *hege*), hedge, d. sg., 819.

hei-sugge (O.E. *hege-sugge*), hedge-sparrow, 505.

helle (O.E. *hell*), hell, d. sg., 1014.

helpe (O.E. *helpan*), help, with dat., 664, pr. 1. sg., 484; **helpþ**, pr. 3. sg., 171.

heme (O.E. *-hǣme*), householders, masters, n. pl., 1115.

hen (O.E. *henn*), hen, 413.

Henri, Henry, 1091.

heo, heore, heom, etc., see he.

heonne, honne (O.E. *heonan*), hence, 1673, 66.

heorte, horte (O.E. *heorte*), heart, mind, 1565, 37; **horte**, g. sg., d. sg., 945, 678.

heouene, houene (O.E. *heofon*), heaven, d. sg., 916, 897; for compounds see **houenkinge**, etc.

hepe (O.E. *hēap*), heap; **ful bi hepe** = full to overflowing, 360.

her, here (O.E. *hēr*), here, 462, 931; **her-bi**, 127; **herof**, from this, concerning this, 1076, 875; **heruore**, therefore, 1165.

herde, see ihere.

herdes (O.E. *hierde*), shepherds, n. pl., 286.

here, see heare.

here (O.E. *here*), ravaging army, troop, d. sg., 1709, 1790, see note; acc. sg., 1702.

herest (O.E. *herian*), praisest, pr. 2. sg., 1518.

hergonge (O.E. *heregang*), invasion, d., 1191.

heriinge (O.E. *heriung*), praise, n. sg., 981.

herre, see heȝe.

hes (O.E. *hǣs*), sentence, judicial pronouncement, 748; see note.

hete (O.E. *hete*), hate, sb., 167.

heued (O.E. *hēafod*), head, 74; acc. sg., 119.

hi, see he.

hider (O.E. *hider*), hither, 462, 1690.

hiȝte (O.E. *hyhtan*), rejoice, pr. 1. sg., 532; **hiȝteþ**, pr. 3. sg., 436.

hiȝte (O.E. *hyht*), joy, n. sg., 272; acc. sg., 1103.

himward, with *to* = towards him, 375.

hine, see he.

hine (O.E. **hina : (man) hi(g)na*), servants, n. pl., 1115.

hoȝe (O.E. *hogu*), care, thought, 701; see note, 537.

hoȝeþ (O.E. *hogian*), is anxious, pr. 3. sg., 455.

hoȝfule (O.E. *hogful, hohful*), anxious, thoughtful, n. pl., 537; **hohful**, 1292, 1295; see note.

hoked (O.E. *hōcede*), curved, hooked, 79; **ihoked**, 1675.

hokeþ (O.E. **hōcian*), winds along, pr. 3. sg., 377.

hole (O.E. *hol*), hole, d. sg., 826; **cropþ to hole**, goes to earth; see also holȝ.

holȝ (O.E. *holh*), hollow, adj., n. sg., 643, 1113; **hole**, d. sg., 965.

holi (O.E. *hālig*), holy, 721, 1382.

holinesse (O.E. *hālignes*), holiness, 900.

hom, see ham, he.

honde (O.E. *hand*), hand, d. sg., 1372; acc. pl., 1651.

hongi (O.E. *hangian*), hang, 816; hongest, pr. 2. sg., 1142; hongeþ, pr. sg., 1132, pr. pl., 1612; hong, imp. sg., 658.

honne, see heonne.

hord (O.E. *hord*), hoard, 467.

horne (O.E. *horn*), horn, d. sg., 318.

hors (O.E. *hors*), horse, 629; horse, horsse, d. pl., 1062, 768.

hose (O.E. *hās*), hoarse, harsh, 504.

hot (O.E. *hātan*), commands, pr. 3. sg., 779; hattest, pass. 2. sg. = art called, 255; hoten, p. p. = called, 256.

hot, hote (O.E. *hāt*), hot, 1275; wk., 1454.

hoþ (O.E. *hōn*), hangs, pr. 3. sg., 1123; ihonge, p. p., 1136.

hou (O.E. *hēow*), hue, colour, a. sg., 619; howe, d. sg., 152.

houeneliȝte (O.E. *heofonleoht*), light of heaven, d. sg., 732.

houeneriche (O.E. *heofonrice*), king-dom of heaven, d. sg., 717.

houenkinge (O.E. *heofoncyning*), king of heaven, d. sg., 862.

houentinge (O.E. *heofon + tenge*), reaching to heaven, 1001; see note.

houhsiþe (O.E. *hoh + siþ*), anxious journeyings, 1586; see note.

hu (O.E. *hū*), how, 46, 263.

hude (O.E. *hȳd*), hide, skin, a. sg., 1114.

hude (O.E. *hȳdan*), hide, 1113, pr. 1. sg., 265; hud, imp. sg., 164.

huing (O.Fr. *huer*), outcry, clamour, 1264; see note.

hule, vle, ule (O.E. *ūle*), owl, 41, 143, 26, 837; houle, 1662, 1785.

hund (O.E. *hund*), dog, hound, 817; hundes, gen. sg., 822, n. pl., 375; hunde, d. sg., 814.

hundred (O.E. *hundred*), hundred, 1101.

hunger (O.E. *hungor*), hunger, d., 1191.

hunke, see ich.

hupþ (O.E. **hyppan*), hops, leaps, pr. 3. sg., 379; hupte, pt. 3. sg., 1636; see note, 379.

hure, see he, ich.

hure (O.E. *hūrū*), especially (see note), 1483; hure and hure, 11, 481.

hurne (O.E. *hyrne*), corner, d. sg., 14.

hus (O.E. *hūs*), house, 623; huses, g. sg., 1155, n. pl., 1203; huse, d. sg., 479, d. pl., 1333.

hwan, see hwo.

hwanne (O.E. *hwanne, hwænne, hwonne*), when, 1244; hwan, 1264; hwon, 1566; wane, 420; wan, 459; wonne, 38; wone, 327; won, 324; wanne, 430.

hwar (O.E. *hwǣr*), where, 932, 1727; whar, 64; war, 526; ware, 1049; warto, why, 464.

hwaruore (see above), wherefore, 1421; wareuore, waruore, 267, 1618.

hwat, wat (O.E. *hwæt*), what! well! (interj.), 1730, 635.

hwatliche (O.E. *hwætlice*), quickly, 1708.

hwaþer, waþer (O.E. *hwæþer*), which (of two), 1198, 1064; hweþer, weþer, 1408, 991; ware, 151.

hwaþer (O.E. *hwæþer*), whether (conj.), hwaþer...þe, whether...or, 1362; weþer, 824.

hwi, wi (O.E. *hwi*), 909, 218; whi, 150.

hwile, wile, wule (O.E. *hwil*), while, period of time, 1591, 6, d. sg., 1458; wile, adv. dat. pl. = formerly, 202; wule, adv. d. pl., sometimes, 1542.

hwit (O.E. *hwit*), white, 1276.

hwo, wo, wa (O.E. *hwā*), who (interr.), 1195, 113, 1782; wu, n. sg., 187; hwan, wan, d. sg., 1509, 530; hwat, wat, neu., 1296, 185.

hwon, see hwanne.

hwuch, wucche (O.E. *hwylc*), which, what (adj. and pro.), 1504, 1443; hwucche, d. sg., 936; wucche, d. pl., 1319.

I, see ich.

ibedde (O.E. *gebedda*), bedfellow, 968, 1490.

ibere (O.E. *gebǣru*), noise, outcry, 222, 1348.

ibolwe (O.E. *belgan*), swollen with rage, p. p., 145.

iborȝe (O.E. *beorgan*), saved, p. p., 883.

ibroded (O.E. *brādian*), extended, p. p., 1312.

ibunde (O.E. *bindan*), bound, held (responsible), p. p., 656, 1354.

ich (O.E. *ic*), I, 1, 3; ic, 1049; I, 293, 448; me, d. and acc., 34, 39; unker, dual gen., 151; hunke, dual dat., 1733; we, nom. pl., 552; us, dat. acc., 187, 188; ure, g. pl., 650, 958.

icnowe (O.E. *gecnāwan*), acknow-ledge, cultivate, cherish, opt. sg., 477.

icunde (O.E. *gecynde*), natural, 114; icundur, comp., 85.

icundeliche (O.E. *gecyndelice*), naturally, 1424.

icweme (O.E. *gecwēman*), please, 1784.

idel, see ydel.

idiht, see diht.

idorue (O.E. (*ge*)*deorfan*), afflicted, p. p., 1158.

iduȝe (cf. O.E. *dugan*), profitable, pleasing, 1582.

ifurn (O.E. *gefyrn*), of long ago, 1306; ivurne, 637.

igrad, see grede.

igramed (O.E. *gramian*), enraged, p. p., 933, 1603.

igrede (cf. O.E. *grǣdan*), crying, clamour, sb., 1643.

ihende (O.E. *gehende*), near, at hand, 1131, 1263, sb. = conveniences, 651.

ihere, ihire (O.E. *gehieran*), hear, 224, 312; ihereþ, pr. pl., 222; iherde, herde, pt. sg., 1635, 293; iherd, ihert, p. p., 1317, 1763.

ihoded (O.E. *gehādian*), ordained, p. p., 1177, 1311.

ihold (O.E. *geheald*), protection, stronghold, 621.

iholde, see halde.

ihonge, see hoþ.

ikepþ (O.E. *cēpan*), takes heed, awaits, 1228.

ikunde (O.E. *gecynd*), nature, a. sg., 1383.

iladde (O.E. *lǣdan*), carried, conducted, p. p., 398, 1294.

ilast, see ileste.

ilefde (O.E. *geliefan*), believed, pt. sg., 123.

ileste (O.E. *gelǣstan*), last, continue, 341; ilesteþ, ilest, ilast, pr. 3. sg., 347, 1451, 1038.

ilete, lete (O.E. *gelǣte*, O.N. *lǣti*), face, expression, appearance, 403, 1446, 35, 1715.

ilich (O.E. *gelic*), like, alike, 316; iliche, sg., 358; iliche, adv., 618.

ilike (O.E. *gelica*), like, (thy) sort, n. pl., 157, 1460.

ilke (O.E. *ilca*), same, 99.

ille (O.N. *illr*), wrong, adj., 1536; evil (man), 421.

iloȝe, see liȝe.

ilome (O.E. *gelōme*), often, 49; lome, 1545; ilomest, super., 595.

ilorned, see lorni.

iloue (O.E. *gelēofa*), lover, pl., 1047.

imeind, see meinþ.

imene (O.E. *gemǣne*), common, 234.

imene (O.E. **gemǣna < gemāna*), companion, see note, 1412; imene (O.E. *gemǣne*), fellowship, 301.

imist, see mist.

imunde (O.E. *gemynd*), care, consideration, dat., 1516; acc., 252.

in (O.E. *in*), in, on, 1, 14, 103, 1123; into, 908, 1118; ine, 350, 438.

innoh (O.E. *genōh*), enough, sufficiently, adv., 1220, 1319.

inoȝe (O.E. *genōh*), enough, many, adj. pl., 16; inoh, 1182.

insiȝt (O.E. *in + sihþ, siht*), discernment, 195; insihte, 1187.

into (O.E. *into*), into, 150.

inume, see nime.

ipeint (O.Fr. *peindre, peint*), painted, p. p., 76.

iqueþe (O.E. *gecweþan*), speak, say, 502; quaþ, quad, cwaṭ, pt. 3. sg., 117, 117, 1739; icwede, p. p., 1653.

iredi (O.E. *gerǣde + ig*), ready, 488.

Irish (O.E. *Irisc*), Irish, 322.

Irlonde (O.E. *Iraland*), Ireland, d., 907.

ischend, see schende.

ischire (O.E. *gesciran*), utter, speak, 1532.

ischrud (O.E. *gescrȳdan*), clad, p. p., 1529.

ise (O.E. *isen, īren*), iron, 1030.

iseche, see seche.

iseid, see segge.

isene (O.E. *gesiene*), visible, 166, 275.

iseo, ison, iso (O.E. *gesēon*), see, 1268, 383, 366; iseo, iso, so, pr. 1. sg., 1219, 327, 34; isihst, sichst, pr. 2. sg., 1225, 242; isiþ, siþ, suþ, isoþ, iseȝþ, pr. 3. sg., 407, 950, 246, 424, 1465; soþ, pr. pl., 884; iseo, (n)iso, opt. sg., 1241, 674; iseȝ, pt. 3. sg., 29; iseȝe, (n)iseȝe, opt. pt. sg., 425, 382.

ishilde, see schilde.

ishote (O.E. *scēotan*), shot, p. p., 23, 1121.

islaȝe (O.E. *slēan*), slain, p. p., 1142.

islide, see slide.

isliked (O.E. **slician*), made plausible, specious, p. p., 841.

isome, ysome (O.E. *gesōm*), reconciled, friendly, n. pl., 1735, d. pl., 180.

ispild, see spille.

isprunge, see springe.

istunge (O.E. *stingan*), thrust, p. p., 515.

isunde (O.E. *gesund*), sound, safe, 1102.

isuolȝe (O.E. *swelgan*), swallowed,
p. p., 146.

iswike (O.E. *geswican*), cease, fail,
opt. pl., 929; nisvicst, pr. 2. sg.,
with neg., 406; see note.

it, see he.

itache (O.E. *getǣcan*), teach, pr. 1.
sg., 1347.

iteid (O.E. *tiegan*), tied, p. p., 778.

iþenche (O.E. *geþencean*), remember,
opt. 3. sg., 723.

iþrunge, see þringe.

itide (O.E. *getidan*), betide, befall,
inf., 1733, opt. sg., 1216; itid, itit,
pr. 3. sg., 1256, 1521.

itoȝen (O.E. *tēon*), reared, brought up,
p. p., 1725.

itrede (O.E. *tredan*), trodden, en-
gendered, p. p., 501.

iued, see fedest.

iui (O.E. *ifig*), ivy, d. sg., 27, 617.

iuo (O.E. *gefōn*), capture, seize, 612,
1628; ifoð, pr. pl., 1645.

iuo (O.E. *gefāh*), foe, acc. sg., 1716.

ivurne, see ifurn.

iwar (O.E. *gewær*), aware, 147;
iwarre, n. pl., 1221.

iwarnesse (O.E. *gewærnes*), wariness,
1228.

iweld (O.E. *geweald*), power, control;
nah iweld=cannot help, 1543.

iwinne (O.E. *gewinnan*), win, 766,
1290.

iwis (O.E. *gewiss*), indeed, certainly,
35, 118.

iwit (O.E. *gewit*), understanding, 774,
1188; iwitte, d., 1217.

iwone, iwune (O.E. *gewuna*), custom,
usual, adj. or sb., 475, 1318; see
note.

iworpe, see worpe.

iworþe, see wurþe.

Jesus, Jesus, 1092.

kan, kon, see can.

kanunes (N.Fr. *canonie*, see *N.E.D.*
*canon*²), canons, 729.

kare (O.E. *cearu*), care, 1590.

keie (O.E. *cǣg*), key, d. sg., 1557.

kene (O.E. *cēne*), keen, bold, 276,
526.

kepe (O.E. *cēpan*), like, wish; ke-
pich=kepe ich, 154; see note.

king (O.E. *cyning*, *cyng*), king, 235,
d. sg., 1728; kinges, g. sg., 1095.

knarres (cf. L.G. *knarre*), rocks, 1001.

kniȝt, see cniht.

kukeweld (O.Fr. *cucuault*), cuckold,
1544.

kume (O.E. *cyme*, *cume*), coming, sb.,
436.

kume, kumeþ, see cumen.

kun (O.E. *cynn*), kin, kind, 714;
kunne, d., 1099, g. pl., 888, 1396.

kunne, kuþe, see can.

kunrede (O.E. *cynn*+*rǣden*), kindred,
1677.

kursest (O.E. *cursian*), cursest, 1178.

la (O.E. *lā*), oh!, 1543.

lacche (O.E. *lǣccan*), seize, 1057.

laȝe (O.N. *lagr*), low, adv., 1456; loȝe,
1052.

laȝe (O.E. *lagu*, *lah-*), custom, law,
969, 1037.

lahfulnesse (< O.E. *lagu*, *lah-*), law-
fulness, 1741.

lai, see ligge.

lame, lome (O.E. *lama*), lame, weak,
1732, 364.

lasse (O.E. *lǣssa*), less, lower, adj.,
1227, 482, 1406; adv., 370.

last (O.E. *lǣstan*), lasts, pr. 3. sg.,
516, 1466; lest, 1450.

lat, see lete.

late (O.E. *læt*), late, adv., 1147; later,
comp., 963; see note.

lauedi (O.E. *hlǣfdige*), lady, wife,
959, 1569; lefdi, 1051; lauedies,
n. pl., 1338.

lauerd, louerd (O.E. *hlāford*), lord,
husband, 959, 968; lauerdes,
louerdes, g. sg., 1586, 1589.

leches (O.E. *lēc*), looks, appearance,
1140; see note.

leide, see legge.

lede (O.E. *lǣdan*), lead, 1684; ledest,
pr. 2. sg., 1672; ledeþ, pr. pl.,
280.

lefdi, see lauedi.

legge (O.E. *lecgan*), lay, place; 1224;
leiþ, pr. 3. sg., 801; leidest, pt. 2.
sg., 104; leide, pt. 3. sg., 467, 1057.

leie, see ligge.

leng (O.E. *leng*), longer, comp. adv.,
42, 493.

lengþe (O.E. *lengþu*), length, 174.

lenst (O.E. *lǣnan*), lendest, givest,
pr. 2. sg., 756.

leof, lof (O.E. *lēof*), dear, precious,
1277, 203; loue, 968; þat leof is
=who delights, 1524.

leofmon (O.E. *lēof*+*man*), lover,
1430.

leorni, see lorni.

lepe (O.E. *lēap*), basket, d. sg., 359.

lere (O.E. *lǣre*), empty, 1528.

lere (O.E. *lǣran*), teach, 1017, pr. 1.
sg., 1347; lerdest, pt. 2. sg., 1053.

lese (O.E. *lēas*), false, worthless, pl., 756.

lesing (O.E. *lēasung*), falsehood, 848.

lest, see last.

lete (O.E. *lǣtan*): (1) let, allow, 1457; lat, let, pr. 3. sg., 308, 919; leteþ, pr. 2. pl., 1699; let, pt. 3. sg., 8; lette, pt. 3. sg., 952 (see note); lat, imp. sg., 258; lateþ, imp. pl., 1729. (2) let alone, leave, let, pr. 3. sg., 1530; leteþ, pr. pl., 1771; lete, infin., 1471. (3) caused, let, pt. 3. sg., 1093. (4) refrain from, leten, lete, inf., 1018, 1445; lat, pr. 3. sg., 250; lete, pt. 2. sg., 1308. (5) think of, value, leteþ, pr. pl., 1774.

lete, see ilete.

leþ, see ligge.

leue (O.E. *lēaf*), leave, sb., 457.

leue (O.E. *lēaf*), leaves, a. pl., 456; leues, pl., 1046, 1326.

libbe (O.E. *libban*), live, 1192; libbeþ, pr. pl., 1012; libbe, opt. pl., 1006.

licome (O.E. *lichama, licuma*), body, 1054.

liest, see liȝe.

lif (O.E. *lif*), life, 1127, 988; liue, d. sg., 1078; liues, adv. gen. = alive, 1632, 1634; for his liue, to save his life, 1078.

lifdaȝe (O.E. *lifdæg*), life, d. pl., 1141.

liȝe (O.E. *lēogan*), lie, prevaricate, 853; liest, pr. 2. sg., 367; liȝe, opt. 2. sg., 599; lioȝe, p. p., 847.

ligge (O.E. *licgan*), lie, 1200; liþ, leþ, pr. 3. sg., 430, 1494; list, pr. 2. sg., 1502; liggeþ, pr. pl., 959; ligge, opt. pr. sg., 1619; lai, leie, opt. pt. sg., 1509, 134.

liȝt, liht (O.E. *leoht*), light, 734, 949; liȝte, lihte, d. sg., 163, 1431.

liȝtliche, lihtlice (O.E. *leohtlice*), easily, lightly, 854, 1774.

lihtlich (O.E. *leohtlic*), easy, 1185.

liim (O.E. *lim*), lime, bird-lime, 1056.

liki (O.E. *lician*), please, 342.

lilie (O.E. *lilie*), lily, 439.

lime (O.E. *lim*), limb, acc. sg., 1098.

linde (O.E. *lind*), lime-tree, 1750.

linnene (O.E. *linen*), of linen, adj., 1174.

list, see ligge.

liste (O.E. *list*), cunning, g. sg., 763; d. sg., 172, 767.

litle, see lutel.

liþ, see ligge.

liueþ (O.E. *(be)-lifan*), remains, pr. 3. sg., 810.

lodlich (O.E. *lāðlic*), hateful, horrible, 32, 91.

lof, see leof.

loȝe, see laȝe.

loke (O.E. *loc*), lock, 1557.

loki (O.E. *lōcian*): (a) look, see, 641; lokeþ, pr. 3. sg., 1555; loke, imp. sg., 166, 295. (b) look after, protect, loki, inf., 604; opt. sg., 56.

lome, see lame.

lond (O.E. *land*), land, 999; londe, d. sg., g. pl., d. pl., 420, 1371, 996.

londfolc (O.E. *landfolc*), people, 1158.

long (O.E. *lang*), long, adj., 344, longe, 857.

longe (O.E. *lange*), long, adv., 81, 253.

longeþ (O.E. *langian*), impers., it yearns, 1486; hom longeþ, they yearn, 881.

longinge (O.E. *langung*), longing, 869.

lore (O.E. *lār*), lore, teaching, n. sg., 1640; d. sg., 1208, 1351.

lorni (O.E. *leornian*), learn, 642; leorni, pr. 1. sg., 1212; ilorned, p. p., 216.

losen (O.E. *lēosan*), lose, 351; lost, pr. 3. sg, 830, 1159; lust, pr. 3. sg., 1193; see note.

loþ, loþe (O.E. *lāþ*), hateful, 65, 943, 1607 (see note); loþe, d. sg., 115.

loþe (O.E. *lāþ*), injury, pain, d. sg., 1146.

loue, see leof.

louerd, see lauerd.

lud (O.E. *hlūd*), loud, 6; lude, d. sg., 314.

lude (O.E. *hlūde*), loud, loudly, 112, 982.

lugge (see note), poles, sticks, d. pl., 1609.

lure (O.E. *lyre*), loss, 1153.

luriñg (cf. M.H.G. *lūren*), louring, 423.

lust (O.E. *lust*), desire, lust, 507; luste, d. sg., 895; lustes, pl., 1414.

lust (O.E. *lystan*), it pleases, impers., 213, 613; luste, opt. sg., 39.

lust, see losen.

luste (O.E. *hlystan*), listen, 896; lust, pr. 1. sg., 1594, imp. sg., 263, 546; lusteþ, imp. pl., 1729; luste, pt. 3. sg., 143.

lute (O.E. *lȳt*), a little, 763.

lutel, lutle (O.E. *lȳtel*), little, 561, 911, 1097; as adv., 769; litle, d. pl., 1776.

luteþ (O.E. *lūtian*), lurks, 373.

luþer (O.E. *lÿþer*), evil, bad, 1137.
lutli (O.E. *lÿtlian*), lessen, 540.
luue (O.E. *lufu*), love, 516, d. sg.,
207.
luuien, luuie (O.E. *lufian*), love,
1341, 1345; luueþ, pr. 3. sg., 230;
luuieþ, pr. pl., 791.

mai (O.E. *mæg*), may, can, it avails,
pr. 1. sg., 228, 274, opt. sg., 1266;
miȝt, pr. 2. sg., 64, 78; mai, may,
pr. 3. sg., 762, 1415; maȝe, pr. pl.,
182; miȝte, mihte, pt. 3. sg., 42,
953; miȝtest, pt. 2. sg., 256; miȝte,
pt. pl., 1104, 1749; muȝe, pr. opt.
pl., 62 (see note), 1117; muhe, pr.
opt. sg., 1581.
maide (O.E. *mægden*), maid, 1343,
d. sg., 1419, n. pl., 1338; maidenes,
pl., 1516.
maine (O.E. *mægen*), power, 760.
maister, maistre (O.Fr. *maistre*),
master, 191, 1778.
make (O.E. *maca*), mate, husband,
1159, 1429.
makie (O.E. *macian*), make, pr. opt.
3. sg., 1544; makest, pr. 2. sg.,
339; makeþ, pr. 3. sg., 354, pr. pl.,
650; makeð, pr. pl., 1648.
man, mon (O.E. *mann*, *monn*), man,
477, 783 ; mannes, monnes, g. sg.,
1476, 338; manne, men, d. sg.,
800, 1246; manne, monne, g. pl.,
d. pl., 234, 131; men, n. pl., 127,
acc. pl., 330, d. pl., 910.
mani, moni (O.E. *manig*), many,
much, 1323, 1411; manie, monie,
acc. pl., 1755, 257.
manifolde (O.E. *manigfeald*), mani-
fold, various, 1551.
mankunne, mankenne (O.E. *mann-
cynn*), mankind, d. sg., 849, 973,
1725.
mansing for amansung (O.E. *āmān-
sumung*), excommunication, 1312;
mansinge, d. sg., 1182.
manteine (O.Fr. *maintenir*), defend,
maintain, 759.
masse (O.E. *mæsse*), mass, 1181.
me, mon (O.E. *man*), indecl., one,
they, 142, 455.
mede (O.E. *mēd*), meadow, d.sg., 438.
meinþ (O.E. *mengan*), stirs up, 945;
meind, imeind, imend, p.p., mixed,
mingled, 131, 18, 870; imeinde,
p. p., wk., 823.
mene (O.E. *mǣnan*), mean, tell,
complain; pr. 1. sg., 1257, 92, 583;
menest, menst, pr. 2. sg., 648, 755;
meneþ, pr. pl., 1563.

meoster (O.Fr. *mester*), office, business, 924.
merci (O.Fr. *merci*), mercy, 1092.
merewode (O.E. *miere* + *wōd*), mad
for mares, 496.
mershe (O.E. *mersc*), marsh, d. sg.,
304.
meshe (O.E. **mǣscan*), crush, mash,
84.
mest (O.E. *mǣst*), most, greatest,
684, 852.
mete (O.E. *mete*), food, 107, 1630.
mid (O.E. *mid*), prep., with, 18, 76;
mide, 1768; mit, 616.
middel-niȝte, midelniȝte (O.E. *mid-
delniht*), midnight, d. sg., 325,
731.
miȝt, miȝte, etc., see mai.
miȝte (O.E. *miht*), power, might, 1188;
miȝtte, 536.
milc (O.E. *meolc*, *milc*), milk, 1009.
milce, milse (O.E. *milts*), mercy,
kindness, 1404, 1083.
milde (O.E. *milde*), gentle, kind,
1032; mildre, comp., 1775.
mile (O.E. *mil*), mile, n. sg., 1592.
min, mine (O.E. *min*), my, 712, 1460;
mire, dat. fem., 1741; mi, 37.
misbeode (O.E. *misbēodan*), ill-use,
abuse, 1541.
misdede (O.E. *misdǣd*), offence, mis-
deed, n. sg., 231.
misdon (O.E. *misdōn*), act wrongly,
sin, 1489; misdeþ, pr. 3. sg., 636;
misdoð, pr. pl., 1770; misdo, pr.
opt. pl., 1353; misdon, p. p., 1393.
misfonge (O.E. *misfōn*), use wrongly,
go astray, 1374, opt. pr. sg., 1440.
misȝenge (O.E. *mis* + *genge*), a miss,
1229.
mishap (O.E. *mis* + O.N. *happ*), misfortune, 1249.
misliche (O.E. *mislice*), indiscriminately, 1773.
mislikeþ (O.E. *mislician*), displeases,
pr. 3. sg., 344.
misnume (O.E. *mis* + *niman*), mis-
taken, gone wrong, p. p., 1514.
misrede (O.E. *misrǣdan*), advise
badly, 1063; misraddest, pt. 2. sg.,
160.
misreke, misreken (O.E. *mis* + *recan*),
go astray, 490, see note; 675.
misrempe (O.E. *mis* + *rempan*), go
headlong, go wrong, pr. opt. 1. sg.,
1787, pr. opt. 3. sg., 1353.
misstorte (see note), go wrong, 677.
mist (O.E. *missan*), escape, fail, pr.
3. sg., 825, 1640; imist, p. p., 581;
miste, p. p., 764; see note.

mistide (O.E. *mistidan*), turn out badly, impers., opt. pr. 3. sg., 1501.

mit, see mid.

mo (O.E. *mā*), more, comp. adv., 1108, 1330; used as sb., 564, 803; see note.

mod (O.E. *mōd*), mood, anger, mind, 8, 952; ac. pl., 1032; mode, d. sg., 517, 1349.

modi (O.E. *mōdig*), passionate, proud, 500.

modinesse (O.E. *mōdignes*), pride, d. sg., 1405, 1416.

mon, monne, see man.

mone (O.E. **mān*), complaint, 1520; see note.

moni, see mani.

more (O.E. *māra*), greater, comp. adj., 690, 786; used as adv. =more, 213, 516; used as sb., 482, 1207.

more (O.E. *mōr*), moor, 818.

more (O.E. *moru*), root, bottom, stumbling-block, 1328, 1392, 1422.

moregeninge (O.E. *morgen + ing*), morning, 1718.

mose (O.E. *māse*), titmouse, 69, 503.

mot (O.E. *mōt*), must, pr. 3. sg., 471, 1553; most, pr. 2. sg., 1302, 1304; moten, mote, opt. pl., 741, 857; moste, pt. 3. sg., 665; mote, may, pr. opt. sg., 52, 987.

mot (O.E. *mōt*), discussion, speech, 468.

mowe (O.E. *māwan*), mow, reap, 1040.

muchel, muche (O.E. *mycel*), much, great, 1094, 764; muchele, wk. dat., 1217; muchel, adv., 847; muche, sb., 1212.

muȝe, muhe, see mai.

mulne (O.E. *mylen*), mill, gen. pl., 778.

munekes (O.E. *munuc*), monks, 729.

murȝþe (O.E. *myrgð*), delight, joy, n. sg., 341, 718; murhþe, mureȝþe, 1402, 355.

murie (O.E. *myrig*), merry, pleasant, 345, 728.

murninge (O.E. *murnung*), mourning, d. sg., 1598.

mus (O.E. *mūs, mȳs*, pl.), mice, 87, 607; muse, d. pl., 591, 610.

muþ (O.E. *mūþ*), mouth, 673; muþe, d. sg. and pl., 234, 698.

na (O.E. *nā*), no, in phrases, na mo, 564; na more, 213.

na, see nan.

nabbeþ (=*ne habbeþ*), 252; see habbe.

nabideþ, see abide.

nabuȝþ (O.E. *ābūgan*), does not obey, pr. 3. sg., 782.

nacoleþ, see acolen.

nadde, naddest (=*ne + hadde, haddest*), 1560, 1061; see habbe.

nah, see ah.

naht (O.E. *naht*), worthless, 1480.

nai, nay (O.N. *nei*), nay, 266, 543.

nam, nart, nartu, nis, nas, nere, etc. (=*ne + am, ne + art*, etc.), 753, 559, 1330, 120, 114, 656; see beon.

nan (O.E. *nān*), no, adj., 1389; nanne, mas. ac., 1238; na, 901; nanne, pro., 812.

narewe (O.E. *nearw-*), narrow, 377; adv., closely, 68.

naþeles, noþeles, neoþeles (O.E. *nāþelǣs*), nevertheless, 827, 149, 1297.

nauestu, naueþ (=*ne + hauestu, haueþ*), 1670, 772; see habbe.

nawedeþ, see awedeþ.

nawiht, nowiȝt, nawt (O.E. *nāwiht*), naught, 1324, 884, 1620; nawt, nowiht, nowt, not at all, not, 1470, 928, 1391.

ne, ni (O.E. *ne*), not, nor, 42, 950; ne...ne, neither...nor, 291-2.

neauer, neuer, neuere, neure (O.E. *nǣfre*), never, 907, 60, 691, 209.

necke (O.E. *hnecca*), neck, 122.

nede (O.E. *nied, nēod*), need, duty, d. sg., 1584, adv., of necessity, 636; neode, 906, 938.

neȝ, neh (O.E. *nēah*), nigh, 44, 1220, 1267.

nele, nelle, nelleþ, neltu (=*ne + wile, wille*, etc.), 1482, 452, 653, 150; see wile.

neode (O.E. *nēod*), desire, pleasure, 1542.

neor, ner (O.E. *nēar*), near, 923, 1657; nearer, 1260.

nesche (O.E. *hnesc*), tender, weak, frail, 1349, 1546.

nest (O.E. *nest*), nest, 627; neste, d. sg., 134, 282.

netle (O.E. *netele*), nettles, d. pl., 593.

nich (=*ne + ich*), not I, no, 266.

Nichole, Nicholas, 191.

niȝt, niht (O.E. *niht*), night, 331; niȝte, nihte, d. sg., 365, 1432; niȝtes, n. pl., 523; niȝtes, adv. gen., 238, 591.

niȝtegale, nihtegale, niȝtingale (O.E. *nihtegale*), nightingale, 1739, 1512, 4.

nime, nimen (O.E. *niman*), catch, take, 1097, 607, 1764; nimeþ, pr. pl., 649; nom, pt. sg., 124, 1073;

inume, p. p., 541; p. p., accepted, 1197.

niseȝe, niso (=*ne*+*iseȝe, iso*), 382, 674; see iseo.

nisvicst, see iswike.

niþ (O.E. *niþ*), envy, wickedness, 1194; niþe, d. sg., 417, 1088.

no (O.E. *nā*), not, not at all, no, 42, 153, 579.

no, see non.

noȝt (O.E. *naht*), not, not at all, 102, 154; pro., naught, 246, 1127.

nolde (=*ne*+*wolde*), see wille.

nom, see nime.

nome (O.E. *nama*), name, 1762.

non, none, no (O.E. *nān*), no (adj.), 534, 493, 571; non, pro., none, 1705.

Noreweie, Norway, 909.

norþ (O.E. *norþ*), north, 921.

not, nost, nute, nuste, etc. (=*ne*+*wot, wost, wite,* etc.), 1180, 755, 1010, 1441; see wite.

note (O.E. *notu*), use, profit, service, 557, 330, 1624.

noþeles, see naþeles.

noþer (O.E. *nāþer, nāhwæþer*), neither, pro., 1127; used with ne =neither...nor, 465; nouþer...ne, 1732.

noþerward (O.E. *neoþor-*), downwards, 144.

noþing (O.E. *nān*+*þing*), nothing, 624; adv., not at all, 562.

noti (O.E. *notian*), render service, 1033.

nowar (O.E. *nāhwǣr*), nowhere, 1168.

nowe (O.E. *nēowe*), newly, adv., 1129.

nowiȝt, nowt, see nawiht.

nu (O.E. *nū*), now, 46.

nulle, nultu, etc. (=*ne*+*wille, wiltu*), see wille.

nuste, nust, see not.

O, see on.

of (O.E. *of*), from, of, concerning, because of, 22, 14, 9, 40.

ofdrad (O.E. *ofdrǣdd*), afraid, p. p., 1744; ofdradde, pl., 1143.

oferen (O.E. *āfǣran*), terrify, 978; oferd, p. p., 399.

ofligge (O.E. *oflicgan*), lie upon, opt. sg., 1505.

oflonged (O.E. *oflangian*), overcome with longing, p. p., 1587.

ofne (O.E. *ofen*), oven, d. sg., 292.

ofschamed (O.E. *ofscamian*), ashamed, p. p., 934.

ofslahe (O.E. *ofslēan*), killed, p. p., 1611.

oft, ofte (O.E. *oft*), often, 81, 1217.

oftoned (O.E. *of*+*tēonian*), vexed, irritated, p. p., 254.

ofþuȝte (O.E. *ofþyncan*), impers. (it) displeased, vexed, 397.

oȝe, oȝer (O.E. *āgen*), own, adj., 259, 118; oȝene, d. sg., 1652; owe, 100; ahene, 1286, 1542.

oȝt (O.E. *āht, āwiht*), aught, 662.

old, olde (O.E. *eald*), old, 25, 207, as sb.; of olde, 685.

on (O.E. *on*), on, in, 51, 429, 174, 275; one, 613.

on (O.E. *ān*), one (pro.), 82; one, d. sg., 357; in on, continuously, 356; ones, of one (kind), 1395; (art.) on=an, 90; one, o, d. sg., 2, 103; ore, d. fem., 1750.

onde (O.E. *anda*), malice, anger, 419, 1401.

ondsware, ondswere (O.E. *andswaru*), answer, 1185, 1573.

one (O.E. *āna*), alone, 1594.

one, ones, see on.

ongred (O.N. *angra*), to vex, p. p., 1588; see note.

onsene (O.E. *ansīen*), appearance, aspect, 1706.

op, see up.

ope (O.E. *open*), evident, 168.

opeliche (O.E. *openlice*), openly, 853.

orde (O.E. *ord*), point, d. sg., 1068; beginning, 1785.

ore (O.E. *ār*), mercy, grace, d. sg., 1404; a. sg., 886, 1083.

ore, see on.

orfe, oreue (O.E. *orf*), cattle, d. sg., 1157, 1199.

orþliche (O.E. *eorþlic*), earthly, mortal, pl., 788.

oþer (O.E. *ōþer*), other (pro.), 117, one of two, either, 1477; pl., 136; oþeres, g. sg., 11; oþre, pl., 1593; (adj.) other; oþer, d. sg., 54; oþre, oðer, d. pl., 1376, 905; oþers, oþres, g. sg., 1476, 1499; on oþer, otherwise, 671, see note.

oþer (O.E. *āhwæþer, ā(w)þer, āþor*), either, or, 243, 666; oþer...oþer, either...or, 328, 1479–80.

ouer, over (O.E. *ofer*), beyond, upon, 347, 64, 1524.

ouercome, ouercume, ouerkume (O.E. *ofercuman*), p. p., overcome, 1662, 542, 1198; ouerkome, opt. pr. 3. sg., 1743; ouerkumeþ, pr. 3. sg., 788.

ouerdede (O.E. *ofer*+*dǣd*), excess, 352.

ouerfulle (O.E. *oferfyllo*), repletion, excess, 354.

ouergan (O.E.*ofergān*), inf. intrans., pass away, 952; ouergo, p. p., 567; trans. ouergeþ, pr. 3. sg., overruns, 947.

ouerhoheð (O. E. *oferhogian*), despises, 1406.

ouerlonge (O. E. *ofer + lange*), too long, adv., 450.

ouerquatie (O.E.*ofer + O.Fr.quatier*), cram to excess, 353; see note.

ouerseʒ (O.E. *ofersēon*), beheld with scorn, pt. 3. sg., 30.

ouersit (O.E. *ofersittan*), neglects, pr. 3. sg., 1438; see note.

ouerswiþe (O.E. *oferswiþe*), too much, 1518.

oueruareþ (O.E. *oferfaran*), overrun, fight, pr. pl., 387.

ov, see þu.

ow, see þu.

owe, see oʒe.

owel (O.E. *āwel*), awl, 80.

ower (O.E. *ēower*), your (adj.), 1685, 1699.

oxe (O.E. *oxa*), ox, 629.

paþes (O.E. *pæþ*), paths, acc. pl., 377.

pes (O.Fr. *pēs, pais*), peace, 1730.

pie (O.Fr. *pie*), magpies, 126, 1613.

pine (O.E. *pin*), pain, torture, 1116.

pinnuc (see *N.E.D.*), hedge-sparrow, 1130.

pipe (O.E. *pipe*), pipe, 22, 343.

pipest (O.E. *pipian*), pipest, 503.

piping (< O.E. *pipe*), sb., piping, 567; pipinge, d., 316.

plaid, plait (O.Fr. *plaid, plait*), plea, debate, 1737, 5; plaites, g. sg., 472.

plaidi (O.Fr.*plaidier*), plead, discuss, inf., 184; plaideð, pr. 3. sg., 944.

plaiding (< O.Fr. *plaid*), pleading, debate, 12.

pleie, pleien (O.E. *plegian*), frolic, play, 213, 486; pleie, pr. 1. sg., 531, opt. sg., 1425.

Pope (O.E. *pāpa*), Pope, 746.

Portesham, Porteshom, Portisham, d., 1791, 1752.

poure (O.Fr. *povre*), sb., the poor, 482.

preost, prest, prost (O.E. *prēost*), priest, 902, 1180, 322; prestes, g. sg., 1179; preoste, d. pl., 913; prostes, n. pl., 733.

prude (O.E.*prȳte, prȳd*), pride, 1685; see note.

pulte (O.E. **pyltan*), assail, pelt, thrust, 873, 1524.

punde (O.E.*pund*), pound (in money), g. pl., 1101.

quaþ, quad, see iqueþe.

qued (cf. O.E. *cwēad*, excrement), adj. = evil, vile, 1137; sb. = evil, 1152.

queme (O.E. *cwēman*), please, inf., 209.

quide (O.E. *cwide*), proverb, saying, 685.

rad (O.E. *hræd*), quick, ready, 1043; rade, pl., 423; raddere, comp., 738.

raddest, see rede.

raþe (O.E. *hraþe*), quickly, 1700, early, 1086, 1147; raþere, comp. = sooner, 738.

reades, see red.

readliche (O.E. *rǣde + līce*), readily, quickly, 1281.

recche (O.E. *reccean*), reck, care for, inf., 803, pr. 1. sg., 60; reche, pr. 1. sg., 58; recþ, rehþ, pr. 3. sg., 491, 1404; reccheþ, pr. pl., 1006; roʒte, opt. pt. sg., 427.

red (O.E. *rǣd*), wise counsel, plan, 396, 682, d. sg., 680, see note; rede, d. sg., 307, 660; reades, a. pl., 1222.

rede (O.E. *rēad*), red, 830.

rede (O.E.*rǣdan*), advise, inf., 1697; pr. 1. sg., 860; inf. = read, speak, 350, 1782; raddest, pt. 2. sg. = didst advise, 159.

redles (O.E. *rǣdlēas*), destitute of counsel, redeless, 691.

redpurs (O.E. *rǣd + purs*), treasury of wisdom, 694.

reʒel (O.E. *hrægl*), dress, armour, 562.

rehte, see riʒt.

rehþ, see recche.

reke (O.E. *recan*), go, inf., 1606.

rem (O.E. *hrēam*), outcry, hue-and-cry, 1215.

rente (O.Fr. *rente*), revenue, living, 1767.

reowe (O.E. *hrēow*), grief, pity, d. sg., 1445; reu, 1498; see note.

res (O.E. *rǣs*), rush, impulse, 512.

rest (O.E. *restan*), resteth, pr. 3. sg., 1452; see note.

reste (O.E. *rest*), rest, acc. sg., 281.

reu, see reowe.

reue (O.E. *rēaf*), spoil, plunder, 458.

riche (O.E. *rice*, O.Fr. *riche*), adj., great, rich, pl., 1770; sb. pl., 482.

riche (O.E. *rice*), kingdom, 357, 717, 855.

rideþ (O.E. *ridan*), rideth, pr. 3. sg., 494.

riȝt, riht (O.E. *riht*), adj., right, 549, 958; **riȝte**, d. sg., 179; = true, 1345; **rihtne**, acc. sg. m., 1238; **rehte**, acc. sg. m., 1602; **riȝte, riȝtte**, straight, 815, 962; **riȝte**, pure, 276, 1088; **riȝt**, adv. = just, 76; **riht**, straight, 1736.

riȝt, riht (O.E. *riht*), sb., right, duty, 188, 950; **riȝte**, d. pl., 88; **mid riȝte**, rightly, 186.

rinde (O.E. *rind*), bark, d. sg., 602.

ripe (O.E. *ripe*), mature, 211.

ris (O.E. *hris*), twig, branch, d. sg., 1636, n. pl., 586; **rise**, d. sg., 19, d. pl., 1664.

rodde (O.E. *rodd*), rod, d. sg., 1123, 1646.

rode (O.E. *rōd*), cross, 1382.

roȝte, see **recche**.

rok (O.E. *hrōc*), rook, 1130.

Rome (O.E. *Rōm*), Rome, d. sg., 746.

rord (O.E. *reord*), speech, 311.

rose (O.E. *rose*), rose, 443.

rude (O.E. *rudu*), ruddy colour, d. sg., 443.

ruȝe (O.E. *rūh*), rough, hairy, d. pl., 1013.

rugge (O.E. *hrycg*), back, d. sg., 775.

rum (O.E. *rūm*), roomy, spacious, 643.

rum-hus (O.E. *rȳm- + hūs*), latrine, 652; d. sg., 592.

rune (O.E. *ryne*), course, pursuit, 1156.

rune (O.E. *rūn*), secrets, acc. pl., 1170.

rure (O.E. *hryre*), fall, ruin, 1154.

sade (O.E. *sæd*), sated, pl., 452.

sake (O.E. *sacu*), quarrel, questioning, 1160, 1430, see note; **sake** = sake, 1589.

salue (O.E. *sealf*), salve, healing power, acc. sg., 888.

schadde, see **schede**.

schal, shal (O.E. *sceal*), shall, must, pr. 1. sg., 960, 547; **schalt, shalt**, pr. 2. sg., 956, 544; **schal, scal, shal**, 187, 1199, 342; **schul, schule, shulle**, pr. pl., 1200, 1192, 856; **schille, shulle**, pr. opt. sg., 1683, 442; **scholde, sholde, solde, soldich, schulde**, pt. opt. sg., 1728, 464, 975, 1025, 1417; **scholde, schulde, solde**, pt. opt. pl., 1691, 1262, 977.

schame (O.E. *scamu*), shame, 1761, 1283; **schome, shome**, 167, 1075.

schamie (O.E. *scamian*), be ashamed, imp. sg., 161.

scharp (O.E. *scearp*), sharp, 79; **scharpe**, adv., 141.

schawles, see **sheueles**.

schede (O.E. *scēadan*), distinguish, inf., 197; **schadde**, shed, pt. 1. sg., 1616.

schelde (O.E. *scield*), shield, d. sg., 1713; **sheld**, acc. sg., 1022.

schende (O.E. *scendan*), inf., reproach, revile, 274, opt. pt. sg., 285; **ischend**, put to shame, p. p., 1336.

schilde, ishilde (O.E. *(ge)scieldan*), protect, inf., 62, 781, opt. sg., 57, opt. pr. pl., 1253; **schild**, imp. sg., 163.

schille (O.E. *sciell*), shrill, 142, 558; adv., 1656.

schille, see **schal**.

schipes (O.E. *scip*), ships, acc. pl., 1205.

schirme (cf. O.H.G. *scirman*), to fight, 306.

schit-worde (O.E. *scitte-word*), foul words, d. pl., 286.

schome, shome, see **schame**.

schonde (O.E. *scand*), disgrace, shame, d. sg., 1498, 1652.

schrichest (cf. O.L.G. *scrīcon*), screechest, 223.

schulde, schule, see **schal**.

schunest (O.E. *scunian*), shunnest, 590; **schunet, schuniet, shuneþ**, pr. 3. sg., 236, 229, 1165; **shunieþ**, pr. pl., 792.

sckile (O.N. *skil*), discernment, reason, 186.

Scotlonde, Scotland, 908, 1758.

screwen (O.E. *scrēawa*), evil persons, shrews, d. pl., 287.

sea, see (O.E. *sǣ*), sea, 1205; d. sg., 1754.

seche, sechen, iseche (O.E. *sēcean*), seek, attain, 1759, 1508, 741; **secheþ**, pr. 3. sg., 380, pr. pl., 538.

sed (O.E. *sǣd*), seed, 1041; **sedes**, n. pl., 1129.

sede, see **segge**.

see, see **sea**.

segge (O.E. *secg*), sedge, 18.

segge (O.E. *secgan*), say, tell, pr. 1. sg., 266, 1421; **seist, seistu**, pr. 2. sg., 50, 1075; **seiþ**, pr. 3. sg., 176; **sede, seide**, pt. 3. sg., 33, 235; **segge**, opt. pr. 2. sg., 60; **sede**, opt. pt. sg., 1296; **seie, sei**, imp. sg., 217, 1407; **segget**, imp. pl., 113; **ised, iseid**, p. p., 395, 1037.

selde (O.E. *seldan*), seldom, 943.

sele (O.E. *sǣl*), happiness, d. pl., 953; see note.

seme (O.E. *sēman*), arbitrate, 187.

semes (O.E. *sēam*), loads, 775.

sende (O.E. *sendan*), send, pr. 1. sg., 1264, opt. 3. sg., 1570; **send,** pr. pl., 1520; see note.

sene (O.E. *sīen*), vision, power of seeing, 240, 368.

seolliche (O.E. *sellic*), strange, 1299.

seolue, solue, sulf, sulue (O.E. *seolf, sylf*), self, 1284, 835, 497, 810; **seolfe, sulue, sulfe,** very (for emphasis), 1679, 69, 495, 746.

seoluer (O.E. *seolfor*), silver, 1366.

seorhe, see **sorȝe.**

seoþþe, soþþe (O.E. *seoþþan, siþþan*), afterwards, 1402, 324.

serueþ (O.Fr. *servir*), serves, pr. 3. sg., 1579.

seten, see **sitte.**

setle (O.E. *setl*), seat, d. sg., 594.

sette (O.E. *settan*), set, inf., 1626; pt. sg., 1057.

sewi (O.E. *scēawian*), show, inf., 151.

shafte (O.E. *(ge)sceaft*), creatures, 788.

sheue (O.E. *scēaf*), sheaves, d. pl., 455.

sheueles (see note), scarecrow, n. sg., 1128; **schawles,** acc. sg., 1648.

shine (O.E. *scin(u)*), shins, n. pl., 1060.

shine (O.E. *scīnan*), shine, opt. sg., 963.

short (O.E. *scort*), short, 73.

shulle, see **schal.**

sibbe (O.E. *sibb*), peace, acc. sg., 1005.

sichst, see **so.**

side (O.E. *sid(e)*), side, part, 429.

siȝte, sihð, see **sikeþ.**

sikerhede (O.E. *sicor + *hǣdu*), certainty, security, 1265.

sikerliche (O.E. *sicorlice*), surely, 1139.

sikeþ, sihð (O.E. *sican*), sighs, pr. 3. sg., 1352, 1587; **siȝte,** pt. 3. sg., 1291; see note.

singe, singen, singin (O.E. *singan*), sing. inf., 39, 709, 910; **singe,** pr. 1. sg., 313; **singest, singist, singst,** pr. 2. sg., 331, 219, 505; **singeþ, singet, singþ,** pr. 3. sg., 414, 196, 721; **singeþ, singeð,** pr. pl., 483, 916; **sunge,** pt. 2. sg., 1049; **song,** pt. 3. sg., 20; **sungen,** pt. 3. pl., 1663; **singe,** opt. sg., 967; **sunge,** opt. pt. 1. sg., 1026; **singinde,** pr. pt., 855.

siþ, see **so.**

siþe, siðe (O.E. *sīþ*), time, occasion, d. sg., 293, 1184; **siþe** = experience, lot, d. sg., 993.

sitte (O.E. *sittan*), sit, perch, inf., 282, pr. 1. sg., 1218; **sittest,** pr. 2. sg., 89; **sit,** pr. 3. sg., 1587; **sitteþ,** pr. pl., 97, 1682; **sat,** pt. 3. sg., 15; **seten,** pt. pl., 1102; **sitte,** opt. pr. sg., 384; **site,** imp. sg., 655.

siueþ (O.Fr. *sewir, sivir*), follows, pr. 3. sg., 1526.

skente (O.N. *skemta*), amuse, pr. 1. sg., 449; pt. 1. sg., 1085.

skentinge (cf. O.N. *skemta*), delight, pleasure, 986, d. sg., 613; (song of) delight, 446, 532.

skere (cf. O.N. *skǣrr*), cleanse, 1302.

slepeþ (O.E. *slǣpan*), are sleeping, pr. 3. pl., 1593.

slide (O.E. *slīdan*), slip, err, inf., 1390; **islide,** p. p., 686.

slider (O.E. *slidor*), slippery, 956.

slitte (O.E. *slite*), pockets, d. pl., 1118.

slo (O.E. *slōh*), slough, mire, d. sg., 1394.

smak (O.E. *smæc*), scent, 823.

smal (O.E. *smæl*), small, thin, 73; **smale,** d. sg., 320, d. pl., 64, 277.

smel (cf. Du. *smeulen*), smell, scent, 822.

smiten (O.E. *smitan*), smite, 78.

snailes (O.E. *snægl*), snails, 87.

snel (O.E. *snell*), quick, active, swift, 531, 829, 918; **snelle,** pl. 768, as sb. 526.

snepe (O.E. *snǣp*), foolish, adj. = sb., d. pl., 225; see note.

sniuw (O.E. *sniwan*), snows, opt. 3. sg., 620; see note.

snou, snov (O.E. *snāw*), snow, 1002, 430; **snowe,** d. sg., 413; **snuwe,** n. sg., 1206.

so, see **swa.**

so (O.E. *sēon*), see, pr. 1. sg., 34; **sichst,** pr. 2. sg., 242; **siþ,** pr. 3. sg., 950, 246; **soþ,** pr. pl., 884.

softe (O.E. *sōfte*), adj., soft, low, 6, gentle, 1350; **softest,** most comfortable, 644.

soldich, solde, see **schal.**

soleþ (O.E. *solian*), becomes soiled, 1276.

solue, solve, see **seolue.**

sone (O.E. *sōna*), soon, 518; **sone so,** as soon as, 501.

song (O.E. *sang*), song, singing, 36, 220; **songe,** d. sg., 46, d. pl., 82; **songes,** g. sg., 1358, a. pl., 722, d. pl., 896.

sor (O.E. *sār*), pain, grief, 1234; **sore,** d. sg., 540.

sore (O.E. *sār*), grievous, sore, pl., 1472; adv., grievously, 885, 1352.

sorȝe (O.E. *sorg*), sorrow, trouble, acc. sg., 431; **seorhe**, **sorwe**, d. sg., 1599, 884.

sori (O.E. *sārig*), sad, wretched, 994, 1162.

sori-mod (O.E. *sārig-mōd*), sad, 1218.

sot (O.E. *sott*), foolish, adj., 1435; **sottes**, sb. g. sg. =fool's, 1351, acc. pl., 297.

sothede (O.E. *sot*+*hǣdu*), folly, 1488.

soti (O.E. *sōtig*), dirty, 578.

soþ, **soð** (O.E. *sōþ*), true, 349, 1769; **soþe**, d. sg., 698.

soþ, **soð** (O.E. *sōþ*), truth, 217, 950; **soþe**, d. sg., 264.

soþ-saȝe (O.E. *sōþsagu*), true saying, 1038.

soþþe, see **seoþþe**.

soule (O.E. *sāwol*), soul, d. sg., 1092.

sowe (O.E. *sāwan*), sow, 1039; **soweþ**, pr. 3. sg., 1041; **isowe**, p. p., 1129.

spac, see **speken**.

spale (O.E. *spala*), substitute, 258; see note.

spanne (O.E. *spanan*), seduce, entice, 1490.

speche (O.E. *sp(r)ǣc*), law-suit, plea, 13, 398, see note, 545; speech, 480.

specþ, see **speken**.

spedde, see **spet**.

speken, **speke** (O.E. *sp(r)ecan*), speak, inf., 678, 261; **spekest**, pr. 2. sg., 1282; **spekeþ**, **specþ**, pr. 3. sg., 1536, 1072; **spac**, pt. 3. sg., 396; **speke**, pt. 2. sg., 554; **speke**, opt. pr. sg., 1079; **ispeke**, p. p., 1293.

spel (O.E. *spell*), story, 128; **spelle**, d. sg. =a long story, 264; **spelle**, d. pl. =sayings, 294.

spene (O.E. *spendan*), spend, 165, see note; **speneþ**, **spenþ**, pr. 3. sg., 1525, 362; **spene**, opt. pr. sg., 1549.

spere (O.E. *spere*), spear, 1022; **speres**, g. sg., 1068.

spet (O.E. *spēdan*), succeeds, pr. 3. sg., 763; **spedde**, pt. pl., 1792; **speddestu**, pt. 2. sg., 169.

speten (O.E. *spǣtan*), spit, inf., 39.

spille (O.E. *spillan*), waste, 1020; **ispild**, p. p., 1027.

spire (O.E. *spir*), tall reeds, d. pl., 18.

sprede (O.E. *sprǣdan*), spread, inf., 437.

sprenge (O.E. *sprencg*), trap, 1066.

springe (O.E. *springan*), spring, burst forth, 437, 1134; **springeþ**, **sprinþ**, pr. 3. sg., 734, 1042; **isprunge**, p. p., 300.

spure (O.E. *spura*, *spora*), spur, 777.

spusbruche (O.Fr. *espūs* + O.E. *bryce*), adultery, 1368.

spuse (O.Fr. *espūs*), marriage vow, 1334.

spuse (O.Fr. *espūse*), wife, spouse, 1527.

spusing (< O.Fr. *espūs*), marriage, 1336, 1555, 1340.

spusing-bendes (O.E. *-bend*), marriage-bonds, 1472.

sputing (< O.Fr. *disputer*), disputing, 1574.

stable (O.Fr. *estable*), stable, d. sg., 629.

stal, see **stele**.

stal (O.E. *steal*), place, 1632, see note; **stalle**, d. sg. =stall, 629.

starc, **starke** (O.E. *stearc*), severe, violent, 5, 1473, 524, 1176.

start (O.N. *sterta*), starts, leaps, pr. 3. sg., 379.

stare-blind (O.E. *stare-blind*), stone-blind, 241.

starest (O.E. *starian*), starest, 77.

staue (O.E. *stæf*), staves, d pl., 1167.

steape (O.E. *stæpe*), step, 1592.

stede (O.E. *stede*), places, acc. pl., 590, 966.

stefne, **steune**, **steuene** (O.E. *stefn*), voice, 317, 522, 986; teaching, 727.

stele (O.E. *stiele*), steel, 1030.

stele (O.E. *stelan*), steal, inf., 1499; **stele**, pt. 2. sg., 103; **stal**, pt. 3. sg., 1432.

steorre (O.E. *steorra*), stars, pl., 1329; **storre**, d. pl., 1321.

sterne (O.E. *stierne*), sternly, 112.

sticke (O.E. *sticca*), stick, 1625.

stif (O.E. *stif*), stiff, 5, 269.

stiþ (O.E. *stigan*), rises, pr. 3. sg., 1405.

stille (O.E. *stille*), still, calm, adj., 261, 979; adv.=quietly, 1255; see note.

stoc, **stok** (O.E. *stocc*), stump, log, 25, 1113.

stod, see **stont**.

stode (O.E. *stōd*), stud, herd, d. sg., 495.

stone, **stoone** (O.E. *stān*), stones, d. pl., 1609, 1167; **stones**, a. pl., 1118.

stont (O.E. *standan*), stands, pr. 3. sg., 618; **stod**, pt. sg., 25; **stode**, pt. 2. sg., 1632, see note; **stond**, imp. sg., 1788.

stor (O.E. *stōr*), violent, severe, 1473.

storre-wis (O.E. *steorra* + *wis*), skilled in star-lore, 1318.

stottes (O.E. *stotte*), horses, n. pl., 495.

strenge (O.E. *streng*), bow-string, d. sg., 1230.

strengþe, strencþe, strenþe (O.E. *strengþo*), strength, 762, 1226, 781.

strete (O.E. *strǣt*), road, acc. sg., 962.

strind (see note), stream, 242.

strong, stronge (O.E. *strang*), strong, adj., 579, 269; violent, severe, 5, 524; hard, 667; **strengur**, comp., 773; **stronge**, adv., violently, 254, 1082, see note.

stubbe (O.E. *stybb*), stumps of trees, d. pl, 506.

stude (O.E. *styde*), place, 936; g. pl., 1767.

stumpeþ (see *N.E.D.*), stumbles, trips, pr. 3. sg., 1424; pr. pl., 1392.

stunde (O.E. *stund*), time, d. sg., 802; moments (of thought), d. pl., 706.

sval (O.E. *swelan*), burned, raged, pt. 3. sg., 7.

svete, see **swete**.

suich, see **swuch**.

svikedom (O.E. *swicdōm*), treachery, 167.

svikeldom (O.E. *swicol + dōm*), treachery, 163.

svikelhede (O.E. *swicol + *hǣdu*), treachery, 162; **swikelede**, 838.

sulieð (O.E. *sylian*), becomes defiled, pr 3. sg., 1240.

sum, sume (O.E. *sum*), pro., some, something, 540, 1599; **summe**, n. pl., 1648; **sum**, a certain one, one, 1016, 1397.

sum (O.E. *sum*), adj., some, a certain, 1151; **sumere**, fem. d. sg., 1, see note; **sumne**, mas. acc. sg., 1152, 1353; **sume**, mas. d. sg., 293; **sume**, n. pl., 879, d. pl., 709; **summe**, acc. pl., 1246.

sumdel (O.E. *sume dǣle*), somewhat, 870, 934.

sumere (O.E. *sumor*), summer, d., 416; **sumeres-**, g. sg., 489.

sunegeþ (O.E. *syngian*), sins, pr. 3. sg., 1416; **sunegi**, opt. pr. pl., 928.

sunfulle (O.E. *synnfull*), sinful = sb. d. pl., 891.

sunne (O.E. *sunne*), sun, n. sg., 963.

sunne (O.E. *synn*), sin, d. sg., 863, n. pl., 1395, acc. pl., 974; **sunnen**, d. pl., 858.

sur (O.E. *sūr*), sour, bitter, 866; **sure**, adv., 1082; see note.

suþ (O.E. *sūþ*), south, 921.

suþ, see **so**.

suþe, see **swiþe**.

swa, swo, so (O.E. *swā*), conj. = as, as if, 1665, 1738, 77; so...so = as...as, 334, 681; adv. = so, 1373, 1577, 209.

sweng (O.E. *sweng*), (wrestling) trick, 799; **swenge**, g. pl., 803, d. pl., 1286; **swenges**, acc. pl., 797.

swete (O.E. *swēte*), sweet, 866; **svete**, 358.

swete (O.E. *swǣtan*), sweat, inf., 1716.

swiche, see **swuch**.

swike (O.E. *swican*), cease, pr. 1. sg., 1459; **swikeþ**, pr. 3. sg., 336.

swikelede, see **svikelhede**.

swiþe, swuþe, sviþe, suþe (O E. *swiþe*), very, 1175, 1591, 377, 12; = much, 1274, 1561; **suiþe**, swiftly, 376.

swonk (O.E. *swincan*), toiled, pt. 3. sg., 462.

sworde (O.E. *sweord*), sword, d. sg., 1068.

swore (O.E. *swēora*), neck, 73, 1125.

swuch, suich (O.E. *swylc*), pro. = such, such a one, 1307, 405; **swucche**, d. pl., 1324; adj. = such, such a, **swuch**, d. pl., 1453; **suich**, n. sg., 1169; **swiche, suich, swucche, swuch**, conj. = as if, 566, 1533.

tacninge (O.E. *tācnung*), symbolism, d. sg, 1213.

tale (O.E. *talu*), speech, indictment, charge, 140 (see note), 1511; dispute, 3, 190; **tales**, g. pl., 257.

taueleþ (O.E. *tæflian*), plays at dice, pr. 3 sg, 1666.

teche (O.E. *tǣcan*), teach, inf., 914; **teche, teache**, pr. 1. sg., 892, 1334, 1449.

tele, telen (O.E. *tǣlan*), abuse, reproach, 1377, 1415.

telle (O.E. *tellan*), tell, inf., 293, pr. 1. sg., 267; **telst**, pr. 2. sg., 310, 625; **telstu** = dost thou reckon, 793; **telþ**, pr. 3. sg., 340.

teme (O.E. *tieman*), breed, inf., 499, pr. 1. sg., 1470.

temes (O.E. *tēam*), teams, 776.

teo (O.E. *tēon*), go, 1232; **tihþ**, draweth, pr. 3. sg., 1435.

teres (O.E *tēar*), tears, 426, 865.

teþ (O.E. *tōþ*), teeth, d. pl., 1538.

tide (O.E. *tid*), time, season, d. sg., 709; hours, acc pl, 26; see note.

tihþ, see **teo**.

time (O.E. *tima*), time, 323; at riȝte time, in season, 984.

tiþinge (O.N. *tiðindi*), tidings, 1035, 1171.

to (O.E. *tō*), prep., to, at, as, for, 38, 731, 1311, 232, 606.

A. 15

to (O.E. *tō*), too, 171, 452.
toberste (O.E. *tōberstan*), break, opt. sg., 122; **tobursteþ**, pr. 3. sg., 1610.
tobeteþ (O.E. *tōbēatan*), beats severely, pr. 3. sg., 1610.
tobreke (O.E. *tōbrecan*), break, inf., 1554, 1730; break off, 1737; **to-broke**, p. p., 1558.
tobrode (O.E. *tōbregdan*), p. p., pulled to pieces, 1008.
tobuneþ (see note), beats severely, 1166.
tobursteþ, see **toberste**.
tochine (O.E. *tō-cinan*), split, crack, inf., 1565.
todraʒe (O.E. *tōdragan*), drawn a-sunder, p. p., 1062; **todrowe**, pt. pl., 126.
tofore (O.E. *tōforan*), before, 746; **touore**, 1728.
togadere (O.E. *tōgædere*), together, 807.
toʒte (< M.E. **togen**, to pull), tight, adv. = sb., the tough, 703; **tohte**, adj. = drawn, 1446.
toheneþ (O.E. *tō* + *hienan*), strike down, injure, pr. pl., 1119.
tolli (cf. O.E. *-tyllan*), entice, inf., 1627.
tome (O.E. *tam*), tame, 1444.
tone (O.E. *tēona*), reproach, 50.
tonge, see **tunge**.
tonge (O.E. *tange*), pair of tongs, 156.
top (O.E. *topp*), top, 1328; **toppe**, d. sg., 1422.
toppes (O.E. *toppa*), threads, d. pl., 428; see note.
tort (O.E. *tord*), excrement, 1686.
toschakeŏ (O.E. *tōscacan*), shake to pieces, pr. pl., 1647.
tosheneþ (O.E. *tōscǣnan*), break to pieces, pr. pl., 1120.
toslit (O.E. *tōslitan*), broken, cut to pieces, p. p., 694; see note.
tosvolle (O.E. *tōswellan*), swollen (with anger), 145.
totorueþ (O.E. *tōtorfian*), pelts with turf, pr. 3. sg, 1166; **totorueŏ**, pr. pl., 1119.
totose (cf. O.E. *tǣsan*), pull to pieces, inf., 70.
totwichet (O.E. *tō* + *twiccian*), pluck to pieces, pr. pl., 1647.
touore, see **tofore**.
toweard (O.E. *tōweard*), concerning, to, 553; adj. = approaching, imminent, 1254.
trendli (O.E. *trendlian*), trundle, roll, opt. 3. sg., 135; see note.
triste (cf. O.N. *treista*), trust, pr. 1. sg., 760.

tro, trowe (O.E. *trēow*), tree, d. sg., 438, 135; **treon, tron**, n. pl., 1201, 1133.
truste (cf. O.N. *traust*), should trust, opt. 3. sg., 1273.
tueie (O.E. *twēgen*), two, n., 795; **tweire**, gen., 888, 1396.
tukest (O.E. *tūcian*), maltreatest, pr. 2. sg., 63.
tune (O.E. *tūn*), town, village, d. sg., 1169, 1753.
tunge, tonge (O.E. *tunge*), tongue, 258, 1071, 37.
turf (O.E. *turf*), turf, d. sg., 1167; see note.
turne (O.E. *tyrnan*), turn, inf., 820, pr. 1. sg., 1598; **turneþ, turnþ**, pr. 3. sg., 1284, 818; **turnde**, pt. 3. sg., 1090.
twelue (O.E. *twelf*), twelve, 836.
twene (O.E. *twēo*), doubtful things, g. pl., 991; see note.
twengeþ (O.E. *twengan*), pinch, nip, pr. 3. sg., 1114; **tuengst**, pr. 2. sg., 156.
two (O.E. *twā*), two, 1047; **twom, twam**, d. pl., 991, 1477.

þah (O.E. *þēah*), though, however, 1235, 1779.
þan, þanne, see **þe**.
þan, þane (O.E. *þonne, þon*), than, 24, 39; **þe**, 564; **þon**, 505.
þanne, þane (O.E. *þanne, þonne*), then, 531, 700; when, 165, 591, 670, 682; **þone**, 804; **þenne**, then, 1380.
þar, þare (O.E. *þǣr, þāra*), there, 25, 295, 595, 913; **þer**, 1485; **þar, þare**, where, 26, 126, 892; also frequent in compounds, e.g. **þar-after**, after that, 45; **þar-bi**, whereby, 98; **þerfore, þareuore**, therefore, 1260, 274; **þar-rihte**, straight away, 1246, etc., etc.
þare, þas, þat, see **þe**.
þarf (O.E. *þearf*), need, pr. 3. sg., 803; **þaref**, 190.
þat (O.E. *þæt*), conj., that, so that, 21, 122.
þat (O.E. *þæt*), rel. pro., that, who, 80, 176, 1082; what, 95, 159; who, pl., 251; to which, to whom, 231, 1524.
þe (O.E. *þē*), (1) def. art. = the (all cases sg. and pl.), 13, 21, 96; **þo**, n. sg., 26, 199; **þas**, g. sg., 338; **þare**, f. gen. sg., 28, f. dat. sg., 31; **þan, þon, þen**, m. dat. sg., 125, 801, 1514, neu. dat. sg., 133, 135; **þan, þane, þanne**, mas. acc. sg., 742,

250, 1406. (2) demon. adj.=that, those, þan, m. dat. sg., 359, d. pl., 389; þane, m. acc. sg., 1097; þare, fem. d. sg., 140; þat, neu. nom. sg., 5; þene, mas. acc. sg., 1093. (3) demon. pro.=that, those, þe, 800; þan, þon, d. sg., 200, 679, d. pl., 650, 1762; þane, mas. acc. sg., 1346; þare, fem. dat. sg., 1525, g. pl., 1584; þat, neu. nom., 82, 573; þeo, n. pl., 1305, 1671; þas, gen. sg.=that matter, 1442; þes, g. sg.=because of that, 882; þe, instr.=the, 19, 34; þi, instr.= therefore, 860.

þe, see þu.

þe (O.E. þe), or, (weþer...þe), 824, 1360.

þe, see þan, þane (than).

þe (O.E. þe), rel. pro., who, 1346, 1386; which, 1447, 1675.

þeȝ (O.E. þēah), though, 48, 813.

þenche (O.E. þencean), think, pr. 1. sg., 485; þencheþ, pr. pl., 1116; þoȝte, þohte, pt. 3. sg., 392, 1442; þoȝtest, pt. 2. sg., 157; þenche, opt. sg., 726; iþoht, p. p., 1560.

þenne (O.E. þanon), thence, 1726; þonne, 132.

þeo (O.E. þēoh), thigh, acc. sg., 1496.

þeo, see þe.

þeode (O.E. þēod), people, d. sg., 1583, d. pl., 905; þode, acc. pl., 387; see note.

þeos, see þes.

þeostre, þustre (O.E. þēostre, þiestre), dark, 1432, 249.

þeoues (O.E. þēof), thieves, 1372; þoues, g. sg., 1156.

þes (O.E. þes), (1) dem. adj.=this, 259; þis, d. sg., 1794; þisse, d. pl., 659, 750; þeos, n. fem., 1667, 41, acc. fem., 177, pl., 730, 139. (2) dem. pro., þis, 113, 1635.

þewes (O.E. þēaw), customs, habits, acc. pl., 1017.

þicke (O.E. þicce), thick, 580; sb.= thick underwood, thick-set, 1626.

þider (O.E. þider), thither, 719, 143.

þilke (O.E. *þylce, see N.E.D.), that same, 1038.

þin, þine (O.E. þin), poss. adj.=thine, thy, 319, 169; þi, 220; þire, d. fem., 429.

þinche (O.E. þyncan), (1) to seem, 346; þinchest, pr. 2. sg., 578; þuncheþ, pr. pl., 1472; þuȝte, pt. sg., 21. (2) impers., þincþ, þingþ, þuncþ, þungþ, þunþ, 541, 1694, 1649,

1473, 1592; þincþe, seems to thee, 46; þuȝte, þuhte, 31, 1661.

þing (O.E. þing), thing, matter, 229; þinge, d. pl., g. pl., 485, 1214; for mine þinge, d. pl., for my sake, 434.

þo (O.E. þā), then, when, 25, 187, 1653.

þoȝ (cf. O.N. þō), though, 304.

þoȝt (O.E. þoht), thought, 492; þoȝte, þohte=mind, 391, 940.

þoleþ (O.E. þolian), endures, pr. 3. sg., 777.

þonc, þonk (O.E. þanc), thanks, thought, 461, 490; hire þonkes, g. abs., willingly, 70.

þonne (O.E. þonne), then, 508.

þornes (O.E. þorn), thorns, 586; þorne wode, thorn copse, briar bush, 444.

þoues, see þeoues.

þrete (O.E. þrēat), threat, d. sg., 58.

þretest (O.E. þrēatian), threatenest, 83; þreteþ, pr. 3. sg., attacks, 1609.

þridde (O.E. þridda), third, 325, 1478.

þringe (O.E. þringan), press, opt. 3. sg., 796; iþrunge, p. p., 38.

þriste (O.E. þrist), bold, 171.

þroȝe (O.E. þrāg), time, turn, 260; þrowe, d. pl., 478.

þrostle (O.E. þrostle), thrush, throstle, 1659.

þrote (O.E. þrote), throat, 24, 558.

þrowe, see þroȝe.

þrusche (O.E. þrysce), thrush, 1659.

þu (O.E. þū), thou, 33; þe, 85, 34; ȝe, pl., 116; ow, ov, eu, d. pl., 1686, 114, 1793.

þuȝte, see þinche.

þunne (O.E. þynne), adv., thinly, 1529.

þurȝ (O.E. þurh), through, because of, by means of, 447, 1162; þurch, þurh, 1401, 1256.

þurȝut (O.E. þurhūt), throughout, 879.

þus (O.E. þus), thus, 758.

þuster (O.E. þiestru), darkness, 198.

þusternesse (O.E. þiester + nes), darkness, 369.

þuuele (O.E. þȳfel), bushes, thicket, d. pl., 278.

uaȝt, see fiȝte.

vair, see fair.

uale, uele, ueole, see fele.

uare, see fare.

uastre, see faste.

uecche (O.E. feccean), obtain, 1504.

uel, vel, see wel.

uel, see felle.

venne (O.E. fenn), fen, mud, d. sg., 962; uenne, 832.

uerde, see ferde.

uere, see beon.

vich (O.E. *gehwilc*), each, 1378.
uinde, uint, see **finde.**
uise, see **wis.**
uisest, see **wisi.**
ule, vie (O.E. *ūle*), owl, nom., 837, 26; **hule,** g. sg., 28; **hule, houle,** n. sg., acc. sg., 41, 1662.
ulize (O.E. *flēoge*), flies, d. pl., 600.
unblipe (O.E. *unblīpe*), sad, 1585.
unclene (O.E. *unclǣne*), unclean, 91, 233.
under (O.E. *under*), under, 515.
underzat (O.E. *undergietan*), perceived, understood, pt. 3. sg., 1055; **underyat,** pt. 3. sg., 1091, see note; **underzete,** p. p., 168.
understonde (O.E. *understandan*), understand, perceive, 1262; **understond,** pr. 3. sg., 1463; **(hi) understod** = bethought herself, 951, 1297; **understode,** opt. pt. sg., 662.
unfele (O.E. *unfǣle*), impure, evil, 1381; **unuele,** 1003.
ungode (O.E. *ungōd*), evil one, sb., 129; **ungod** = evil, 1364.
ungrete (O.E. *un + grīetu*), small size, 752.
unhwate (O.E. *un + hwata*), evil omen, misfortune, 1267; **unwate,** d. pl., 1148.
unihoded (O.E. *un + gehādod*), not ordained, 1178.
unilike (O.E. *ungelica*), unlike, contrast, sb., 806.
unisele (O.E. *unsǣle*), evil, wicked, 1004.
unisome (O.E. *ungesōm*), at variance, pl., 1522.
unker, see **ich.**
unlede (O.E. *unlǣde*), wretched, accursed, 976, 1644.
unlengpe (O.E. *un + lengpu*), shortness, 752.
unmepe (O.E. *unmǣp*), excess, 352.
unmilde (O.E. *unmilde*), rough, harsh, 61, 1254.
unmurie (O.E. *unmyrig*), unpleasant, sad, 346.
unneape (O.E. *unēape*), scarcely, with difficulty, 1605; difficult, 1618, see note.
unorne (O.E. *unorne*), feeble, 317, 1492.
unred (O.E. *unrǣd*), folly, unwisdom, acc. sg., 1464; **unrede,** 161, 212, 1355.
unrizt (O.E. *unriht*), sb. and adj., wrong, injustice, unjust, 1488, 165; **vnrizt, unriht,** 1054, 1548.

unrihtfulnesse (O.E. *un + rihtful + nes*), lawlessness, 1742.
unripe (O.E. *unripe*), immature, 320.
unselpe (O.E. *unsǣlp*), unhappiness, n. sg., 1263.
unsipe (O.E. *unsip*), misfortune, d. sg., 1164.
unsode (O.E. *unsoden*), p. p., uncooked, raw, 1007.
unstrengpe (O.E. *un + strengpu*), weakness, 751.
unstrong (O.E. *unstrang*), weak, 561.
unpeu (O.E. *unpēaw*), vice, bad habit, 194; **unpewes,** acc. pl., 1018.
unuele, see **unfele.**
unwate, see **unhwate.**
vnwizt (O.E. *un + wiht*), monster, 90; **unwiztis,** n. pl., 218.
unwille (O.E. *ungewill*), unpleasing, 422, 1535.
unwrenche (O.E. *unwrenc*), spiteful tricks, d. pl., 169.
unwreste (O.E. *unwrǣst*), unavailing, futile, pl., 178, 1170; adv. = badly, 342.
vnwrozen, unwroze (O.E. *un + wrēon*), discovered, revealed, p. p., 162, 848.
unwurp (O.E. *un + wurp*), worthless, 339.
uo (O.E. *fāh*), foe, d. sg., 403.
uode, see **fode.**
uolde (O.E. *feald*), fold, d. sg., 696, d. pl., crevices, 602; **manie volde,** many ways, d. pl., 72.
vonde, see **fondi.**
uonge (O.E. *fōn*), seize, inf., 1135.
uor, see **feor.**
uor, vor, see **for.**
uorbisne (O.E. *for(e)bisen*), proverb, parable, saying, 98, 244, 637.
uorbredep (O.E. *forbregdan, -brēdan*), become transformed, corrupt oneself, pr. pl., 510.
uorcrempep (see note), twist convulsively, ramp, pr. pl., 510.
uorzete (O.E. *forgietan*), forget, opt. 3. sg., 725.
uorletep, see **forleten.**
uorlost, see **forleose.**
vorre (O.E. *feorran*), afar, 327.
uote (O.E. *fōt*), foot, d. sg., 51.
up, vp (O.E. *ūp*), adv., up, 96, 851; op, 1394; prep. = upon, 15, 1625.
upbreide (O.E. *ūp + bregdan*), upbraid, reproach, inf., 1414.
upbrozte (O.E. *ūp + bringan*), uttered, pt. 3. sg., 200.
uppon, upon, uppen (O.E. *uppan*), prep. = upon, 1636, 494, 1683; upe

þon = as against that, 679; **upe londe**, throughout the country, 733; see note.

ure (O.E. *ūre, ūser*), our, adj., 118.

urne, see **eorne**.

ut, vt (O.E. *ūt*), out, 8, 53.

ute (O.E. *uton*), let (us), 1779.

uthalue (O.E. *ūthealf*), outside, adv. dat., 110.

utheste, utest (O.E. *ūthǣs*), hue-and-cry, 1698, 1683; see note.

utlete (cf. O.E. *ūt + lǣtan*), outlet, d. sg., 1754; see note.

utschute (O.E. *ūtscyte*), outbreaks, excesses, 1468.

uuel, vuel (O.E. *ȳfel*), evil, ill, adj., 1051, 769; **vuele, uuele**, adv. = badly, 63, 1206.

wai, wailawai (O.E. *weilawei*), alas! 120, 220; see **wolawo**.

wai, see **wei**.

wake (O.E. *wæcen*), wakefulness, sb., 1590.

walde, see **wille**.

walles (O.E. *weall*), walls, acc. pl., 767; see note.

wan, see **hwo**.

wan, wane, wanne, see **hwanne**.

wanene (O.E. *hwanone*), whence, 1300; **whonene**, 138.

wanst, see **wonie**.

war, ware, see **hwar**.

war (O.E. *wær*), cautious, 170; **wear**, 1638.

ware, waþer, see **hwaþer**.

wareuore, waruore (O.E. *hwǣr + for*), wherefore, why, 267, 1618.

warm (O.E. *wearm*), warm, 622; **wearme**, sb., d. sg., 538.

warni (O.E. *wearnian*), warn, pr. 1. sg., 330, 739.

warp, see **worpe**.

warto, see **hwar**.

waste (O.Fr. *wast*), deserted, solitary, 17; see note.

wat, see **wite**.

wear, see **war**.

wede (O.E. *wēod*), weeds, d. pl., 937; **wode**, d. sg., 320, d. pl., 587, 593.

weȝe (O.E. *wegan*), carry, 1022.

wei (O.E. *hwǣg*), whey, 1009.

wei, wai (O.E. *weg*), path, way, 956, 249; **weie**, d. sg., 214; **weie** = manner, 1428.

wel, uel, vel (O.E. *wel*), well, very, 36, 537, 95; **wel**, almost, 216, readily, 201.

wel (O.E. *wiell*), well, spring, 917.

welcume (O.E. *wilcuma*), welcome guest, 1600.

wenden (O.E. *wendan*), turn, 1326; **wende**, pr. 1. sg., 288; **wend**, pr. 3. sg., 1464; **wende**, opt. pr. 3. sg., 864; **iwend**, p. p., 1519.

wene (O.E. *wēnan*), expect, suppose, 1266, pr. 1. sg., 237; **wenest, wenist, wenestu, wenst**, pr. 2. sg., 259, 315, 303, 47; **ueneð, weneð**, pr. 3. sg., 1554, 901; **weneþ**, pr. pl., 844.

weolcne (O.E. *wolcen*), clouds, sky, d. pl., 1682.

weole (O.E. *wela*), prosperity, riches, d. sg., 1273.

wepen (O.E. *wēpan*), weep, 987; **wepe**, pr. 1. sg., 876; **wepeþ**, pr. pl., 885; **wepe**, opt. 2. sg., 226; **wepen**, wepe, opt. pl., 931, 861.

wepmon (O.E. *wǣpmann*), man, d. sg., 1379.

wepne (O.E. *wǣpen*), weapons, n. pl., 1369.

were (O.E. *wer*), man, husband, n. sg., 1522; acc. sg., 1341.

were, see **beon**.

wereþ (O.E. *werian*), protects, 834; **werieþ**, pr. pl. = wear, 1174.

werne (O.E. *wiernan*), deny, refuse, 1358, 614.

west (O.E. *west*), west, 923.

west (O.E. *weaxan*), increases, pr. 3. sg., 689.

weste (O.E. *wēste*), desolate, barren, 1000, 1528.

weþer, see **hwaþer**.

whonene, see **wanene**.

wicchecrefte (O.E. *wiccecræft*), witchcraft, d. sg., 1301; **wiecchecrafte**, acc. sg., 1308.

wicke-tunes (O.E. *wic-tūnas*), religious communities, n. pl., 730.

wide (O.E. *wide*), far, wide, adv., 288.

wider (O.E. *hwider*), whither, 724.

wif (O.E. *wif*), woman, wife, 1159, 1173; **wiue**, d. sg., 1077; **wif**, a. pl., 1334; **wiues**, g. sg., 1468, n. pl., 1562.

wiȝt, wiht (O.E. *wiht*), creature, n. sg., 434, 1642, voc., 556; **wiȝte**, n. pl., 87, 204, g. pl., 628; **wiȝtes**, n. pl., 431, a. pl., 598.

wike (O.E. *wic*), dwellings, a. pl., 604.

wike (O.E. *wice*), services, duties, 605; a. pl., 603, 1179; g. pl., 805.

wilde (O.E. *wilde*), wild-wood, 125.

wildernisse (O.E. *wildernes*), wilderness, 1000.

wile, see **hwile**.

wille, wule, wulle (O.E. *willan*), wish, intend, will, pr. 1. sg., 262, 1467, 903; wilt, wiltu, wult, pr. 2. sg., 165, 640, 1064; wile, wule, pr. 3. sg., 214, 630; wulleþ, pr. pl., 896, 1257; wolde, walde, pt. 3. sg., 425, 1710; woldest, pt. 2. sg., 1050, 84; walde, pt. pl., 1678; wille, wile, wule, opt. sg., 77, 185, 1362; wille, wulle, opt. pl., 306, 1730; wulde, opt. pt. sg., 1727; wolde, opt. pt. pl., 1024.

wille (O.E. *willa*), will, pleasure, 1256; a wille = to the delight, 1722.

wimmon, wummon (O.E. *wifman*), woman, 1357, 1359; wimmane, d. sg., 1379; wimmen, wummen, n. pl., 1355, 1350.

win (O.E. *win*), wine, acc. sg., 1011.

winne (O.E. *winn*), trouble, d. sg., 670.

winter, wintere (O.E. *winter*), d. sg., 412, 415; winteres, g. sg., 458.

wippen (cf. L.Ger. *wippen*), flap, tremble, 1066.

wirche, wurchen (O.E. *wyrcean*), inf., make, 722, 408.

wis, wise (O.E. *wis*), wise, 192, 1071; uise, n. pl., 961; wisure, comp., 1250; wise = sb., 176.

wisdom (O.E. *wisdōm*), wisdom, 772, 454.

wise (O.E. *wise*), melody, song, tune, acc. sg., 54, 519, 1703, g. pl., 1663, d. pl., 20; manner, way, d. sg., 893, d. pl., 1029.

wisi (O.E. *wissian*), show, teach, inf., 915; wisse, pr. 1. sg., 927; uisest, pr. 2. sg., 973.

wiste, see wite.

wit, see wiþ.

wit (O.E. *witt*), reason, mind, understanding, 681, 689; witte, d.sg., 783.

wite (O.E. *witan*), know, 1139; wat, wot, pr. 1. sg., 1179, 61; wost, pr. 2.sg., 95, 1407; wot, pr. 3. sg., 236; wiste, pt. sg., 160; wuste, pt. pl., 10; wite, opt. 2. sg., 1467, 440; wiste, opt. pt. pl., 116.

wite (O.E. *witan*), blame, reproach, 1248; witestu, pr. 2. sg., 1356.

witest (O.E. *(be)witian*), dost watch over, guardest, pr. 2. sg., 1045.

wiþ, wiδ, wit (O.E. *wiþ*), against, 403, 1608, 56; = with, 131, 1419; see note, l. 18.

wiþute, witute (O.E. *wiþūtan*), without, prep., 1430, 183; adv. = outside, 646; wiδute, 1594.

witi (O.E. *wittig, witig*), wise, 1189.

witles (O.E. *witlēas*), senseless, 692.

wlate (O.E. *wlætta*), disgust, nausea, 1506.

wlatie (O.E. *wlātian*), to be disgusted, 354.

wlite (O.E. *wlite*), beauty, 439.

wlonc (O.E. *wlanc*), proud, arrogant, 489.

wo (O.E. *wā*), grief, woe, 882.

wod, wode (O.E. *wōd*), mad, frenzied, 1041, 512, 1029.

wode (O.E. *wād*), woad, d. sg., 76.

wode, see wede.

wode, see wude.

woȝe (O.E. *wōh*), crooked, pl., 815; sb. = wrong, 164, 198.

wolawo (O.E. *wālawā*), welladay! alas! 412.

wolcumeþ (O.E. *wilcumian*), welcomes, pr. 3. sg., 440.

wolde (O.E. *weald*), forest, d. sg., 1724.

wonie (O.E. *wānian*), complain, bewail, 975; wonest, wanst, pr. 2. sg., 985, 1644.

woning (O.E. *wānung*), lamentation, 311; woninge, d. sg., 870.

wonne, see hwanne.

wop (O.E. *wōp*), lamentation, 878; wope, d. sg., 857.

word (O.E. *word*), word, speech, sentence, 233; worde, n. sg., 1270, d. pl., 180; wordes, n. pl., 841, acc. pl., 756; bare worde, 547, see note.

worlde (O.E. *woruld*), world, g. sg., 476; worldes, g. sg., 1280.

wormes (O.E. *wurm, wyrm*), worms, acc. pl., 601.

worpe (O.E. *weorpan*), throw, utter, 768; worpeþ, pr. pl., 596; warp, pt. 3. sg., 45, 125; iworpe, p. p., stricken, 1121.

worre (O.Fr. *werre*), war, 385.

worse, worste, see wurs.

worþ, iworþe, see wurþe.

wost, wot, see wite.

wowe (O.E. *wāwa*), woe, misery, 414.

wowes (O.E. *wāh*), walls, acc. pl., 1528.

wraȝte (O.E. *wreccean*), hatched, pt. sg., 106; see note.

wrake (O.E. *wracu*), revenge, cruelty, 1194.

wranne (O.E. *wrænna*), wren, 564, 1740.

wraslinge (O.E. *wrǣstlung*), wrestling, d. sg., 795.

wraþþe (O.E. *wrǣþþo*), wrath, 941, 954.

wrecche, wrecch, wreche (O.E. *wrǣcca*), wretch, 534, 1377, 1669; adj. = miserable, wretched, 335, 1316; wreche, 1688.

wrechede (O.E. *wræc* + **hǣdu*), misery, 1219, 1251.

wrench (O.E. *wrenc*), trick, 811; wrenche, d. pl., 247, g. pl., 813; wrenches, acc. pl., 798.

writ (O.E. *writan*), writes, pr. 3. sg., 1756; wrot, pt. sg., 235.

writelinge (< O.E. **writelian*), trilling, 48 (see note), 914.

wrong (O.E. *wrang*), wrong, 877; wronge, adv., 196.

wroþ, wroð (O.E. *wrāþ*), angry, 111, 1608; wroþe, sb., 944; wroþe, adv., angrily, badly, 63, 972, 1529.

wrouehede (see note), Accidia, Sloth, 1400.

wude (O.E. *wudu*), wood, forest, d. sg., 615, 1626; wode, 444.

wudewale (cf. M.H.G. *witewal*), woodwall, woodpecker, 1659.

wule, see wille.

wule, see hwile.

wulues (O.E. *wulf*), wolves, n. pl., 1008.

wummen, see wimmon.

wunder (O.E. *wundor*), wonder, 361; wundere, 1473; wunder, g. pl., 852.

wundri (O.E. *wundrian*), wonder, pr. 1. sg., 228.

wunest (O.E. *wunian*), dwellest, remainest, 338, 589; wuneþ, pr. 3. sg., 1752.

wunienge (O.E. *wunung*), dwelling, acc. sg., 614; woning, acc. sg., 1760.

wunne (O.E. *wynn*), joy, pleasure, 272 (see note), 1100.

wurchen, see wirche.

wurs, worse (O.E. *wiers*), worse, comp. adj., 34, 303; worste, sb. = worst, 10; wurs, wurse, worse, adv., 793, 1408, 505.

wurþ (O.E. *wurþ*), worthy, estimable, 769, 572; worth, 1550.

wurþe (O.E. *weorþan, wurþan*), be, become, 846; wurþ, pr. 3. sg., 1158, 548; worþ, pr. 3. sg., 405; wurþe, opt. pr. sg., 1382, opt. pt. sg., 400; iworþe, p. p., 660.

wurþful (O.E. *weorþful*), distinguished, much honoured, 1481.

wurþschipe, wurschipe, wurþsipe (O.E. *weorþscipe*), honour, dignity, 1344, 1288, 1099.

wuste, see wite.

ydel (O.E. *idel*), useless, 917; on idel = uselessly, 920.

ysome, see isome.

For EU product safety concerns, contact us at Calle de José Abascal, 56–1°,
28003 Madrid, Spain or eugpsr@cambridge.org.

www.ingramcontent.com/pod-product-compliance
Ingram Content Group UK Ltd.
Pitfield, Milton Keynes, MK11 3LW, UK
UKHW042150130625
459647UK00011B/1273